INDIA AND TIBET

INDIA AND TIBET

A HISTORY OF THE RELATIONS WHICH HAVE SUBSISTED BETWEEN THE TWO COUNTRIES FROM THE TIME OF WARREN HASTINGS TO 1910; WITH A PARTICULAR ACCOUNT OF THE MISSION TO LHASA OF 1904

BY

SIR FRANCIS EDWARD YOUNGHUSBAND

GYAN

ISBN : 978-81-212-1588-6(HB)

First Published, 1910

Published, 2018

Published by

Gyan Publishing House
5, Ansari Road
Daryaganj, New Delhi-110002
Phone: 011-47034999, 9811692060
www.gyanbooks.com
E-mail: books@gyanbooks.com

Printed at: G. Print Process, Delhi.

THE DALAI LAMA.

Frontispiece.

TO

MY WIFE,

ON WHOM FELL THE ANXIETY
AND SUSPENSE OF
DISTANTLY AWAITING THE RESULTS OF HIGH ADVENTURE,

I DEDICATE THIS BOOK,

IN THE HOPE THAT
FROM IT MAY COME SOME RECOMPENSE FOR
THE SUFFERING SHE ENDURED

PREFACE

An apology is needed for the length of this book. When it was passing through the press, a Parliamentary Blue-book appeared containing much important information as to recent developments, and what I had intended as only the account of our relations with Tibet up to the return of the Mission of 1904 I thought with advantage might be extended to include our relations to the present time. The whole forms one connected narrative of the attempt, protracted over 137 years, to accomplish a single purpose—the establishment of ordinary neighbourly intercourse with Tibet. The dramatic ending disclosed is that, when that purpose had at last been achieved, we forthwith abandoned the result.

The reasons for this abandonment have been—firstly, the jealousy borne by two great Powers for one another; and, secondly, the love of isolation engrained in us islanders. I have suggested that our aim should be to replace jealousy by co-operation, and, instead of coiling up in frigid isolation, we should expand ourselves to make and keep friendships.

The means I have recommended are living personalities rather than dry treaties, and what Warren Hastings and Lord Curzon wanted—an agent at Lhasa—is to me also the one true means of achieving our purpose.

I am fully conscious of having made mistakes in that part of the conduct of these affairs which fell to me to discharge. The exactly true adjustment of diplomatic with military requirements, and of the wishes of men in England with the necessities of the situation in Tibet, could only be made by a human being arrived at perfection. Not yet having arrived there, I doubtless made many errors. I can only assume that, if I had never made a mistake, I should never have made a success.

Likewise, in my recommendations for the future, I may often be in error in detail, but in the main conclusion of substituting intimacy for isolation and effecting the change by personality, I would fain believe I shall prove right.

What I say has no official inspiration or sanction, for I have left the employment of Government, and am seeking to serve my country in fields of greater freedom though not less responsibility; but, in compiling the narrative of our relations with the Tibetans, I have made the fullest use of the four Blue-books which have been presented to Parliament. These contain information of the highest value, though in the very undigested form characteristic of Parliamentary Papers. Beyond personal impressions I have added nothing to them, but merely sought to deduce from them a connected account of events and of the motives which impelled them. To Sir Clement Markham's account of Bogle's Mission and Manning's journey to Lhasa, to Captain Turner's account of his Mission to Tibet, and to Perceval Landon's, Edmund Candler's, and Colonel Waddell's accounts of the Mission of 1904, I am also indebted, as well as to Mr. White, Captain Bailey and Messrs. Johnston and Hoffman for photographs.

I lastly desire to acknowledge the trouble which Mr. John Murray has so kindly taken in correcting the proofs.

FRANCIS YOUNGHUSBAND.

September 7, 1910.

P.S.—Too late to make use of it, I have received the just published reprint from the T'sung Pao of Mr. Rockhill's "The Dalai Lamas of Lhasa and their Relations to the Manchu Emperors of China." The conclusion of this famous authority on Tibet, that the Tibetans have no desire for total independence of China, but that their complaints have always been directed against the manner in which the local Chinese officials have performed their duties, is particularly noteworthy.

CONTENTS

CHAPTER I

WARREN HASTINGS' POLICY: BOGLE'S MISSION—1774

CHAPTER II

WARREN HASTINGS' POLICY (*continued*): TURNER'S MISSION—1782

CHAPTER III

MANNING'S VISIT TO LHASA—1811

CHAPTER IV

THE BENGAL GOVERNMENT'S EFFORTS—1873-1886

CONTENTS

CHAPTER X

KHAMBA JONG—1903

CHAPTER XI

DARJILING TO CHUMBI—1903

CHAPTER XII

TUNA—1904

CHAPTER XIII

GYANTSE—1904

CONTENTS

CHAPTER XIV

THE STORMING OF GYANTSE JONG—1904

CHAPTER XV

THE ADVANCE TO LHASA—1904

CHAPTER XVI

THE TERMS—1904

CHAPTER XVII

THE NEGOTIATIONS

CHAPTER XVIII

THE TREATY CONCLUDED—1904

CHAPTER XIX

IMPRESSIONS AT LHASA—1904

CHAPTER XX

THE RETURN—1904

CHAPTER XXI

RESULTS OF THE MISSION

CHAPTER XXII

NEGOTIATIONS WITH CHINA—1905-1910

CHAPTER XXIII

ATTITUDE OF THE TIBETANS SINCE 1904—1904-1910

CHAPTER XXIV

SOME CONCLUSIONS

CHAPTER XXV

A FINAL REFLECTION

APPENDIX

LIST OF ILLUSTRATIONS

MAPS

INDIA AND TIBET

INTRODUCTION

This book is an account of our relations with Tibet, but many still wonder why we need have any such relations at all. The country lies on the far side of the Himalayas, the greatest range of snowy mountains in the world. Why, then, should we trouble ourselves about what goes on there? Why do we want to interfere with the Tibetans? Why not leave them alone? These are very reasonable and pertinent questions, and such as naturally spring to the mind of even the least intelligent of Englishmen. Obviously, therefore, they must have sprung to the minds of responsible British statesmen before they ever sanctioned intervention. The sedate gentlemen who compose the Government of India are not renowned for being carried away by bursts of excitement or enthusiasm, nor are they remarkable for impulsive, thoughtless action. They have spent their lives in the dull routine of official grind, and by the time they attain a seat in the Viceregal Council they are, if anything, too free from emotional impulses. Certainly, the initiation of anything forward and interfering was as little to be expected from them as from the most rigorous anti-Imperialist. The head of the Government of India at the time of the Tibet Mission was, it is true, a man of less mature official experience, but he happened to be a man who had studied Asiatic policy in nearly every part of Asia, besides having been Under-Secretary for Foreign Affairs; and even supposing he had been the most impulsive and irresponsible of Viceroys, he could take no action without gaining the assent of the majority of his colleagues in India, and without convincing the Secretary of State in England. India is not governed by the Viceroy alone, but by the Viceroy in Council. On such a question as the despatch of a mission to Tibet, the Viceroy would not be able to act without the concurrence of three out of his six councillors, and without the approval of the Secretary of State, who, in his turn, as expenditure is incurred, would have to gain the support of his Council of tried and experienced Indian administrators and soldiers, besides the approval of the whole Cabinet.

It is, then, a very fair presumption at the outset that if all these various authorities had satisfied themselves that action in Tibet was necessary, there probably was some reasonable ground for interference. What was it that influenced these sedate authorities, alike in India and in England, to depart from the natural course of leaving the Tibetans alone, to behave or misbehave themselves as they liked? What was it that persuaded these gentlemen that action, and not inaction, intervention, and not *laissez-faire*, were required, and that we could no longer leave this remote State on the far side of the mighty Himalayas severely alone? There must have been some strong reason, for it was not merely a matter of permitting an adventurous explorer to try and reach the "forbidden city." After thirty years of correspondence what was eventually sanctioned was the despatch of a mission with an escort strong enough to break down all opposition. What was the reason?

The answer to this I will eventually give. But to make that answer clear we must view the matter from a long perspective, and trace its gradual evolution from the original beginnings. And, at the start, I shall have to emphasize the point that there has always been intercourse of some kind between Tibet and India, for Tibet is not an island in mid-ocean. It is in the heart of a continent surrounded by other countries. That it is a mysterious, secluded country in the remote hinterland of the Himalayas most people are vaguely aware. But that it is contiguous for nearly a thousand miles with the British Empire, from Kashmir to Burma, few have properly realized. Still less have they appreciated that this contact between the countries means intercourse of some kind between the peoples inhabiting them, even though it has to be over a snowy range. The Tibetans drew their religion from India. From time immemorial they have been accustomed to visit the sacred shrines of India. Tibetan traders have come down to Bengal, Kashmiri and Indian traders have gone to Tibet. Tibetan shepherds have brought their flocks to the pastures on the Indian side of the range in some parts. In other parts the shepherds from the Indian side have taken their sheep and goats to the plateaux of Tibet. Sometimes the Tibetans or their vassals have raided to valleys and plains of India, sometimes Indian feudatories have raided into Tibet. At other times, again, the intercourse has been of a more pacific kind, and intermarriages between the bordering peoples and interchanges of presents have taken place. In a multitude of ways there has ever been intercourse between Tibet and India. Tibet has never been really isolated. And, as I shall in due course show, the Mission to Lhasa of 1904, was merely the culmination of a long series of efforts to regularize and humanize that intercourse, and put the relationship which must necessarily subsist between India and Tibet upon a business-like and permanently satisfactory footing.

CHAPTER I

BOGLE'S MISSION, 1774

It is an interesting reflection for those to make who think that we must necessarily have been the aggressive party, that the far-distant primary cause of all our attempts at intercourse with the Tibetans was an act of aggression, not on our part, not on the part of an ambitious Proconsul, or some headstrong frontier officer, but of the Bhutanese, neighbours, and then vassals, of the Tibetans, who nearly a century and a half ago committed the first act—an act of aggression—which brought us into relationship with the Tibetans. In the year 1772 they descended into the plains of Bengal and overran Kuch Behar, carried off the Raja as a prisoner, seized his country, and offered such a menace to the British province of Bengal, now only separated from them by a small stream, that when the people of Kuch Behar asked the British Governor for help, he granted their request, and resolved to drive the mountaineers back into their fastnesses. Success attended his efforts, though, as usual, at much sacrifice. We learn that our troops were decimated with disease, and that the malaria proved fatal to Captain Jones, the commander, and many other officers. "One can hardly breathe," says Bogle, who passed through the country two years later—"frogs, watery insects, and dank air." And those who have been over that same country since, and seen, if only from a railway train, those deadly swamps, who have felt that suffocating, poisonous atmosphere arising from them, and who have experienced that ghastly, depressing enervation which saps all manhood and all life out of one, can well imagine what those early pioneers must have suffered.

Fortunately there was at the head of affairs the greatest, though the most maligned, of all the Governors-General of India, who was able to turn to profit the advantages accruing from the sacrifices which had been made. Fortunately, too, in those days a Governor-General still had some power and initiative left, and was able, without interminable delays, debates, correspondence, and international considerings, to act decisively and strongly before the psychological moment had passed.

Warren Hastings resisted the aggression of the Bhutanese, and drove them back from the plains of Bengal into their own mountains; but when the Tashi Lama of Tibet interceded on their behalf, he at once not only acceded, but went further, and made a deliberate effort to come into permanent relationship with both the Bhutanese and Tibetans. Nor did he think he would gain lasting results by any fitful effort. He knew well that to achieve anything effort must be long, must be continuous, and must be persistent, and that the results would be small at first, but, accumulating in the long process of years, would eventually amount to what was of value.

The Bhutanese, I have said, when they found themselves being sorely punished for their aggression, appealed to the Tashi Lama of Tibet to intercede for them with the Governor of Bengal; and the Tashi Lama, who was then acting as Regent of Tibet during the infancy of the Dalai Lama, wrote to Warren Hastings a very remarkable letter, which is quoted both by Turner and Markham, and which is especially noteworthy as marking that the intercourse between us and the Tibetans was *started* by the Tibetans. The Tibetans have stated on many a subsequent occasion to the Government of India, and on innumerable occasions to myself, that they are not permitted to have intercourse with us. But *originally*, and when they wanted a favour from us, the intercourse was started by themselves, and in a very reasonable, dignified, and neighbourly manner.

The Tashi Lama wrote to Warren Hastings, after various compliments: "Neither to molest nor to persecute is my aim. . . . But in justice and humanity I am informed you far surpass . . . I have been repeatedly informed that you have been engaged in hostilities against the Deb Judhur, to which, it is said, the Deb's own criminal conduct in committing ravages and other outrages on your frontier has given rise. As he is of a rude and ignorant race (past times are not destitute of instances of the like misconduct which his own avarice tempted him to commit), it is not unlikely that he has now renewed those instances, and the ravages and plunder which he committed on the skirts of the Bengal and Behar provinces have given you provocation to send your avenging army against him. However, his party has been defeated, many of his people have been killed, three forts have been taken from him, he has met with the punishment he deserved, and it is evident as the sun that your army has been victorious, and that, if you had been desirous of it, you might in the space of two days have entirely extirpated him, for he had no power to resist your efforts. But I now take upon me to be his mediator, and to represent to you that, as the said Deb Raja is dependent upon the Dalai Lama . . . should you persist in offering further molestation to the Deb Raja's country, it will irritate both the Lama and all his subjects against you. Therefore, from a regard to our religion and customs, I request you will cease all hostilities against him, and in doing this you will confer the greatest favour and friendship upon me. I have reprimanded the Deb for his past conduct, and I have admonished him to desist from his evil practices in future, and to be submissive to you in all matters. I am persuaded that he will conform to the advice which I have given him, and it will be necessary that you treat him with compassion and clemency. As for my part, I am but a Fakir, and it is the custom of my Sect, with the rosary in our hands, to pray for the welfare of mankind and for the peace and happiness of the inhabitants of this country; and I do now, with my head uncovered, entreat that you may cease all hostilities against the Deb in future."

On receipt of this letter, Warren Hastings laid it before the Board at Calcutta, and informed them that, in reply, he had written to the Tashi Lama, proposing a general treaty of amity and commerce between Bengal and Tibet. The letter of the Lama, he said, had invited us to friendship, and the final arrangement of the disputes on the frontier had rendered the country accessible, without danger either to the persons or effects of travellers. He had, therefore, written for and obtained a passport for a European to proceed to Tibet for the negotiation of the treaty, and he now purposed sending Mr. Bogle, a servant of the Company, well known for his intelligence, assiduity, and exactness in affairs, as well as for the "coolness and moderation of temper which he seems to possess in an eminent degree." Warren Hastings, with great wisdom and knowledge of Asiatic affairs, adds that he "is far from being sanguine in his hopes of success, but the present occasion appears too favourable for the attempt to be neglected."

This latter is precisely the point which we who have dealt with Asiatics can appreciate so well—taking the opportunity, striking while the iron is hot, not letting the chance go by, knowing our mind, knowing what we want, and acting decisively when the exact occasion arises. It is hard to do nowadays, with the Provincial Government so subordinate to the Government of India, with the Government of India so governed by the Secretary of State, with Cabinet Ministers telling us that the House of Commons are their masters, and members of the House of Commons saying they are the mouthpieces of their constituents. Nevertheless, the advantages of such a method of conducting affairs must not be forgotten. Decision and rapidity of action are often important factors in the conduct of Asiatic affairs, and may save more trouble than is saved by caution and long deliberation.

Warren Hastings' policy was, then, not to sit still within his borders, supremely indifferent to what occurred on the other side, and intent upon respecting not merely the independence but also the isolation of his neighbours. It was a forward policy, and combined in a noteworthy manner alertness and deliberation, rapidity and persistency, assertiveness and receptivity. He sought to secure his borders by at once striking when danger threatened, but also by taking infinite pains over long periods of time to promote ordinary neighbourly intercourse with those on the other side. Both qualities are necessary. Spasmodic action unaccompanied by steady, continuous efforts at conciliation produces no less bad results than does plodding conciliation never accompanied by action. It was because Warren Hastings possessed this capacity for instantly seizing an opportunity, because he could and would without hesitation or fear use severity where severity alone would secure enduring harmony, but would yet persistently and with infinite tact, sagacity, and real good-heartedness work for humane and neighbourly relationship with adjoining peoples, that he must be considered the greatest of all the great Governors-General of India.

But to be successful a policy must be embodied in a fitting personality. And to appreciate Warren Hastings' Tibetan policy we must know something of the agent he chose to carry it into effect. What was the character of the man who was to lead the first Mission ever sent to Tibet? We learn from Markham that he was born in 1746, and had at first been brought up in a business office; but on proceeding to India had been given a post in the Revenue Department. His letters to his father and sisters show him to have been a man of the strongest home feelings, and his conversations with the Tibetans indicate that he was a man of high honour and strict rectitude. Warren Hastings himself not only had a high opinion of his abilities and official aptitude, but also entertained for him a warm personal friendship.

The youth of Warren Hastings' agent is the first point to note: he was only twenty-eight. Nowadays we use men who are much too old. It is when men are young, when they are still crammed full of energy, when their faculties are alert, that they are most useful and effective. I often doubt whether the experience of maturer age possesses all the advantages which are commonly attributed to it, and whether young men act more rashly

MR. BOGLE.

To face page 8.

or irresponsibly than old men. The former have their whole careers before them, and their reputations to make. They are no more likely, therefore, to act rashly than "old men in a hurry." Warren Hastings was therefore wise, in my opinion, to choose a young man, and he was equally wise to choose an agent of good breeding and with great natural kindliness of disposition. Asiatics do not mind quickness or hotness of temper, or severity of manner, as long as they can feel that at bottom the man they have to do with has a good, warm, generous heart. He need not wear it on his sleeve, but they will know right enough whether he possesses one or not. And that Warren Hastings' agent had such a heart his home correspondence, his friendship with Hastings himself, and his eventual dealings with the Tibetans amply testify.

Having determined his policy and selected his agent, Warren Hastings gave him the following instructions,* dated May 13, 1774: "I desire you will proceed to Lhasa. . . . The design of your mission is to open a mutual and equal communication of trade between the inhabitants of Bhutan [Tibet] and Bengal, and you will be guided by your own judgment in using such means of negotiation as may be most likely to effect this purpose. You will take with you samples, for a trial of such articles of commerce as may be sent from this country. . . . And you will diligently inform yourself of the manufactures, productions, goods, introduced by the intercourse with other countries, which are to be procured in Bhutan. . . . The following will be also proper objects of your inquiry: the nature of the roads between the borders of Bengal and Lhasa, and of the country lying between; the communications between Lhasa and the neighbouring countries, their government, revenue, and manners. . . . The period of your stay must be left to your discretion. I wish you to remain a sufficient time to fulfil the purposes of your deputation, and obtain a complete knowledge of the country and the points referred to your inquiry. If you

* Markham, "Mission of Bogle," p. 6.

shall judge that a residence may be usefully established at Lhasa without putting the Company to any expense, but such as may be repaid by the advantages which may be hereafter derived from it, you will take the earliest opportunity to advise me of it; and if you should find it necessary to come away before you receive my orders upon it, you may leave such persons as you shall think fit to remain as your agents till a proper resident can be appointed. . . . You will draw on me for your charges, and your drafts shall be regularly answered. To these I can fix no limitation, but empower you to act according to your discretion, knowing that I need not recommend to you a strict frugality and economy where the good of the service on which you are commissioned shall not require a deviation from these rules."

Did ever an agent despatched on an important mission receive more satisfactory instructions? The object clearly defined, and the fullest discretion left to him as to the manner of carrying it out. Hastings, having selected the fittest agent to carry out his purpose, leaves everything to his judgment. Whatever would most effectively carry out the main purpose, that the agent was at perfect liberty to do, and time and money were freely at his disposal. "I want the thing done," says Warren Hastings in effect, "and all you require to get it done you shall have."

The only equally good instructions I have personally seen issued to an agent were given by Cecil Rhodes in Rhodesia. I travelled up to Fort Salisbury with Major Forbes, whom Rhodes had summoned from a place two months' journey distant to receive instructions, for he did not believe in letters, but only in personal communication. After dinner Rhodes questioned Forbes most minutely as to his requirements, as to the condition of things, as to the difficulties which were likely to be encountered, and as to his ideas on how those difficulties should be overcome. He said he wanted to know now what Forbes required in order to accomplish the object in view, because he did not wish to see him coming back later on, saying he could have carried it out if only he had had this, that, or the other. Let him therefore say now whatever he required to insure success.

All that he asked, and more than he asked, Rhodes gave him, and then despatched him, saying, "Now, I don't want to hear of you again till I get a telegram saying your job is done."

These are, of course, ideal methods of conveying instructions to an agent, which it is not always possible for a high official to give. Lord Curzon would, I know, have liked to give similar instructions to me, and, as far as providing money, staff, military support, etc., he did. But, with the closer interconnection of public affairs, public business is now so complicated that it is not, I suppose, possible to leave to an agent the same amount of discretion that Warren Hastings did to Bogle. Still, great results in many fields, and, what is more, great men, have been produced by the use of Warren Hastings' method of selecting the fittest agent, and then leaving everything in his hands. I do not see that any better results have been obtained by utilizing human agents as mere telephones. If the conduct of affairs has become complicated, that does not appear to be any reason in itself for abandoning the method. It appears only a reason for principals and agents rising to the higher occasion while still pursuing the old successful method. Ease of communication has brought nations more closely together and complicated affairs, but it has also made possible readier personal communication between principal and agent. And therefore there is need not so much for curtailing the discretion of the agent while he is at work as for utilizing the greater facility for personal intercourse now possible. In conversation the agent will be able to impress his principals with whatever local and personal difficulties he has to contend with, and the means required for carrying out their object, and they will be able to impress him with the limits outside which it is impossible to allow him to act. It is a clear certainty that the present tendency to concentrate, not merely control, but also direction, in London, cannot go on for ever. An Empire like ours, immense in size and immensely complicated, cannot be managed in detail from headquarters. The time must come when the House of Commons and the constituencies, overburdened with the great affairs with which they have to deal, will, by the sheer force and weight of circumstances, see the advantages of leaving more to the men on the spot. They will probably insist on agents being more carefully selected. They will require them to keep in much closer personal contact with headquarters. They will expect, too, that politicians who control should already be personally acquainted, or make themselves personally acquainted, with the countries they control. But with these conditions fulfilled they will, it may be hoped, be able to leave more to the men on the spot, removing them relentlessly if they act wrongly, but while they are acting, leaving them to act in their own way.

Bogle, with these free instructions and this ample support, set out from Calcutta in the middle of May, 1774, that is, less than two months from the date of the despatch of the Tashi Lama's letter from Shigatse, so that Warren Hastings, if he had left ample leisure to his agent to carry out his purpose, had himself acted with the utmost promptitude, even in so important a matter as sending a mission to Lhasa with the possibility of establishing there a permanent resident. Rapidity of communication has not resulted in the rapidity of the transaction of public affairs, and the consideration of despatching a mission to Lhasa nowadays takes as many years as weeks were occupied in the days of Warren Hastings.

During his passage through Bhutan, Bogle found many obstacles placed in his way; but he eventually left the capital in the middle of October, and on the 23rd of that month reached Phari, at the head of the Chumbi Valley, up which we marched to Lhasa 130 years later. Here he was received by two Lhasa officers, and farther on, at Gyantse, where the Mission of 1904 was attacked and besieged for nearly two months, he was entertained by a priest, "an elderly man of polite and pleasant manners," who sat with him most of the afternoon, and drank "above twenty cups of tea." Crowds of people appear to have assembled to look at him, but beyond the irksomeness of these attentions he suffered no inconvenience or opposition.

On November 8, 1774, he arrived at the place near Shigatse where the Tashi Lama was at the time in residence. The day following he had an interview with the Lama, and delivered to him a letter and a necklace of pearls from Warren Hastings. This was the first official interview which had ever taken place between a British officer and a Tibetan, and as such is particularly worthy of note.

The Tashi Lama received Bogle* "with a very courteous and smiling countenance," seated him near him on a high stool covered with a carpet, and spoke to him in Hindustani, of which he had "a moderate knowledge." After inquiring about Warren Hastings' health, and Bogle's journey through Bhutan, he introduced the subject of the war in Behar—that is, the Bhutanese invasion of the plains of Bengal. "I always," said the Lama, "disapproved of Deb Judhur (the Bhutanese Chief) seizing the Behar Raja (the Raja of Kuch Behar) and going to war with the Fringies (the English); but the Deb considered himself as powerful in arms, and would not listen to my advice. After he was defeated, I wrote to the Governor, who, in ceasing hostilities against the Bhutanese, in consequence of my application, and restoring to them their country, has made me very happy, and has done a very pious action. My servants who went to Calcutta were only little men, and the kind reception they had from the Governor I consider as another mark of friendship."

Bogle explained that Kuch Behar was separated from the British province of Bengal only by a rivulet; that the Bhutanese from time immemorial had confined themselves to their mountains, and when they visited the low countries it was in an amicable manner, and in order to trade; that when many thousand armed men issued at once from their forests, carried off the Raja of Kuch Behar as prisoner, and seized his country, the Company very justly became alarmed, and concluded

* Markham, p. 135.

that the Bhutanese, encouraged by their successes in Kuch Behar to-day, and undeterred by so slight a boundary as a small stream, might invade the British provinces to-morrow. Bogle continued that Warren Hastings, on the people of Kuch Behar applying to him for assistance, immediately despatched a battalion of sepoys to repel the invaders, but was extremely glad, on receipt of the Tashi Lama's letter, to suspend hostilities and subsequently to conclude a peace with the Bhutanese and restore them their country. In conclusion, he said that Warren Hastings, being happy to cultivate the friendship of a man whose fame was so well known, and whose character was held in veneration by so many nations, had sent him to the Lama's presence with the letter and tokens of friendship which he had laid before him.

The Lama said that the Deb Judhur did not manage his country properly, and had been turned out. Bogle replied that the English had no concern with his expulsion; it was brought about by his own people: the Company only wished the Bhutanese to continue in their own country, and not to encroach upon Bengal, or raise disturbances upon its frontier. "The Governor," said the Lama, "had reason for going to war, but, as I am averse from bloodshed, and the Bhutanese are my vassals, I am glad it is brought to a conclusion."

The point, then, that it was an act of aggression on the part of a vassal of the Tibetans which was the initial cause of our relationship with the Tibetans; that that act was considered unjustifiable by the then ruler of Tibet, and that our own action was approved of and appreciated by him, is established by this conversation. Except for the unjustifiable aggression of the Bhutanese upon our neighbours, we would never have been brought into conflict with these vassals of Tibet; and but for the intervention of the Tibetan Regent on their behalf, we should not then have thought of any relationship with the Tibetans. The initiation of our intercourse did not rest with us. We were not the interferers. It was the

Tibetans themselves who made the first move. This much is clear from the Tashi Lama's conversation.

We may well pause for a moment to consider the man who had thus first communicated with us. It so happens that he was the most remarkable man Tibet has produced in the last century and a half, and one cannot help thinking that if he had lived longer, and Warren Hastings had remained longer in India, these two able and eminently sensible and conciliatory men would have come to some amicable and neighbourly agreement by which the inter-relations of their respective countries might have been peacefully conducted from that time till now.

Bogle says of him that he was about forty years of age, that his disposition was open, candid, and generous, and that the expression of his countenance was smiling and good-humoured. He was extremely merry and entertaining in conversation, and told a pleasant story with a great deal of humour and action. "I endeavoured," says Bogle, "to find out, in his character, those defects which are inseparable from humanity, but he is so universally beloved that I had no success, and not a man could find it in his heart to speak ill of him."

The Lama treated Bogle in the most intimate manner. He would walk the room with the strange Englishman, explain to him the pictures, and make remarks upon the colour of his eyes. "For, although," says Bogle, "venerated as God's vicegerent through all the eastern countries of Asia, endowed with a portion of omniscience, and with many other Divine attributes, he throws aside, in conversation, all the awful part of his character, accommodates himself to the weakness of mortals, endeavours to make himself loved rather than feared, and behaves with the greatest affability to everybody, particularly to strangers."

Continuing his conversation on the subject of Behar, the Lama, in subsequent interviews, said that many people had advised him against receiving an Englishman. "I had heard also,"* he said, "much of the power of the Fringies: that the Company was like a great King, and fond of war and conquest; and as my business and that of my people is to pray to God, I was afraid to admit any Fringies into the country. But I have since learned that the Fringies are a fair and a just people." To this Bogle replied that the Governor was, above all things, desirous of obtaining his friendship and favour, as the character of the English and their good or bad name depended greatly upon his judgment. In return the Lama assured Bogle that his heart was open and well disposed towards the English, and that he wished to have a place on the banks of the Ganges to which he might send his people to pray, and that he intended to write to Warren Hastings about it. This he did, after Bogle's return, and a piece of land was given him on the banks of the Hooghly branch of the Ganges, opposite Calcutta, and a house and temple were constructed on it by Bogle for the Lama.

The conversation now turned to the question of trade. The Tashi Lama said that, owing to the recent wars in Nepal and Bhutan, trade between Bengal and Tibet was not flourishing, but that, as for himself, he gave encouragement to merchants, and in Tibet they were free and secure. He enumerated the different articles which went from Tibet to Bengal—"gold, musk, cow-tails (yak-tails), and coarse woollen clothes"—but he said the Tibetans were afraid to go to Bengal on account of the heat. In the previous year he had sent four people to worship at Benares, but three had died. In former times great numbers used to resort to Hindustan. The Lamas had temples in Benares, Gaya, and several other places; their priests used to travel thither to study the sacred books and the religion of the Hindus, and after remaining there ten, twenty, or thirty years, return to Tibet and communicate their knowledge to their countrymen; but since the Mohammedan conquest of India the inhabitants of Tibet had had little connection with Bengal or the southern countries.

* Markham, p. 137.

Bogle assured him that times were now altered, that under the Company in Bengal—and it must be remembered that when he was speaking our rule did not extend beyond Bengal on that side of India—every person's property was secure, and everyone was at liberty to follow his own religion.

The Lama said he was informed that under the Fringies the country was very quiet, and that he would be ashamed if Bogle were to return with a fruitless errand. He would therefore consult his officers and some men from Lhasa, as well as some of the chief merchants, and after informing them of the Governor's desire to encourage trade, and of the encouragement and protection which the Company afforded to traders in Bengal, "discuss the most proper method of carrying it on and extending it."

The following day the Lama told Bogle that he "had written to Lhasa on the subject of opening a free commercial communication between his country and Bengal." "But," says Bogle, "although he spoke with all the zeal in the world, I confess I did not much like the thoughts of referring my business to Lhasa, where I was not present, where I was unacquainted, and where I had reason to think the Ministers had entertained no favourable idea of me and my commission."

Later on, at the request of the Tashi Lama, two deputies from Lhasa came to visit Bogle. They said the English had shown great favour to the Lama and to them by making peace with the Bhutanese and restoring their country. Bogle replied that the English were far from being of that quarrelsome nature which some evil-minded persons represented them to be, and wished not for extent of territories. They were entrusted with the management of Bengal, and only wished it should remain in tranquillity. The war with the Bhutanese was of their own seeking. The deputies might judge whether the Company had not cause for alarm when eight or ten thousand Bhutanese, who had formerly confined themselves to their mountains, poured into the low country, seized the Raja of Kuch Behar, took possession of his territories, and carried their arms to the borders of Bengal. The deputies could judge for themselves whether the Company were not in the right in opposing them. In the course of the war some of the Bhutan territory was taken from them, but was immediately restored at the request of the Tashi Lama, and so far from desiring conquest, the boundaries of Bengal remained the same as formerly.

The Lhasa deputies said the Lama had written to Lhasa about trading, but that the Tibetans were afraid of the heat, and proceeded, therefore, only as far as Phari, where the Bhutanese brought the commodities of Bengal and exchanged them for those of Tibet. This was the ancient custom, and would certainly be observed.

Bogle stated that besides this there was formerly a very extensive trade carried on between Tibet and Bengal; Warren Hastings was desirous of removing existing obstacles, and had sent him to Tibet to represent the matter to the Tashi Lama, and he trusted that the Lhasa authorities would agree to so reasonable a proposal. They answered that Gesub Rimpoche (the Regent at Lhasa) would do everything in his power, but that he and all the country were subject to the Emperor of China.

"This," says Bogle, "is a stumbling-block which crosses me in all my paths." And in the paths of how many negotiators since has it not stood as a stumbling-block! The Tibetans are ready to do anything, but they can do nothing without the permission of the Chinese. The Chinese would freely open the whole of Tibet, but the Tibetans themselves are so terribly seclusive. So the same old story goes on year after year, till centuries are beginning to roll by, and the story is still unfinished. When in the Audience Hall of the Dalai Lama's Palace at Lhasa itself I had obtained the seals of the Dalai Lama, of the Council, of the National Assembly, and of the three great monasteries, to an agreement, and had done all this in the presence of the Chinese Resident, I thought we had at last laid that fiction low for ever. But it seems to be springing up again in all its old exuberance, and showing still perennial vitality.

Bogle, at the request of the Tashi Lama, related to him the substance of his conversation with the Lhasa deputies. The Lama assured him again of the reasonableness of his proposals in regard to trade, but said that, in reply to the letter he had written on the subject, he had received a letter from the Lhasa Regent mentioning his apprehension of giving umbrage to the Chinese. There were, too, disturbances in Nepal and Sikkim which rendered this an improper time to settle anything, but in a year or two he hoped to bring it about. As to the English, the Lhasa Regent had received such accounts as made him suspicious, "and," added the Tashi Lama, "his heart is confined, and he does not see things in the same view as I do."

Bogle then hinted at the advisability of the Tibetans coming into some form of alliance with the English so that the influence of the latter might be used to restrain the Gurkhas of Nepal from attacking Tibet and its feudatories. This argument evidently much struck the Lama, who asked if he might write it to the Lhasa Regent. Bogle told him he might, and that he had no doubt that Warren Hastings would be ready to employ his mediation to make the Gurkha Raja desist from his attempts on the territories subject to Lhasa, and that he had reason to think that from the Gurkha Raja's dread of the English it would be effectual. The Lama said that the Regent's apprehensions of the English arose not only from himself, but also from his fear of giving offence to the Chinese, to whom Tibet was subject. The Regent wished, therefore, to receive an answer from the Court at Peking.

Bogle contended that Warren Hastings, in his proposals to facilitate trade, was promoting the advantage of Tibet as well as of Bengal; that in former times merchants used to come freely into Tibet; that the Gurkha Raja's wars and oppressions had prevented their coming for some years past, and he only prayed the Lama to remove the obstacles which these had occasioned. To this the Lama replied that he had no doubt of carrying the point, but that it might require a year or two to do it effectually.

So we see the well-intentioned Tashi Lama held back by the obstructive Lhasa authorities; and this was still more evident at Bogle's next interview, which was with the Lhasa deputies. They came to pay him a farewell visit, and in the innocence of his heart he made the very simple request that they would convey a letter from him to the Lhasa Regent. Nothing could be more natural than such a request; but, till recently, one might just as well have asked a Tibetan to touch a red-hot poker as to carry a letter from an Englishman. The deputies said that if it contained anything to do with business they could not carry it. "I confess," says Bogle, "I was much struck with this answer." Poor man, he might well be! And I was equally struck, 130 years later, when I was formally deputed on a mission to Tibet, with the full consent of the Chinese suzerain, when Tibetans still refused to take a letter from an Englishman. It was only when we were in full march to Lhasa, and but a few miles distant, that they at last consented to so simple a proceeding as receiving a letter, though now they have changed so completely round, that this year the Dalai Lama himself, at Calcutta, appealed to the Viceroy of India "to secure the observance of the *right* which the Tibetans had of dealing direct with the British."

Bogle told the Lhasa deputies that he wished to know the grounds of the Regent's suspicions, but they replied "that much conversation was not the custom of their country," and wished him a good journey back to Bengal. Bogle endeavoured to get them to listen to him, as he wished to introduce the subject of trade, but it was to no purpose.

"This conversation gave me more concern," he records, "than any I had in Tibet." He immediately asked to see the Tashi Lama, and told him "with some warmth," as he was "a good deal affected," that he could not help being concerned that the Regent should suspect him of coming into his country to raise disturbances; that God was his witness that he wished the Regent well, and wished the Lama well, and the country well, and that a suspicion of treachery and falsehood he could not bear. The Tashi Lami tried to calm him, and eventually dictated a letter in Tibetan in Bogle's name to the Lhasa Regent. This letter contained only one sentence of pure business. It simply said: "I request, in the name of the Governor, my master, that you will allow merchants to trade between this country and Bengal." Not a very aggressive request to make or a very great favour to ask, especially as the Tibetans had begun their intercourse by asking a favour from us. But it was not for a century and a quarter, and not till we had carried our arms to Lhasa itself, that that simple request was answered, although all the time the *people* and *traders* of Tibet were only too willing to trade with us.

Why Bogle did not himself go to Lhasa, as he was empowered to do by his instructions, seems strange. The Tashi Lama said that he himself would have been quite willing, but that the Lhasa Regent was very averse, and he dissuaded Bogle, saying that the Regent's heart was small and suspicious, and he could not promise that he would be able to procure the Regent's consent.

And now the feeling of suspicion was to be increased by an unfortunate occurrence. The Gurkha Raja of Nepal wrote to both the Tashi Lama and the Lhasa Regent, announcing that he had subdued certain districts. He said he did not wish to quarrel with Tibet, but if they had a mind for war he let them know he was well prepared, and he would desire them to remember he was a Rajput. He wished to establish factories at places upon the Tibetan border, where the merchants of Tibet might purchase the commodities of his country and of Bengal, and he desired the concurrence of the Tibetans. He also further desired the Tibetans "to have no connection with

Fringies or Moghuls, and not to allow them into the country, but to follow the ancient custom, which he was resolved likewise to do." A Fringy had come to him upon some business, and was now in his country, but he intended to send him back as soon as possible, and desired the Tibetans to do the same with Bogle.

Thus were Bogle's difficulties still further increased. And in one respect, at least, we have advanced since his day; for the Mission to Lhasa in 1904, instead of being hampered, was warmly supported by the Nepalese. The Dewan of Nepal wrote strongly to the Lhasa authorities, urging them to reason, and his agent at Lhasa was of the greatest assistance to me in my negotiations with the Tibetans.

Besides China and Nepal thus entering into this Tibetan question, there was also some mention of Russia even so far back as that. The Tashi Lama had already questioned Bogle about the Empress of Russia. He now told Bogle that there was a quarrel between the Russians and the Chinese over some Tartar tribe. The Russians had not yet begun hostilities, but he imagined they would soon go to war about it. Bogle told him that as the Russians were engaged in a very heavy war with the Turks —how far back that other story reaches!—he supposed they would hardly think of entering into another with the Chinese. He said the Russians were a very hardy and warlike people, capable of great efforts, and he doubted whether the Chinese would be able to cope with their troops.

Bogle then had conversations with the Kashmiri traders, who had been sent to him by the Tashi Lama, and who wanted to be allowed to trade with Bengal through Bhutan. They stated the difficulties which the Bhutanese placed in their way, and said that the Chief of Bhutan would soon remove these if the Company would threaten him with war, as after the last war he was in great dread of the English. It is a point which should be specially noted by those who believe that Warren Hastings' policy was aggressive, that Bogle, in reply to this hint, told the merchants* that he had no power to use such language to the Bhutanese, and that *whatever he did with the Raja must be by peaceable and friendly means.* The Company had entered into a treaty of peace with them, "which, according to the maxim of the English Government, would . . . remain for ever inviolate."

Tibetan merchants also came, at the Tashi Lama's request, to see Bogle. They dealt chiefly in tea, some of them to the extent of two or three lakhs of rupees a year—of the then value of £20,000 to £30,000. They said the Lama had advised them to send agents to Bengal, but they were afraid to go into the heat of the plains. They had a tradition that about eight hundred years ago people of Tibet used to go to Bengal, but that eight out of ten died before their return. Bogle told them that if they were afraid of sending their servants thither, the Kashmiri would supply them with what they wanted. They said that formerly wool, broadcloth, etc., used to come through Nepal, but since the wars in Nepal the trade had diminished. They added that people imagined from gold being produced in Tibet that it was extremely rich, but that this was not the case, and if extraordinary quantities of gold were sent to Bengal, the Emperor of China, who was Sovereign of the country, would be displeased.

At his farewell interview Bogle said that Warren Hastings would send letters to the Lama by his own servants, upon which the Lama said: "I wish the Governor will not at present send an Englishman. You know what difficulties I had about your coming into the country, and how I had to struggle with the jealousy of the Gesub Rimpoche (the Regent) and the people at Lhasa. Even now they are uneasy at my having kept you so long. I could wish, therefore, that the Governor would rather send a Hindu. I am in hopes my letter to the Regent will have a good effect in removing his jealousy, and I expect in a year or two that the government of this country will

* Markham, p. 162.

be in the Dalai Lama's hands, when I will inform the Governor, and he may then send an Englishman to me and to the Dalai Lama."

The Tashi Lama repeated his concern at Bogle's departure and the satisfaction he had received in being informed of the customs of Europe. He spoke all this, in and with a look very different from the studied compliments of Hindustan. "I never could reconcile myself," continues Bogle, "to taking a last leave of anybody; and what from the Lama's pleasant and amiable character, what from the many favours and civilities he had shown me, I could not help being particularly affected. He observed it, and in order to cheer me mentioned his hopes of seeing me again."

Of Bogle's own warm-hearted and affectionate feelings to the people of Tibet there can be no question. On the eve of his departure he wrote in a letter to his sister: "Farewell, ye honest and simple people! May ye long enjoy the happiness which is denied to more polished nations; and while they are engaged in the endless pursuits of avarice and ambition, defended by your barren mountains, may ye continue to live in peace and contentment, and know no wants but those of nature."

At the close of Bogle's Mission we may review its results. He was sent by Warren Hastings to establish relationship and intercourse of trade with the Tibetans. How far did he succeed in carrying out that object?

It is sufficiently clear that, as regards personal relationship, he was eminently successful, and that was about as much as he could have expected to establish at the start. As we have already seen, Warren Hastings never expected any very striking result from the first communication. He wished to lay the *foundation* for neighbourly intercourse, and in this much he succeeded. He had had experience enough of Asiatics in other quarters to be aware that they are very naturally suspicious of a European Power, then by some apparently irresistible process gradually expanding over smaller Asiatic peoples. As the instance of the Gurkha

Raja's letter showed, there are few Asiatic rulers who, if they have the *power* to subdue a weaker neighbour, will not as a perfectly natural course proceed to bring that neighbour under subjection. This is looked upon by most Asiatics as a quite normal and inevitable proceeding. Naturally, therefore, the Tibetans would assume that it would only be a matter of time before the English Governor of Bengal would attack Tibet. He had the power to subdue the country; he would therefore subdue it. In the first instance he would, of course, send up an agent to spy out the land, to see what it was worth, and to find out the best way into it; and such an agent doubtless Bogle was, in their opinion. It was inevitable, therefore, that Bogle should be viewed with suspicion, and that the Tibetans should not, at the first jump off, throw their country freely open to trade. How much wiser, in their opinion, would be the views of some shrewd old counsellor who said: "Keep the English at a distance; don't let one into our country; stay behind our mountain barrier and have nothing whatever to do with anyone beyond it. This is the 'ancient custom.' Do not let us depart from it. Let us be civil to this Bogle now he is here, lest we offend his powerful master, but for God's sake let us get rid of him as soon as we can, and put every polite difficulty we know of in the way of any other Englishman coming amongst us."

We can imagine how sound such an opinion would seem to the generality of the old greybeard's hearers, and how difficult it would be for anyone—even the Tashi Lama—to contend against it. And with such a feeling in existence Bogle could not do more than produce a favourable personal impression, and put in an argument or two, whenever he had the opportunity, to show that there were also some *advantages* in having relationship with the English, in the hopes that these arguments might gradually sink into the Tibetan mind, and when the opportunity should arise, bring forth fruit. And this much he did most effectively in carrying out the Governor's policy.

CHAPTER II

TURNER'S MISSION, 1782

WARREN HASTINGS was not content with a single effort to reopen the commercial and friendly intercourse which in former times had subsisted between Tibet and India. As he had expected little from the first move, so he had always intended to work continuously with the same end in view, hoping to eventually gain that end by repeated efforts over long periods.

Bogle returned to Calcutta in June, 1775, and in November of the same year Hastings deputed Dr. Hamilton, who had accompanied him to Tibet, on a second mission to Bhutan. Hamilton spent some months in Bhutan, inquiring into and settling certain causes of dispute; and in July, 1777, he was sent on a third mission to Bhutan to congratulate a new Deb Raja on his succession. Thus, as Markham points out, Warren Hastings, by keeping up a regular intercourse with the Bhutan rulers, by maintaining a correspondence with the Tashi Lama, and by means of an annual fair at Rangpur, prevented the opening made by Bogle from again being closed.

Warren Hastings also intended to send another mission to Tibet itself, and in 1779 Bogle was appointed Envoy for a second time. But in the meanwhile the Tashi Lama had decided to undertake a journey to Peking to visit the Chinese Emperor. Bogle, therefore, was to have been sent to Peking to meet the Lama there, but, most disastrously for all friendly intercourse between Tibet and India, the Lama died in Peking in November 1780, and Bogle himself died at Calcutta in April, 1781.

The success of Asiatic affairs depends so much on the

influence of personalities that the death of these two men, who had conceived such a real respect and affection for one another, was an almost fatal blow to Warren Hastings' plans for the improvement of the relationship between Tibet and India. Nevertheless, he kept steadily on with his deliberate policy, and watched for some other opportunity of carrying it to fruition. Persistency of aim and watchfulness for opportunities, making the most of the occasion offered, and decisiveness of action—these were always Hastings' guiding principles. So when, in February, 1782, news reached Calcutta that the Tashi Lama, in accordance with the Tibetan ideas of reincarnation, had reappeared in the person of an infant, he resolved to send another mission to Tibet to congratulate the Regent.

For this duty he selected Captain Samuel Turner, an officer who had distinguished himself at the Siege of Seringapatam and on a mission to Tippoo Sultan, and who was then thirty-three years of age.

Turner himself was very favourably received at Shigatse, and at his first interview informed the Regent that Warren Hastings had an earnest solicitude to preserve and cultivate the amicable intercourse that had so happily commenced between them; that this correspondence, in its earliest stages, had been dictated by the purest motives of humanity, and had hitherto pointed with unexampled sincerity and steadiness towards one great object, which constituted the grand business of the Tashi Lama's life—peace and universal good; that the Governor-General, whose attention was always directed towards the same pursuits, was overwhelmed with anxiety lest the friendship which had been established between himself and the Regent might undergo a change, and he had therefore sent a trusted agent to convey his congratulations on the joyful reappearance in the world of the late Tashi Lama, and to express the hope that everything that was expected would at length be effectually accomplished.

To this the Regent replied that the present and the

late Tashi Lama were one and the same, and that there was no manner of difference between them, only that, as he was yet merely an infant, and his spirit had but just returned into the world, he was at present incapable of action. The Regent assured Turner of the firm, unshaken attachment which the Tashi Lama had entertained for Mr. Hastings to his latest breath, and he was also loud in his encomiums on the occasion that gave birth to their present friendship, which originated entirely in his granting peace to the Bhutanese in compliance with the intercession of the Tashi Lama.

In other interviews the Regent assured Turner that during the interview of the late Tashi Lama with the Emperor of China, the Lama had taken several opportunities to represent in the strongest terms the particular amity which subsisted between the Governor-General and himself. The Regent said that the Lama's conversation had even influenced the Emperor to resolve upon commencing a correspondence with his friend. Turner was also assured that the Tashi Lama particularly sought from the Emperor liberty to grant admission to Tibet to whatever person he chose, without control. And to this the Emperor is said to have consented; but, owing to the death of the Tashi Lama and the jealousy of the Chinese officials, nothing resulted.

The power and influence of these Chinese officials in Tibet was evidently very great, for in his intercourse with the Tibetan officials Turner could plainly trace, though they were averse to own any immediate dependence upon the Chinese, the greatest awe of the Emperor of China, and of his officers stationed at the Court of Lhasa, who had usurped even from the hands of the Dalai Lama the greatest portion of his temporal power. When Turner offered to attend a certain ceremony, the Regent excused himself from accepting the offer of his company on account of the Chinese, whose jealousy of strangers was well known, and to whom he was particularly anxious to give no occasion for offence. On a subsequent occasion the Regent told Turner that many letters had passed between himself and the Dalai Lama, who was always favourably inclined towards the English; but he attributed the discouragement and obstruction Turner had received to the Chinese officials at Lhasa. "The influence of the Chinese," adds Turner, "overawes the Tibetans in all their proceedings, and produces a timidity and caution in their conduct more suited to the character of subjects than allies." At the same time, they were very jealous of interference by the Chinese, and uneasy of their yoke, though it sat so lightly upon them. And while they respected the Chinese Emperor, and had this fear of Chinese officials, they "looked upon the Chinese as a gross and impure race of men."

And now again, as in Bogle's time, we see traces of Russian influence. The Regent and the Ministers told Turner that they were no strangers to the reputation of the reigning Czarina, Catherine, her extent of dominion, and the commerce carried on with China. Many overtures, they told him, had been made on the part of Russia to extend her commerce to the internal part of Tibet, but the disinclination of the Tibetans to enter into any new foreign connection, and the watchful jealousy of the Chinese, had hitherto defeated every attempt of that nature.

Turner spent nearly a year in Tibet, and though he was unable to visit Lhasa owing to the antipathy of the Lamas, he was able to obtain some substantial concessions from the Regent of the Tashi Lama at Shigatse. He obtained* "his promise of encouragement to all merchants, natives of India, that may be sent to traffic in Tibet, on behalf of the Government of Bengal," and he reports to Warren Hastings that his authority alone is requisite to secure these merchants the protection of the Regent, who had promised to grant free admission into Tibet

* Turner, p. 374.

to all such merchants, natives of India, as shall come recommended by the Governor of Bengal; to yield them every assistance requisite for the transport of their goods; and to assign them a place of residence for vending their commodities, either within the monastery at Shigatse, or, should it be considered as more eligible, in the town itself. He did not consider it consistent with the spirit of Warren Hastings' instructions, he reports, to be importunate for greater privileges than those to native traders. Such as he had obtained he hoped would suffice to open the much-wished-for communication. When merchants had learnt the way, tasted the profit and established intercourse, the traffic might bear a tax, which, if laid upon it in its infancy, might suppress its growth.

Turner rejoined Warren Hastings at Patna in March, 1784, and I remember seeing, among some original letters of Warren Hastings in the Indian Foreign Office, an enthusiastic appreciation of Turner's work, and an expression of the great pleasure the meeting afforded him; for Hastings was as warmly appreciative with some men as he was coldly reserved with others.

As long as Hastings remained in India our intercourse with Tibet prospered. But soon after his departure a contretemps occurred, and all his work was undone. In 1792 the Nepalese invaded Tibet, sacked Shigatse, and carried off all the plunder of the monasteries. The Lamas had to flee across the Brahmaputra and apply for protection to the Chinese. A Chinese army was despatched to their assistance. The Nepalese were defeated and driven back across their own frontier, and peace was only concluded upon the conditions of an annual tribute to the Emperor and the full restitution of all the spoils which they carried off.

By an unfortunate circumstance, through the first British Envoy having arrived in Nepal just about the time of this invasion, the Chinese commander formed the impression that we had instigated, or at least encouraged, the Nepalese in their attack on Tibet; and the representations which he made to his Government, coupled, says Turner, with our declining to afford effectual assistance to the Lamas' cause, had considerable weight. As a consequence, all communication between Tibet and India was stopped, and "the approach of strangers, even of Bengal and Hindustan, was utterly prohibited." The Hindu holy men were charged with treachery in acting as spies and guides for the Nepalese, and were forbidden to remain any longer in Shigatse; and "from this period," continues Turner, "unhappily is to be dated the interruption which has taken place in the regular intercourse between the Company's possessions and the territory of the Lama."

It was a sad ending to what had begun so promisingly, and one is tempted to reflect what Warren Hastings would have done if he had still held the reins of government in Bengal, and whether he would have been able to restrain the Gurkhas, to assist the Lamas, and to reassure the Chinese. Certainly it is a most unfortunate circumstance that we so often are unable to help our friends just when they most need our help, and press our friendship upon them just when they least want it.

Thus the results of Warren Hastings' forethought and careful, steady endeavour were all lost. Yet it must be conceded by the sturdiest advocate of non-interference that those endeavours were not merely statesman-like, but humane. There was never any attempt to aggress. No threats were ever used; no impatience was shown. Warren Hastings, as the representative of a trading company, looked, firstly, to improve trade relations; but as the ruler of many millions of human beings, he knew that trade or any other relationship must be based on mutual good feeling, and he knew that good feeling with a suspicious people can only be established by a very, very slow process. He therefore took each step deliberately, and he strove to secure permanently the advantages of each small step taken; and, having done this, he had some right to expect that when he himself had shown so much restraint and moderation, those who followed after would continue the same deliberate policy.

Unfortunately, as we have seen, the policy of drift and inaction in regard to Tibet set in on Warren Hastings' departure. The promotion of intercourse had proved a difficult business; and with so much on hand elsewhere in the building up of the Indian Empire, it was perhaps natural that the ordinary Governor-General should let the matter drop.

CHAPTER III

MANNING'S VISIT TO LHASA

Now when statesmen were most lukewarm about Tibet the inevitable English adventurer came to the front. And it is a curious circumstance that it was just when our relations with the Tibetans were at their coldest that the only Englishman who ever reached Lhasa before the Mission of 1904 achieved this success. He was not an accredited agent of Government sent to bring into effect a deliberate policy such as that conceived by Warren Hastings. He was a private adventurer, and he went up in spite of, and against the wishes of, the Government of the time.

His name was Manning. At Cambridge he was the friend of Charles Lamb, and was of such ability that he was expected to be at least Second Wrangler, but he was of an eccentric nature, and "had a strong repugnance to oaths," and left the University without a degree. He conceived, however, a passionate desire to see the Chinese Empire. He studied the Chinese language in France and England, afterwards made his way to Canton, remained there three years, and in 1810 procured a letter of introduction from the Select Committee of Canton to Lord Minto, then Governor-General of India, asking him to give him every practicable assistance in the prosecution of his plans. But he received little or no aid from the Government, and was left to his own resources, without official recognition of any description.

Manning, attended by a Chinese servant, proceeded to Tibet through Bhutan, and on October 21, 1811, arrived at Phari, at the head of the Chumbi Valley. His description of the Jong then precisely corresponds with our own experiences in Tibet on many an occasion since: "Dirt, dirt, grease, smoke. Misery, but good mutton."

A Chinese Mandarin arrived there about the same time, and Manning gave him two bottles of cherry-brandy and a wineglass. This, and probably Manning's very original manners, evidently unfroze his heart, for he asked him to dinner, and promised to write immediately to the Lhasa Mandarin for permission for him to proceed. Manning also received applications to cure soldiers, and his medicines "did wonderfully well, and the patients were very grateful." They even petitioned for him to go with the Mandarin towards Gyantse, and the Mandarin granted their request.

Altogether, Manning made a very favourable impression on the Chinese who, he remarked, lorded it in Tibet like the English in India, and made the Tibetans stand before them. And he considered then that there were advantages in having the Chinese in this superior position. "Things are much pleasanter now the Chinese are here," he says; "the magistrate hints about overtures respecting opening a commercial intercourse between the Chinese and the English through Bhutan. I cannot help exclaiming in my mind (as I often do) what fools the Company are to give me no commission, no authority, no instructions. What use are their Embassies when their Ambassadors cannot speak to a soul, and can only make ordinary phrases pass through a stupid interpreter? No *finesse*, no *tournure*, no compliments. Fools, fools, fools, to neglect an opportunity they may never have again!"

Poor Manning experienced very severe cold, and travelled to Gyantse in great discomfort, and felt these discomforts acutely, so that the greater part of his diary is filled with quaint denunciation of his Chinese clerk; of a vicious horse which kicked and bit him; of the "common horse-furniture," which was "detestable"; of the saddle which was so high behind and before that he sat in pain unless he twisted himself unequally; of another pony "which sprang forward in a full runaway gallop, with the most furious and awkward motion he ever experienced"; of yet another that was "so weak, so tottering, and so stumbling, and which trembled so whenever he set his foot on a stone, which was about every other step," that he could "hardly keep up with the company"; of his being "so eaten up by little insects" that he had to sit down in the sunshine and get rid of as many as he could, for he "suffered a good deal from these little insects, whose society he was not used to"; of his at last finding "a very pleasant-going horse with a handsome countenance," which he was tempted to buy, "but was checked by the prudent consideration that he might encumber me at Lhasa," and too much disencumber his lean purse. Strange that the first Englishman ever to visit Lhasa should have been incommoded for want of a five-pound note with which to buy a rough hill pony.

At Gyantse the Chinese Mandarin and General, in whose train Manning had come, appointed him a little lodge in the courtyard of the principal house, and whatever he required was soon supplied by the Chinese soldiers and others who wished medical treatment from him. "One brought rice, one brought meat, another brought a table, another brought a little paste and paper and mended a hole in the window, another brought a present of a pen and candles." Every Chinaman in the town came to see him. The General was "vastly civil and polite," and invited him to dinner. But though he was "very much of a gentleman," Manning concluded that he was "really no better than an old woman." The dinner was tolerably good, and the wine excellent, but the cooking was indifferent.

On the other hand, the Mandarin was impressed by Manning's beard. He had known men with better moustaches than Manning's, for he had, "for convenience of eating, song, and drink," cut his short in India, and it had not yet grown again. But the beard never failed to excite the General's admiration, and he declared he had never seen one nearly so handsome. The General, likewise, approved of his "countenance and manner." He pretended to skill in physiognomy and fortune-telling, and foretold very great things of Manning.

Manning also visited the Tibet Mandarin, who lived "in a sort of castle on the top of a hill," the Jong, which General Macdonald attacked and captured in 1904, and they discussed Calcutta and Tibet together for half an hour, but what they said Manning does not record. The Tibetan intimated that he would return the visit the next day, and he sent "some rice and a useful piece of cloth, but did not come himself."

With his medical practice Manning had a greater success. To one Chinaman and his wife, who were suffering from "an intermittent fever," he gave "opium, Fowler's solution of arsenic, and afterwards left them a few pages of bark. The mother-in-law, also, who had the complaint of old age, he cheered up with a little comforting physic."

The General often came to see him, "for, like many other Generals, he had nothing to do, and was glad of a morning lounge." He managed, however, to foist a Chinese servant on to Manning as cook. This man's cooking was bad, but "in drying and folding up linen he saved him infinite trouble," for, says Manning, "I never could to this day fold up a shirt or other vestment. A handkerchief or a sheet I can manage, but nothing further."

Manning, hearing that the General was fond of music, and "no bad performer," took the opportunity "one day, while he was smoking his pipe in my courtyard, of introducing the subject, and paying my court to him by requesting the favour of hearing music. This brought me an invitation to take an evening repast and wine with him, which was just what I liked. He gave us a very pretty concert. . . . The Chinese music, though rather meagre to a European, has its beauties. . . . The General insisted upon my giving him a specimen of European (Calcutta) music on the Chinese flute. I was not acquainted with the fingering of that instrument, but I managed to produce something, which he politely praised."

The answer from the Lhasa magistrate to his request to be permitted to proceed to Lhasa arrived a few days after his arrival at Gyantse. A passport was given him, transport and supplies furnished, and as he neared Lhasa he was met by a "respectable person on horseback, who dismounted and saluted," and who had been sent out by the Tibetan authorities to welcome him and conduct him to Lhasa.

The view of the Potala, "of the lofty, towering palace, which forms a majestic mountain of a building," excited his admiration, but if the palace had exceeded his expectations, he says, the town as far fell short of them. There was "nothing striking, nothing pleasing, in its appearance. The habitations were begrimed with smut and dirt. . . . In short, everything seemed mean and gloomy, and excited the idea of something unreal."

His first care was to provide himself with a proper hat, and, having found one, he proceeded to pay his respects to the Chinese Mandarin. Coming into his presence, he for the first time in his life performed the ceremony of *ketese*, or kneeling. The Mandarin received him politely, and said he had provided him with quarters. On the following day he visited two of the chief Tibetan officials.

On December 17, 1811, he went to the Potala to salute the Grand Lama. He took with him as an offering some broadcloth, two pair of china ewers, and a pair of good brass candlesticks, which he had "clean and furbished up," and into which he put "two wax candles to make a show." He also took "thirty new bright dollars, and as many pieces of zinc," and, besides this, "some genuine Smith's lavender-water . . . and a good store of Nankin tea, which is a rarity and delicacy at Lhasa, and not to be bought there."

Arrived in the great hall he made due obeisance, touching the ground three times with his head to the Grand Lama, and once to the Ti-mi-fu. While he was bowing, "the awkward servants contrived to let fall and break the bottle of lavender-water." Having delivered his present to the Grand Lama, he took off his hat, and "humbly gave his clean-shaved head to lay his hands upon."

This ceremony over, he sat on a cushion, not far from the Lama's throne, and had suché brought them. But "the Lama's beautiful and interesting face and manner engrossed almost all his attention." His face was, he thought, poetically and affectingly beautiful. He was at that time about seven years old, and had the simple and unaffected manners of a well-educated, princely child. Sometimes, particularly when he looked at Manning, his smile almost approached to a gentle laugh. "No doubt," naïvely remarks Manning, "my grim beard and spectacles somewhat excited his risibility."

The little Grand Lama addressed a few remarks to Manning, speaking in Tibetan to the Chinese interpreter, the interpreter in Chinese to Manning's Chinese Munshi, and the Munshi in Latin to Manning. "I was extremely affected by this interview with the Lama," says Manning. "I could have wept through strangeness of sensation."

Here in Lhasa, as at Gyantse, Manning had many applications made to him for medicine, and he treated both Chinese and Tibetans. But spies also came, and "certainly," says Manning, "my bile used to rise when the hounds looked into my room." The Tartar General detested Europeans. They were the cause, he said, of all his misfortunes. Sometimes he said Manning was a missionary, and at other times a spy. "These Europeans are very formidable; now one man has come to spy the country he will inform others. Numbers will come, and at last they will be for taking the country from us." So argued the Mandarins, and, indeed, there were rumours that the Chinese meant to execute Manning. He had always fully expected this possibility, and writes: "I never could, even in idea, make up my mind to submit to an execution with firmness and manliness."

Yet, on the whole, he was not badly treated. He

remained on at Lhasa for several months, paying many visits to the Grand Lama, and eventually orders came from Peking for him to return the way he came. He left Lhasa on April 19, and reached Kuch Behar on June 10, 1812.

Manning's own object was "A moral view of China, its manners, the degree of happiness the people enjoy, their sentiments and opinions so far as they influence life, their literature, their history, the causes of their stability and vast population, their minor arts and contrivances; what there might be in China to serve as a model for imitation, and what to serve as a beacon to avoid." Having been foiled in this his main object, he does not appear to have regarded the subsidiary circumstance that he had reached Lhasa as of particular interest. And he seems to have been so disgusted with the Government's refusal to support him, that when he returned to Calcutta he would give no one any particulars of his journey. The account which Markham published sixty years later was only discovered long after his death.

It is a meagre record of so important a journey, yet it exemplifies one or two points which are worthy of note. It showed that an individual Englishman, with delicacy of touch and with a real sympathetic feeling towards those among whom he was travelling, could find his way even into the very presence of the Dalai Lama in the Potala itself. It showed, too, that he could get on perfectly well with the Chinese personally. But it showed likewise that at the back of the minds of both the Tibetans and Chinese was a strong dread of the British power, which made them fear to allow a single Englishman to remain in Tibet or even pass through the country.

Yet Manning confirmed what Bogle and Turner had also noticed — that, while the Tibetans dreaded the Chinese, they disliked them intensely. He says that the Chinese were very disrespectful to the Tibetans. Only bad-charactered Chinamen were sent to Tibet, and he could not help thinking that the Tibetans "would view the Chinese influence in Tibet overthrown without many emotions of regret, especially if the rulers under the new influence were to treat the Grand Lama with respect; for this is a point in which those haughty Mandarins are somewhat deficient, to the no small dissatisfaction of the good people of Lhasa." These words would be very fairly applicable to the situation at the present day.

After Manning, no Englishman, in either a private or official capacity, visited Lhasa till the Mission of 1904. This seems to show want of enterprise on the part of Englishmen in India; but some did make the attempt, and many more would have if they could have obtained the necessary leave from all the authorities concerned. British officers in India are keen enough to go on such adventures, but leave can very rarely be obtained. I had myself planned out such a journey in 1889. I had interviewed the Foreign Secretary, now Sir Mortimer Durand, and not only obtained permission, but even some pecuniary assistance, when, at the last moment, I was refused permission by the Colonel of my regiment. Such restrictions must, I know, have prevented many another besides myself. Still, efforts were made by individual officers, unsupported by Government, to explore Tibet, and, if possible, reach Lhasa. Moorcroft explored Western Tibet, and, according to some reports, actually reached Lhasa and died there; Richard and Henry Strachey visited the sources of the Brahmaputra and the Sutlej; Carey, Littledale, Bower, Wellby, Deasy, and Rawling explored in Northern Tibet; and native surveyors mapped even Lhasa itself, to which point Sarat Chandra Das also penetrated at great risk and brought back most valuable information.

These and other efforts to explore the country by the Russian travellers Prjevalsky, Pievtsoff and Kozoloff; by the Frenchmen Huc and Gabet, Bonvalot, Prince Henri d'Orléans, Dutreuil de Rhins and Grenard; and by that indefatigable and courageous Swedish traveller, Sven Hedin, have all been brought together by Sir Thomas

Holdich in his recent work on exploration in Tibet. It is not necessary here to do more than refer to the fact that efforts to gain a knowledge of the country were almost continuously being made through the second half of last century; my object is rather to describe the effort, not so much to explore the country, as to regularize and foster the intercourse which already existed with its people.

CHAPTER IV

THE BENGAL GOVERNMENT'S EFFORTS, 1873–1886

It was not till a century had elapsed since Warren Hastings had begun his attempts to form a friendship with the Tibetans that the Government in India again made any real effort to come into proper relationship with their neighbours. For a century they were content to let things take their course, in spite of their informality, and in spite of the fact that Indian subjects were having all the worst of the intercourse, for while Tibetans were allowed to come to India when and where and how they liked, to trade there without duty and without hindrance, to travel and to reside wherever they wished, on the other side, obstructions of every kind were placed in the way of Indians, and still more of British, trading, travelling, or residing in Tibet. But in the year 1873 the Indian Government began to stir, and take stock of the position, and to reflect whether this one-sided condition of affairs might not be changed to the advantage of Indians and Europeans without hurting the Tibetans.

In that year the Bengal Government addressed the Government of India a letter, a copy of which was sent to the Royal Geographical Society, in which they urged that the Chinese should be pressed "for an order of admittance to Tibet," and that "the authorities at Peking should allow a renewal of the friendly intercourse between India and Tibet which existed in the days of Bogle and Turner." The Bengal Government said that the Government of India and the Secretary of State had repeatedly expressed the great interest which they took in this subject, and the wish that no favourable opportunity should be neglected of promoting the development of commercial intercourse between British India and those trans-Himalayan countries which were then practically closed to us. If only the Chinese and Tibetans would remove the embargo at present imposed upon the entry of our trade, there were, by routes under our own control, no serious difficulties or dangers of any kind to overcome, and none of the risks of collision which existed elsewhere.

Tibet, the Bengal Government said, was a well-regulated country with which our Hillmen were in constant communication. When Europeans went to the frontier and tried to cross it, there was no display of violence or disturbance. They were civilly turned back, with an intimation that there were orders not to admit them. All the inquiries of the Lieutenant-Governor led to the belief that the Tibetans themselves had no objections to intercourse with us. The experiences of the great botanist, Sir Joseph Hooker, who in 1849 had travelled to the Tibetan border, and Blanford among the recent travellers, and of Bogle and Turner in the past, were singularly at one upon this point. The Commandant of Khamba Jong, who had met Mr. Blanford on the frontier in 1870, assured him that the Tibetans had no ill-will to foreigners, and would, if allowed, gladly receive Europeans. The fact appeared to be, the Lieutenant-Governor said, that "the prohibition to intercourse with Tibet is part of the Chinese policy of exclusion imposed on the Tibetans by Chinese officials and enforced by Chinese troops stationed in Tibet." He fully sympathized with the Chinese desire to keep out foreigners in China. "But," he said, "in Tibet there is not wealth enough to attract many adventurers; there is room only for a moderate and legitimate commerce;" and among a people so good and well regulated as the Tibetans there would be no such difficulties as existed in China. If the road were opened, it would be used only by fair traders and by responsible Government servants or travellers under the control of Government.

In seeking to press the Chinese for admittance to Tibet, he said, the most emphatic declaration might be made that, having our natural and best boundary in the

Himalayas, we could not, and would not in any circumstances, encroach on Tibet, and we might offer to arrange that none save Hillmen or classes domiciled in Tibet should be allowed to go in without a pass, which would be given under such restrictions that Government would be responsible for the conduct of the holders.

The Lieutenant-Governor adduced as a further reason for entering into formal relationship with the Tibetans that, if we had an understanding between us, we should together be able to keep in order the wild tribes inhabiting the hilly country between British territory and Tibet. And he instanced the case of the Mezhow Mishnies, who for murdering two French missionaries in 1854 were punished both by us and by the Tibetans, and who, in consequence, ever after had "a most salutary dread of using violence."

The Bengal Government also contended then in 1873, as they are still contending now, for the admission of our tea. Indian tea is grown in large quantities on the hills in British territory bordering Tibet. But, said the Lieutenant-Governor, nearly forty years ago: "The Tibetans, or rather their Chinese Governors, will not, on protectionist principles, admit our tea across the passes. An absolute embargo is laid on anything in the shape of tea." The removal of this, he thought, might well be made a subject of special negotiation. And besides tea, the Bengal Government thought that Manchester and Birmingham goods and Indian indigo would find a market in Tibet, and that we should receive in return much wool, sheep, cattle, walnuts, Tibetan cloths, and other commodities.

Thus, thirty years before the Tibet Mission started the local Government had made a real effort to have the Chinese pressed to abandon their policy of exclusion so far as Tibet was concerned. The lineal official descendant of Warren Hastings in the Governorship of Bengal neither attempted nor advocated any high-handed local measures. He stated his case calmly and reasonably, and advocated the most correct course—the attempt to settle the matter direct with the Chinese.

Local officers are often told that they are too impatient, and that they too frequently want to settle a matter by local action, when it might be so much better disposed of by correspondence from headquarters; by negotiations, for instance, between London and Peking, or London and St. Petersburg. They are urged to take a wider view, and to display a calmer spirit, and greater confidence in the wisdom and sagacity of their London rulers. But when thirty years after this very moderate and perfectly reasonable request was made by the local authority, the matter was still no nearer settlement than it was when the request was made; and when the House of Commons, which controls the destinies of the Empire, was still asking why we did not apply to the Chinese, the local officer's faith in the superior efficacy of headquarters treatment is somewhat shaken. And he often questions whether matters which, after forming the subject of voluminous correspondence between the provincial Government and the Government of India, between the latter and the India Office, between the India Office and the Foreign Office, between the Foreign Office and the Ambassador abroad, between him and the Foreign Government, which are discussed in the Cabinet, and form a subject for debate in the House of Commons and the House of Lords, and for platform speeches and newspaper articles innumerable, do not in this lengthy process assume a magnitude which they never originally possessed; whether, having assumed such magnitude, they ever really do get settled or only compromised; and whether, after all, they might not have been settled expeditiously and decisively on the spot before they had been allowed to grow to these alarming proportions.

There are, one knows, many cases which can only be settled by the Central Government, and which are so settled very satisfactorily, but I am doubtful if Tibet is one of these, and whether we have been wise in the instance of Tibet, and in many others connected with China, to make so much of, and expect so much from, the Chinese Central Government, which has so little real control over the local Governments. Perhaps if the

Government of Bengal, with the countenance and support of the Imperial Government, had long ago dealt directly with the Lhasa authorities, Chinese and Tibetan matters might have been arranged more expeditiously and satisfactorily. At any rate, it cannot be safely assumed that the Central Government method is necessarily the best.

In this case, for instance, all that resulted was that the Chinese Government, in the Chefu Convention concluded three years later, undertook to protect any mission which should be sent to Tibet—an undertaking which was literally valueless, for when a mission was actually sent to Tibet they were unable to afford it the slightest protection, and the Chinese representative in Lhasa confessed to me in writing that he could not even get the Tibetans to give him transport to enable him to meet me.

The Government of Bengal had therefore to content themselves with improving the road inside our frontier, and with doing what they could on our side to entice and further trade.

But in 1885 a renewed effort was made to come to an understanding with the Tibetans. The brilliant Secretary of the Bengal Government, Colman Macaulay, visited the frontier to see if any useful relationship could be established with the Shigatse people by the route up the head of the Sikkim Valley. The Tashi Lama, who resides at Shigatse, had always been more friendly than the Lhasa people, and this seemed more promising. Macaulay saw a local Tibetan official from the other side, entered into friendly intercourse, and found, as Bogle and Turner had found, that apart from Chinese obstruction there was no objection on the part of the Tibetan people themselves to enter into friendly relationship. Macaulay was filled with enthusiasm. He threw his whole soul and energy into the matter. He secured the support of the Government of India. And, more important still, he fired the Secretary of State for India with ardour. Never before had such enthusiasm for improving our relations with Tibet been shown. And as it happened that this Secretary of State was the best the India Office have ever had—the man who without any faltering hesitation annexed Burma, to the lasting benefit of the Burmese, of ourselves, and of humanity—there seemed now a real prospect of success. Lord Randolph Churchill and Colman Macaulay were something of kindred spirits, and Macaulay was sent to Peking with every support and encouragement to get the necessary permit for a mission to Lhasa. The Chinese assented. Permission was granted. Macaulay organized his mission, bought rich presents, collected his transport, and was on the eve of starting from Darjiling when "international considerations" came in and Government countermanded the whole affair.

"Everything had gone so fairly," wrote Macaulay to Sir Clements Markham from Darjiling in October, 1886, "that it was difficult for us here to believe that we should be shipwrecked within sight of the promised land." Yet so it was, and he took his disappointment so deeply to heart that he completely broke down in health, and died a few years later.

Immediately following on the abandonment of the mission came the most unprovoked aggression on the part of the Tibetans. They crossed the Jelap-la, the pass from Chumbi into Sikkim and the frontier between Tibet and our feudatory State, and they occupied Lengtu, eighteen miles on our side of the frontier, building a guard-house there, and turning out one of our road overseers, placed there to superintend the road which Sir Richard Temple had made when Lieutenant-Governor of Bengal. And on hearing that the mission had been countermanded, they became so elated that they boasted that they would occupy Darjiling, only seventy-eight miles off, and something like a panic ensued in this almost unprotected summer resort. At the same time, on the opposite side of Tibet they were still more actively aggressive, expelling the Roman Catholic missionaries from their long-established homes at Batang, massacring many of their converts, and burning the mission-house.

This is a very essential fact to bear in mind in the consideration of the Tibetan question—that after both Tibetan and Chinese susceptibilities had been given way to on every occasion, it was the Tibetans who invaded us. It was a Bhutanese invasion of the plains of Bengal, followed by a letter from the Tashi Lama, that had initiated our relations with Tibet in the time of Warren Hastings. And it was this invasion of Sikkim that forced upon us the regularization of our relations with the Tibetans.

When the Tibetans thus invaded the territory of our feudatory, we should have been well within our right in forthwith expelling them by force; but, in accordance with the policy of forbearance we had so consistently pursued, we referred the matter to the Chinese, and requested them to procure the withdrawal of the Tibetans. We also allowed the Chinese ample time, a year, within which to bring their influence to bear. Then, at the end of 1887, we wrote to the Tibetan commander that unless he evacuted his position before March 15, 1888, he would be expelled by force. This letter was returned unopened. In February we wrote to the Dalai Lama himself to the same effect, but again we received no reply. It was only on March 20, 1888, that a British force assumed the offensive, and advanced upon the Tibetans in the position they had occupied within our frontier at Lengtu.

The Tibetans, for the time being, offered no resistance, and retired to Chumbi, on their own side of the frontier, and our troops occupied a position at Gnatong, on our side. Two months later, however, the Tibetans again showed truculence, and with 3,000 men attacked our camp at Gnatong. They were repulsed, and once more withdrew. But in September they, for the third time, advanced across our border, and in a single night, with that skill in building for which they are so remarkable, threw up a wall three miles long and from 3 to 4 feet high in a position just above Gnatong, and some miles within our border.

This position General Graham attacked on the following day, and drove the Tibetans from it over the Jelap-la Pass, and in the ensuing days pursued them into the Chumbi Valley. But here again, in accordance with our principle of respecting Chinese susceptibilities, our troops did not remain in Chumbi a single day, but returned at once to Gnatong. For two years now the Tibetans had been encroaching on our side of the frontier, but not for one day would we permit our troops to remain on the Tibetan side. Forbearance could scarcely go further than this, but yet it was to be still more strained on many a subsequent occasion.

CHAPTER V

THE CONVENTION WITH CHINA

THE Chinese Amban, or Resident, at Lhasa now appeared upon the scene to effect a settlement, and during 1889 we endeavoured to have the frontier line properly fixed and our exclusive supremacy in Sikkim, which was recorded in well-known treaties, definitely recognized. We also wished, if possible, to have trade regulated. Considering that we had abandoned the proposed mission to Lhasa out of deference to Chinese and Tibetan susceptibilities, that the Tibetans had assumed the offensive, and that the Chinese had shown themselves utterly unable to control them, this was not an unreasonable expectation to hold. We made no demand for indemnity or for any accession of territory. We merely asked that the boundary and trade should be regulated. Yet a year of negotiation passed and no result was obtained, and the Government of India told the Chinese negotiators that they had decided "to close the Sikkim incident, so far as China is concerned, without insisting upon a specific agreement."

But now that the Indian Government, knowing that they could perfectly well hold their own up to their frontier, and finding that the Chinese were of little use in controlling events beyond it, were quite prepared to drop negotiations, the Chinese themselves came forward and pressed for their conclusion. This is an important point. It was now the Chinese who were pressing for an agreement. Further, and this is still more important, they stated that "China will be quite able to enforce in Tibet the terms of the treaty," and they asked the Government of India to depute officers to meet the Chinese Resident at Gnatong. For the agreement which was subsequently reached the

Chinese are therefore in the fullest sense responsible. They had themselves sought it, and they had themselves undertaken to control the affairs of the Tibetans.

Agreement was eventually reached in 1890, and a Convention was signed by Lord Lansdowne and the Chinese Resident in Calcutta on March 17. It laid down that "the boundary of Sikkim and Tibet shall be the crest of the mountain range separating the waters flowing into the Sikkim Teesta, and the affluents from the waters flowing into the Tibetan Mochu, and northwards into other rivers of Tibet." It admitted the British protectorate over the Sikkim State. By it both the Chinese and British Governments engaged "reciprocally to respect the boundary as defined in Article I., and to prevent acts of aggression from their respective sides of the frontier." The three questions of providing increased facilities for trade, of pasturage, and of the method in which official communications between the British authorities in India and the authorities in Tibet should be conducted were reserved for discussion by joint Commissioners from either side, who should meet within six months of the ratification of the Convention.

This Convention proved in practice to be of not the slightest use, for the Tibetans never recognized it, and the Chinese were totally unable to impress them. But it was at least a start towards effecting our ultimate object of regularizing our intercourse with Tibet, and for another three years we solemnly occupied ourselves in discussing the three reserved points; the Chinese Resident, Sheng, being himself the joint Commissioner on the side of the Chinese, and Mr. A. W. Paul representing the British Government.

Our principal aim was to get some mart recognized, to which our merchants could resort and there meet Tibetan merchants. We did not attempt to gain permission for our traders to travel all over Tibet, as Tibetan traders can travel all over India. We merely sought to have one single place recognized where Indian and Tibetan traders could meet to do business with each other. And the place we sought to get so recognized was not in the centre of Tibet, or even in Tibet proper at all. It did not lie on the far side of the Himalayan watershed. It was Phari, at the head of the Chumbi Valley, on the southern side of the main Himalayan range. Yet to even this the Chinese and Tibetans would not agree, and eventually Yatung, at the extreme southern end of the Chumbi Valley and immediately on our border, was agreed upon.

Having made this concession, and having refrained from pressing for permission to allow British subjects to travel beyond this or to buy land and build houses there, we had hoped that the Chinese would meet our wishes in regard to the admission of tea. Speakers in Parliament scoffed at the idea of pressing tea upon the Chinese, but for the Bengal Government it is an important point. All along the low hills bordering Tibet there are numerous tea-plantations, affording both an outlet for British and Indian capital and employment for many thousands of Indian labourers. To a responsible local Government it is of importance to encourage and foster this industry. Now, just across the frontier are three millions of tea-drinkers. Tea is just the kind of light, portable commodity most suited for transit across mountains, and it was perfectly natural, reasonable, and right that the Bengal Government should press for its admission to Tibet, that the Tibetans might at least have the chance of buying it or not, as they pleased. But the Chinese, in spite of concessions in other matters by the Government of India, remained obstinate, and still remain obstinate, in regard to the admission of tea, and eventually only agreed to admit Indian tea into Tibet "at a rate of duty not exceeding that at which Chinese tea is imported into England," which, as the latter rate of duty is 6d. per pound, and the tea drunk in Tibet is very inferior, was in reality the imposition of an *ad valorem* duty of from 150 to 200 per cent., and was therefore a concession of not the slightest value.

On December 5, 1893, the Trade Regulations were signed at Darjiling. The trade-mart at Yatung was to "be open for all British subjects for purposes of trade from the first day of May, 1894," and the Government were to be "free to send officers to reside at Yatung to watch the conditions of British trade." British subjects were not at liberty to buy land and build houses for themselves, but were to be free "to rent houses and godowns (stores) for their own accommodation and for the storage of their goods," and "to sell their goods to whomsoever they please, to purchase native commodities in kind or in money, to hire transport of any kind, and, in general, to conduct their business without any vexatious restrictions." Goods other than arms, liquors, and others specified, were to be "exempt from duty for a period of five years"; but after that, if found desirable, a tariff might be "mutually agreed upon and enforced." The Political Officer in Sikkim and the Chinese Frontier Officer in conference were to settle any trade disputes arising.

No arrangements for communication between British and Tibetan officials were made, but it was laid down that despatches from the Government of India to the Chinese Resident should be handed over by the Political Officer in Sikkim to the Chinese Frontier Officer.

And as to grazing, it was agreed that at the end of one year such Tibetans as continued to graze their cattle in Sikkim should be subject to such regulations as the British Government might lay down.

May 1, 1894, had been fixed as the date upon which the trade-mart at Yatung was to be opened, and at the appointed time Mr. Claude White, the Political Officer in Sikkim, was sent to visit Yatung, to attend the opening of the mart, and to report on the general situation as regards trade. He was instructed not to raise the question of demarcating the frontier, but to undertake, if the subject was mooted by the Chinese officials, that their views and suggestions should be laid before the Government of India.

Mr. White, writing on June 9 from Yatung, reported that, in the first place, the site of the mart had been "exceedingly badly chosen." It will be remembered that it was chosen by the Tibetans, and simply accepted by us out of deference to their feelings. It was at the bottom of a narrow valley, shut in by steep hills, with no room for expansion. He further reported that the godowns (stores), or shops, built for the trade would answer the purpose of native shops, but were quite inadequate for the storage of goods or for the use of European merchants, and that the rent proposed was exorbitant, being Rs. 25 a month, when a fair rent would be from Rs. 4 to Rs. 5. He found the Tibetans most discourteous and obstructive, and he believed that the Lhasa authorities had issued orders that the free-trade clauses of the treaty were not to be carried out. The local official at Phari, at the head of the Chumbi Valley, charged 10 per cent. on all goods passing through Phari, both imports and exports; and this action, in Mr. White's opinion, certainly did away with any freedom of trade, as provided for in the treaty, for it was obviously useless to have provided by treaty that Indian goods should be allowed to enter Tibet free of duty if a few miles inside the frontier, and on the only road into Tibet, a heavy duty was to be imposed upon them.

Mr. White also reported that the Chinese, though friendly to him, and apparently willing to help, had "no authority whatever." They admitted that the treaty was not being carried out in a proper spirit, and Mr. White gathered that the Tibetans actually repudiated it, and asserted that it was signed by the British Government and the Chinese, and therefore they had nothing to do with it. In any case, they maintained that they had a right to impose what taxes they chose at Phari so long as goods were allowed to pass Yatung free. The Chinese confessed that they were not able to manage the Tibetans. The Tibetans would not obey them, and the Chinese were afraid to give any orders. China was suzerain over Tibet only in name, was Mr. White's conclusion. Negotiation was, therefore, he said, most difficult, for though the Chinese agreed to any proposal, they were quite unable to answer for the Tibetans, and the Tibetans, when spoken to, either sheltered themselves behind the Chinese or said that they had no orders to give any answer for Lhasa, and could only report.

Mr. White's immediate superior, the Commissioner of the Rajshahi Division, agreed with him that the levying of a duty of 10 per cent. *ad valorem* at Phari was a clear breach of the main article of the Trade Convention. He contended that by Article IV. of the Regulations it is provided that goods entering Tibet for British India across the Sikkim-Tibet frontier, or *vice versa*, shall be exempt from duty for a period of five years, and that this meant a general exemption from all duties, wherever imposed, the place of realization being altogether irrelevant. He recommended, therefore, that this breach of the main article of the treaty, to which all the other provisions were ancillary, should be made the subject of a representation to the Chinese Government.

The Government of Bengal took the same view. They thought the levy of the duty at Phari undoubtedly seemed to be inconsistent with the terms of the treaty, which provided for free trade for a period of five years. And the Lieutenant-Governor felt that no time should be lost in making this matter the subject of a representation to the Government of China.

And in this view our Minister at Peking, Mr. (afterwards Sir Nicholas) O'Conor, Ambassador at St. Petersburg and Constantinople, thoroughly concurred, and suggested to the Viceroy that the imposition of a 10 per cent. *ad valorem* duty at Phari should be very strongly protested against as contrary to treaty stipulations.

The Government of India, however, "recognizing the necessity for extreme patience in dealing with the Tibetans, decided that it would be premature to make any formal complaint of their obstructiveness."* They wrote to the Government of Bengal that "The information in regard to the levy of duty at Phari and to the obstructiveness of the Tibetans was certainly unsatisfactory, but the Regulations

* Blue-book, p. 24.

only laid down that goods entering Tibet from British India across the Sikkim-Tibet frontier, or *vice versa*, shall be exempt, etc. Phari is a considerable distance from the frontier, and unless it could be shown that the duty to which Mr. White referred was a special one newly imposed it appeared doubtful whether the Government of India could enter a valid objection." "It has always been recognized," continues the despatch, "that the utmost patience is necessary in dealing with the Tibetans, and having regard to the short time which has elapsed since the date fixed for the opening of the Yatung mart, the Governor-General in Council would prefer to make nothing in the nature of a complaint to the Chinese Government at the present stage."*

The Viceroy, accordingly, merely wrote to the Amban that he had been sorry to learn from Mr. White's reports that he was disappointed at the existing conditions of trade between Tibet and Sikkim; that it would seem that Mr. White was of opinion that trade was unduly hampered by the action of the Tibetan officials at Phari; that His Excellency (the Amban) would be interested to hear the views which Mr. White had formed; and that he, the Viceroy, was confident that traders will, under the Amban's directions, be allowed all the freedom and privileges permissible under the Regulations, and he hoped that before long they might be able to congratulate each other on successful trade development at Yatung. Certainly nothing could have been milder, more patient, and more forbearing—and also, as it proved, less effectual.

It was not only in trade matters that the Tibetans had shown a disregard of the treaty. In the matter of the frontier also they proved troublesome, and during his stay at Yatung Mr. White was informed that certain places in the north-east of Sikkim, and within the boundary laid down in the Convention of 1890, had recently been occupied by Tibetan soldiers. The Viceroy wrote to the Amban in August, 1899, pointing out that

* Blue-book, p. 31.

such incidents were not unlikely to occur as long as the frontier officials had no practical acquaintance with the actual border-line, and suggesting that it would probably be convenient to arrange that Frontier Officers should meet before long on the border and travel together along the boundary fixed by the Convention.

To this the Amban replied, in October, that the Tibetan Council raised objections to our officers "travelling along" the frontier, and were unable to agree that British officers should travel on the Tibetan side of the frontier, but that they considered the proposal to send officers to define the frontier was one with which it was proper to comply. The Amban had, accordingly, deputed a Chinese Major commanding the frontier troops, and the Tibetan Council had deputed a General and a Chief Steward, to proceed to the frontier to meet the officer appointed by the Viceroy, "there to inspect the border between Sikkim and Tibet as defined by the Convention, and to make a careful examination in order that boundary pillars might be erected, which shall be for ever respected by either side." In conclusion, the Amban asked to be informed what officer had been deputed by the Viceroy for this duty, and the date on which he would arrive on the frontier, in order that he might instruct the Chinese and Tibetan deputies "to proceed at the appointed time for the work of demarcation."

This seemed clear and business-like enough. Mr. White pointed out to Government that, with winter coming on, it would be impossible to commence demarcation before May the 1st in the following year, so there was plenty of time in which to make all preliminary arrangements. He also said that the Chinese deputy was an official whom he had met at Yatung, and who had been most courteous to him. And the Commissioner and Bengal Government agreed that the Tibetan objection to British officers travelling within the Tibetan borders might be respected, and that it would be sufficient to erect pillars at the passes, which could be approached from the Sikkim side. So the Viceroy replied, in December, that he thought a start should be made any time between May 1 and July 1 ; that

Mr. White had been deputed for the purpose, and would meet the other deputies at whatever point on the frontier might be convenient; and would be strictly enjoined not to travel on the Tibetan side of the boundary, as it would be sufficient if boundary pillars were erected at the passes which can be approached from the Sikkim side.

The Amban replied on January 13, 1895, that he had sent orders to the deputies "to hold themselves in readiness to commence work at the time suggested by the Viceroy," and he suggested that the respective officers should "come together at Yatung, where they can decide upon the best place for beginning operations, and where the three parties (Indian, Chinese, and Tibetan) can agree upon a date for starting together on the work of demarcation."

Everything was then carefully and deliberately arranged, and there seemed good prospect of a settlement of the frontier; but when, in the following May, Mr. White approached the frontier to meet the Chinese deputy, in accordance with an arrangement they had made between them, he was met by a letter, written by direction of the deputy, and stating that the Lamas were obstinate in their refusal to supply transport, and that he was much disturbed at his failure to keep his appointment, but had laid his difficulties before the Amban. On May 19 Mr. White and the Chinese Major met—a different one from the deputy originally appointed, for the latter had since died. He asked for more delay, but Mr. White refused, as he had already been kept waiting with his escort at inclement altitudes, and Mr. White and he fixed the site of the pillar on the Jelap-la (pass), which is a spot where the site of the watershed forming the boundary, according to treaty, is quite unmistakable, as it runs along a very sharply-defined ridge. Mr. White erected a pillar here, and arranged with the Chinese deputy to meet him at another pass, the Dokala, on June 1, while Mr. White should in the interval erect a pillar at the Donchukla, to be afterwards inspected by the Chinese.

At this time Mr. White also received a letter from the Amban, saying that a day for the beginning of the work having been decided upon, it was, of course, proper that a commencement should be made on that day, and he had already received the consent of the Tibetan State Council to that end. But the Lamas of the three great monasteries, the Amban proceeded to explain, were still full of suspicion, and were pressing certain matters upon him, which made it necessary for him to enlighten them further.

He therefore requested Mr. White kindly to postpone commencing work for a time, in order to avoid trouble on this point. But Mr. White replied that his letter had arrived too late, as the work of demarcation had already commenced before its receipt, and he urged Government to grant no further delay, for the Chinese had had five years since the treaty was signed within which to settle with the Tibetans.

The Government of India, however, thought that no serious inconvenience had apparently arisen through the frontier being undemarcated, and that if the Chinese delegate failed to meet him at the Dokala on or about June 1, he should write to the Chinese Resident, explaining that he had proceeded so far under arrangements with the Chinese deputies at the Jelap-la; but as they had not joined him, he would return to Gantok. He was further to ask the Resident whether work could be jointly proceeded with that season, and giving latest dates for recommencement.

A few days later came the news that the pillar which Mr. White had erected on the Jelap-la had been demolished by the Tibetans, and the stoneware slab on which the number of the pillar had been inscribed had been removed by them. And on June 11 Mr. White telegraphed that the pillar he had erected on the Donchuk-la had been wilfully damaged, and as this was an unfrequented pass he considered the outrage must be deliberate. He subsequently stated that the numbered slab here also had been taken away, and that the destruction of the pillar was most probably the work of three Lamas sent from Lhasa to watch the proceedings of the Tibetan Commissioners at Yatung.

This was brought to the notice of the Chinese Resident by the Viceroy, and a reply was received that the Council of State had sent no orders for the destruction of the pillar, and that he had given orders that a strict examination should be made into the affair, and the people who stole the slab from the pillar be severely punished. At the same time, the Amban suggested that the work of delimiting the frontier should be postponed "until after the expiry of the free period when the treaty was to be revised."

When informed of this proposal, our Minister at Peking stated his opinion that it would be best to be firm in the refusal of a postponement, and he solicited the Viceroy's authority to repeat to the Chinese Government what he had previously informed them, that, if obliged, the British Commissioner would proceed alone.

The Bengal Government also urged that Mr. White "should be authorized to proceed with his own men alone to lay down the boundary and set up pillars on the passes along the eastern frontier where no dispute was known to exist." But the Lieutenant-Governor was informed that the Government of India were not prepared to insist upon the early demarcation of the frontier, and directed that Mr. White should return to Gantok forthwith, or, at any, rate withdraw at once from the immediate neighbourhood of the border.

The Lieutenant-Governor, Sir Charles Elliott, acknowledged that it was difficult for Mr. White to remain indefinitely in his camp on the frontier, but declared that it was impossible to disguise the fact that a return to Gantok practically meant the abandonment of the demarcation. He believed that the authorities in Peking were anxious that the delimitation should continue without delay, but it was plain that the Amban at Lhasa was unable to give effect to the wishes of his Government in consequence of the opposition manifested by the Lamas, who exercised the real authority in Tibet. The contemplated withdrawal of Mr. White to Gantok would undoubtedly, he thought—and events proved him to be absolutely right—cause a loss of prestige, would be looked upon by the Tibetans as a rebuff to British authority, and would encourage them in high-handed acts and demands, and possibly outrages. He had no doubt that if the British Government had only to deal with Tibet, the wisest policy would be to give them warning that unless they at once made arrangements to co-operate in the work of delimitation it would be done without them, and that unless they appointed a ruler on their side who could protect the pillars set up, the British Government would march in and hold the Chumbi Valley in pawn, either temporarily or permanently. Such a brusque and high-handed line of conduct, added the Lieutenant-Governor, was the only one that frontier tribes who have reached the stage of civilization of the Tibetans could understand. But the affair, he allowed, was complicated by the relations of Government with China, and our desire to uphold the weak and tottering authority of the Chinese in Lhasa, the result of which was that the people who were in real power were not those we dealt with, and that the people we dealt with had no power to carry out their engagements with us. In the circumstances, Sir Charles Elliott advocated such negotiations with the Chinese Government as would leave the British Government free to march in and hold the Chumbi Valley, with their consent, and without any detriment to the Chinese suzerainty, but with the object of assisting them to establish their authority more firmly at Lhasa. At any rate, we ought, he considered, to intimate in a firm and friendly way to the Peking Government that either they must get their orders carried out or we must. He reminded the Government of India that nothing had been exacted as the result of the British victories at Lengtu and on the Jelap-la—not even compensation for the cost of the campaign—and he urged that we should now insist that we would protect our own interests if China could not carry out her engagements.*

These, in the light of future events, appear reasonable and sensible proposals; but the Government of India, in pursuance of their policy of forbearance and moderation, would not accept them. They ordered Mr. White definitely to return to Gantok. They noticed that the returns of trade between British territory and Tibet showed a marked increase, and they hoped that the continued exercise of moderation and patience would gradually remove Tibetan suspicions as to our aims and policy.

A few months after this was written, in November of 1895, Mr. Nolan, the Commissioner of Darjiling, an officer who had for many years been conversant with the Tibetan question, and who held civil charge of that division of Bengal which adjoins Sikkim and Bhutan, and who supervised our relations with those two States as well as our trade with Tibet, visited Yatung, and had conversations with Chinese and Tibetan local officials. His report of the state of affairs there is one of the most interesting published.† He found that the imposition of the 10 per cent. duty at Phari was no new exaction, but had existed for a long time. He found, also, that the reason the Tibetans did not meet Mr. White in the previous summer to delimit the boundary was that they wished the general line of the frontier should be agreed upon, in the first instance, with reference to maps, and the ground visited only after this was done. But he found, too, that the Tibetans repudiated the treaty. The "Chief Steward," the sole Commissioner on the part of the Tibetan Government for reporting on the frontier matter, "made the important statement that the Tibetans did not consider themselves bound by the Convention with China, as they were not a party to it." He reported further, that the Tibetans had prevented the formation of a mart

* Blue-book, p. 44. † *Ibid.*, p. 54.

by building a wall across the valley on the farther side of Yatung, by efficiently guarding this and by prohibiting their traders from passing through. Mr. Korb, a wool merchant from Bengal, had come to Yatung to purchase wool from some of his correspondents on the Tibetan side, who had invited him thither; but the Tibetans prevented his correspondents from coming to do business with him. Tibetan merchants were similarly prevented from seeing Mr. Nolan.

Mr. Nolan's conclusion was that, even though the duty which was collected at Phari was neither special nor newly imposed, yet exaction was inconsistent with the treaty provision that trade with India should be exempt from taxation; and also that the first clause in the Trade Regulations, providing that "a trade-mart shall be established at Yatung," which "shall be open to all British subjects for the purposes of trade," had not been carried into effect.

The failure to carry out the treaty he attributed entirely to the Tibetans. He was quite satisfied that the Chinese officials in Tibet, whatever might have been their prepossessions in favour of the policy of seclusion, then sincerely desired to see the Convention carried out, being afraid that they would be disgraced by their own Government if it were not. The Tibetans were the real as well as the ostensible opponents. And Mr. Nolan believed their true motives in opposing the treaty were correctly expressed by a monk, who said that if the English entered Tibet, his bowl would be broken, meaning that the influence of his Order would be destroyed, and its wealth, typified by the collection of food made from door to door in bowls, would be lost. And this opposition on the part of the Lamas the Chinese had not the means of overcoming. They certainly had an acknowledged social superiority, and they were feared to a certain extent on account of their power to send an army through the Himalayas, as they had done on several occasions with surprising success. On the other hand, their present forces in Tibet were ridiculously small, and from Yatung to Gyantse they only had 140 soldiers, and at Lhasa only a few hundreds, while the monks at Lhasa numbered 19,100, of whom 16,500 were concentrated in three great monasteries, and they were vigorous and formidable in a riot, having attacked the Chinese in 1810 and 1844 and the Nepalese in 1883.

Mr. Nolan, with his long experience on this frontier, had, as events have shown, most accurately gauged the situation. The Lieutenant-Governor, Sir Charles Elliott, considered that his report showed that the improvement hoped for from conciliation and forbearance had not taken place in the two seasons during which the mart had nominally been opened, and by the systematic obstruction of the Tibetans the object of the treaty with China had been frustrated. He therefore renewed his recommendation that a diplomatic reference should be made to China, pointing out how completely the Tibetans had violated the spirit of the treaty and Trade Regulations, and had refused to be bound by their terms.

But the Government of India again replied that they wished to pursue a policy of conciliation, and did not wish to make any serious representations to the Chinese Government. They repeated that trade had increased, and as regards demarcation of the frontier, they understood from a further report of Mr. Nolan's that the Tibetans claimed a strip of territory near Giagong, in the north of Sikkim, and these claims the Government of India considered it would not only be impolitic but inequitable to ignore. The Viceroy therefore wrote to the Chinese Resident, suggesting that Chinese and Tibetan delegates should be sent to Gantok, the capital of Sikkim, to meet Mr. White there, and proceed with him to Giagong to make a local inquiry, but that no actual demarcation should take place until the reports of the results of the inquiry had taken place.

And so the game rolled on, and nothing whatever resulted. The Chinese Resident was superseded, and the Chinese asked that action should be deferred till the new one arrived. The new Resident came, and wrote that the Tibetans are "naturally doltish, and prone to doubts and misgivings," and it would be best therefore that they should "personally inspect the line of demarcation mentioned in the treaty," though a Tibetan representative had been with the Chinese Amban when the Convention was made, and had ample opportunity during the years that agreement took in negotiating to inspect and to give the views of his Government upon it. And so it resulted that when, at the conclusion of five years from the signing of the Trade Regulations, the Secretary of State asked the Government of India for "a full report, both on the progress made since the date of that agreement towards the settlement of the frontier, and on the extent to which the trade stipulations of the treaty and Convention had been operative," the Bengal Government had to reply* that the boundary between Sikkim and Tibet, as laid down in Article I. of the Convention, had not yet been demarcated, owing to the refusal of the Tibetans to abide by the terms of the Convention, and to their claiming a tract of land to the north of Donkya-la, Giagong, and the Lonakh Valley; and that the trade stipulations contained in the Regulations, had been inoperative. The Tibetans had prevented Yatung becoming a real trade-mart; absolutely no business was transacted there, and it was merely a registering post for goods passing between Tibet and India, and the proclamation of the place as a mart had in no way influenced the trade between the two countries, for what small increase there was appeared to be mainly due to, and might have been expected from, the restoration of peace between the British Government and Tibet.

This was the net result of the policy of conciliation and forbearance towards the Tibetans and of reliance on the Chinese Central Government, which had been pursued from 1873.

* Blue-book, p. 92.

CHAPTER VI

SECURING THE TREATY RIGHTS

Now that five years had elapsed since the Trade Regulations were concluded, and they were, according to their provisions, subject to revision, the Government of India began to consider any practical measures for securing fuller facilities for trade. The Convention of 1890 and the Trade Regulations of 1893 were intended to provide these facilities, but so far none had been obtained; and the Indian Government thought that, as the Tibetans attached great importance to retaining the Giagong piece of territory in Northern Sikkim, and as we had no real desire to hold it, there might be advantage in conceding that point if the Tibetans would, on their side, make some equivalent concession. They might, it was thought, concede to us the point for which we had contended when negotiating the Trade Regulations, and recognize Phari as the trade-mart in place of the quite useless Yatung. Lord Salisbury* agreed that some action was necessary, but it seemed to him that, as during recent years Chinese advisory authority in Tibet had been little more than nominal, and the correspondence of the Government of India even seemed to show that it was practically non-existent, it would be preferable to open direct communication between the Government of India and the Tibetan authorities.

Lord Curzon therefore commenced, in the autumn of 1899, a series of attempts to open up direct communication with them. Ugyen Kázi, the Bhutanese Agent in Darjiling, who was accustomed to visit Tibet for trade

* Blue-book, p. 101.

purposes, was first employed to write a letter on his own behalf to the Dalai Lama, suggesting, in general terms, that a high Tibetan official should be sent to discuss the frontier and trade questions. This letter met with an unfavourable response. Captain Kennion, the Assistant to the Resident in Kashmir, who annually visits Leh and the Western Tibet frontier, was then charged with a letter from the Viceroy to the Dalai Lama, which he was to give to the Tibetan officials in Gartok; but six months after this was returned to Captain Kennion, with the intimation that the officials had not dared, in the face of the regulations against the intrusion of foreigners into Tibet, to send it to Lhasa. These two methods having failed, Ugyen Kázi was entrusted with another letter from the Viceroy to the Dalai Lama, which he was himself to present at Lhasa. In August, 1901, he returned from Lhasa, reporting that the Dalai Lama declined to reply to it, stating as his reason that the matter was not one for him to settle, but must be discussed fully in Council with the Amban, the Ministers, and the Lamas, and the letter was brought back with the seal intact.

A factor of determining importance now suddenly thrust itself into the situation. At the very time when the Viceroy was making these fruitless efforts to enter into direct communication with the Dalai Lama came the information that this exclusive personage had been sending an Envoy to the Czar. Our Ambassador at St. Petersburg forwarded to the Foreign Office an announcement in the official column of the *Journal de Saint Petersbourg* of October 2 (15), 1900, announcing the reception by His Majesty the Emperor of a certain Dorjieff, who was described as first Tsanit Hamba to the Dalai Lama of Tibet. And, some months later, our Consul-General at Odessa forwarded to the Foreign Office an extract from the *Odessa Novosti* of June 12 (25), 1901, stating that Odessa would welcome that day an Extraordinary Mission from the Dalai Lama of Tibet, which was proceeding to St. Petersburg with diplomatic instructions of importance. At the head of the mission was the Lama, Dorzhievy (Dorjieff), and its chief object was a rapprochement and the strengthening of good relations with Russia. It was said to have been equipped by the Dalai Lama, and despatched with autograph letters and presents from him to His Imperial Majesty. And, among other things, it was to raise the question of the establishment in St. Petersburg of a permanent Tibetan Mission for the maintenance of good relations with Russia.

This Dorjieff, it appeared from an article in the *Novoe Vremya* of June 18 (July 1), 1901, was a Russian subject, who had grown up and received his education on Russian soil. He was by birth a Buriat of Chovinskaia (in the province of Verchnyudinsk, in Trans-Baikalia, Eastern Siberia), and was brought up in the province of Azochozki. He had settled in Tibet twenty years before his present visit to Russia. "This reappearance of the Tibet Mission in Russia proved," said the *Novoe Vremya*, "that the favourable impressions carried back by Dorjieff to his home from his previous mission have confirmed the Dalai Lama in his intention of contracting the friendliest relations with Russia. . . . A rapprochement with Russia must seem to him [the Dalai Lama] the most natural step, as Russia is the only Power able to frustrate the intrigues of Great Britain."

Count Lamsdorff, however, in conversation with the British Ambassador* on July 3, 1901, characterized "as ridiculous and utterly unfounded the conclusion drawn in certain organs of the Russian press, that these Tibetan visitors were charged with any diplomatic mission." He said Dorjieff was a Mongolian Buriat of Russian origin, who came occasionally to Russia with the object, he believed, of making money collections for his Order from the numerous Buddhists in the Russian Empire. Count Lamsdorff added that on the occasion of Dorjieff's visit in the previous autumn to Yalta, the Emperor had received him, and he himself had had an opportunity of learning some interesting details from him of life in Tibet; the Russian Geographical Society also took an interest in his

* Blue-book, p. 166.

visit, which had, however, no official character whatever, although he was accompanied on this visit by other Tibetans.

But, in spite of this declaimer, Dorjieff was still styled an Envoy Extraordinary, and the *Messager Officiel* of June 25 (July 8, 1901) had the announcement that his Majesty the Emperor had received on June 23, in the Grand Palace at Peterhof, the Envoy Extraordinary from the Dalai Lama of Tibet. And as the Russian press announced that the Envoys had paid visits to Count Lamsdorff and M. Witte, Sir Charles Scott, the British Ambassador, took an opportunity at an interview with Count Lamsdorff of ascertaining some further particulars.* The latter said that, although the Tibetan visitors had been described as Envoys Extraordinary of the Dalai Lama, their mission could not be regarded as having any political or diplomatic character. The mission was of the same character as those sent by the Pope to the faithful in foreign lands. Dorjieff had some post of confidence in the Dalai Lama's service, but Count Lamsdorff believed that he still maintained his original Russian nationality. He had brought the Count an autograph letter from the Dalai Lama, but this letter merely expressed a hope that Count Lamsdorff was in the enjoyment of good health and was prosperous, and informed him that the Dalai was able to say that he himself enjoyed excellent health.

These proceedings naturally enough attracted the attention of the Secretary of State for India, who on July 25 pointed out to the Foreign Office† that the Dalai Lama had recently refused to receive the communications addressed to him by the Viceroy, and that while the Viceroy was thus treated with discourtesy a mission was publicly sent to Russia, and the publicity given to the Tibetan Mission which had recently arrived in St. Petersburg could not fail to engender some disquietude in the minds of the Indian Government as to the object and result of any negotiations which might ensue. The Secretary of State for India suggested, therefore, that our Ambassador should be instructed to inform Count

* Blue-book, p. 117.

† *Ibid.*, p. 123.

Lamsdorff we had received his assurance with satisfaction, as any proceedings that might have a tendency to alter or disturb the existing status of Tibet, would be a movement in which His Majesty's Government could not acquiesce. This suggestion was adopted, and on September 2, 1901, our Ambassador informed Count Lamsdorff that His Majesty's Government would naturally not regard with indifference any proceedings that might have a tendency to alter or disturb the existing status in Tibet. The Russian Minister repeated his assertion that "the mission was chiefly concerned with matters of religion, and had no political or diplomatic object or character."

For the time being the Government of India itself took no action in regard to this new factor, though in concluding a despatch to the Secretary of State on February 13 of the following year (1902) they declared that it was desirable that the unsatisfactory situation in Tibet should be brought to an end with as little delay and commotion as possible, since there were factors in the case which, at a later date, might invest the breakdown of the unnatural barriers of Tibetan isolation with a wider and more serious significance.

They continued to plod steadily along at the settlement of the frontier, and corresponded with the Secretary of State and the Bengal Chamber of Commerce about the introduction of tea to Tibet now that the five years, during which it was to be excluded had expired. But they acted with much more decision than previously, and instead of waiting year after year for the arrival of Chinese or Tibetan deputies to meet our representatives, they sent Mr. White, in the summer of 1902, to Giagong, to reassert British rights to the tract of country which the Tibetans had been occupying in contravention of the treaty of 1890, and, if necessary, to expel them from the British side of the frontier. Mr. White had suggested that an effective and simple way would be to occupy the Chumbi Valley, but the Government of India, though they considered grounds for strong action were far from lacking, were not for the time in favour of such a proposal. And another alternative of stopping all Tibetan trade they thought would be hard on our own traders, and might drive trade permanently away to Nepal and Bhutan. They accordingly adopted the above-mentioned course.

Mr. White went to Giagong on June 26, 1902, with 200 men, and camped half a mile from the Tibetan wall, where the Khamba Jongpen and 40 men were stationed. He gave them twenty-four hours' notice in which to move to the other side of the boundary. On the following morning, after some protests, the Tibetans removed across the boundary. On July 4 a number of Tibetan officials visited him, and said they had come under instructions from the Tashi Lama to show him the Giagong boundary. Mr. White told them that his orders were to lay down the boundary as shown in the Convention of 1890, which had been signed by the Chinese Amban on behalf of the Tibetans. To which they replied that they had heard of the treaty, but that it was invalid, as it had not been signed by any Tibetan. The Tibetans, however, asked for a copy of the treaty and for the names of the passes, and Mr. White told them they could see for themselves if the water ran into the Sikkim Valley or into Tibet, and where the water parted into Sikkim and Tibet was the boundary. He found on the tract 6,270 sheep, 737 yaks, out of which only 1,143 sheep and 80 yaks belonged to the Sikkimese, and the remainder were Tibetan. Near the top of the Naku La he found a Tibetan wall running across the valley, with a blockhouse on the east.

The immediate consequence of this action was, that at the end of July the Viceroy received a letter from the Chinese Resident at Lhasa, asking for an explanation of the object and reasons of Mr. White's proceedings, and saying that he had appointed Mr. Ho Kuang-Hsi to proceed to Giagong, and had further arranged with the Dalai Lama for the despatch of a Tibetan official to act conjointly with Mr. Ho in any discussion with Mr. White which should arise.

The Viceroy, in reply, wrote to say that the object

of the journey from which Mr. White had recently returned was to inspect the boundary as laid down in the Convention of 1890, and to compel the withdrawal from Sikkim territory of any troops which the Tibetans might have established in violation of that Convention. He reminded the Chinese Resident that he had offered to make concessions with respect to these frontier lands, on the understanding that matters as to trade would be put on a proper footing. But Lord Curzon pointed out that the negotiations for the improvement of trade relations between India and Tibet had made no real progress during the past twelve years. In these circumstances, he had no alternative but to compel the observance of the boundary as prescribed by the Convention; and until matters as to trade had been placed on a satisfactory footing, he must continue to insist on the boundary being observed, though any proposals which the Chinese Resident would make for the improvement of trade relations would receive careful consideration, and Mr. White had been instructed to discuss with the Commissioners appointed by the Amban any suggestions which they might put forward.

As a fact, the Commissioner never did meet Mr. White. Mr. Ho was prevented by "ill-health" from proceeding to Gantok. Then he was recalled to Lhasa. Then the Chinese Resident himself was to be replaced, and the new one would not reach Lhasa till the following summer. And so on, with the usual and unfailing excellent reasons for doing nothing.

But, in the meanwhile, the new factor in the situation was assuming significant proportions and causing the Government of India anxiety. I have already related how the Dalai Lama was sending missions to the Czar, with autograph letters to the Russian Chancellor, at the very moment when he was declining all communications from the Viceroy of India. And now, from a totally different quarter, came rumours that China was making a secret agreement with Russia in regard to Tibet.

Our Minister at Peking, on August 2, 1902, telegraphed* to Lord Lansdowne that there had been going the rounds of the press an agreement in regard to Tibet, alleged to have been secretly made between Russia and China. In return for a promise to uphold the integrity of China, the entire interest of China in Tibet was to be relinquished to Russia. This rumour, said our Minister, seemed to have originated in a Chinese paper published in Satow. Fuller information was sent by letter. According to this, among other things, Russia would establish Government officers in Tibet to control Tibetan affairs.

On Sir Ernest Satow making, in accordance with Lord Lansdowne's instructions, a representation to the Chinese Foreign Board about this, the President of the Board strongly denied that there was any such agreement, and declared that no such arrangement had ever formed a subject of discussion between the Chinese and Russian Governments. But the rumour seems to have had a wide prevalence and to have been regarded seriously, for our Ambassador at St. Petersburg reported in October that the Chinese Minister there had told him that several of his colleagues had been making inquiries from him respecting this pretended agreement, which had appeared in several Continental as well as Russian newspapers, and which he, the Chinese Minister, had first seen in the Chinese newspapers. The Government of India; also, reported to the Secretary of State that circumstantial evidence, derived from a variety of quarters, all pointed in the same direction, and tended to show the existence of an arrangement of some sort between Russia and Tibet.

It may be asked—and, indeed, it was asked—why the Government of India should have been so nervous about Russian action in Tibet. The Russian Government had said that the mission which the Dalai Lama had sent to St. Petersburg was of a "religious" nature, and the Chinese Foreign Board had said there was no agreement

* Blue-book, p. 140.

with Russia about Tibet. Why not, then, have disregarded these idle rumours? Such lofty disregard is easy for irresponsible persons at a comfortable distance in England to display. But the responsible Government in India cannot dismiss such rumours with so light a heart. Russia might not have had any agreement about Tibet, and the Tibetan Mission might have been purely religious; but that she was extremely interested in Tibet was unquestionable. She had for years been sending semi-official, semi-scientific expeditions into the country. These had always reported on the richness of Tibet in regard to gold, and the desirability of getting concessions there. There was at the very moment one of these expeditions with an armed escort in Tibet. Apart from this, the interest of Russiain Tibet was thoroughly natural. The Dalai Lama was regarded with superstitious reverence by many thousands of Russian Asiatic subjects. Moreover, at that time it was generally looked upon as inevitable that Russia would shortly absorb Mongolia, and all Mongols look upon the Dalai Lama as a god. It was, indeed, because of his immense influence over the Mongols that the Chinese had for centuries, and at great cost to themselves, secured and maintained a dominant influence in Lhasa. It is easy to understand, therefore, that the Russians would be glad enough of any opportunity of gaining an influence with the Dalai Lama. The mission of the latter to the Czar might, as the Russian Chancellor said, be mainly religious, and similar to missions which the Pope sends out. But even in Europe it is often difficult to distinguish between religion and politics, and in Asia the two are almost indistinguishable. A religious understanding between the Dalai Lama and the Czar might by the former be regarded as a political agreement. And whatever might have been the intentions of the Russian Government at the time, they might on some subsequent occasion have sent a mission to Lhasa, as they had sent a mission to Kabul in 1879 and caused an Afghan War.

Even so, why should we trouble? What possible harm could a few Russians do in Lhasa? Russia might invade India through Afghanistan, but she could never invade India across Tibet and over the Himalayas. Why, then, should we be so touchy about her action there? Why not let her send as many missions and officers as she liked? This also seems a broad-minded attitude, such as a platform orator in the heart of England might safely take up. But, again, it was not so easy for those away on the frontier of the Empire, with immediate responsibilities on their shoulders, to feel so complacent. If Russia had been the friend she is now, and if our influence in Lhasa had been unmistakable, it would have been easier to take such a view, and it is, indeed, in my opinion, the right view now to take. But in 1902 she was still on the crest of a great advancing wave of expansion. She had not yet been checked by Japan. She had spread over Manchuria with startling rapidity. Where, at the time of my journey there with Sir Evan James, no Russian had ever been seen, there were now Russian railways and Russian cantonments. She had expanded in Western Turkestan and annexed the Pamirs, and it was generally looked upon only as a matter of time before she would absorb Chinese Turkestan and Mongolia. If, then, we complacently, and without a protest, allowed her to establish herself in Tibet, we could hardly expect those States dependent on us and bordering Tibet to think otherwise than that this was the real Power in Asia, and this, therefore, the Power to look up to.

A full-dress Russian invasion of India, through Tibet, no responsible person ever dreamed possible. But, without a real invasion, Russia established in Lhasa, while we were unrepresented there, could cause Government a great deal of anxiety. In practical detail it would mean the increase of our army on the North-East frontier by several thousand men.

It was obviously prudent, therefore, to prevent her acquiring a more predominant influence than our own in Tibet. While it was quite natural that she should be glad to have an influence at Lhasa, it was still more natural that we should be jealous of her having more influence than we had. For, while our border was contiguous with

Tibet for 1,000 miles, from Kashmir nearly to Burma, the Russian border nowhere touched or even approached Tibet. The whole breadth of Chinese Turkestan lay in between the Russian frontier and the nearest frontier of Tibet, and Lhasa itself was 1,000 miles distant from the nearest point on the Russian frontier. To appreciate the position, let the reader draw out the map at the end of this volume.

The Government of India, accordingly, recommended prompt action. The attempts to negotiate an understanding with the Tibetans through the Chinese had proved a failure. It had been found impossible to open up direct communications with the Tibetans. The result of the exclusion of the Tibetans from the pasture lands at Giagong, though it had materially improved our position on the border, was not in effect more than a timely assertion of British authority upon the spot. These different rumours from such varied sources tending, in the opinion of the Government of India, to indicate the existence of some kind of an arrangement between Russia and Tibet, necessitated dealing with the situation far more drastically and decisively than it had ever been dealt with before. Continuously since 1873 the Government of India had been trying by every correct and reasonable method to regularize their intercourse with Tibet. Their patience was now exhausted, and, instead of trifling about on the frontier with petty Chinese or Tibetan officials, they proposed, in the very important despatch of January 8, 1903,* to send a mission, with an armed escort, to Lhasa itself, there to settle our future relations with Tibet, and to permanently establish a British representative.

This proposal, when it reached England, seems to have caused considerable surprise. But Warren Hastings, a century before, had meant to do this very thing; and the Russians had a Consular representative in Chinese Turkestan alongside their frontier, so there seemed no particular reason why we should not have had a similar representative in Tibet alongside our frontier. The risk had to be considered, it is true, but why the case of

* Blue-book, p. 152.

Cavagnari's murder at Kabul should be everlastingly brought up as an argument against sending an officer outside our frontier it is difficult to understand. It is ignoble to the last degree to be scared for all time by what happened then. Cavagnari was murdered. What then? I agree with my old chief and first master in Central Asian politics, Sir Charles Macgregor, that if our agent A was murdered we should have sent up B, and if B was murdered we should have sent up C. Our whole Afghan policy for thirty years past has been frightfully ignominious, and the day will come when we shall bitterly regret not having had an agent at the capital of a country for whose foreign policy we are responsible. At any rate, the fact of barbarian Afghans murdering our representative at Kabul in 1879 was no adequate reason for not sending a representative to Lhasa in 1903.

These, however, are merely my own views. The contention of the Government of India was that, in suggesting a mission to Lhasa, they were merely reviving a proposal which had been supported as far back as 1874 by Sir T. Wade, then British Minister at Peking, and which was almost taking definite shape in 1885-86, when the importance of a Burmese settlement appears to have so impressed itself upon all parties that the Lhasa Mission was sacrificed in order that the signature of the Chinese Government to the Burmese Convention might be obtained. The Government of India considered it a grave misfortune that they should have been diverted from a project of unquestionable importance by the exigencies of political considerations that had not the remotest connection with Tibet. They recommended, therefore, the revival of this precedent, and the firm pursuance of the policy which was then abandoned.

The Government of India regarded the so-called suzerainty of China over Tibet as a constitutional fiction. China was always ready to break down the barriers of ignorance and obstruction and to open Tibet to the civilizing influence of trade, but her pious wishes were defeated by the short-sighted stupidity of the Lamas. In the same way Tibet was only too anxious to meet our advances, but she was prevented from doing so by the despotic veto of the suzerain. The Government of India wished to put an end to this "solemn farce," and would have preferred to deal with Tibet alone. But they recognized that China could not be entirely disregarded, and only asked that, if the Home Government trusted to the interposition of China, this might be accompanied by a resolute refusal to be defeated by the time-honoured procedure, and that if and when a new treaty was concluded, it should not be signed by the British and Chinese alone, but by a direct representative of the Tibetan Government also.

At the same time, said the Government of India, the most emphatic assurances might be given to the Chinese and Tibetan Governments that the mission was of an exclusively commercial character, that we repudiated all designs of a political nature upon Tibet, that we had no desire either to declare a protectorate or permanently to occupy any portion of the country, but that our intentions were confined to removing the embargo that then rested upon all trade between Tibet and India, and to establishing those amicable relations and means of communication that ought to subsist between adjacent and friendly Powers.

These proposals the Government of India commended to the favourable consideration of His Majesty's Government, in the firm conviction that if some such step were not taken, "a serious danger would grow up in Tibet, which might one day, and perhaps at no very distant date, attain to menacing dimensions." They regarded the situation, as it seriously affected the frontiers which they were called upon to defend with Indian resources, as one in which their opinion was entitled to carry weight with His Majesty's Government; and they entertained a sincere alarm that, if nothing was done and matters were allowed to slide, they might before long have occasion gravely to regret that action was not taken while it was still relatively free from difficulty.

CHAPTER VII

NEGOTIATIONS WITH RUSSIA

I WOULD again recall the fact that when the Government of India wrote the above-quoted despatch, Russia was not yet at war with Japan, and was very much in the ascendant and active in Asia. She had recently occupied Port Arthur, and run a railway through Manchuria; and she was in a dominant, almost domineering, position at Peking. And as showing the interest she took in Tibet, there came, just after the receipt by the India Office of Lord Curzon's despatch, a representation from the Russian Chargé d'Affaires in London, founded apparently upon our very humble efforts of the previous summer within our own frontier. In this representation, which was made in the form of a memorandum* communicated to the Foreign Office, it was stated that, according to the information which the Russian Government had received from an authoritative source, a British military expedition had reached Komba-Ovaleko, on its way north by the Chumbi Valley, and that the Russian Government would consider such an expedition to Tibet as likely to produce a situation of considerable gravity, which might oblige them to take measures to protect their interests in those regions.

It was impossible to trace what place was intended by Komba-Ovaleko. Mr. White and his little escort of 150 men had never gone outside the limits of Sikkim, and had long since returned to their headquarters. There was no difficulty, then, in giving the Russian Ambassador the assurance that this "authoritative" information was without the smallest foundation. And Lord Lansdowne went further than merely refuting the false information.

* Blue-book, p. 178.

He told the Ambassador* that the language of the communication had seemed to him unusual, and, indeed, almost minatory in tone. He referred especially to the statement that the Imperial Government might, in consequence of our action in a country which immediately adjoined the frontiers of India, find it necessary to take measures to protect Russian interests in those regions. Lord Lansdowne said he could not conceive why it was necessary for Russia to evince her interest in this manner.

Count Benckendorff expressed his opinion that these exaggerated rumours had been spread designedly in order to foster ill-feeling between Great Britain and Russia, and thought we should spare no pains in order to dissipate them. There was, he said, no reason whatever why the two Governments should have trouble over Tibet. Russia had no political designs upon the country, and he presumed we had not.

Lord Lansdowne replied that if he was invited to say that we had no desire to annex Tibetan territory, he would unhesitatingly answer in the affirmative, but he was bound to be careful how he gave general assurances, the import of which might hereafter be called in question, as to our future relations with Tibet. It was natural that the Indian Government should desire to promote Indian trade in that country, and they would no doubt take whatever measures seemed to them necessary for that purpose. The Ambassador admitted that this was only natural.

A few days later, on February 18, Lord Lansdowne, in a further conversation with the Russian Ambassador, recurred to the same subject.† He said that the Indian Government had been seriously perturbed by the communication made to the Foreign Office. The interest of India in Tibet was, Lord Lansdowne said, of a very special character. With a map of Central Asia before him, he pointed out to the Ambassador that Lhasa was within a comparatively short distance of the Indian frontier, while, on the other hand, it was considerably over 1,000 miles from the Asiatic possessions of Russia, and

* Blue-book, p. 180. † *Ibid.*, p. 181.

any sudden display of Russian interest or activity in the regions immediately adjoining the possessions of Great Britain could scarcely fail to have a disturbing effect upon the population, or to create the impression that British influence was receding, and that of Russia making rapid advances into regions which had hitherto been regarded as altogether outside her sphere of influence.

Lord Lansdowne added that he had received from apparently trustworthy sources reports to the effect that Russia had lately concluded agreements for the establishment of a Russian protectorate over Tibet, and also that, if she had not already done so, she intended to establish Russian agents or Consular officers at Lhasa, and he thought it of the utmost importance that as the Ambassador had disclaimed on the part of Russia political designs upon Tibet, he should be in a position to state whether these rumours were or were not without foundation.

Count Benckendorff replied that he did not believe that there was any foundation in them, but he expressed his readiness to make special inquiries of the Russian Government as to the truth of the statements referred to.

Lord Lansdowne then went on to say that as we were much more closely interested than Russia in Tibet, it followed that, should there be any display of Russian activity in that country, we should be obliged to reply by a display of activity, not only equivalent to, but exceeding that made by Russia. If they sent a mission or an expedition, we should have to do the same, but in greater strength. As to our dealings with Tibet at the moment, Lord Lansdowne stated that we were endeavouring to obtain from the Tibetan authorities the fulfilment of pledges which had been given to us in 1890 in regard to the location of the frontier, and in regard to trade facilities on the borders of Sikkim. We had found that it was of no use to deal with Tibet through China, owing to the dilatory methods of the Chinese Government and the slenderness of their influence over Tibet. It was absolutely necessary that these local questions should be disposed of to our satisfaction, and we should continue to take the necessary steps for that purpose.

Some delay occurred in getting a reply from the Russian Government, but on April 8, 1903, the Russian Ambassador informed Lord Lansdowne* that he could "assure him officially that there was no convention about Tibet, either with Tibet itself, or with China, or with any-one else; nor had the Russian Government any agents in that country, or any intention of sending any agents or missions there. But, although the Russian Government had no designs whatever about Tibet, they could not remain indifferent to any serious disturbance of the *status quo* in that country. Such a disturbance might render it necessary for them to safeguard their interests in Asia; not that even in that case they would desire to interfere in the affairs of Tibet, as their policy 'ne viserait le Tibet en aucun cas,' but they might be obliged to take measures elsewhere. They regarded Tibet as forming part of the Chinese Empire, in the integrity of which they took an interest."

Count Benckendorff went on to say that he hoped that there was no question of any action on our part in regard to Tibet which might have the effect of raising questions of this kind, and Lord Lansdowne told him that we had no idea of annexing the country, but he was well aware that it immediately adjoined our frontier, that we had treaties with the Tibetans, and a right to trade facilities. If these were denied us, and if the Tibetans did not fulfil their treaty obligations, it would be absolutely necessary that we should insist upon our rights. In cases of this kind, where an uncivilized country adjoined the possessions of a civilized Power, it was inevitable that the latter should exercise a certain amount of local predominance. Such a predominance belonged to us in Tibet. But it did not follow from this that we had any designs upon the independence of the country.

With these very definite assurances from Russia, it might well be asked why we should still have desired to take pronounced measures in Tibet. Anxiety in regard to Russian action in Tibet was the main reason why the Government of India sought to take action in Tibet.

* Blue-book, p. 187.

Now that we were reasonably assured that Russia had no intention of interfering in Tibet, why should we still have thought it necessary to send a mission into the country? The answer is that we had not yet settled those questions of trade and intercourse which had existed years before the Russian factor intruded itself into the situation; besides which we had always the consideration that, although it might be true enough that the Russians had no mind to have any dealings with the Tibetans, yet the Tibetans might still think they could rely on the Russians in flouting us. The Germans had officially no intention of interfering with the Boers, yet it was because Kruger thought he could rely upon German support that he went to war with England. He was much too astute an old gentleman to have fought us if he had thought he would have had to fight us by himself. So it was with the Tibetans. The Russian Government might not have the remotest intention of helping them in any possible way, yet the Tibetans might, and did, think they could count upon Russian support. The Dalai Lama's Envoy Extraordinary had been very well received by the Czar and by the Russian Chancellor and others. Doubtless, he had collected some very handsome subscriptions and received valuable presents. A little Oriental imagination would soon expand these ordinary amenities into a promise of thick-and-thin support against the English. We had still this erroneous impression to reckon with.

CHAPTER VIII

A MISSION SANCTIONED

WHILE the negotiations with Russia were proceeding the Home Government would come to no final decision as to the action to be taken. The question at issue, they informed the Indian Government* in February, was no longer one of details as to trade and boundaries—though on these it was necessary that an agreement should be arrived at—but the whole question of the future political relations of India and Tibet. They agreed with the Indian Government that, having regard to the geographical position of Tibet on the frontiers of India, and its relations with Nepal, it was "indispensable that British influence should be recognized at Lhasa in such a manner as to render it impossible for any other Power to exercise a pressure on the Tibetan Government inconsistent with the interests of British India." They admitted, also, the force of the contention that the interest shown by the Russian Government in the action of the Government of India on the Tibetan frontier demonstrated the urgency of placing our relations with Tibet on a secure basis. They recognized that Nepal might be rightly sensitive as to any alteration in the political position of Tibet which would be likely to disturb the relations at present existing between the two countries, and that the establishment of a powerful foreign influence in Tibet would disturb those relations, and might even, by exposing Nepal to a pressure which it would be difficult to resist, affect those which then existed on so cordial a basis between India and Nepal. They regretted the necessity for abandoning the passive attitude that had hitherto sufficed in the regulation

* Blue-book, p. 184.

of affairs on the frontier, and were compelled to recognize that circumstances had recently occurred which threw on them the obligation of placing our relations with the Government of Lhasa upon a more satisfactory footing. And they acknowledged that the proposal to send an armed mission to enter Lhasa, by force if necessary, and establish there a Resident, might, if the issue were simply one between India and Tibet, be justified as a legitimate reply to the action of the Tibetan Government in returning the letters which on three occasions the Viceroy had addressed to them, and in disregarding the Convention with China of 1890. But they stated that they could not regard the question as one concerning India and Tibet alone. The position of China in its relations to the Powers of Europe had been so modified in recent years that it was necessary to take into account those altered conditions in deciding on action affecting what still had to be regarded as a province of China. It was true that we had no desire either to declare a protectorate or permanently to occupy any portion of the country. But measures of that kind might become inevitable if we were once to find ourselves committed to armed intervention.

For the above reasons, the Home Government thought it necessary, before sanctioning a course which might be regarded as an attack on the integrity of the Chinese Empire, to be sure that such action could be justified by the previous action of Tibet, and they had, accordingly, come to the conclusion that it would be premature to adopt measures so likely to precipitate a crisis in the affairs of Tibet as those proposed by the Government of India. They would await, therefore, the result of their reference to the Russian Government, and after those explanations had been received they would be in a better position to decide on the scope to be given to the negotiations with China, and on the steps to be taken to protect India against any danger from the establishment of foreign influence in Tibet.

When the Russian assurances were at length received, the purport of the conversation Lord Lansdowne had held with the Russian Ambassador was at once communicated by telegram to the Viceroy, and on April 14 the Secretary of State, presuming that it would be necessary to include in the scope of the negotiations with China and Tibet the entire question of our future relations with Tibet, commercial and otherwise, asked the Viceroy for his views as to the form which these negotiations should now take, with special reference to the means to be adopted to insure that the conditions that might be arrived at would be observed by Tibet.

The Viceroy on April 16 replied that he had recently received from the delegate deputed by the Chinese Resident an intimation that if Yatung was not considered a suitable locality, they were willing to negotiate at any place acceptable to us. And he proposed, accordingly, to invite the Chinese Resident to depute delegates to meet our representative at Khamba Jong, which was the nearest inhabited place on the Tibetan side to the frontier in dispute near Giagong. The Viceroy proposed that our representative, with an escort of 200 men, should proceed to that place, while reinforcements were held in reserve in Sikkim, and that, should the Chinese and Tibetan representatives fail to appear, or should the former come without the latter, our representative should move forward to Shigatse or Gyantse, in order that the arrival of the deputations from Lhasa might be accelerated.

The Secretary of State telegraphed on April 29 that there was no objection to the Chinese, Tibetan, and Indian representatives meeting at Khamba Jong or to the military arrangements recommended; but His Majesty's Government considered that without previous reference to them the Mission should not advance beyond that place, as in existing conditions, even in the event of the failure of the Chinese and Tibetan parties, any sudden advance to Lhasa was not, in their opinion, justified.

In regard to the subject-matter of the forthcoming negotiations, the Viceroy telegraphed on May 7 that, having regard to the stultification of existing treaty provisions, and to the unsuitability of either Yatung, Phari, or any other place in the Chumbi Valley, for a trade-mart, in which business could be transacted directly between British and Tibetan merchants, without incurring the monopoly of local traders, it was necessary to insist upon opening a new trade-mart and upon having a British agent at Gyantse. The Viceroy thought that having a British representative at Lhasa, which would be the best possible security for the future observance of the conditions, would be far preferable; but assuming the unwillingness of His Majesty's Government to press this claim, the proposal for an agent at Gyantse was a suitable alternative. In any case, the fullest facilities should be given to the British representative for direct communication with the Tibetan Government, and if he met with obstruction, it would be necessary to resort to the alternative of moving him forward to Lhasa. Furthermore, it would be necessary to secure for British Indian subjects the same freedom for trade and travel in Tibet as was enjoyed by Kashmiris and Nepalese, and to insist that all British subjects duly authorized by the Government of India should be allowed to proceed by recognized routes to Gyantse, beyond which a pass from the Tibetan Government would be required.

As Commissioner, the Viceroy proposed to appoint Major Younghusband, Resident at Indore. He could confidently rely on his judgment and discretion, and he had great Asiatic experience. With him he would associate as Joint Commissioner Mr. White, Political Officer in Sikkim.

The Secretary of State hesitated to accept at once the proposal regarding Gyantse, and wished before coming to any decision to be informed whether the Viceroy could propose any alternative in place of the extreme course of advancing by force into Tibet; and the Viceroy said the only alternatives were (*a*) the costly and ineffectual measure of blocking all trade-routes and excluding Tibetans from British India, and (*b*) an occupation of the Chumbi Valley.

The final decision of the Home Government on the whole matter was telegraphed to the Viceroy on May 28. They approved a procedure by which both the Chinese and Tibetan Governments would be bound by the action of their representatives, but they wished that the negotiations should be confined to questions concerning trade relations, the frontier, and grazing rights, and that no proposal should be made for the establishment of a Political Agent at Gyantse or Lhasa, as such a political outpost might entail difficulties and responsibilities incommensurate with any benefits which would be gained by it. They had recently received assurances that Russia had no intention of developing political interests in Tibet, and they were unwilling to be committed by threats to any definite course of compulsion to be undertaken in future.

While the Home Government and the Indian Government were thus deliberating as to the final action which should be taken, communications with the Chinese were being exchanged. The Chinese Government had, in December, informed our Minister at Peking that "the Throne, attaching deep importance to international relations, and regarding the Tibetan question of great importance, had specially appointed Yu Tai to be Imperial Resident in Tibet, with orders to proceed with all speed, and negotiate with Mr. White in an amicable spirit." This newly-appointed Resident called on the British Minister on January 5, and informed him that he had hoped to be able to travel to his new post by way of India, but that, in order to avoid arousing the suspicion of the Tibetans, it had been decided that he should travel by the Yangtse River and Szechuan, and would not be able to reach Lhasa much before July. He did not, in fact, reach it till six months later still, till thirteen critical months had elapsed since the Chinese Government had told us that he was to proceed to Lhasa with all possible speed.

Mr. Townley, the British Chargé d'Affaires at Peking, on May 12, informed the Chinese Government that the Government of India would invite the Resident at Lhasa to send Chinese delegates to meet the representatives of the British Government at Khamba Jong, for the settlement of pending questions, and would inform the Resident that the Chinese delegates should be accompanied by a duly accredited Tibetan representative. The Chinese Government were told that we attached great importance to this latter point, for the Tibetans had more than once intimated to the British authorities that they did not consider themselves bound to observe the provisions of the treaties previously made between the British and Chinese representatives, because no representative of the Dalai Lama had taken part in the negotiations.

The Chinese Government, on receipt of this, telegraphed to the Resident at Lhasa, asking him again to admonish the Dalai Lama, and to persuade him not to fail to send, with speed, a Tibetan official to be associated with the deputy Ho in his discussion with Mr. White. In reply, the Chinese Government received, on July 18, a telegram from the Resident, saying that he had at once communicated these instructions to the Dalai Lama, "directing him to send a Tibetan [lit., barbarian] official of fairly high standing and despatch him to the frontier, provided with credentials as a negotiator, in order to concert with the Prefect Ho and his colleagues, to await British officials, and effect a harmonious and sincere settlement."

The Resident at Lhasa had also at this time submitted to the Throne a memorial, which furnishes exceedingly instructive reading. He said he had summoned the Tibetan Councillors to his office, and admonished them in person to the effect that the English intended to bring troops to Tibet, and that it was difficult to fathom their objects. All this, he said, was the result of their obstructing last year a deputy with his retinue, so that a favourable opportunity was lost. If the English did make this long march, it would, of course, be the duty of him, the Imperial Resident, to proceed in person to the frontier and find some way of persuading them to stop. But the Tibetans, on their side, must not show their previous obstinacy; and if the English did not stop, and insisted on entering Tibet, they must on no account repel them with arms, but must discuss matters with them on the basis of reason. Thus he hoped a rupture might be avoided, and things brought back to a satisfactory conclusion. But if, as before, the Councillors allowed themselves to be guided by the three great monasteries, and hostilities once began, then the horrors of war would be more than he could bear to think of, and even the mediation of him, the Imperial Resident, would be of no avail.

Such, said the Resident, were the admonitions which he addressed to the Tibetan Councillors, and as he did so he watched their demeanour. It was submissive certainly, but obstinacy was engrained in the character of the Tibetan barbarians, and whether, when matters should become pressing, they would consent to obey and discuss questions in a friendly spirit, it was difficult for him to tell in advance.

The laconic observation by the Emperor on this curious document, which correctly described the Tibetans, and which incidentally depicted both the contempt of the Chinese for these "barbarians" and the ineffectiveness of their control over them, was—"Seen."

But the Resident had also written to the Viceroy, on April 6, saying that he had deputed Mr. Ho and Captain Parr for the discussion of affairs, and they were waiting at Yatung. The deputy appointed by the Viceroy might, he said, either come to Yatung, or the Chinese deputies would proceed to Sikkim, or such other place as might be decided on by the Viceroy.

To this the Viceroy replied, on June 3, 1903, that, as the Resident had already clearly recognized, it would be useless to negotiate upon matters affecting Tibet without insuring the full and adequate representation of the Dalai Lama's Government throughout the proceedings. He was nominating as his Commissioner Colonel Younghusband, who, accompanied by Mr. White, Political Officer in Sikkim, as Joint Commissioner, would proceed to meet the Commissioners appointed by the Resident, who should, of course, be of equivalent rank, and must be attended by a Tibetan officer of the highest rank, whose authority to bind the Tibetan Government was absolute and unquestioned. On this understanding, that the Lhasa authorities would be duly and fully represented, the

Viceroy was prepared to accept the Resident's invitation that the Commissioners should meet at a very early date, and discuss, not only the exact position of the frontier under the Convention of 1890 and the mutual rights of grazing to be allowed on either side of that frontier to the people of Tibet and British territory, but also the method in which our trade relations could be improved and placed upon a basis more consonant with the usage of civilized nations and our direct and predominating interests in Tibet. And as the Resident was prepared to let his deputies meet the British representative at any place which the Viceroy might select, and as Khamba Jong, being the nearest inhabited place to the frontier in question, seemed to be the most suitable place for the meeting, he had directed Colonel Younghusband to proceed thither as soon as he conveniently could, and he trusted that the Resident would secure the attendance of the Chinese and Tibetan representatives at Khamba Jong on, or as soon as possible after, July 7.

On the same date as this letter was written I also received my own formal instructions.* I was informed that a strict insistence on the boundary-line as laid down in the Convention of 1890 was, perhaps, not essential either to the Government of India or to the Sikkim Durbar, and I was directed to give my opinion on this point after inspecting the tract in question. The matter of grazing rights was not one of great importance, and after discussion with the Chinese and Tibetan delegates I was to submit my proposals as to the agreement which might be come to in this matter. The revision of the Trade Regulations and the recognition of Gyantse as a trade-mart in place of Yatung were to form the subject of discussion with the Chinese and Tibetan delegates, and the provision of guarantees for the observance of such agreements as might be concluded were to be considered a matter of the first importance. It was further considered very desirable that arrangements for free communication between the Government of India and the authorities at Lhasa should be made, and possibly also annual meetings between

* Blue-book, p. 198.

British and Tibetan officials for the due settlement of the trade and frontier difficulties which might occur.

In conclusion, I was warned to be very careful to abstain from using any language or taking any action which would bind the Government to any definite course hereafter without first obtaining the sanction of the Government of India.

All was now prepared for the start of a mission. In this extraordinarily complex and intricate matter the many different lines had at last been made to converge on one point. The manifold communications which had taken place for thirty years between the Bengal Government and the Government of India, between local Indian officers and local Chinese and Tibetans; the correspondence between Simla or Calcutta and London, between the India Office and the Foreign Office, between the Foreign Office and the Russian and Chinese Governments, and between the Viceroy and our Minister at Peking and the Chinese Resident at Lhasa, had all been boiled down into the definite act of the despatch of a mission to a place a bare dozen miles inside Tibet to discuss trade-relations, frontier and grazing rights.

This was not, after all, any remarkably bold or outrageously aggressive act. Such as it was, was it justified? The narrative of the causes which led to the move has been long, but, even so, it has been hard to put their true significance so that it may be appreciated by people unacquainted with Orientals. Still, there are some fairly plain facts and considerations which emerge from the long narrative, and which all who are accustomed to the conduct of affairs may be expected to understand.

The first fact is this—that it was aggression on the part of the Tibetans or their vassals which led to action on our part, and that before ever a single soldier of the British Government had crossed the frontier into Tibet Tibetan troops had crossed it to the Indian side. It was the irruption of the Bhutanese into the plains of Bengal which caused Warren Hastings to send Bogle to Tibet in

1774. It was the invasion of Sikkim by the Tibetans which made the necessity for the treaty of 1890. And it was because the Tibetans repudiated that treaty, and occupied territory inside the boundary therein laid down, that we had to take measures to see it observed.

But even supposing they were aggressive, it may be said that we ought to have treated the Tibetans with leniency, gentleness, and consideration, because of their ignorance. So we ought, and so we did. Warren Hastings conceded the request of the Tashi Lama. And though the Tibetans for a century have been free to come down to India, with no restrictions on their trade or on their travel, we for years never pressed for any ordinary rights of trade and travel for our own subjects, whether British or Indian. We allowed the Tibetans to come down where, and when, and how they liked. For a century we let the principle of heads they win, tails we lose, continue. Even when we at last stirred, and thought of sending Macaulay to Lhasa to make some less one-sided arrangement, we gave up the idea when we saw that the Tibetans raised objection. And even, again, when the Chinese asked us to make a definite treaty with them on behalf of the Tibetans, and guaranteed its observance by them, and when the Tibetans broke it, and repudiated it, and refused to meet our officers, we continued for ten years showing them forbearance and patience. It was only at last when the Tibetans, having broken the treaty, having declined to have any communication with us, yet sent Envoys to the Russians, that we took high action, and despatched a mission with an escort into Tibet. If we had shown no inclination to hold the Tibetans and Chinese to their engagements, others might well think that they also would not be held to theirs, and our authority and influence would slacken in proportion as this impression got abroad. No Government can conduct the affairs of contiguous States if it allows a treaty to be broken with impunity.

My personal view is that the local question would have been better settled, and much subsequent international complications would have been saved if, at an earlier stage in the proceedings, when it first became amply clear that our treaty was valueless; that the Tibetans repudiated and ignored it, and that the Chinese were unable to have it observed, we had at once resumed the proceedings where we had left them when we drove the Tibetans across our border, and had again advanced into the Chumbi Valley, and stopped there till we had effected a properly recognized and lasting settlement. This was the course recommended by Sir Charles Elliott, the then Lieutenant-Governor of Bengal, and whether that would have been a wise course or not, I do not see how anyone who has carefully considered the whole course of transactions which at last led up to the despatch of a mission to the first inhabited place across the border can deny that such a course was justified.

Whether the mission was conducted with due consideration or with unnecessary harshness, and whether any good came of it, either to ourselves or to the Tibetans or to anyone else, are matters for separate review, and to that purpose I will now address myself in the following narrative of the course of the mission.

CHAPTER IX

SIMLA TO KHAMBA JONG

THE previous chapters have been necessarily, though perhaps somewhat tediously, filled up with a narrative of the many intricate considerations which went towards the final determination to send a mission to Tibet. But of all that had been going on—of the voluminous correspondence in the great offices, of the meetings and attempts at meetings on the frontier—I was wholly ignorant. Anglo-Indian papers seldom contain information on such happenings. And for some years past, in accordance with the well-intentioned, but, as it has since turned out, thoroughly unsound, advice of a previous Viceroy, that it would be to my advantage in the Political Department not to remain for ever on the frontier, but to acquire experience of internal affairs as well, I had been serving in the interior in political agencies in Rajputana and Central India, and had heard nothing of any intention to send a mission to Tibet. Nor had I ever had any connection with Tibet, though as long ago as 1888 the then Lieutenant-Governor of Bengal had, I discovered many years after, asked the Government of India for my services, as I had then just returned from a journey around Manchuria and across Central Asia, from Peking to Kashmir, and it was thought that, knowing Chinese customs, I might be of use, in addition to the Chinese interpreter. This request was twice made, it appears; but I was then a young subaltern, still in military employ, and in the throes of examination, and the Government of India replied that I was not available, as I was about to go up for examination, and, if sent away then, would fail to qualify for promotion. So I went up for one of those examinations of which such a fetish is made, and never till now had been near the Tibet frontier. I made, indeed, an abortive effort in 1889 to go to Lhasa, disguised as a Turki from Central Asia; but this, too, was nipped in the bud by the refusal of my Colonel to give me leave from the regiment. What spirit of adventure I possessed never received much encouragement from Government, and, as I have said, I had left the frontier for some years, and was superintending the affairs of a native State in the very heart of India, when, on a sweltering day in May, I suddenly received a summons to proceed at once to Simla to receive instructions regarding a mission I was to lead to Tibet.

Here, indeed, I felt was the chance of my life. I was once more alive. The thrill of adventure again ran through my veins. And I wasted little time in rounding up my business, packing my things, and starting off for Simla.

There I was handed over all the papers in the Foreign Office to digest while the final instructions of the Secretary of State were still awaited. And one afternoon I was asked to lunch with Lord Curzon and Lord Kitchener, at a gymkhana down at Annandale, where, after lunch, sitting under the shade of the glorious pine-trees, Lord Curzon explained to me all his intentions, ideas, and difficulties. Men and ladies performed every feat of equestrian skill and equestrian nonsense, and the place was crowded with all the beauty and gaiety of Simla in the height of the season. But the Viceroy and I sat apart, and talked over the various difficulties I should meet with in Tibet, and the best means by which they could be overcome.

One thing he made perfectly clear to me from the start—that he meant to see the thing through; that he intended the mission to be a success, and would provide me with every means within his power to make it so. Fortunately, we knew each other well—ever since his first appointment as Under-Secretary of State for India. We had travelled together nine years previously round Chitral and Gilgit; we had corresponded for years; and when he came to India he, with a kindness of heart for which he is ordinarily given very little credit, had asked me to regard him, not as Viceroy, but as an old friend and fellow-traveller. No better initiator and supporter of such an enterprise as a mission to Tibet could be imagined. He had his whole heart and soul in the undertaking, and I do not think it took long for me to put my whole heart into it, too.

I had in previous years been despatched from Simla on two political missions—in 1889 to explore the unknown passes on the northern frontier of Kashmir, and to put down the raids from Hunza, and in 1890 to the Pamirs and Chinese Turkestan—so I had some general idea of what to expect on the present occasion; and as I had also spent three months in the Legation at Peking, besides travelling from one end to the other of the Chinese Empire, I knew enough about the Chinese to know that I should never be able to deal successfully with them without the assistance of someone who had had a life-training in the work. I therefore, in the first place, asked for an officer of the China Consular Service to act as adviser and interpreter. Next, as regards dealing with the Tibetans, it was most necessary to have an officer who could speak the Tibetan language, and it was fortunate for the success of the mission that Government were able to send with it, first as Intelligence Officer and afterwards as Secretary, Captain O'Connor, an artillery officer, who, when stationed with his mountain battery at Darjiling, had learned the Tibetan language and studied the history and customs of the Tibetans, and who, I afterwards found, was never so happy as when he was surrounded by begrimed Tibetans, with whom he would spend hour after hour in apparently futile conversation.

The services of some of the Gurkhas and of the Pathan, Shahzad Mir, who had been with me on my mission in 1889, I also tried to secure; but the Gurkhas had all left their regiment, and Shahzad Mir, who had been employed on many a mission and reconnaissance since, was then absent in Abyssinia.

Mr. White reached Simla a day or two after my arrival, and we at once set to work to discuss arrangements. He had had experience on that frontier for fourteen years, and was naturally well up in all the local aspects of the question, and knew—what I did not—what dealing with Tibetans really meant. His accounts of their obstinacy and obstructiveness appeared to me exaggerated, and, with the optimism of inexperience, I thought that we should, together with Captain O'Connor's assistance, be able to soon break through it. But Mr. White turned out in the end to be right, and I think from the first he knew that we should not be able to do anything elsewhere than in Lhasa.

Mr. White's long local experience on that frontier made his recommendation in regard to arrangements specially valuable. We were to have an escort of 200 men from the 32nd Pioneers, who had been for some months in Sikkim improving the road towards the frontier, and we wished arrangements made for them to precede us to the vicinity of the frontier, so that we, travelling lightly, might reach Khamba Jong as quickly as possible, for we were now getting well on into the summer, and had not much time to spare for negotiation before the winter came on.

Indian troops and officers have, fortunately, plenty of experience in rough work of this and every other description. The 32nd Pioneers I had known in the Relief of Chitral in 1895, and they had come almost straight to Sikkim from another frontier expedition, so they could be relied on to be thoroughly up to the duty now expected of them. All I asked Government for, on Mr. White's recommendation, was that, as they would be moving up from the hot, steamy valleys of Lower Sikkim to a plateau 15,000 feet above sea-level, they should be provided with clothing on the winter scale, with poshtins (sheepskin coats) for sentries, and that special rations should be issued to the men. And for ceremonial effect, which is an item never to be lightly passed over in dealings with Asiatics, I asked that they should take with them their full-dress uniforms, and that twenty-five of them should be mounted on ponies, which could be procured locally.

The Government of India always equips and organizes

its expeditions well, and such little arrangements were soon and readily made. And by a piece of foresight on its part, there was on the spot in Sikkim the best practical rough-and-ready supply and transport officer in their service, Major Bretherton, D.S.O., a very old friend of mine in Chitral days, a man of unbounded energy, of infinite resource, and of quite unconquerable optimism, who was drowned in the Brahmaputra within a few days' march of Lhasa, when we were just about to reap the reward which he, more than any other single man, had put within our reach.

All headquarter arrangements having been made, and my formal instructions received, Mr. White and I left Simla early in June to proceed by Darjiling to the Sikkim frontier. In India such enterprises as we were now embarking on are always started off very quietly, and few outside a limited official circle, and possibly the Russian Government, knew anything at all about our mission. The Government of India is over-sensitive to questions and criticisms in Parliament, and, dependent as it is upon the support of public opinion in England, would be better advised, in my opinion, to take the public in England more into its confidence. But this sensitiveness is intelligible. It must by the necessity of the case be especially difficult to govern India from England, but that task is rendered vastly more difficult by careless questions and criticisms of Members of Parliament. My mission suffered much through the want of support by the British public, and they could hardly have been expected to give it support when it was eventually sprung so suddenly on them, and when they had not had the opportunity of watching affairs gradually growing to a crisis. On the other hand, the Indian Government cannot be expected to expose delicate affairs to the risk of rough, crude handling from men who, though they ultimately control these affairs, are so very little versed in their conduct.

I departed, then, from Simla in the most matter-of-fact manner possible, telling my friends, what was perfectly true, that I was going to see Darjiling. I had therefore no "enthusiastic send-off." But I had what was better, the heartfelt good wishes of the Viceroy, who has known the conditions under which frontier officers work, and has been more interested in the problems which confront them than any other Viceroy for many a year past. I was also greatly cheered, and subsequently most warmly and continuously supported, by Sir Louis Dane, the Foreign Secretary, whose hospitality I had enjoyed during my stay in Simla.

The journey from Simla to Darjiling by Calcutta was a curious beginning for an expedition to the cold of the Himalayas. The monsoon had not yet broken. The heat of the railway journey was frightful. At Calcutta the temperature was almost the highest on record. And we hurried on, for I was impatient, not only to be out of the heat, but to be getting to work.

At the very outset I looked forward to one experience of, to me, peculiar interest. My life through, mountains have excited in me a special fascination. I was born in the Himalayas, within sight of the Kashmir Mountains; and some inexplicable attraction has drawn me back to them time after time. Now that I was called upon to pierce through the Himalayas to the far country on the hither side, I was to make my start from that spot, from which of all others the most perfect view is to be obtained. Darjiling is now known throughout the world for the magnificence of its mountain scenery, and fortunate it is that such a spot should be now so easily accessible.

As in the earliest dawn I looked out of the train window, to catch the first glimpse of those mighty mountains I had to penetrate, I saw far up in the sky a rose-tinged stretch of seeming cloud. All around was level plain. The air was stifling with the heat of a tropical midsummer. But I knew that pinky streak across the sky could be nothing else than the line of the Himalayas, tinted by the yet unrisen sun. It gave me the first thrill of my new adventure, and I forthwith drank in greedily every new impression.

All around in the plains there was rank, dank, depressing vegetation. Unwholesomeness exuded from the soil. Putrefying pools of water lay about on every side. The whole air was thick with fever. But those high heavenly mountains carried hope. As the train progressed, the lower "hills"—themselves 7,000 or 8,000 feet in height—came into sight. Eventually we reached their base, and left the ordinary train for the little mountain railway which ascends to Darjiling. And now, indeed, were charms on every hand. The little railway winds its way upward through a tropical forest of superb magnificence. The orchids could almost be plucked from the miniature carriages. The luxuriant vegetation nearly met over the train. Immense tree-ferns and wild bananas shot up beneath the overhanging arches of the dripping forest trees. Wreaths and festoons of vine, convolvulus, and begonia stretched from bough to bough. Climbing bauhinias and robinias entwined the trunks and hung like great cables from tree to tree. Bamboos shot up in dense tufts to a height of 100 feet. Refreshing streams dashed foaming down the mountain-side. Glorious waterfalls here and there thundered over steep cliffs. And through all the diminutive train panted its way upward—by zigzags, by spirals, through tunnels, across dizzy bridges, along the sides of cliffs—but only too slowly, for, glorious as was the tropical forest, I thirsted for the sight of Kinchinjunga, which we should get when we at last topped the ridge and reached Darjiling.

Alas! when we at last reached the summit, all was hid in cloud. Fresh from the steamy plains, we shivered in the damp mists, and when we reached Darjiling itself rain was descending in cataracts. It was depressing, but it had the advantage that it enabled me to recuperate a little from the hot, trying railway journey through the plains of India, and be all the more fit therefore to thoroughly enjoy and appreciate the great view when at last it should be revealed.

Many times afterwards I saw it, and each time with a

new and more wonderful impression. Sometimes in the eddying cloudy billows a break would come, giving a glimpse into heaven itself; and through the little inlet would be seen a piece of sky of the intensest blue, and against it a peak of purest white, so lofty and so much a partner of the sky and clouds it seemed impossible it could ever be of earth. This was Kinchinjunga in one of its aspects. At another time, when all was clear of cloud, I would look steeply down from the tropical forests of Darjiling for 6,000 feet to the bottom of the narrow valley beneath, and then up and up through tier after tier of ever-heightening ridges, till, far up in the skies, suffused in the blue and dreamy haze, my eyes would rest on the culminating range of all, spotless and ethereal, and reaching its climax in one noble peak nearly 28,000 feet above the valley depths from which it rose. And at yet another time, when the houses were all lit in the bazaar, and the lamps lighted along the roads, and night had almost settled down upon Darjiling, high up in the skies would be seen a rosy flush: Kinchinjunga was still receiving the rays of the sun, long since set to us below. In these and many other aspects Kinchinjunga had never-ending charms.

Darjiling itself, with such scenery and vegetation, was, it need hardly be said, an exquisitely beautiful place. And it had about it none of the busy air of Simla. It was at this season nearly always shrouded in mist, and seemed wrapped in cotton-wool. No one was in a hurry, and the whole tone of the place was placid and serene.

Sir James Bourdillon, the acting Lieutenant-Governor; Mr. Macpherson, the Chief Secretary; Mr. Marindin, the Commissioner; Mr. Walsh, the Deputy-Commissioner, were all most helpful to me, and I appreciated their assistance all the more because I could not help feeling somewhat of an interloper and poacher upon other people's preserves. Since 1873 the Bengal Government had been working for the settlement of their frontier affairs with Tibet, and now at the crucial moment a stranger dropped down from the Olympian heights of Simla to carry out the culminating act. I could naturally expect ordinary official civility from them. But they, every one of them, went out of their way to put their whole information and experience at my disposal. More than that, both they and their wives were more thoughtful and kind to my wife than I could possibly record during all that time of anxiety and depression when we subsequently advanced to Lhasa, and we have ever felt most deeply grateful to them.

The Bengal Government, I have often thought, has experienced a hard fate over Tibet affairs. It was a Governor of Bengal—Warren Hastings—who initiated the idea of sending a mission to Tibet. It was another Lieutenant-Governor who revived the idea of intercourse in 1873. It was a Bengal officer, Colman Macaulay, who originated and pushed through the idea of a mission to Lhasa in 1885. It was a Bengal officer, Mr. Paul, who negotiated the Trade Regulations of 1893; and it was a Lieutenant-Governor, Sir Charles Elliott, who, in 1895, made what seems to me to have been the most suitable recommendation for the settlement of the question, an occupation of the Chumbi Valley.

But gradually, in the course of years, the conduct of frontier matters has been taken out of their hands by the Government of India and out of the hands of the latter by the Imperial Government. There has been a greater and greater centralization of the conduct of frontier relations, which may be necessary from some points of view, but one of the effects of which is apparent locally. The local Government loses its sense of responsibility for frontier matters. Local officers feel little inducement to fit themselves for the conduct of such affairs. And, consequently, when good frontier officers really are wanted in future, they will not be found, and the next mission to Lhasa will in all probability be led by a clerk from the Foreign Office in London.

I left Darjiling on June 19, in drenching rain. To realize it the English reader must picture to himself the heaviest thunderstorm he has ever seen, and imagine that pouring down continuously night and day. I was, of course, provided with a heavy waterproof cloak, with a riding apron and an umbrella; but the moisture seemed to soak through everything, for there was not only the rain beating down from above, but the penetrating mists creeping in all round. But I could not be depressed by mere rain, however much. The road passed through a forest of unsurpassable beauty. Chestnuts, walnuts, oaks, laurels, rhododendrons, and magnolias grew in great magnificence, and among them Himalayan kinds of birch, alder, maple, holly, apple, and cherry. Orchids of the most brilliant varieties I could have gathered in basketfuls. The perpetual moisture and the still atmosphere nourished the most delicate ferns; while the mosses were almost as beautiful, and hung from the trees in graceful pendants, blending with the festoons of the climbing plants.

After riding for some miles along the ridge, we descended towards the Teesta River, and again met with the magnificent tree-ferns, palms, bamboos, and wild bananas. We passed by several flourishing tea plantations, each with its cosy, but lonely, bungalow, surrounded by a beautiful garden. By the roadway caladiums of every variegated colour brightened the prospect. But as we descended the atmosphere grew more oppressive and stifling, till when we reached the Teesta itself, which here lies at an altitude of only 700 feet above sea-level, the atmosphere was precisely that of a hothouse. The thermometer did not rise above 95°, but the heat was well-nigh unbearable. Perspiration poured from every pore. Energy oozed away with every drop, and the thought of a winter amid the snows of Tibet became positively cheering. It was a curious beginning for such an expedition as was to follow, but the Indian officer has to be prepared to undergo at a moment's notice every degree of heat or cold, of storm and sunshine, of drought or deluge, and take everything he meets cheerily as in the day's work.

We were now in Sikkim proper, the thin wedge of a valley which runs from the plains to the watershed of the Himalayas, and separates Nepal from Bhutan. For luxuriance and for variety of vegetation, and of animal, bird, and insect life, it must, I should say, be unequalled by any other country in the world, for it lies in the tropics, and rises from an elevation of only a few hundred

SIKKIM SCENERY.

To face page 105.

feet above sea-level to a snowy range, culminating in a peak 28,178 feet in height.

The valley bottom was narrow, and the Teesta River, 100 yards or so broad, dashed down over great boulders and beside precipitous cliffs with immense velocity. Both the main and the side valleys were very deep, the slopes steep, and the whole packed with a dense forest of rich and graceful and variegated foliage. Tropical oaks of gigantic size, a tree with a buttressed trunk growing to a height of 200 feet, "sal," sago-palms, bamboos, bananas, bauhinias, "took," screw-pine, and on the ridges *Pinus excelsus*. An immense climber, with pendulous blossoms, and which bears a fruit like a melon, was very prevalent, and aristolochias, with their pitcher-like flowers, orchids, and ferns. Tropical profusion of vegetable growth was nowhere better exemplified. But almost more remarkable were the number and the variety of the butterflies. I counted seventeen different species in a couple of hundred yards, some of the most exquisitely beautiful colouring, flashing out every brilliant and metallic hue; others mimicking the foliage, and when at rest shutting their wings together, and exactly resembling the leaves of a tree. Less beautiful, but equally abundant, was the wealth of insect life. And here with a vengeance was the thorn which every rose possesses. Midges, mosquitoes, gnats, every conceivable horror and annoyance in this particular line, was present here; also beetles in myriads; some spiders, too, of enormous size; cockchafers and cockroaches, winged ants, and, in addition to all these insect pests, the countless leeches on every leaf and every blade of grass. It is indeed a paradise for a naturalist, but only for such a naturalist as has his flesh under due subjection to the spirit. And such a naturalist was the great Sir Joseph Hooker, the friend of Darwin, who first explored this country in 1848 and 1849, and who is even now living amongst us.

The stillness of these parts I have already referred to. There is seldom a breath of air stirring, and one feels in a gigantic hothouse. But it is not noiseless, for, apart from the roar of the main river as it dashes impetuously through the languid forest, and, apart from the thundering of the voluminous waterfalls, which, fringed with rich masses of maidenhair and many other delicate and graceful ferns, form yet another striking feature in the landscape. one hears also in the forest depths the incessant chorus of the insects. Bird-life there is scarcely any, and therefore very little song of the birds; but there is an incessant rhythmic rise and fall of insect whirring, broken at intervals by the deafening, dissonant screechings of invisible crickets.

All this was very beautiful and very interesting as an experience, but I felt no temptation to linger in the stifling valley, and was glad when the road began to rise to Gantok and the temperature to lower. Then the more distinctly tropical vegetation began to disappear, and at between 4,000 and 5,000 feet a kind of birch, willows, alders, rhododendrons, and walnuts grew side by side with the plantains, palms, and bamboos. Among the plants grew balsam, climbing vines, brambles, speedwells, forget-me-nots, strawberries, geraniums, orchids, tree-ferns, and lycopodiums.

Embedded amidst all the luxuriance of forest and plant life, and facing the snowy range with a view of Kinchinjunga itself, is the Gantok Residency, a charming English house, clustered over with roses, and surrounded by a garden in which rhododendrons, magnolias, canna of every rich variety, tree-ferns, lilies, and orchids, and all that could excite the envy of the horticulturist, grow almost without the trouble of putting them into the ground.

Here I enjoyed the hospitality of Mr. White, who had preceded me to make preparations. He and Mrs. White had lived there for fourteen years. They were devoted to their garden, in which they found a never-ending interest with all the English flowers—narcissus, daffodils, pansies, iris—in the spring, and the beautiful tropical plants in the summer.

They were also devoted to the people amongst whom they lived. These Lepchas are, says Mr. White, in his recent book, "Sikkim and Bhutan," "quite an exceptional people, amongst whom it is a pleasure to live." And he says they make excellent and trustworthy servants. Certainly these people were devoted to Mr. White, who, in a kindly patriarchal way, did many a kindness for them as he toured through their valley. And I was particularly interested in observing them, and hearing Mr. White's opinion of them, because they have been the subject of so many encomiums on the part of Herbert Spencer. On account of their truthfulness and gentleness they had been held up by him as an example to civilized people, and I was anxious to see whether at close quarters they were as estimable as they had appeared at a distance to the philosopher.

They are of the Mongolian type of feature, yet they have very distinctive features of their own, and would never be mistaken for either the Tibetans, the Nepalese, or the Bhutanese, who touch them on either side, and they seem to have come along the foothills from Assam and Burma. Their chief characteristic is undoubtedly their gentleness. Timidity is the word which might better describe it. They live in a still, soft, humid climate, and their character is soft like the climate; but their disposition is also attractive, like their country. They are great lovers of Nature, and unequalled as collectors. In their own country and unspoiled they are frank and open, good-natured and smiling, and when they are at their ease, amiable, obliging, and polite. They are indolent and improvident, but they seldom have private or political feuds. They never aggress upon their neighbours. And by nature they are scrupulously honest. Their women are chaste, and neither men nor women drink in excess.

These 6,000 Lepchas certainly have every estimable quality, and many for which we Europeans are not strikingly remarkable. Yet mere gentleness, without strength and passion at the back, can hardly count much in the world, and it is not possible seriously to regard the Lepchas as an ensample for our living. Even the naughty little Gurkhas, who would, except for our protection of the Lepchas, have long since swallowed them up, we really prefer.

We remained only a few days in Gantok, and then pushed on toward the Tibetan frontier, for we were well on in the summer now, and we wanted, if possible, to get the matter settled before winter. The rain never ceased: bucketfuls and bucketfuls came drenching down. The ordinary waterproofing in which we wrapped our luggage was soaked through as if it had been paper. In the valley bottom we passed the camp of the 32nd Pioneers engaged in improving the road, and anything more depressing and miserable I have never seen. Tents, clothes, furniture—everything was soaking. The heat was stifling, the insect pests unbearable. Fever sapped the life out of the men, and one shuddered at the misery of life under such conditions: day after day, week after week, month after month, digging and blasting away at a road which as soon as it was made was washed into the river again; wet through with rain and with perspiration while at work, and finding everything equally moist on returning to camp; tormented with insect pests at work and in camp by night and by day. Yet it was only by mastering such conditions as these that the eventual settlement with Tibet was ever rendered possible.

Fortunately for them, some 200 were now to leave these dismal surroundings and accompany me to the Tibetan frontier as escort. We marched on up the valley by a road carried in many places along the side of precipices overhanging the roaring river, and with neither wall nor railing intervening between one and destruction. Only in Hunza, beyond Kashmir, have I seen a more precarious roadway. The same luxuriant vegetation extended everywhere. But what impressed me most in this middle region of Sikkim were the glorious waterfalls. Never anywhere have I seen their equal. We were in the midst of the rains. The torrents were full to the limit, and they would come, boiling, foaming, thundering down the mountain-sides in long series of cascades, gleaming white through the ever-green forest, and festooned over and framed with every graceful form of palm and fern and foliage.

And now, as we reached the higher regions, the loathsome leeches, the mosquitoes, gnats, and midges, were left behind, and we came into a region of Alpine vegetation—spruce-firs, ash, birch, maple, crab-apple, and nut, with jasmine, ivy, spiræa, wood-sorrel, and here and there, rising lightly through the shade of the forest, a gigantic white lily, most exquisitely lovely.

On June 26 we reached Tangu, at a height of 12,000 feet above the sea, and here in a comfortable wooden rest-house, in a cool and refreshing climate, we were able to forget all the depressions of the steamy valleys. The spiræa, maple, cherry, and larch, which we had met lower down, had now disappeared, and in their place were willow, juniper, stunted birch, silver fir, white rose, berberry, currant, and many rhododendrons. The mountain-sides were covered with grass and carpeted with flowers, and especially with many beautiful varieties of primulas, as well as with gentians, potentillas, geraniums, campanulas, ground orchids, delphiniums, and many other plants, while near by we found a fine dark blue poppy; and, most remarkable plant of all, growing here and there on the mountain-side in isolated grandeur, a gigantic rhubarb (*Rheum nobile*), described by Hooker as the handsomest herbaceous plant in Sikkim, with great leaves spread out on the ground at the base, while the main plant rose erect to a height of 3 feet in the form of a pyramid, but with the clusters of flowers protected from the wind and rain, by reflexed bracts.

Here, at Tangu, only a march below the district round Giagong, which the Tibetans claimed, the real business of the mission commenced. By July 1 the whole of both the escort and the support—the former 200 men and the latter 300—were assembled, under the command of Colonel Brander. Both the men and the transport animals had suffered greatly in marching through the drenching rain and the steamy, fever-laden lower valleys; but now, in the cooler air of Tangu, they recovered their strength, and all were eager for the advance into Tibet. I was myself equally keen, but as I could hear no news of either Chinese or Tibetan officials of rank or authority having arrived at Khamba Jong to meet me, I decided to let Mr. White, with Captain O'Connor and the whole escort, go on in advance to arrange preliminaries.

On July 4 they left Tangu, and encamped some nine miles distant, on the near side of the wall at Giagong, which the Tibetans claimed as their boundary, and from which they had been removed by Mr. White in the previous year. Before reaching camp—that is to say, well on the Sikkim side of even the wall—Mr. White was met by the Jongpen, or Commandant, of Khamba Jong—"Jong" being the Tibetan for fort. He informed Mr. White that there were encamped at Giagong, on the other side of what the Tibetans claimed as their frontier, two officials—a General and a Chief Secretary of the Dalai Lama—who had been deputed to discuss frontier matters, and who were anxious to confer with Mr. White on the following day.

Mr. White informed the Jongpen that he would be prepared to greet the officials on the road, and to receive them in a friendly manner in his camp on the next evening, but that he was not prepared to halt or hold any discussion at Giagong.

On the following day Captain O'Connor rode forward, and was met by the Jongpen of Khamba Jong at the wall at Giagong, which the Tibetans claimed as their frontier, but which was on a river flowing into the Teesta River, and therefore clearly on our side of the frontier laid down by the Convention of 1890, concluded by the Chinese Resident, who had with him a Tibetan representative. The Jongpen importuned Captain O'Connor to dismount and to persuade Mr. White to do the same. But Captain O'Connor said that no discussion was possible, and on Mr. White's arrival with the escort they all passed through the wall, and just beyond saw the two Lhasa officers arrayed in yellow silks, and accompanied by a crowd of unarmed retainers riding towards them from their camp. Captain O'Connor advanced to meet them, and they dismounted and spoke to him very civilly. They asked him to persuade Mr. White to dismount, to proceed to their tent close by, to partake of some refreshments, and to "discuss matters." Captain O'Connor replied that Mr. White was not prepared to break his journey or to discuss matters at Giagong, but would be glad to see them in his camp that evening, though any discussion must be deferred until after the arrival of myself and the Chinese Commissioner at Khamba Jong.

They pressed forward on foot, and, catching hold of Mr. White's bridle, importuned him to dismount and repair to their tents. At the same time their servants pressed round the horses of the British officers, and, seizing their reins, endeavoured to lead them away. After speaking very civilly to the two Lhasa officials, Mr. White was obliged to call two or three sepoys to clear the way, and the British officers then rode on, while the two Lhasa officers mounted and rode back to camp. The Jongpen afterwards followed the British officers, and made repeated efforts to induce them to halt for a day at the next camp in order to confer with the two Lhasa officials. He was in a very excited state, and hinted more than once at possible hostilities, and said: "You may flick a dog once or twice without his biting, but if you tread on his tail, even if he has no teeth, he will turn and try and bite you."

I suppose it is always difficult for one party to see the other party's point of view; but, of course, his contention regarding us precisely applied to what we thought of the Tibetans. It was simply because the Tibetans had encroached on us, and were even now addressing us *inside* the frontier fixed by treaty, that we were at last turning and insisting on our treaty rights.

That evening Mr. Ho, the Chinese delegate, sent word that he had arrived at Giri, just on the other side of the frontier, and asking that Mr. White would remain at Giagong.

The next day Mr. White and his escort rode quietly across the frontier, without meeting anyone except the Chinese Commandant of the small post of Giri, who passed by without speaking. Mr. White encamped near Giri, and received a visit from Mr. Ho, who communicated to him the contents of the Resident's reply to the Viceroy, and made a request, which was politely declined, that the British Commissioner should remain at Giri in preference to proceeding to Khamba Jong. In this despatch the Chinese Resident informed the Viceroy that he had again deputed Mr. Ho, in conjunction with Captain Parr, the Customs Commissioner at Yatung, who, he said, were truly of equal rank to the Commissioner deputed by the Viceroy, to discuss all matters in a friendly manner. He further said that the Dalai Lama had deputed his Chief Secretary and a Depon (General) of Lhasa to negotiate in conjunction with the Chinese Commissioners. But the Resident understood, he said, that Khamba Jong was in Tibetan territory, and therefore the meeting could only be at the boundary near the grazing-grounds fixed by the Convention of 1890. The Resident contended, that is to say, that though the Tibetans had for thirteen years with armed men occupied territory on our side of the frontier laid down by the Convention, we were not even to meet temporarily for discussion on the Tibetan side of the same frontier.

On July 7 Mr. White, with his escort, marched to Khamba Jong, and encamped on a small stream not far from the Jong, or fort, which was an imposing building on the summit of a lofty crag some hundreds of feet above the plain. Mr. Ho wrote to Mr. White saying that he had instructed the Khamba Jongpen to provide him with supplies, and that he himself, accompanied by the two Lhasa officials, would arrive there on the following day. A letter of thanks was sent, and on the strength of Mr. Ho's letter Mr. White wrote to the Tibetan Jongpen asking him to supply some grass; but the letter was returned unopened, with a somewhat unceremonious verbal message.

Major Bretherton, the energetic supply and transport officer, who had come up from Sikkim to arrange supply matters, on the following day found a rich and fertile valley some three or four miles from Khamba Jong, where grazing was abundant, and where barley crops were raised and sheep and cattle reared.

In the evening the Khamba Jongpen, with two junior officers bearing presents from the Lhasa delegates, arrived in camp. Mr. White received them, and sent polite messages in return, and Captain O'Connor afterwards interviewed the messenger in his own tent, and conversed very amicably for some time, the messenger being evidently very pleased with his reception, and altogether refusing to accept money, which was all Mr. White had at the moment, in return for their presents. The Jongpen also behaved with great civility, and repeatedly apologized in regard to his refusal to accept the letter, and promised to supply grass on the following day.

The two Lhasa officials, who were those referred to in the Chinese Resident's letter to the Viceroy, visited Mr. White on July 11. They were well-mannered, but made protests regarding what they called our transgression of the frontier. After the interview with Mr. White they visited the Sikkim heir-apparent, who had arrived in Mr. White's camp on the previous day; and here Captain O'Connor, in a less formal way, had a long conversation with them, endeavouring to find out under what amount of authority they had come. But they evaded all queries, and merely reiterated that if they had not had proper orders they would not, of course, be there. On the same day Mr. White visited Mr. Ho.

Captain O'Connor had a two-hours conversation with the Lhasa delegates on the 12th. He elicited that the Chief Secretary had been to Peking and back by Calcutta and Shanghai. The position they took up was that the place appointed by their Government for the discussion of affairs was the Giagong frontier, and on arrival there they would produce their credentials. As regards official correspondence, they said that by the terms of some treaty between the Chinese and the Tibetans all official correspondence between the Tibetans and foreigners had to be conducted through the Ambans, and, under these circumstances, they could neither receive nor reply to our letters. But they affirmed, nevertheless, that they were fully empowered to treat with our Commissioners at the proper place—the Giagong frontier.

Their dislike of the Chinese they plainly expressed. They said the Chinese despised the Tibetans, and were often instrumental in letting foreigners into the country—the poor Chinese who are accused by us of keeping foreigners *out!* The relations of Tibetans and Chinese were indeed extraordinarily anomalous. Whilst the Tibetans deferred to Mr. Ho in almost every matter, going so far as to forward to him official letters received from our camp for fear that they might get into trouble if they retained them, Mr. Ho himself admitted that in many matters he was powerless. The Tibetan officials appeared to be childishly impotent and terrified of their own Government, whilst at the same time they were deliberately obstructive in every matter, great or small, in which the British were concerned, and were quite ready to use the Chinese as a very convenient scapegoat whenever it suited them.

Mr. White made a formal visit to them on July 13, and at the close of the interview gave them presents, including two packets of tea each. They tried to raise some objections to receiving the tea, but no attention was paid, and the presents were accepted.

While all these proceedings were taking place, I confess that I at Tangu was in some anxiety. To march across the frontier in face of all protest, as Mr. White did, appears, when set down like this, as a very high-handed action. But it was also very risky. I had purposely, though not very wisely, but at any rate to avoid a direct collision at the very start, decided not to attack, and remove the Tibetans from Giagong, as they had been removed on the previous year. Mr. White was simply to march through to the place appointed by our Government in communication with the Chinese Government for the place of negotiation. But in so doing we left Tibetan troops in a good position on our line of communications, and as the Tibetans were evidently in an irritable state, this was no mean risk to take, and Colonel Brander and I at Tangu used to look out with considerable anxiety for the arrival of the daily dak from Mr. White.

On the face of it there seems some force in the Tibetan argument that discussion should take place at Giagong; and when officials from Lhasa had at last arrived, and with a Chinese deputy as well, and even provided with credentials, and were ready to negotiate, it would seem more reasonable on our part to have met there and negotiated. But such negotiations would not in fact have led to any result. The powers they had would simply have been not to let us inside the wall. They would have had none to negotiate in the real sense of the word, and they would have been afraid to make any kind of concession for fear their property or even their lives would be forfeited. Even when we arrived close to Lhasa, and men of much higher rank came to meet us, they had absolutely no power. Even the Regent had none, nor the whole Council. The Tibetans had no machinery for the conduct of foreign relations. They were under some arrangement to let the Chinese conduct their foreign relations, and yet, as we had experienced, they refused to abide by what the Chinese did for them.

CHAPTER X

KHAMBA JONG

Now that Chinese and Tibetan representatives of some kind had appeared, even though they were not of much rank or accredited with much power, I thought it well to proceed to Khamba Jong to get into touch with them, and form my own impression of how matters stood. I therefore rode straight through from Tangu to Khamba Jong on the 18th, accompanied by Mr. Dover, the Sikkim engineer, who had made such excellent rough roads and bridges, and escorted by a few mounted men.

After Tangu the mountain-sides became more and more barren; trees were replaced by low shrubs and dwarf rhododendrons, and higher up they, too, disappeared, till, when we crossed the Kangra-la (pass), there was nothing but rough coarse scrub. The pass itself was easy enough, though it was just over 17,000 feet in height. As we descended from it we were at length really in Tibet, and the change was most marked. In place of narrow valleys were great wide plains, intersected indeed by distant ranges of mountains, and absolutely devoid of trees, but open and traversable in every direction. The sky, too, was clear. The great monsoon clouds were left behind, and the sun shone with a power which brought the temperature up to 82° in the shade, and made it quite uncomfortably hot at midday, though at night there were 4° of frost.

As we rode on into Tibet and got out into the open, and well away from the Himalayan range, we obtained a glorious view of that stupendous range from Chumalhari, 24,000 feet, on the extreme east, to Kinchinjunga,

MISSION CAMP, KHAMBA JONG (MOUNT EVEREST IN FAR DISTANCE).

To face page 116.

28,275 feet, in the centre, and Everest itself, 29,002 feet, and ninety miles distant in the far west.

On July 20 I made a formal call upon Mr. Ho and the Tibetan delegates. Mr. Ho was not a very polished official, and did not favourably impress me. The Tibetan Chief Secretary, however, did, and I reported at the time that he had an "exceedingly genial, kind, accomplished style of face." But appearance belied him, and right up to the conclusion of the treaty, nearly fourteen months later, he was the most inimical to us of all the Tibetans.

As this was a first interview, I did not proceed with any business discussion, but I told the delegates that, though I must await the orders of the Viceroy on the letter which the Resident had addressed him, and could not, therefore, yet commence formal negotiations, yet I would at our next meeting state plainly in detail the view which the Viceroy took of the situation, so that they might know our views, and be ready when the formal negotiations commenced to make proposals for their settlement.

Two days later they all came to return my visit, and after the usual polite conversation I said I would now redeem my promise, and I told the interpreter to commence reading a speech which I had prepared beforehand, and which Captain O'Connor had carefully translated into Tibetan. But before he could commence the Tibetans raised objections to holding negotiations at Khamba Jong at all. The proper place, they said, was Giagong. I told them that the place of meeting was a matter to be decided upon, not by the negotiators, but by the Viceroy and Amban. The Viceroy had selected Khamba Jong because of its proximity to the portion of frontier in dispute, and he had chosen a place on the Tibetan rather than the Indian side of the frontier because the last negotiations were conducted in India; and when, after much trouble a treaty had been concluded between the Chinese and British Governments, the Tibetans had repudiated it, saying they knew nothing about it. On the present occasion, therefore, the Viceroy decided that negotiations should take place in Tibet, and had asked that a Tibetan official of the highest rank should take part in them, in order that, when the new settlement was completed, the Tibetans should not be able to say they knew nothing of it.

The Tibetans then raised objections to the size of my escort. I explained that it was merely the escort which was becoming to my rank, and was even smaller than the escort which the Chinese Resident took to Darjiling and Calcutta at the former negotiations. They said they had understood that the negotiations were to be friendly, and so they themselves had brought no armed escort. I replied that the negotiations certainly were to be friendly, and that if I had had any hostile intentions I should have brought many more than 200 men, a number which was only just sufficient to guard me against such attacks of bad characters as had very recently been made upon the British Ambassador at the capital of the Chinese Empire.

My speech was then read by the interpreter. It recounted how, seventeen years before, the Viceroy proposed a peaceful mission to Lhasa to arrange the conditions of trade with Tibet. British subjects had the right to trade in other parts and provinces of the Chinese Empire, just as all subjects of the Chinese Emperor were allowed to trade in every part of the British Empire. But in this one single dependency of the Chinese Empire, in Tibet, obstacles were always raised in the way of trade. It was to discuss this matter with the Tibetan authorities at Lhasa, and to see if these obstacles could not be removed, that the then Viceroy of India proposed, with the consent of the Chinese Government, to send a mission to Lhasa in 1886. But when the mission was about to start, the Chinese Government at the last moment informed the Viceroy that the Tibetans were so opposed to the idea of admitting a British mission to their country that they (the Chinese Government) begged that the mission might be postponed; and out of good feeling to the Chinese Government, and on the distinct understanding that the Chinese would exhort the Tibetans to promote and develop trade, the Viceroy counterordered the mission.

Seventeen years had now passed away since the Chinese made the promise, and the British Government had just cause to complain that in all these years, owing to the persistent obstruction of the Tibetans, the Chinese had been unable to perform their pledge.

And the forbearance which the Viceroy had shown in countermanding the mission had met with a bad return on the part of the Tibetans, for they had proceeded, without any cause or justification, to invade a State under British protection. Even this the Viceroy bore with patience for nearly two years, trusting they would be obedient to the authority of the Chinese Government and withdraw. But when they still remained in Sikkim, and even attacked the British troops there, he was compelled to punish them and drive them back from Sikkim and pursue them into Chumbi. And in Chumbi the British troops would have remained as a punishment for the unprovoked attack upon them if it had not been for the friendship which existed between the Emperor of China and the Queen of England.

Out of regard, however, for that friendship, the Viceroy agreed to enter into negotiation with the Chinese Resident acting, on behalf of the Tibetans, and after some years an agreement was made, by which the boundary between Tibet and Sikkim was laid down, and arrangements were made for traders to come to Yatung to sell the goods to whomsoever they pleased, to purchase native commodities, to hire transport, and to conduct their business without any vexatious restrictions. It was also agreed that if, after five years, either side should wish to make any alterations, both parties should meet again and make a new agreement.

At the end of five years the Queen's Secretary of State wrote to the Viceroy and inquired how the treaty was being observed, and the reply went back that the Tibetans had destroyed the boundary pillars which British and Chinese officials had erected on the frontier laid down by the treaty; that they had occupied land at Giagong inside that boundary; that they had built a wall on the other side of Yatung, and allowed no one to pass through to trade with the traders who came there from India; and, lastly, that they had repudiated the treaty which had been signed by the Resident and the Viceroy on the ground that it had not been signed by one of themselves.

When the Queen's Great Secretary heard of the way they had set at naught the treaty which the Amban and the Viceroy had signed, he was exceedingly angry, and ordered Mr. White to go to Giagong to remove the Tibetans who had presumed to cross the frontier which the Amban and Viceroy had fixed. Mr. White had gone there and removed the Tibetans, and thrown down their guard-house, and reported to the Viceroy what he had done.

Now the Amban, when he heard what Mr. White had done, wrote to the Viceroy that, if there was any matter which needed discussion, he would send a Chinese officer and a representative of the Dalai Lama to settle it with a British officer. And the Viceroy had written in reply that he had sent a high officer with Mr. White to Khamba Jong to settle everything about the frontier and about trade; but as the Tibetans had broken the old treaty because they said they had known nothing about it, His Excellency had written to the Amban that there must be at the negotiations a Tibetan official of the highest rank, whose authority to bind his Government must be unquestioned. Mr. White and I had accordingly come, and as soon as I heard from the Viceroy that he was satisfied on this last point I was ready to commence negotiations.

The Viceroy, I could assure them, had no intention whatever of annexing their country, and it was possible, indeed, that he might make concessions in regard to the lands near Giagong, if in the coming negotiations they showed themselves reasonable in regard to trade. But I warned them that, after the way in which they had broken and repudiated the old treaty, concluded in their interests by the Amban at the close of a war in which they were defeated, they must expect that he would demand from them some assurance that they would faithfully observe any new settlement which might be made.

"You come and travel and trade in India just as you please," I said. "You go where you like, and stay there as long as you like. But if any one from India wishes to trade in Tibet he is stopped on the frontier, and no one is allowed to go near him. He can trade in Russia, in Germany, in France, and in all other great countries, and in all other dependencies of the Chinese Empire, in Manchuria, in Mongolia, and in Turkestan; but in Tibet alone of all countries he cannot trade. This is a one-sided arrangement, unworthy of so fair-minded and cultured a people as you are; and though His Excellency has no intention of annexing your country, and may, indeed, if you prove reasonable in regard to the admission of trade, make concessions to you in respect to the frontier lands near Giagong, yet he will insist that the obstacles which you have for so many years put in the way of trade between India and Tibet shall be once and for ever removed."

This speech was, of course, made for the benefit of the Lhasa Government. The Tibetan officials would receive no written communications, but I thought it barely possible that they might pass on a verbal communication, especially when it was made before a responsible Chinese official, and after I had given due notice of my intention.

The Tibetan delegates listened attentively while it was being delivered, but at its conclusion said that they could not enter into any discussion upon it. I replied that neither could I discuss it with them, for I had not yet heard from the Viceroy that he was satisfied that they were of sufficiently high rank to carry on negotiations. I had, however, as a matter of courtesy, taken the trouble to acquaint them informally with the Viceroy's views, which I trusted they would report to their Government. They replied that they could not even do that much, that they could make no report at all unless we went back to Giagong.

Mr. Ho here interposed, and said that the Tibetans were very ignorant and difficult to deal with, and he asked me if I could not meet them by agreeing to go to the frontier. I said I would with pleasure, and when representatives whom the Viceroy would permit me to negotiate with were present I would gladly ride with them to the frontier and discuss the question on the spot; but the frontier was not at Giagong, as the Tibetans supposed, but at the Kangra-la (pass), only ten miles from where we where. Mr. Ho said the actual position of the frontier was not known yet, but that it was where the waters flowed down to India. I said five minutes' investigation would make clear where that was, and Mr. Ho said that then the matter could be very easily settled.

Mr. Ho's Chinese secretary then suggested that I should give the Tibetans the copy of my speech which the interpreter had read from. I assented with readiness, and, with Mr. Ho's approval, presented it to them. But they could not have got rid of a viper with greater haste than they got rid of that paper. They said that they could on no account receive it, and handed it on to Mr. Ho's secretary, to whom, as he spoke English, I had also given an English version.

These so-called delegates never came near us again at Khamba Jong, but shut themselves up in the fort and sulked. And in reporting the result of this interview to Government, I said that both Mr. White and I were of opinion that Government must be prepared for very protracted negotiations, and also for the possibility of coercion. The attitude of the Tibetans was fully as obstructive, I said, as Mr. White and every other person acquainted with them had predicted it would be, and I saw at present little prospect of coming to a settlement without coercion, though I would use every possible means of argument and persuasion.

And if the delegates did not choose to give me any work, I was quite content to do none, for I was thoroughly happy in camp there at Khamba Jong. All my staff were delightful companions, and we were very happy together. Mr. White was the best possible hand at making a camp comfortable and feeding arrangements good; and we had neither the stifling heat of the Indian plains nor the discomforts of the rainy season in the hills. We were beyond the reach of the monsoon. We had occasional refreshing showers, but for July, August, and September, the rainfall was only 4·9 inches, and, for the most part, the weather was bright and fine and clear. We could see immense distances over the rolling plains. We would watch the mighty monsoon clouds sweeping along the Himalayas; we would catch glimpses of some noble peak rising superbly above them, and Kinchinjunga close by and Everest in the farthest distance were a perpetual joy.

Some of us went out shooting antelopes and *Ovis ammon;* while others went botanizing or geologizing; and when, later on, our scientific staff was complete, I could accompany Mr. Hayden to hunt for fossils, Captain Walton to collect birds, and Colonel Prain, now Director of the Botanical Gardens at Kew, to collect plants, and thus hear from each of these specialists in turn all the interests of their sciences, so I did not care a pin how long these obstinate Tibetans kept us up there.

But while the Lhasa delegates would have no more to say to us, a deputation came to see me on behalf of the Tashi Lama, who is of equal spiritual importance with the Dalai Lama, though of less political authority. They said that they had been sent to represent to us that the Tashi Lama was put to great trouble with the Lhasa authorities by our presence at Khamba Jong; that the Lhasa authorities held him responsible for permitting us to cross the frontier, and he begged me to be so kind as to save him from the trouble by withdrawing across the frontier or to Yatung, which was the place fixed for meetings of this kind. I repeated to them all the arguments I had used with the Lhasa delegates. They were much more courteous, and talked over the matter in a perfectly friendly, and even cheery, way. They said, though, that they knew nothing about the treaty, as it was concluded by the Amban, and not by themselves, and they could not be responsible for observing it. I said that that was precisely the reason why we had now come to Tibet. We wished now to make a new treaty there, where Tibetans could take part in the negotiations, so that they would not in future be able to say they knew nothing about it. They laughed, and said this was a very reasonable argument, but that it was the Lhasa people, and not themselves, who had broken the treaty, and we ought to go to Yatung and make the new treaty there.

I told them that, in the first place, they also had broken the treaty by crossing the boundary fixed in it and occupying Giagong; and, in the second place, we must regard Tibetans as all one people, and hold all responsible for the actions of each.

The impression left upon me by this interview, I reported at the time, was that the Tibetans, though excessively childish, were very pleasant, cheery people, and, individually, probably quite well disposed towards us.

Mr. Wilton, of the China Consular Service, joined us on August 7. He had been acting as Consul at Chengtu, in Szechuan, and I had not spoken to him for more than five minutes before I realized what a help he would be to us. He at once said that neither the Chinese nor the Tibetan delegates were of at all sufficient rank or authority to conduct negotiations with us, and no one else than one of the Ambans and one of the Tibetan Councillors would be of any use. The new Chinese Resident, who had been deputed in the previous December specially for the purpose of conducting these negotiations he had himself seen at Chengtu, and it is significant of the dilatoriness of the Chinese that, while Mr. Wilton reached me early in August, the Resident did not reach Lhasa till the next February, thirteen months after he had set out from Peking.

Having received Mr. Wilton's advice regarding the status of the delegates, the Viceroy, on August 25, wrote to the Chinese Resident, suggesting that either he himself or his Associate Resident should meet me, and that, as the present Tibetan delegates had shown themselves entirely unsuited for diplomatic intercourse, and would not even accept the copy of the speech explanatory of the relations between India and Tibet which I had made, he proposed that the Tibetan Government should be invited to depute a Councillor of the Dalai Lama, accompanied by a high member of the National Assembly.

As regards the objection which the Resident had made to the selection of Khamba Jong as the meeting-place, Lord Curzon said that it was the nearest point in Tibet to the disputed boundary; and it was necessary that the present negotiations should be conducted in Tibet, as the former Convention which the Tibetans had repudiated was concluded in India, and His Majesty's Government were not prepared to allow a similar repudiation of any new agreement. But, as winter was approaching, if the negotiations were not completed, I might have to select some other place in Tibet for passing the winter. In conclusion, the Viceroy emphasized the importance of my position and duties, and stated that I was entitled to expect that he should reply to my communications, and look to him for co-operation.

At Khamba Jong itself no progress was being made. There was, indeed, fear at one time that we should be attacked, and I have not much doubt that we should have been if we had shown any slackness or unguardedness. But Captain Bethune was an officer of much experience, and his men were all accustomed to frontier warfare, and every precaution was taken. Our camp was well fortified and the country round regularly patrolled.

Two Sikkim men who had gone to Shigatse, as was customary, were seized, however, and, we heard, had either been tortured or killed. In spite of our representations, the Tibetans refused to give them up, and, in retaliation, we had to seize Tibetan herds and to remove all the Tibetans I had so far, though at considerable risk, allowed to remain at Giagong.

Some slight chance of a settlement appeared when, on August 21, the head Abbot of the Tashi Lumpo monastery, near Shigatse, came to make another representation on behalf of the Tashi Lama. He was a courteous, kindly man, and was accompanied by two monks and a lay representative, besides the former deputy from the Tashi Lama. The Abbot said that a Council had been held by the Tashi Lama, and it had been decided to make another representation to me. This representation did not, however, differ from the first, and I repeated the same arguments in reply. He was especially insistent about Giagong, and I asked him when one man had a certain thing which another man wished to get from him, which was the wiser course to pursue—to make friends with him, or to do everything to make him annoyed. The Tibetans all burst out laughing at this argument, and I then went on to say that the Lhasa authorities, instead of doing everything they could to dispose us favourably towards them, and incline us to make concessions in regard to Giagong, had adopted a steadily unfriendly attitude; they had sent only small officials to meet Mr. White and myself, and these small officials did nothing but say they would negotiate nowhere else but at Giagong. This was not the way to predispose us in their favour.

The Abbot said the delegates were not small officials, but were next in rank to the Councillors. I said I had concluded they were men of little power, because when I had made a speech to them on my first arrival, and had asked them to report the substance of it to the Lhasa Government, they had refused. If they could not even report a speech, I supposed they would not be fit to negotiate an important treaty.

I asked the Abbot to give this advice to His Holiness —that if he wished us to withdraw from Khamba Jong, he should use his influence with the Lhasa authorities to induce them to send proper delegates, and instruct such delegates to discuss matters with us in a reasonable and friendly spirit. Then matters would be very soon settled, and we would return to India.

I then made some personal observations to the Abbot, and he told me that from a boy he had been brought up in a monastery in a religious way, and was not accustomed to deal with political matters. I told him I envied him his life of devotion. It was my business to wrangle about these small political matters, but I always admired those who spent their lives in the worship of God. He asked me if he might come and see me again, and I said he might come and see me every day and all day long; and Captain O'Connor, who could speak Tibetan, would often pay him visits.

On August 24 the Abbot again came to see me, and said that after his previous visit he had gone to the Lhasa delegates and urged them to negotiate at Khamba Jong, instead of at Giagong. But they had replied that, just as my orders were to negotiate at the former place, so their orders were to negotiate at the latter, and they could not agree to anything different. The Abbot, therefore, now came to say that there were several hundred Tibetan troops near by, but he would get those withdrawn if I would send away my escort. He thought that then the Lhasa Government would probably consent to negotiations at Khamba Jong. I told him that I had not the slightest objection to the presence of the Tibetan troops, but it surprised me that, when they had so many hundreds near, they should have any objection to the small number which I myself had.

The innocent-minded Abbot then asked if I would send away half, and he would himself remain with us as a hostage. He explained that the Tibetans thought we had come with no friendly intent, as we had forced our way into the country, and a reduction of our escort would appease them. I told the Abbot I could not acknowledge that we had forced our way into Tibet, as I had up to now ignored the presence of Tibetan soldiers inside the treaty frontier, who had no business to be where they were; and I repeated my old arguments in regard to the strength of my escort.

The Abbot very politely apologized for all the trouble he was giving me by making so many requests. I told him he might make requests to me all day long, and he would always find me ready to listen to him and give him what I, at any rate, considered reasonable answers. I much regretted the inconvenience which was being caused to the Tashi Lama, and I felt sure that if the conduct of these negotiations rested with His Holiness and the polite and reasonable advisers of his whom he had sent to me, we should very soon come to a settlement.

I advised the Abbot to get the Tashi Lama to represent matters directly to Lhasa. He replied they were not allowed to make representations against the orders of the Lhasa Government. Nevertheless, he would again, that very day, go to the Lhasa delegates, tell them how he had once more tried to induce me to go back to Giagong, and would ask them to make a request to Lhasa to open negotiations at Khamba Jong, and he said he would even go so far as to undertake to receive in their stead any punishment which the Lhasa Government might order upon the delegates for daring to make this request.

He then asked me what we wanted in the coming negotiations. I told him that I had set our requirements forth fully in a speech I had made on my first arrival, a copy of which I would very gladly give him. But he was well acquainted with it, and asked me what was meant exactly by opening a trade-mart. I explained that we wanted a proper trade-mart, which would not be closed with a wall behind it, as Yatung had been—a mart where Indian traders could come and meet Tibetan traders ; a mart such as we had in other parts of the Chinese Empire, and had formerly had in Shigatse itself.

The Abbot himself was a charming old gentleman. Whatever intellectual capacity he may have had was not very apparent to the casual observer, and he corrected me when I inadvertently let slip some observation implying that the earth was round, and assured me that when I had lived longer in Tibet, and had time to study, I should find that it was not round, but flat, and not circular, but triangular, like the bone of a shoulder of mutton. On the other hand, he was very sociable and genial. He would come and have lunch and tea with us, and would spend hours with Captain O'Connor and Mr. Bailey, playing with gramophones, typewriters, pictures, photographs, and all the various novelties of our camp.

But the situation now began to grow worse. On August 31 I was informed by a trustworthy person, who had exceptional sources of information, that he was convinced that the Tibetans would do nothing till they were made to and a situation had arisen. They were said to be quite sure in their own minds that they were fully equal to us, and, far from our getting anything out of them, they thought they would be able to force something out of us. Some 2,600 Tibetan soldiers were occupying the heights and passes on a line between Phari and Shigatse. My informant did not think, however, that they would attack us for the present, though they might in the

THE SHIGATSE ABBOT.

To face page 128.

winter, when our communications would be cut off. Their immediate policy was one of passive obstruction. They had made up their minds to have no negotiations with us inside Tibet, and they would simply leave us at Khamba Jong, while if we tried to advance farther, they would oppose us by force. They were afraid that if they gave us an inch we would take an ell, and if they allowed us at Khamba Jong one year we should go to Shigatse the next, and Lhasa the year after. So they were determined to stop us at the start.

The Shigatse Abbot had, I heard, done his best to make the Lhasa officials take a more reasonable view, but without success. The Lhasa officials were entirely ruled by the National Assembly at Lhasa, and this Assembly was composed chiefly of Lhasa monks.

It was difficult to understand why there was all this trouble about negotiating at Khamba Jong, for the Chinese Government had informed our Minister at Peking on July 19 that "the Imperial Resident had now arranged with the Dalai Lama to appoint two Tibetan officials of fairly high standing to proceed with the Prefect Ho to Khamba to meet Major Younghusband and Mr. White, and discuss with them what steps are to be taken." The Chinese Government added that they trusted it would be possible to effect a speedy and friendly settlement of this long-standing dispute, and requested Mr. Townley to acquaint his Government by telegraph with the contents of this communication, so that Major Younghusband and Mr. White might be instructed to open negotiations in a friendly spirit with the Tibetan and other delegates appointed, and it was hoped that the pending questions would then be speedily and finally settled.

The Chinese Government did, indeed, ask the British Government to withdraw the troops we had with us at Khamba Jong, but this was on the strength of a report they had received that when I was to follow Mr. White to Khamba Jong, I was to bring with me the 300 men who formed the support left at Tangu.

That the Dalai Lama himself had agreed to Khamba

Jong being the meeting-place seems evident from the copy of the telegram from the Chinese Resident at Lhasa, which the Chinese Government forwarded to Mr. Townley with the above-mentioned communication. The Resident's words were: "The Dalai Lama's answer is to the effect that, since the British Government has appointed Major Younghusband as Boundary Commissioner and Mr. White as his fellow-Commissioner, and fixed the 7th instant for the meeting of the delegates at the frontier station of Khamba, and as the Prefect Ho Kuang Hsieh is to proceed there in a few days from Chingshi, it is his duty, the matter being a very important one, also to appoint interpreter officials above the usual rank to proceed to Khamba, and, in company with the Prefect Shou [? Ho], to meet the British delegates and discuss the frontier question with them."

Nothing would seem clearer than this. Both the Chinese Government and the Dalai Lama accepted Khamba—that is, Khamba Jong—as the place of meeting, and directed their delegates to proceed to meet Mr. White and myself there. Yet, when we met at the appointed place, they refused to have anything to do with us!

I think a solution of this extraordinary proceeding may be found in the last paragraph of the telegram of the Resident to his Government. In this very same telegram in which he announces that the Dalai Lama is sending delegates with Mr. Ho to meet me at Khamba Jong, the Resident asks that we should "be careful not to cross the frontier, and thus again excite the suspicion and alarm of the Tibetans."

My impression is that neither the Chinese Government, the Resident, nor the Dalai Lama knew that Khamba Jong was on the Tibetan side of the frontier. And this appalling ignorance of the frontier by men who, nevertheless, kept the control of frontier affairs absolutely in their hands was one of the main difficulties with which we had to deal, and was what made it an absolute necessity to negotiate with them face to face at Lhasa itself.

In any case, whether they really were ignorant or not

of the position of Khamba Jong, they had all formally agreed to send delegates to meet Mr. White and myself there, and the continued refusal of these delegates even to receive communications was utterly indefensible.

On September 1 Mr. Ho came to me to say he had been recalled to Lhasa owing to ill-health. I took the opportunity to recount the difficulties the Chinese Government had placed us in by undertaking responsibilities in regard to the Tibetans, and then not being able to fulfil them. The British Government had time after time shown consideration to the Chinese Government, but the net result was that the Tibetans had broken the old treaty, and now placed every obstacle in the way of negotiating a new one. I trusted he would represent to the Resident the seriousness of the position, and impress upon him the importance of using his influence with the Tibetan Government to induce them to change their present intolerable attitude. The Tibetans did not seem to understand that for years they had been offending the British Government, and that it ill became them, therefore, to object to the mere place where negotiations were to be held. We had given them the opportunity for negotiating, and if the Lhasa Government still persisted in refusing to hold negotiations at Khamba Jong, and the Chinese still showed their incapacity to make them negotiate there, then the Resident must understand that the position would become very grave indeed, and the Chinese and Tibetans would only have themselves to thank if, under these circumstances, the British Government took matters into their own hands and adopted their own measures for effecting a settlement.

Mr. Ho said he would explain all this to the Amban, and he also then and there explained it to the Tibetans—the Shigatse Abbot and others, though not including the Lhasa delegates—who were present, and these seemed impressed, though they said we were acting in a very oppressive manner.

On September 2 the Government of India asked me to submit proposals for dealing with the situation if the Tibetans continued to be so impracticable. I replied on the 9th, that I thought that the Viceroy's reply to the Resident might have some effect upon the Chinese at least. Both Chinese and Tibetans had so far been under the impression that the present mission was only one more of the futile little missions which had come and gone on the Sikkim frontier for years past. They thought that if they could be obstructive enough during the summer and autumn, we should no doubt return before the winter. On this point the Viceroy's letter would leave them in no doubt. It was clear from that that we intended to stay for the winter. Besides this I had, I said, in conversation with Mr. Ho and the Shigatse people, tried to bring both the Chinese and the Tashi Lama round to putting pressure on the obstinate Lhasa monks. But there was little hope, I thought, that mere verbal persuasion would be sufficient. Direct action would be required. The despatch of a second Pioneer regiment to put the road to the Jelap-la (pass) in order, had, I understood, been ordered. I recommended, therefore, that about the same time my escort should be strengthened by 100 men from the support.

What I thought, however, would have a greater effect than anything else upon the Tibetans would be the demonstrating to them that the Nepalese were on our side, and not theirs. The Nepalese Minister had offered 8,000 yaks. I would have 500 of these march across to us by the Tinki Jong route, and would recommend that a suitable representative of the Nepalese Durbar should accompany them for the purpose of formally handing them over to us. This would be a sign which the Tibetans could not mistake that the Nepalese were on our side.

The strengthening of my escort and the appearance of the Nepalese yaks might be made to coincide with the concentration of the 23rd Pioneers in the neighbourhood of the Jelap-la (pass) in about a month's time. This I thought was all that could be done to bring the Tibetans to a more suitable frame of mind. If these measures failed, an advance into the Chumbi Valley was the most obvious course to take, for the Jelap-la could be crossed at any time during the winter, and along the Chumbi Valley lay the best trade-route and military road to Lhasa. When the Chumbi Valley had been occupied, the mission might, transported by Nepalese yaks, march across to Gyantse. The 32nd Pioneers and all transport would then be transferred to the Chumbi Valley line, and that line be made our chief line of communication.

These were my recommendations to Government when two months' experience had shown me the difficulty of even entering into communication with the Tibetans. Neither Mr. White nor I, nor any of us, had any real hope of effecting a final settlement anywhere short of Lhasa itself; for it was quite evident to us on the spot that to carry the negotiations through we should have to come to close grips with the priestly autocrats who kept all power in their own hands, and to whom the officials on the frontier were frightened to represent the real state of affairs. But at that time it was high treason for me to whisper the word Lhasa to my nearest friend, such agitation did the sound of it cause in England. So I racked my brains and everyone else's brains to think of alternative measures to an advance to Lhasa, which might be exhausted before this alarming proposal could be made. And I subsequently strove honestly to get the utmost out of each of those measures before I suggested the next, for I quite realized the difficulty which any Government at home has in securing support from the House of Commons in a matter of this kind. Such methods are very costly, very risky, and very ineffective; but as long as what an officer in the heart of Asia may do is contingent on the "will" of "men in the street" of grimy manufacturing towns in the heart of England, so long must our action be slow, clumsy, and hesitating, when it ought to be sharp and decisive.

I have referred to the offer of the Nepalese Government to help us with yaks, a species of buffalo peculiar to Tibet, which are of value as transport animals at high altitudes. This offer was not only of great practical use, but of still greater political significance. And it is time now to consider this yet other important factor in the situation—the attitude of the Nepalese Government; for Nepal was in rather a peculiar position in this matter. On the one hand, it sends a mission to Peking every three years, and also has a treaty with the Tibetans, under which it is bound to come to their assistance if they are attacked; on the other hand, it has political relations with ourselves. The attitude which the Nepalese Government would take under the circumstances was a matter of considerable importance to us, and no doubt of much questioning among themselves.

Recognizing this, the Government of India at the start laid down in their despatch to the Secretary of State of January 8, 1903, that they contemplated acting in complete unison with the Nepalese Durbar throughout their proceedings, and would invite them, if thought advisable, to take part in our mission. The Indian Government believed that the policy of frank discussion and cooperation with the Nepalese Durbar would find the latter prepared most cordially to assist our plans. An interview at Delhi at the time of the Durbar between Lord Curzon and the Prime Minister of Nepal, Maharaja Chandra Shamsher Jang—the same who came to England in 1908—confirmed the impression. The Nepalese Government regarded this rumour of intrigue in Tibet with the most lively apprehension, and considered the future of the Nepalese State to be directly involved. Further, the Maharaja (the Prime Minister) was prepared to cooperate with the Government of India in whatever way might be thought most desirable, either within or beyond the frontier, for the frustration of designs which he deemed to be utterly inconsistent with the interests of his own country.

This intention the Maharaja afterwards most amply fulfilled right up to the close of the mission. The welcome offer of 500 yaks, now accompanied as it was by a further offer of 8,000 yaks within a month, was the first practical sign of the intention. A second was to follow. And early in September I received from Colonel Ravenshaw, our Resident in Nepal, who had so much con-

THE PRIME MINISTER OF NEPAL.

To face page 134.

tributed to this good understanding between us and the Nepal Prime Minister, the translation of a letter which the latter had just addressed to the Council of Lhasa.

In this letter the Nepal Minister said that he had heard from his frontier officers and from newspaper reports that, in the absence of fully-empowered Commissioners from Tibet to deal with the British Commissioners at Khamba Jong, no settlement could be arrived at, and the latter were being unnecessarily detained. This omission to depute Commissioners vested with full authority, and the neglect or failure of the Tibetan Council to bring about a reasonable settlement for so long, compelled him to say that "such unjustifiable conduct" might lead to grave consequences. It was laid down, the Minister said, in the treaty between Nepal and Tibet that Nepal would assist Tibet in the case of the invasion of its territory by any foreign Rajas. Consequently, when a difference of opinion arose between the Tibetans and anyone else, it was incumbent on him to help them to the best of his power with his advice and guidance, in order to prevent any trouble befalling them from such difference of opinion. And the manner in which the Tibetans had managed the present business not appearing commendable, the assistance he would give at this crisis "of their own creation" would consist in giving such advice as would conduce to the welfare of their country. Should they fail to follow his advice and trouble befall them, there would be no other way open to him of assisting them in the troublous solution brought about by following a wayward course of their own. This should be understood well, for the British Government did not appear to him to have acted in an improper or high-handed way in this matter, but was simply striving to have the conditions of the treaty fulfilled, and it was against the treaty and against all morality or policy to allow matters to drift, and to regard as enemies the officers of such a powerful Government who had come to enforce such rights. Besides, when the Emperor of China had, for their good, posted Ambans of high rank, it was a serious mistake on their part to disregard even their advice and neglect to carry on business with the British Commissioners.

The advice the Nepal Minister gave to the Tibetan Council was this: If the report was correct that they had refused to be bound by the treaty of 1890, on the ground that it was concluded by the Chinese and not by themselves, then they had acted very improperly. The Tibetans and the Nepalese had for a long time held the Emperor of China in high respect. It was improper, then, to declare that the treaty, having been made by the Chinese, was not binding upon the Tibetans, since whatever was done was done on their behalf. The Minister pointed out that, since the conclusion of the treaty between the British and Nepal Governments representatives of each of the Governments had resided in the other's country, and the due observance of the terms of the treaty had been continually advantageous to the Government of Nepal, and their religion had not suffered in any way. The advantages derived from such an arrangement were too many to enumerate. Since the treaty was made, the British Government had on different occasions restored to them territories lost by Nepal in war, and producing a revenue of many lakhs of rupees. The Tibetans must bear in mind that the Government that they had to deal with was not a despotic, but a constitutional, one, and this would be corroborated by the fact that the British had helped the Nepalese to maintain the autonomy of their country for so long a time, whereas they might easily have deprived them of it if they had had a mind to behave in a despotic and unjust manner. The most notable feature in the relations of the Nepalese with the British, continued the Minister, was that they sacredly observed Nepalese religious and social prejudices. Hence if the Tibetans would even now take time by the forelock, settle the pending questions, and behave with the British as true friends, he was sure Tibet would derive the same benefit from such an alliance as Nepal had hitherto done. That the British Government had any evil designs upon Tibet did not appear from any source. It was well known that the sun never sets upon the

British dominions, and that the Sovereign of such a vast Empire should entertain designs of unjustly and improperly taking the Tibetan mountainous country should never cross their minds. So wrote the Nepalese Minister to the Lhasa Council.

Another month passed, and there was still no improvement in the situation. On the contrary, continued rumours arrived that the Tibetans were massing troops, and that at Lhasa they were quite prepared to go to war. The old Shigatse Abbot was very friendly, but quite ineffectual in bringing about negotiations. One day he lunched with us, and assured us that he had made a divination that Yatung was the place where negotiations would be carried on quickest. I said that what we wanted to find was a place where the negotiations could be carried on, not quickest, but best; and I asked him to consult his beads again, and see if Shigatse would not be suitable in that respect. He laughed, and replied that the divination had to be made in front of an altar, to the accompaniment of music. Captain O'Connor had succeeded in making the Abbot and his people so friendly that Mr. Wilton heard from Chinese sources that the Chinese believed that we had either bought over the Abbot or promised him some considerable concession—neither of which was, of course, the case. Still, all this friendliness of the Shigatse men amounted to very little practical use as long as the Lhasa people were still obstinate. So on October 7 I telegraphed to Government that I was strengthening my escort by 100 men from the support, and on the following day telegraphed them a résumé of the whole situation.

I said that the Viceroy's despatch had reached the Resident one month previously, and no reply had yet been received, though letters from Lhasa could reach Khamba Jong in four days. The Mission had been there for three months without being able to even commence negotiations. The Chinese showed indifference and incompetence, and the Tibetans pure obstruction. The present Resident was acknowledged by even the Chinese to be weak and incompetent, and his Associate Resident had been allowed to resign some months back. The new Amban, though appointed in December, was only just leaving Chengtu, and could not reach the frontier till January. The new Associate Resident had been given sick-leave before even joining his post. Mr. Ho, though I had given him the above-mentioned very serious warning, made no haste to proceed to Lhasa, but had loitered at Phari. Even if the Chinese showed less indifference, they could do little with the Tibetans. Mr. Ho was refused transport, and Colonel Chao (his successor) had informed me that the new Resident could not bring large numbers of troops into Tibet, as Tibetans would refuse to furnish transport and supplies. As regards the attitude of the Tibetans, the people in the vicinity and the Shigatse deputies were perfectly friendly, but the Lhasa authorities were as obstructive as ever. The delegates, since the first formal visits, had refused all communication, social or official, with me. The two Sikkim men made prisoners remained in custody, and Tibetan troops lined all the heights between our camp and Gyantse or Shigatse ; and there was much probability that Siberian Buriat Lamas were present in Lhasa. The result of all our moderation in the present and previous years was *nil*, and I could, I said, no longer hold out any hope to Government of a peaceful solution of the question.

On October 11 I left Khamba Jong to proceed to Simla to confer with the Government of India on future action, and thus ended this futile effort to settle the question on the frontier.

The unsatisfactory nature of the situation had in the meanwhile been taken notice of by the Government in England, and, under their instructions, Sir Ernest Satow, our Minister at Peking, on September 25 presented a note to the Chinese Government, stating that, in spite of the Dalai Lama having agreed that negotiations should take place at Khamba Jong, the Tibetan representatives had refused to negotiate there ; they had imprisoned two British subjects at Shigatse, and refused to release them ; and they were collecting troops, and making hostile preparations. Sir Ernest Satow further verbally informed the Foreign Board, in accordance with his instructions, that His Majesty's Government expected them to bring immediate pressure to bear upon the Dalai Lama, with a view to the release of the two British subjects who had been imprisoned, and to the commencement without delay of negotiations between the Tibetan delegates and the British Commissioners. Should the Dalai Lama not give immediate satisfaction to these demands, His Majesty's Government would feel themselves compelled to take such measures as they might consider necessary for the safety of their Mission and for the release of the two British subjects.

Prince Ching promised Sir Ernest Satow to despatch a telegram at once to Lhasa by Batang, and said he hoped an improvement would manifest itself as soon as the new Resident arrived; but he described the Tibetans as intensely ignorant and obstinate, and very difficult to influence.

At first the Imperial Government was not prepared to sanction anything further than the occupation of the Chumbi Valley; but on October 1 Lord George Hamilton telegraphed to the Government of India that Government had again considered the position, and were now prepared, if complete rupture of negotiations proved inevitable, to authorize, not only the occupation of the Chumbi Valley, but also the advance of the Mission to Gyantse, if it could be made with safety; and he asked the Viceroy to inform him of his plans, and particularly how he proposed to secure the safety of the Mission at Gyantse.

It was upon this that I was summoned to Simla to advise the Government of India, and after consultation with me at a meeting of the Council, which I was invited to attend, they telegraphed, on October 26, to Mr. Brodrick, who had now succeeded as Secretary of State, that, for the following reasons, an advance into Tibet seemed indispensable: (1) Though the Dalai Lama had agreed to the Commissioners meeting at Khamba Jong, the Tibetan delegates had refused to hold any communication with the

British Commissioner; (2) no Chinese delegates of suitable rank had as yet been sent; (3) the procrastination of the Chinese Government; (4) the warlike preparations of the Tibetans; (5) the arrest and imprisonment of two British subjects; (6) the complete failure of the policy pursued for twenty-five years, the only result of which was that the Tibetans mistook our patience for weakness, and despised our strength. They recommended, therefore, the advance should extend to Gyantse, and should not be confined to the Chumbi Valley, for these reasons: (1) That the Chumbi Valley is on the Indian side of the watershed, and is not regarded as part of Tibet, and a move from Khamba Jong only to there would be regarded as a retrograde movement by the Tibetans; (2) that if we moved only into the Chumbi Valley, we should find the existing situation at Khamba Jong repeated at Phari; (3) that Colonel Younghusband considered it extremely important that we should come into contact with the Tibetan people, for they were quite prepared to enter into relations with us, and were friendly, it being only the hierarchy of Lhasa Lamas who were opposed; (4) that, as we were pressing to have a mart at Gyantse, that object could be secured in no better way than by advancing thither at once. On arrival at Gyantse the force would not attack the place, but, as had been done at Khamba Jong, would establish a fortified port, and invite Tibetans and Chinese to resume negotiations.

It was estimated, in a subsequent telegram, that the total force to be employed would be one battalion of Gurkhas, two companies of Sappers and Miners, two battalions of Pioneers, two guns, British Mountain Battery, two Maxims, and two seven-pounder guns. The command of the whole was to be entrusted to Brigadier-General Macdonald.

The Secretary of State,* in a telegram dated November 6, at last gave his sanction to an advance. In view of the recent conduct of the Tibetans, His Majesty's Government felt that it would be impossible not to take action, and they accordingly sanctioned the advance of the

* Blue-book, I., p. 294.

Mission to Gyantse. They were, however, clearly of opinion that "this step should not be allowed to lead to occupation or to permanent intervention in Tibetan affairs in any form. The advance should be made for the sole purpose of obtaining satisfaction, and as soon as reparation was obtained a withdrawal should be effected. While His Majesty's Government considered the proposed action to be necessary, they were not prepared to establish a permanent Mission in Tibet, and the question of enforcing trade facilities in that country should be considered in the light of this telegram."

It was a curious telegram, which I never quite understood. It said that the advance was to be made for the sole purpose of obtaining satisfaction. But it was always understood, and it was most emphatically laid down, that this was not a punitive expedition to obtain satisfaction and get reparation. It was a Mission despatched to put our relations with the Tibetans on a regular footing, to establish ordinary neighbourly intercourse with them. Lord Lansdowne himself said in the House of Lords*: "We desire that a new Convention should be entered into between the Government of India, on the one hand, and the Tibetans and Chinese, as the suzerain Power, on the other. That is the object of the Mission." It is remarkable that a document which was so often quoted to the Russian Government, to the Indian Government, to the Chinese Government, and which the Indian Government on one occasion quoted to me in terms of admonition, should have described with so little precision the real purpose of the advance—and this at the culminating point of thirty years' effort on the part of the Government of India. It was not till after the Mission had been attacked at Gyantse, and on account of that attack, that we demanded satisfaction—in the shape of an indemnity. The obvious purpose of the advance was to do what Warren Hastings had attempted, what the Government of Bengal since 1873 had been advocating—to put our intercourse with the Tibetans on proper terms. We had found it impossible to effect this object on the frontier or

* February 26, 1904.

by negotiation with the Chinese Government. We were going to advance into Tibet, to Gyantse, to see if we could not effect it there, to get the frontier defined and recognized, to have the conditions under which trade could be carried on determined, and to have the method of communication between our officials and Tibetan officials clearly laid down. This, and not the obtaining of satisfaction, which is the business of a military commander in charge of a punitive expedition, was obviously the purpose of our advance into Tibet, and it is odd that this was not recognized in what was so often afterwards quoted as the fundamental statement of our policy.

The telegram was not very purposeful or instructive, but such as it was we were glad enough to get it. It at least allowed us to go to Gyantse, and though at the time when my advice was asked I said I did not think we should get the business really settled till we reached Lhasa, we certainly stood a better chance at Gyantse than at Khamba Jong. In all civilized countries envoys who have to negotiate a treaty go straight to the capital, and how it could ever have been expected that in Tibet, where all power was concentrated in a supposed god, who relied upon the support of Russia in any difficulties, we should have been able to negotiate a treaty at anywhere short of Lhasa, it is hard now to realize.

However, as I told Lord Curzon at his camp in Patiala, where I took leave of him on my return to Tibet, I meant to do my very best to get the thing through. He once more gave me the same warm encouragement he always extended to those in India whom he believed to be working well, and I left again for Darjiling.

While we were making preparations at Darjiling for the next move, correspondence was also taking place from headquarters. The Viceroy, in reply to a letter of the Lhasa Resident's of October 17, stating that he had nominated a Colonel Chao in place of Mr. Ho, that he had asked the Dalai Lama to send a Councillor of State to accompany him (the Resident) to Khamba Jong, but that all this required time to settle, and asserting that the Tibetan passes were guarded by soldiers, and requesting the Viceroy, therefore, to instruct the British Commissioner not to move from the present camp, told the Resident that he understood that Colonel Chao was of lower, not higher, rank than Mr. Ho, and that, as the Resident's departure was contingent on the Dalai Lama's nomination of a Councillor, and as the Dalai Lama had for four months past failed to send, as desired, an officer of the highest rank, he saw no prospect of the Resident arriving at Khamba Jong within any reasonable time. The Viceroy then recapitulated our various grounds of complaint, and concluded by saying that, in these circumstances, he had no alternative but to transfer the place of negotiations to some more suitable spot, where he hoped they might be resumed. And as the Resident had stated that the Tibetan passes were guarded by soldiers, he had been compelled to take measures to insure the safety of the Commissioners in moving from Khamba Jong, and to prevent any possible interruption of communication with them.

The Chinese Government made on November 16 a protest to Lord Lansdowne against an advance, and hoped that I would be instructed to await the arrival of the new Resident, who, it will be remembered, had been instructed nearly a year previously to proceed as rapidly as possible to Lhasa; but Lord Lansdowne informed them that His Majesty's Government had learnt by experience that the Tibetans systematically disregarded the injunctions of the Emperor and the Chinese Government, who had no real influence in restraining them from acts such as those we complained of. We had treated the Tibetans with the utmost forbearance, but these recent proceedings compelled us to exact satisfaction, and we could not remain inactive until the arrival of the new Resident, who had unnecessarily protracted his journey.

The Chinese Minister said that his Government recognized the forbearance shown by the British authorities towards the Tibetans, and also the friendly spirit brought by the British Commissioners to the discussion of frontier questions, and they hoped that we would recognize the difficult position in which China had been placed by her obstinate and ignorant vassal, and enjoin our Commissioners to exercise patience and forbearance, and thus assist the Resident, who had been instructed to proceed in person to the frontier to bring the Tibetans to a juster sense of their duties and responsibilities as good neighbours.

To this Lord Lansdowne replied that the Chinese had hitherto signally failed in such attempts, and the attitude of the Tibetan authorities had of late been of increased hostility. It was impossible, therefore, for us to desist from the measures already sanctioned.

In the event, it turned out that the Resident never did meet me on the frontier, and that even his successor, when at last he arrived at Lhasa, did not care to meet me even at Gyantse, for the Tibetans, so he informed me, would not provide him with transport. Lord Lansdowne's refusal to desist from action and pursue still further the policy of patience and forbearance was, therefore, amply justified by events.

But it was not only the Chinese Government who were now beginning to protest against our action. The Russian Government also began to move in the matter. Lord Lansdowne had on November 7, the day on which the forward move was sanctioned by Government, informed the Russian Ambassador* that, owing to the outrageous conduct of the Tibetans, it had been decided to send our Mission, with a suitable escort, farther into the Tibetan territory, but that this step should not be taken "as indicating any intention of annexing, or even of permanently occupying, Tibetan territory." And on November 17 Count Benckendorff called on Lord Lansdowne,† and spoke in the most earnest tones of the effect which had been created in Russia by the announcement that we were about to advance into Tibet. He was instructed to remind Lord Lansdowne of the former

* Blue-book, I., p. 294. † *Ibid.*, p. 298.

statement he (Count Benckendorff) had made to him as to the manner in which the Russian Government regarded the Tibetan question. They could not help feeling that the invasion of Tibetan territory by a British force was calculated to involve a grave disturbance of the Central Asian situation, and it was most unfortunate that at that moment, when the Russian Government were disposed to enter into an amicable discussion of our relations at the various points where British and Russian interests were in contact—an allusion to the preliminary negotiations for the Anglo-Russian Agreement and *entente cordiale*—an event of this kind, so calculated to create mistrust on the part of Russia, should have occurred.

Lord Lansdowne expressed his great surprise at the excitement which the announcement of the advance seemed to have enacted. He had, he said, already pointed out to the Ambassador that Tibet was, on the one hand, in close geographical connection with India, and, on the other, far remote from any of Russia's Asiatic possessions. Our interest in Tibetan affairs was therefore wholly different from any which Russia could have in them. He reminded Count Benckendorff that he had already explained to him that we had received the greatest provocation at the hands of the Tibetans, who had not only failed to fulfil their treaty obligations, but had virtually refused to negotiate with us. We had always been reluctant to entangle ourselves in quarrels with the Tibetans, but our forbearance had led them to believe that we could be ill-treated with impunity. Lord Lansdowne said he was firmly convinced that the Russian Government would not have shown as much patience as we had, and that they would have been at Lhasa by that time. He felt bound to add that it seemed to him beyond measure strange that these protests should be made by the Government of a Power which had, all over the world, never hesitated to encroach upon its neighbours when the circumstances seemed to require it. If the Russians had a right to complain of us for taking steps to obtain reparation from the Tibetans by advancing into Tibetan territory, what kind of language should we not be entitled to use in regard to Russian encroachments in Manchuria, Turkestan, and Persia.

Count Benckendorff asked him whether he had any objection to his saying that Government had approved of the advance into Tibetan territory with reluctance, and only because circumstances had made it inevitable, and that our sole object was to obtain satisfaction for the affronts we had received from the Tibetans; and Lord Lansdowne said that he had no objection to his making such a statement.

Despite Russian and Chinese protests, the advance to Gyantse was now irrevocably decided on, and once again we have now to ask, Was the Mission justified in advancing into Tibet? I have given all the reasons for thinking that the despatch of the Mission to Khamba Jong was justified. Was this further advance into the Chumbi Valley and to Gyantse equally necessary? Perhaps, if we had shown yet more patience and yet more forbearance, we might have effected our object without advancing by force into the country. Was this so?

What eventually occurred showed that there were no possible grounds for such a belief. Even when the Chinese Central Government were aroused, and had ordered the Resident to proceed to the frontier to settle matters, he was unable to get there. The Tibetans refused him transport, and when we reached Lhasa, in August of the following year, we found him to be practically a prisoner, and almost without enough to eat, as the Tibetans had prevented supplies of money from reaching him, and he had actually to borrow money from us. But it was with the Tibetans that we really wished to negotiate. Perhaps they would have come to terms with us if we had been a little less impatient and remained on the frontier? Perhaps they would have sent a Councillor, as we had asked, and negotiated a treaty? On this point, too, our later experience showed that we could not have relied. When we at length reached Lhasa I had to negotiate, not with one Councillor only, but with the whole

Council; and not with the Council, but the Regent himself, to whom the Dalai Lama had entrusted his own seal and whom he had appointed in his place; and not with the Council and the Regent only, but with the National Assembly and three great monasteries in addition; and with all in the presence of the Chinese Resident himself. No one man would ever have been entrusted by them with power, and no one man would take responsibility. It was only with the whole together that it was possible to negotiate; and we could negotiate with the whole together no where but in Lhasa itself.

Granted all this, some may say, but even then was it worth incurring Russian resentment in order to settle a trumpery affair of boundary pillars and petty trade interests in a remote corner of our Empire? Now, I most fully sympathize with the Russian view. Our advancing into Tibet would—and, in fact, did—"involve a grave disturbance of the Central Asian situation." The news of our signing a treaty in the Potala at Lhasa, and of the Dalai Lama having to flee, did produce a profound impression. But if the subject-matter of our dispute was small, there was small reason why the Russians should trouble us about it. The matter grew in dimension because the Tibetans, whom the Chinese suzerains themselves had characterized as obstinate and difficult to influence, had grown still more obstinate and still more difficult to influence, through their having led themselves to believe that they could count on Russian support. In view of Russian disclaimers, we can assume that the Russian Government gave them no intentional grounds for that belief. Nevertheless, they had it, and for practical purposes that was all that concerned us then. The reception of the Dalai Lama's religious missions by the Czar, the Czarina, the Chancellor and Minister, and the subscriptions they had collected, together with the extraordinary belief they had that Russia was nearer to Lhasa than India was, had led the ignorant Dalai Lama to believe that he could count on Russian support against the British. One can quite realize that the Russians, with their thousands of Buddhist Asiatic subjects, and with the prospect that then seemed near of their absorbing Mongolia, and so possessing still more Buddhist subjects, would be sensitive of our acquiring a predominant influence with the Dalai Lama. But that is scarcely a reason why we should not take measures to counteract an influence which was already, and in hard fact proving, detrimental to our own interests by encouraging the Tibetans in the belief that they could with impunity ignore their treaty obligations. The Russian Government had no intention of sending an agent to Lhasa. Nevertheless, there was in Lhasa all the time a Russian subject who had more influence over the Dalai Lama than the Chinese Resident. When such was the condition of affairs, we could hardly defer to Russia in a matter concerning a country adjoining our frontier, but nowhere adjoining hers.

Just as the move to Khamba Jong a dozen miles inside the Tibetan frontier was most amply justified, so also was the move to Gyantse, halfway to the capital.

CHAPTER XI

DARJILING TO CHUMBI

DURING our stay at Khamba Jong Mr. White, Captain O'Connor, and I had often talked over the question of advancing into Tibet in winter. It had always so far been assumed that with the approach of winter all operations on this frontier must cease, missions must withdraw, and troops go into winter-quarters. But on the Gilgit frontier we had taken troops across snow-passes in winter, and Colonel Kelly took troops and guns across the Shandur Pass to the relief of Chitral in April, which, from the softness of the snow, is the very worst time. I asked Mr. White, who knew the Sikkim frontier so well, whether there was really any insuperable obstacle to our crossing these passes in winter, and as he said there was not, and as he was heartily in favour of such a move, I urged Government not to delay till the spring, but to let us advance even in winter. We do not hesitate when there is real necessity to send troops and missions into unhealthy and hot places in the hottest season of the year. Why, then, should we be put off by cold? Against cold we could take plenty of precautions by clothing troops and followers with furs and sheepskins, and we should doubtless lose some, but not more than we lose from malaria and heat-strokes in hot places. And as for passes being closed, I had had as much experience as most people of Himalayan passes, and I knew that passes which are closed for single men or small parties, are not necessarily closed for large parties, which can organize regular shelters and trample down paths in the snow. It was a risk to take, and Lord Curzon and the Government of India were courageous in taking it. But, like many other risks we took on this enterprise, it was justified by the result. By April the casualties from sickness and frost-bite were only thirty-five deaths among combatants and forty-five among followers, which, considering the circumstances, was wonderfully low, and we had proved for all time to the Tibetans, to ourselves, and to the world, that Indian troops could march across the Himalayas in the very depth of winter.

As we settled down to our preparations at Darjiling, it did indeed seem a bold task that we were undertaking. The weather now, in November, was clear and bright. Day after day from our headquarters at the Rockville Hotel we could look out on that stupendous range of snowy mountains, to view which hundreds of people come at this season from all over the world. And to think that we had to pierce through that mighty barrier at the coldest season of the year in face of the certain opposition of the Tibetans, and to establish ourselves far beyond in a spot to which for half a century no European had approached, did indeed at times appal one. But the very risk and romance and novelty of the task soon again inspired one with enthusiasm. It was no ignoble little raid, as ignoble Little Englanders were saying, that we were embarking on. It was an undertaking with every moral justification behind it. And it was a feat which, if successfully performed, would add one more to the triumphs of man over Nature, and bring added glory to the Indian army by whom it was accomplished.

It had been originally intended that I should return to Khamba Jong to the Mission which I had left there, and with them march across to Kalatso, on the Gyantse line, while General Macdonald marched up through Chumbi. But on talking the matter over with him at Darjiling, he thought that such a move would involve unnecessary risk, and would be difficult to arrange for with the transport and supplies, as the Tibetans had forcibly dispersed the yaks which the Nepalese had sent across the frontier. It was arranged, therefore, that the Mission, now under the charge of Mr. Wilton, should be withdrawn from

Khamba Jong; but both Mr. White and I were anxious that no retirement should take place from one direction till we were actually advancing in another, for any symptom of withdrawal before such people as the Tibetans is apt to be misconstrued into fear, and to encourage them into hostile action. So it was arranged that until we advanced into Chumbi the Mission would remain at Khamba Jong, and then retire into Sikkim and join General Macdonald and myself in Chumbi.

General Macdonald, his Chief Staff Officer, Major Iggulden, who was well acquainted with the frontier, having served in the little Sikkim campaign of 1888, Major Bretherton, and Captain O'Connor now had their hands full with the arrangements for the advance, and, as always happens, every additional unnecessary difficulty arose. For advance into Tibet in mid-winter, animals like yaks, which hate being below 12,000 feet, and are stifled with the heat if the thermometer rises above the freezing-point, were, of all others, the most suitable, and the Nepalese Government, with great trouble had collected several thousand and despatched them to Sikkim. But just as they arrived some kind of disease broke out among them, and all, except a very few, which had to be secluded, died. It was a terrible blow, but Major Bretherton, with his unfailing cheery resourcefulness, set about getting the transport he knew and had worked so well on the Kashmir frontier—Kashmir ponies, Balti and Poonch coolies. Sir Edmond Elles, the Military Member of Council, was near by in Calcutta at the time, and with his unrivalled experience in organizing such expeditions, was able to direct the whole scheme of arrangement to its greatest possible advantage. He would not, indeed, at this stage spare those magnificently organized mule corps which he treasured up in the event of greater need elsewhere, and which he only eventually sent when operations in Tibet assumed a greater importance. But in every other way he gave General Macdonald support in these most difficult transport and supply arrangements, and with great rapidity bullocks, ponies, and coolies, arrived in the Teesta Valley. And sheepskins, blankets, woollen comforters, thick jerseys, and warm socks, were provided for both fighting men and followers. If the Government of India does a thing at all, it does it well, and nothing was spared—except the mules—to make the movement a success.

The local authorities were also extremely helpful. Mr. Walsh, the Deputy Commissioner of Darjiling, on account of his knowledge of the frontier, and because he spoke Tibetan, was to accompany me as an Assistant Commissioner; and Mr. Garrett, who took his place at Darjiling, put his whole energies to collecting coolies, ponies, and supplies. The local engineers got the road along the Teesta Valley—which with unfailing regularity falls into the river in the rainy season—into proper working order again. Mr. White, in Sikkim, set to work to raise a coolie corps for work on the passes. And in a month from the date of receiving the sanction of the Secretary of State, General Macdonald was able, in spite of the blow which had befallen him in the loss of the yaks, to make the start towards Tibet.

It was a sad day when I said good-bye to my wife and little girl to plunge into the unknown beyond the mighty snowy range which lay before us. To me there was nothing but the stir and thrill of an enterprise which would ever live in history; before her there lay only long and dreary months of sickening anxiety and suspense, for which my eventual success might or might not be a sufficient recompense. A little knot of visitors assembled at the Rockville Hotel on the morning of December 5 to bid us good-bye and good luck, and Mrs. Wakefield, the manageress, patriotically waved a Union Jack. Then we were off—as it turned out, to the mysterious Lhasa itself.

The first night I passed with Mr. James, a nephew of my old travelling companion in Manchuria, at a most charming little bungalow in a tea-plantation, and on the way met other tea-planters, all very anxious that my Mission would have the result of opening up Tibet for their produce. I once more rode through all that glorious tropical vegetation in the Teesta Valley. I passed the camp of the 23rd Pioneers, and first made the acquaintance of Colonel Hogge and his officers, with whom I was to be so closely associated in future, and in whom I always found such firm supporters. And by December 10 General Macdonald and his staff, the bulk of the troops for the advance, Mr. White, Mr. Walsh, Captain O'Connor, and myself had all rendezvoused at Gnatong, ready to move into Tibet.

The force then assembled consisted of two guns, No. 7 Mountain Battery, Royal Artillery; a Maxim gun detachment of the Norfolk Regiment; two guns, 7-pounders, 8th Gurkhas; half-company 2nd Sappers; eight companies 23rd Sikh Pioneers; six companies 8th Gurkhas; with field hospitals, engineer field park, ammunition column, telegraph, postal, and survey department detachments. In spite of foot-and-mouth disease among the pack-bullocks, of sickness and desertion amongst the Nepalese Coolie Corps, and of rinderpest, Major Bretherton had succeeded in accumulating a month's supply for the troops and ten days' fodder for the animals, and General Macdonald was able to make a short march on the 11th to the foot of the Jelap-la (pass) with the first column, consisting of 1,150 fighting men, four guns, and four Maxims.

On December 12 we crossed the pass itself. It is 14,390 feet in height, and leads, not across the main watershed of the Himalayas, but across the range dividing Sikkim from Chumbi, a sharp, bare, rocky ridge. The ascent to it was very steep, and, as the ridge formed the boundary between Sikkim and Tibet, it was possible we might be opposed at the summit.

But on the question of opposition I had had some communication with the Tibetans. News of the assembly of troops and of the preparations we were making had naturally reached the Tibetans, and on November 28 Captain Parr, who was in Chinese employ, associated with the Chinese delegate, informed me that the Tibetans were expecting that, before any advance was made into their country, the British Government would make a formal declaration of their intention; that if they intended to make war they would make a formal declaration of war.

I replied that no more formal declaration would be made than that conveyed in the letter from the Viceroy to the Chinese Resident. If the progress of the Mission were obstructed, General Macdonald would use force to clear a way for the passage of the Mission. If no opposition were offered, he would not attack the Tibetans. We were prepared to fight if fighting were forced upon us; we were equally ready to negotiate if the Chinese and Tibetans would send proper delegates to negotiate with us.

All accounts seemed to show at that time that the Tibetans intended to fight, and from several independent sources came information that they were relying on Russian support. And these latter reports were confirmed later by Colonel Chao, the Chinese delegate, who said that Dorjieff was then in Lhasa, and that the arrogance of the Tibetans was due to their reliance on the support of the Russians, since many discussions had been held in Russia between Dorjieff and Russian officials, with the result that of late the Tibetans had been taunting the Chinese openly, and saying that they had now a stronger and greater Power than China upon which to rely for assistance.

Still, I meant to do my best to secure our passage to Gyantse without fighting, and to the General commanding the Tibetan troops at Yatung I gave the pledge that we were conducting the Mission, under adequate protection, to a place better fitted for negotiation, but that we were not at war with Tibet, and unless we were ourselves attacked, we should not attack the Tibetans. I repeated these assurances to some Tibetan messengers at Gnatong, and told them to tell the Tibetan Generals that if they did not attack us we would not attack them.

On reaching the summit of the Jelap-la, on a bright, clear sunny day, with glorious views all round, we found no one to oppose us. We looked down into the Chumbi Valley into a sort of labyrinth of deep forest-clad valleys, and beyond these to the high main range, which still separated us from Tibet proper, for Chumbi is not geographically part of Tibet, nor are its inhabitants true Tibetans.

The march was very trying for the troops and transport, for the "road" was simply a mountain-path of the roughest description. One coolie corps struck work, and a number of the local drivers of a pony corps and many Nepalese coolies had deserted, for a curious feeling was prevalent on the frontier that we were advancing to our doom. But the troops and the bulk of the transport got over all right, though very exhausted, and we encamped in three bodies near Langram, well below the pass, in a deep, narrow, forest-clad gorge.

Here I was met by the ubiquitous Captain Parr, who in many ways was extremely helpful at this time, by the local Chinese official, and by the Tibetan General. They asked me to go back to Gnatong, where the Chinese Resident and Tibetan Councillors would come and discuss matters with me. On my declining, they asked me to remain where I was for two or three months. I told them I had waited for months without result at Khamba Jong; now I had to go on into Tibet. If my passage were opposed, General Macdonald would break down opposition; if they did not oppose us, we would not attack them. They asked me what we should do if on the morrow we found the gate in the Yatung wall closed. I said we would blow it open.

What would happen on the morrow was now the interesting question. We would reach Yatung, which for the last ten years we had been trying to make into a trade-mart, according to the treaty, and we would approach that wall which the Tibetans had thrown up to prevent anyone coming to trade. The dramatic moment had arrived; and as General Macdonald and I on the following morning rode down the wooded gorge with all military precautions, it was impossible to say what our reception would be.

Suddenly, as we turned a sharp corner, we saw a solid wall, stretching right across the valley from the river up the mountain-side. General Macdonald sent a flanking party up the hills, and a skirmishing party to advance straight at the wall. As we approached we were met by the same officials who had visited us on the previous night.

They asked us not to advance, but we noticed that they had left the gate open, so the advance-guard passed through. Then General Macdonald and I followed, and exactly as I passed under the gateway the local official seized my bridle and made one last ineffectual protest.

On the other side I called together all the officials, and sitting on a stone, with a large crowd gathered round, I explained to them the reason for our advance. I let them repeat their protests, for it evidently appeased the Tibetan General to say it in public; but it did not strike me that he personally particularly minded our coming, and the meeting broke up in great good-humour. Then we adjourned to Captain Parr's house, where we had to eat not only his lunch, but lunches sent us by the Chinese and Tibetan officials as well, these latter themselves joining in the meal.

This was an excellent beginning, which filled me with great hopes of effecting a settlement peacefully; and as we advanced up the valley in the next few days we found the villagers ready to bring in supplies for purchase, and to hire out their mules and ponies, while the women and children who had run away to the hills returned to the villages in perfect confidence.

After we had struck off from the subsidiary Yatung Valley into the main Chumbi Valley, through which runs the Amo-chu (river), the valley opened to a width of two or three huudred yards, the road was good, there was a considerable amount of cultivation, and grass was plentiful; the houses were better built, and the villages had a more prosperous look than is generally seen in Himalayan valleys; and with a road right down the Amo-chu to the plains of Bengal, which would save crossing the Jelap-la, this seemed the obvious route by which to approach Tibet.

General Macdonald had to halt for some days, completing his arrangements for supplies and transport, and while we were halted we were joined by Mr. Wilton, Captain Ryder, R.E., the Survey Officer, and Mr. Hayden, the geologist, who had all come in from Khamba Jong. They had had a very cold and very trying time after I left, and their retirement was an extremely delicate operation. The Tibetan troops hovered about, and with a 17,000 feet pass to cross in December, Captain Bethune had about as difficult a manœuvre to perform as often falls to the lot of a soldier. The Tibetans occupied our camp in triumph, but never actually attacked, and the retirement was safely effected.

Both Captain Ryder and Mr. Hayden had done excellent work. The former had surveyed all the neighbourhood, fixing many new peaks far into Tibet; and Mr. Hayden, roaming over the hills, had made interesting discoveries of fossil-bearing beds, which enabled him to determine the age of the strata in those parts.

General Macdonald, with a flying column of 795 fighting men, started on the 18th for Phari, through a piece of country which had never before been traversed by a European. It was reported that there was a Tibetan force there ready to oppose us. The first march beyond the permanent camp at the meeting of the Amo-chu and the Rilo-chu was easy; but the second march was over a very bad road, ascending steeply through a narrow wooded gorge, where a few determined men could have greatly delayed the advance of the column. The hardships of the march were increased by the almost total absence of fuel at Kamparab camping-ground, which was two miles beyond the wood limit. A certain amount of fuel had been taken on spare mules, and this, with yak-dung in small quantities, had to suffice. On the 20th General Macdonald reached Phari, marching over open country, where the only obstacle to rapid marching was the great altitude and numerous frozen streams. The Jong (fort) he found unoccupied. It was a strong, lofty, masonry-castellated structure, at the junction of the road to the Tang-la (pass), with a road to Bhutan, up which Bogle, Turner, and Manning had proceeded to Tibet so many years before.

In this Jong General Macdonald stationed two companies of the 8th Gurkhas and one 7-pounder gun, while the remainder of the column camped on the plain outside. To the Tibetan and Chinese officials General Macdonald explained that he was only safeguarding the road for the advance of the Mission, and guarding against the regrettable display of force with which the Tibetans had endeavoured to intimidate the Mission at Khamba Jong. He stayed there a couple of nights, during which the cold was intense, the thermometer registering about 40° of frost at night. The ground was frozen so hard that a working party of twelve men only succeeded, after two hours' hard work, in excavating some 33 cubic feet of earth, and as neither turf nor stones were available, it was impossible to construct any entrenchments.

Leaving Major Row in command of the two companies in the Jong, General Macdonald returned with the remainder of the force to Chumbi, which he reached on the 23rd. And on Christmas Day we received a mostly kindly and encouraging telegram from Lord Curzon. The inhabitants of the Chumbi Valley were now selling us grass, buck-wheat, turnips and potatoes, and Major Bretherton had arranged for 400 mules to ply on a contract system between here and the Teesta Valley. This, though very helpful, did not amount to very much, and we were dependent for most of our supplies and transport from the rear. In addition to this, the loss of the yaks was now severely felt. So our progress was necessarily slow. But I was very anxious, as soon as we could, to be over the main range, in Tibet proper, in some position equivalent to Khamba Jong. Just over the Tang-la (pass) we knew there was a small place called Tuna, and there I wished the Mission established with a good escort and plenty of ammunition and supplies, while all arrangements were being completed for the further advance to Gyantse. There was a certain amount of risk in this; but to be among the Tibetans proper, and to compensate for the withdrawal from Khamba Jong, I thought it was necessary to run it. Our prestige at this time on the Sikkim frontier was quite astonishingly low. I had never seen it so low elsewhere. In other places there was always that indefinable something behind which gave one something to work with, but on this frontier the people stood in much greater awe of the Lhasa Lamas than they did of us, and we had to do everything we could, short of fighting, to establish some prestige.

On January 4 the Mission and a flying column, under General Macdonald's personal command, left Chumbi, and on the 6th reached Phari. The cold was now terrible. Piercing winds swept down the valley, and discomfort was extreme. Near our camp was a big waterfall frozen solid.

At Phari we found that representatives of the three great monasteries at Lhasa and a General from Lhasa had arrived, and Major Row reported many cases in which the inhabitants had expressed their willingness to deal with us, but feared to do so on account of the threats of these Lhasa functionaries. Captain O'Connor saw these monks, whom he found to be exceedingly surly, saying they would discuss nothing whatever until we went back to Yatung.

A Major Li, who had been deputed by the Resident to take Colonel Chao's place, visited me, and told me it was impossible to get the Tibetans to do anything. He said they were a most obstinate people, and at present would pay no respect to the Chinese, as they were so fully relying on Russian support.

Captain O'Connor reported that the whole demeanour of these Lhasa monks, who were the men who really guided the destinies of Tibet, was impracticable in the extreme. They made no advance in civility, though I instructed Captain O'Connor to be studiously polite in his behaviour, and they adopted the high tone of demanding our withdrawal. All I asked them was an assurance that they would not prevent willing people from selling supplies to us, and even this little they refused both the Chinese and myself.

But the worst feature of the situation, as I reported at the time, was that the local people, and even the Chinese, thought that in advancing into Tibet we were advancing to our destruction. They were not impressed by our troops; they knew how few there were; they knew of thousands of Tibetan troops on the far side of the pass; and they believed that the new Lhasa-made rifles and the new drill would prevent the loss they had incurred in their last campaign against us. Many of our camp-followers deserted, and local men in our employ brought in stories of the numbers and prowess of the Tibetans, and how they would attack us in the night and swamp us.

These were the circumstances in which we set out, now in the extreme depth of winter, to cross over the main range of the Himalayas into Tibet.

On January 7 we encamped at the foot of the pass, the thermometer that night falling to 18° below zero. As I looked out of my tent at the first streak of dawn the next morning there was a clear cutting feel in the atmosphere, such as is only experienced at great altitudes. The stars were darting out their rays with almost supernatural brilliance. The sky was of a steely clearness, into which one could look unfathomable depths. Behind the great sentinel peak of Chumalhari, which guards the entrance to Tibet, the first streaks of dawn were just appearing. Not a breath of air stirred, but all was gripped tight in the frost which turned buckets of water left out overnight into solid ice, and made the remains of last night's stew as hard as a rock. Under such conditions we prepared for our advance over the pass, and as the troops were formed on parade, preparatory to starting, it was found that many of the rifles and one of the Maxims would not work, on account of the oil having frozen.

The rise to the pass was very gradual, and the pass itself, 15,200 feet above sea-level, was so wide and level that we could have advanced across it in line. But soon now the wind got up, and swept along the pass with terrific force. At this altitude, and clad in such heavy clothing, we could advance but slowly, and the march seemed interminable. The clearness of the atmosphere made the little hamlet of Tuna appear quite near; but hour after hour we plodded wearily over the plateau, and it was late in the afternoon before we reached it, and even then, for the sake of water, we had to go a mile or more beyond, and encamp in the open.

A Tibetan force was near at hand, and as they were credited with a habit of attacking at night, General Macdonald took special precautions against such an even-

COLUMN CROSSING THE TANG-LA, JANUARY, 1904.

To face page 160.

tuality; but as darkness set in and the cold increased in intensity, we felt we should be pretty helpless in an open camp, and there were some thoughts of retiring again across the pass, for the military risks were very great. But, on the whole, we thought it would be better to face it now we were there; and as, next morning, we examined the hamlet of Tuna, and found it could be turned into a good defensible post, and had a well within the walls, we decided that the Mission should remain there, with an escort of four companies of the 23rd Pioneers, Lieutenant Hadow's Maxim-gun detachment, and a 7-pounder—the whole under Colonel Hogge; while General Macdonald, with the flying column, returned to Chumbi to complete his arrangements.

The immediate surroundings in which we now found ourselves were miserable in the extreme. Tuna was nearly 15,000 feet above the sea, and was the filthiest place I have ever seen. We tried to live in the houses, but after a few days preferred our tents, in spite of the cold, which was intense, and against which we could not have the comfort and cheer of a fire, for only sufficient fuel for cooking could be obtained, most of it being yak-dung, and much having to be brought from Chumbi. The saving feature was the grand natural scenery, which was a joy of which I never tired. Immediately before us was an almost level and perfectly smooth gravel plain ten or twelve miles in width, and on the far side of this rose the great snowy range, which forms the main axis of the Himalayas, and here separates Tibet from Bhutan. Snow seldom fell. The sky was generally clear, and the sunshine brilliant, and well wrapped up, away from the dirty hamlet and sheltered from the terrific wind, there was pleasure to be had out of even Tuna. And the sight of the serene and mighty Chumalhari, rising proudly above all the storms below and spotless in its purity, was a never-ending solace in our sordid winter post.

CHAPTER XII

TUNA

THE first event of importance after our arrival at Tuna was the receipt, on January 12, of a message from the Lhasa officials, saying that they wished for an interview. At noon, the time I had appointed, several hundreds of men appeared on the plain below the village. They halted there, and asked that I should come out and meet them halfway. Perhaps unnecessarily, I refused this request. It was bitingly cold in the open plain, and I thought the Tibetan leaders might have come into my camp, where I had said I would receive them, and where a guard of honour was ready. However, I sent out the indispensable and ever-ready Captain O'Connor to hear what they had to say, and on his return he replied that they once more urged us to return to Yatung, but afterwards stated that they were prepared to discuss matters there, at Tuna.

This constituted a distinct improvement on the attitude adopted by them at Phari, and their general demeanour was much more cordial, according to Captain O'Connor. But they told him that if we advanced and they were defeated, they would fall back upon another Power, and that things would then be bad for us. In conversation with the Munshi they said that they would prevent us from advancing beyond our present position, and they repudiated our treaty with the Chinese, saying they were tired of the Chinese, and could conclude a treaty by themselves.

Encouraged by the fact that they showed some little signs of a desire to discuss matters, I determined now to make a bold move to get to close quarters with them.

CHUMALHARI

To face page 162.

I was heartily tired of this fencing about at a distance; I wanted to get in under their reserve. And I thought that if we could meet and could tell them in an uncontentious and unceremonious manner what all the pother was about, we might at any rate get a start—get what the Americans call a "move on." It was worth while, it seemed to me, to make a supreme effort to get this intrinsically small matter settled by peaceful means, even if a very considerable risk was incurred in the process; and I wished particularly to see them, and to judge of them, in their own natural surroundings. I was constantly being called upon by Government to give my opinion upon the probable action of the Tibetans, but so far I had only seen them in our own camps, and they had steadily refused to admit me into theirs. I therefore determined on the following morning, without any formality, without any previous announcement, and without any escort, to ride over to their camp, about ten miles distant, at Guru, and talk over the general situation—not as British Commissioner, with a list of grievances for which he had to demand redress, but as one who wished to understand them, and by friendly means to effect a settlement. I was only too well aware that such an attempt was likely to be taken by the Tibetans as a sign of weakness; still, when I saw these people so steeped in ignorance of what opposing the might of the British Empire really meant, I felt it my duty to reason with them up to the latest moment, to save them from the results of their ignorance.

Captain O'Connor and Captain Sawyer, of the 23rd Pioneers, who was learning Tibetan, accompanied me, but we did not take with us even a single sepoy as escort. On our way we were met by messengers, who had come to say that the Tibetan chiefs would not come to see me at Tuna, and I was all the more pleased that I had left Tuna before the message arrived.

On reaching Guru, a small village under a hill, we found numbers of Tibetan soldiers out collecting yak-dung in the surrounding plain; but there was no military precaution whatever taken, and we rode straight into the village. About 600 soldiers were huddled up in the cattle-yards of the houses. They were only armed with spears and matchlocks, and had no breech-loaders. As we rode through the village they all crowded out to look at us, and not with any scowls, but laughing to each other, as if we were an excellent entertainment. They were not very different in appearance from the ordinary Bhutia dandy-bearers of Darjiling or the yak-drivers we had with us in camp.

We asked for the General, and on reaching the principal house I was received at the head of the stairs by a polite, well-dressed, and well-mannered man, who was the Tibetan leader, and who was most cordial in his greeting. Other Generals stood behind him, and smiled and shook hands also. I was then conducted into a room in which the three Lhasa monks were seated, and here the difference was at once observable. They made no attempt to rise, and only made a barely civil salutation from their cushions. One object of my visit had already been attained: I could from this in itself see how the land lay, and where the real obstruction came from.

The Lhasa General and the Shigatse Generals—we had become accustomed to calling them Generals, though the English reader must not imagine they at all resembled Napoleon—took their seats on cushions at the head of the room and opposite to the monks. We were given three cushions on the right, and two Shigatse Generals and another Shigatse representative had seats on the left. Tea was served, and the Lhasa General, as the spokesman of the assembly, asked after my health.

After I had made the usual polite replies and inquiries after their own welfare, I said I had not come to them now on a formal visit as British Commissioner, or with any idea of officially discussing the various points of difference between us; but I was anxious to see them and know them, and to have an opportunity of freely discussing the general situation in a friendly, informal manner. So I had ridden over, without ceremony and without escort, to talk matters over, and see if there was no means of arriving at a settlement by peaceful means. I said that

I had been appointed British Commissioner on account of my general experience in many different countries, that I had no preconceived ideas upon this question and no animus against them; from what I had seen of them, I was convinced there was no people with whom we were more likely to get on, and I hoped now we had really met each other face to face we should find a means of settling our differences and forming a lasting friendship.

The Lhasa General replied that all the people of Tibet had a covenant that no Europeans were ever to be allowed to enter their country, and the reason was that they wished to preserve their religion. The monks here chimed in, saying that their religion must be preserved, and that no European, on any account, must be admitted. The General then went on to say that, if I really wanted to make a friendly settlement, I should go back to Yatung.

I told him that for a century and a half we had remained quietly in India, and made no attempt to force ourselves upon them. Even though we had a treaty right to station an officer at Yatung, we had not exercised that right. But of recent years we had heard from many different sources that they were entering into friendly relations with the Russians, while they were still keeping us at arm's length. One Dorjieff, for instance, had been the bearer of autograph letters from the Dalai Lama to the Czar and Russian officials at the very time when the Lama was refusing letters from the Viceroy of India. We could understand their being friendly with both the Russians and ourselves, or their wishing to have nothing to do with either; but when they were friendly with the Russians and unfriendly with us, they must not be surprised at our now paying closer attention to our treaty rights.

The General assured me that it was untrue that they had any dealings with the Russians, and the monks brusquely intimated that they disliked the Russians just as much as they disliked us; they protested that they had nothing to do with the Russians, that there was no Russian near Lhasa at that time, and that Dorjieff was a Mongolian, and the custom of Mongolians was to make large presents to the monasteries. They asked me, therefore, not to be so suspicious.

I said it was difficult not to be suspicious when they persistently kept us at such a distance. I then addressed them in regard to religion, and asked them if they had ever heard that we interfered with the religions of the people of India. They admitted that we did not interfere, but they maintained, nevertheless, that it was to preserve their religion that they adhered to their determination to keep us out.

As the Buddhist religion nowhere preaches this seclusion, it was evident that what the monks wished to preserve was not their religion, but their priestly influence. This was the crux of the whole situation. And it entirely bore out what Mr. Nolan, the Commissioner of Darjiling, had observed many years before*—that it was "the breaking of the beggars' bowl" that was in question, the loss of these presents from Mongolians and others.

So far the conversation, in spite of occasional bursts from the monks, had been maintained with perfect good-humour; but when I made a sign of moving, and said that I must be returning to Tuna, the monks, looking as black as devils, shouted out: "No, you won't; you'll stop here." One of the Generals said, quite politely, that we had broken the rule of the road in coming into their country, and we were nothing but thieves and brigands in occupying Phari Fort. The monks, using forms of speech which Captain O'Connor told me were only used in addressing inferiors, loudly clamoured for us to name a date when we would retire from Tuna before they would let me leave the room. The atmosphere became electric. The faces of all were set. One of the Generals left the room; trumpets outside were sounded, and attendants closed round behind us.

A real crisis was on us, when any false step might be fatal. I told Captain O'Connor, though there was really no necessity to give such a warning to anyone so imperturbable, to keep his voice studiously calm, and to

* See p. 63.

smile as much as he possibly could, and I then said that I had to obey the orders of my Government, just as much as they had to obey the orders of theirs; that I would ask them to report to their Government what I had said, and I would report to my Government what they had told me. That was all that could be done at present; but if the Viceroy, in reply to my reports, ordered me back to India I should personally be only too thankful, as theirs was a cold, barren, and inhospitable country, and I had a wife and child at Darjiling, whom I was anxious to see again as soon as I could.

This eased matters a little. But the monks continued to clamour for me to name a date for withdrawal, and the situation was only relieved when a General suggested that a messenger should return with me to Tuna to receive there the answer from the Viceroy. The other Generals eagerly accepted the suggestion, and the tension was at once removed. Their faces became smiling again, and they conducted me to the outer door with the same geniality and politeness with which they had received us, though the monks remained seated and as surly and evil-looking as men well could look.

We preserved our equanimity of demeanour and the smiles on our faces till we had mounted our ponies and were well outside the camp, and then we galloped off as hard as we could, lest the monks should get the upper hand again and send men after us. It had been a close shave, but it was worth it.

I had sized up the situation, and felt now I knew how I stood. I knew from that moment that nowhere else than in Lhasa, and not until the monkish power had been broken, should we ever make a settlement. But it was still treason to mention the word "Lhasa" in any communication to Government, and I had to keep these conclusions to myself for many months yet, for fear I might frighten people in England who had not yet got accustomed to the idea of our going even as far as Gyantse.

While I perceived that the monks were implacably hostile, that they had the preponderating influence in the State, and were entirely convinced of their power to dictate to us, I perceived also that the lay officials were much less unfriendly, less ignorant of our strength, and more amenable to reason, and that the ordinary people and soldiers, though perhaps liable to be worked on by the monks, had no innate bad feeling against us. Hereon I based my hopes for the security of the eventual settlement.

A few days later the Lhasa General, known as the Lhi-ding Depon, in company with a high Shigatse official and the General who had met me at Yatung, paid me a visit at Tuna. The Lhasa General announced that, like me, he was most anxious to come to a friendly settlement, and therefore he would ask me to withdraw to Yatung, where discussions could then take place in the most amicable manner. I told him I did not wish to say anything disagreeable to himself personally, as he had always been polite to me, but I would ask him to let his Government know that the time was past for talk of this kind, and to warn them that they must take a more serious view of the situation; they must realize that the British Government were exceedingly angry at the treatment that I, their representative, had received, and were in no mood to be trifled with. Far from going back, or even staying here, we were going to advance still farther into Tibet, and I expected to be met both by the Amban and by a Tibetan official of the highest rank, who would have sufficient authority to negotiate a proper treaty with me in the place of the one concluded by the Amban, which the Tibetans repudiated. I had waited for six months for a proper representative to be sent to meet me, but even now none had arrived.

I heard from him later that he had communicated to the Lhasa monks the substance of this interview, but they had stated they could make no report of my views to the Lhasa Government until we had retired to Yatung.

Two Captains were sent to me on February 7 with a message that I must retire to Yatung, and I sent the usual reply verbally by them and in writing by the hands of my Tibetan Munshi. This latter communication was returned, with the customary intimation that letters were not received.

MOUNTED INFANTRY.

To face page 169.

Two more messengers arrived on the 10th, asking me to fix a date for withdrawal, and threatening trouble if I remained. These threats and rumours of attacks, and reports of the monks having set apart five days to curse us solemnly, continued for the following weeks, and caused us to keep well on the lookout: double sentries were posted at night, and, on account of the cold, relieved every hour. It was wearisome and anxious work, but we felt quite confident of ourselves, and in the end no attack was made.

General Macdonald and the main body were also having a perhaps equally trying time. Communications had to be kept up across two high passes right through the winter; a flying column had to be ready to proceed at any moment to our assistance at Tuna; and supplies and transport had to be collected for our advance as soon as possible to Gyantse. On the Tang-la there was never any great depth of snow, and what snow fell soon cleared away; but there were terrible winds, and the convoys sometimes crossed in blinding, icy blizzards. In February General Macdonald himself came over with one of these convoys for a short inspection. On the passes into Sikkim there was much more snow, and they were occasionally closed after an unusually heavy storm. Still, fairly continuously the transport corps plied across them, and supplies accumulated in Chumbi.

All this time we had been in considerable anxiety in regard to Bhutan. During our advance through Chumbi we had Bhutan on our right flank. The Bhutanese were of the same religion as the Tibetans, and closely connected with them. It was possible, therefore, that they might take the Tibetan side, and it was of the highest importance that we should secure at least their neutrality. Mr. Marindin, the Commissioner of Darjiling, had written to ask them to send someone to discuss matters with him; but the answer, which was received as we were passing through Chumbi, was not wholly satisfactory, so I sent another message, with the result that an official of some standing, the Trimpuk Jongpen, arrived at Phari, and was brought on by Mr. Walsh to see me at Tuna.

He was a rough, jovial person, and when I said that I merely wished to know on which side the Bhutanese intended to place themselves, that, as they were of the same religion and race as the Tibetans, we could quite understand their siding with them, but only wished to know plainly, so that we could make our arrangements accordingly, he replied most emphatically that the Bhutanese would be on our side. I said that these were mere words, and he said that he would put them on paper and seal it, which he did. I said that that was, after all, only a piece of paper. Would he show his friendship by deeds? Would he help us with supplies? And he readily promised, and gave us permission, on payment, to make a road up the Amo-chu. Like the Nepalese on our left flank, these Bhutanese on our right were most whole-souled in their support, and it greatly strengthened my position subsequently to be able to advance into Tibet arm-in-arm with Nepal and Bhutan.

This Trimpuk Jongpen at once became a useful ally. I explained to him the whole of our case with the Tibetans, pretty much as I had explained it to the Tibetans in my speech at Khamba Jong. He asked me whether he might see the Lhasa delegates, explain our views to them, and try and induce them to come to a settlement, for he said his Government were most anxious that a peaceful settlement should be arrived at. I had no hope that he would be able to effect anything, but I thought that the fact of his attempting to mediate might be the means of bringing the Bhutanese Government into closer relation with us. I therefore consented to his seeing the Lhasa delegates, and asked when he proposed to go to Guru. His answer surprised me. He said he found there was no one there of sufficient rank for him to visit them, so he would send over and invite them to come and see him. The Lhasa General, another General, and one of the Lama representatives did come and see him, and this incident furnished sufficient proof of what we had all along contended—that the men whom the Lhasa Government had sent to negotiate with me were of an altogether too insignificant position for me to meet in serious negotiation.

After the first interview the Bhutan Envoy came to me to report the result. He said he had repeated to them what I told him, and the Lhasa delegates had replied that Yatung was the place appointed for discussions, and we ought to have discussed matters there; but, instead of that, we came with an armed force to Khamba Jong, and then had come into Chumbi, so they did not believe that we honestly intended to make a peaceful settlement, but they asked what were the terms of the settlement we wished to make.

I told the Envoy that I would willingly go back to Yatung if I thought that by doing so there was the slightest prospect of making a durable settlement with the Tibetans. But, as a matter of fact, we had tried for years to make a settlement at Yatung. Our political officers, Mr. White and Captain Le Mesurier, had met Tibetan officials, and also the Amban, there, but without result. As to what terms we would ask in the settlement, that was, of course, a matter which I should have to discuss with the high official possessed of full powers to negotiate, as soon as one was appointed; but I might say, in general terms, that there were three main points we should want to settle with the Tibetans: Firstly, the boundary with Sikkim; secondly, the regulation of trade and the selection of a more suitable trade-mart than Yatung; and thirdly, the means of communication between ourselves and the Tibetans. The Envoy then returned to the Lhasa delegates, who had been awaiting my reply. On the following day they had a full meeting at Guru to consider it, and the Lhasa General paid another visit to the Bhutan Envoy. The Tibetans said that, as we were in the wrong, having advanced into Tibet, we should retire to Yatung, and then negotiations could take place; but as regards our wish to regulate communications with them, they could only say that no communications would ever be allowed, as it was against the rule of the country.

These negotiations had led to nothing; but one more stone had been turned in our attempt to effect a settlement peacefully, and incidentally the attempt had been instrumental in putting us on good terms with the Bhutanese. I wrote at the time that I was hopeful that from this beginning we might establish more intimate relations with Bhutan, for the Envoy was the first sensible man I had met on that frontier, and there might be advantage in closer intimacy between us. Everything turned out well afterwards. Mr. White twice visited the country and established the best possible relations with the people, and Bhutan is now definitely under our protection.

This was the last attempt to negotiate before we advanced. The old Resident at Lhasa spoke much of coming to meet me, but never came. The new Resident, who had been appointed specially for this work in December, 1902, did not reach Lhasa till February the 11th, 1904, and neither he nor any proper Tibetan negotiator appeared. And we remained patiently at Tuna through all February and March.

The military officers had a poor time, for they had to be so rigorously on the watch, and Colonel Hogge had such a bout of sleeplessness from the effect of the high altitudes that he had to go for a fortnight's change to Chumbi, which is only 9,000 feet above sea-level, to give himself the chance of sleeping again, after which he was all right. We had, too, twelve cases of pneumonia among the sepoys, eleven of which, from the altitude, proved fatal. And one poor young fellow in the postal department, Mr. Lewis, had to have both his feet amputated for frost-bite, and eventually died of the effects.

But we had much to employ us, too. Captain Ryder would go off surveying; Mr. Hayden would make geologizing expeditions; Captain Walton would collect every living animal of any size and description he could detect; Captain O'Connor would always be surrounded with Tibetans, of every degree of dirt; and I would spend my days on the mountain-sides, sheltered as much as I could be from the wind, getting as much as I could of the bright warm sunshine of these southern latitudes, and on the whole thoroughly enjoying myself, for the natural scenery was an unfailing pleasure.

Generally the days were clear and bright, but almost

THE START FROM TUNA FOR GURU.

To face page 173.

invariably at ten or eleven a terrific wind would arise, and blow with fury for the rest of the day. And sometimes mighty masses of cloud would come sweeping up from the direction of India. Snow would fall, and then for two or three days together we would be the sport of a terrific blizzard. The mountains would be hidden, and nothing would be visible but dull masses of fiercely-driven snow, as fine and dry as dust, and penetrating everywhere. For days together the thermometer would not rise above 15° even in the middle of the day. Our camp would be the very picture of desolation. It seemed impossible that the poor sentries at night would ever be able to stand against the howling storm and the penetrating snow, or that our soldiers would ever be able to resist an attack from the Tibetans in such terrific circumstances.

By the middle of March General Macdonald's arrangements were nearing completion, and I wrote to the new Resident, who had recently announced his arrival, saying that I was about to move to Gyantse to commence negotiations, that I hoped to meet him there, and trusted he would secure the attendance of fully-empowered Tibetan representatives of suitable rank. I asked him to warn the Tibetans that the consequences of resistance to the passage of my Mission would be very serious.

On March 24 General Macdonald left Chumbi, and arrived at Tuna on the 28th, with two 10-pounder guns, one 7-pounder, four companies 32nd Pioneers, three and a half companies 8th Gurkhas, field-hospital, and engineer park.

Colonel Hogge's patrols had been watching the Tibetans carefully lately. Reinforcements had arrived since I visited Guru, and the Tibetans had built a wall across the road about six miles from Tuna. There was also a considerable force on the other side of the Bam-tso (lake).

On March 31, after we had given fair warning to the Tibetans, the advance was made. Light snow lay on the ground. The cold was even now intense. News that the Tibetans were still in position had reached us, and the crucial moment which was to decide upon peace or war was now approaching.

We moved along as rapidly as is possible at those high altitudes and encumbered with heavy clothing. A short way out we were met by a messenger from the Tibetan General, urging us to go back to India. I told the messenger to gallop back at once and tell the Lhasa General that we were on our way to Gyantse, and were going as far as Guru, ten miles distant, that day. I said that we did not want to fight, and would not unless we were opposed, but that the road must be left clear for us, and the Tibetans must withdraw from their positions across it. Farther on, as we advanced across an almost level gravelly plain, we came in sight of the Tibetan position in a series of sangars on a ridge. At 1,000 yards' distance we halted, and awaited the arrival of the Tibetans for our last palaver. They rode up briskly with a little cavalcade, and we all dismounted, set out rugs and coats on the ground, and sat down for the final discussion. I reiterated the same old statement—that we had no wish or intention of fighting if we were not opposed, but that we must advance to Gyantse. If they did not obstruct our progress or did not attack us, we would not attack them. But advance we must, for we had found it impossible to negotiate anywhere else. They replied with the request—or, indeed, almost order—that we must go back to Yatung, and they would negotiate there. They said these were their instructions from Lhasa. They also did not wish to fight, but they had orders to send us back to Yatung.

There was no possible reasoning with such people. They had such overweening confidence in their Lama's powers. How *could* anyone dare to resist the orders of the Great Lama? Surely lightning would descend from heaven or the earth open up and destroy anyone who had such temerity! I pointed to our troops, now ready deployed for action. I said that we had tried for fourteen years inside our frontier to settle matters. I urged that for eight months now I had patiently tried to negotiate, but no one with authority came to see me, my letters were returned, and even messages were refused. I had therefore received the commands of the Emperor to advance to Gyantse, in the hope that perhaps there responsible negotiators would meet us. Anyhow, the time for further parleying here was gone. The moment for advance had arrived. I would give them a quarter of an hour after their return to their lines within which to make up their minds. After that interval General Macdonald would advance, and if the Tibetans had not already left their positions blocking our line of advance, he would expel them by force.

All this was interpreted to them by Captain O'Connor with his inimitable suavity and composure. But we might just as well have spoken to a stone wall. Not the very slightest effect was produced. After all, our numbers were not very overwhelming. The Tibetans had charms against our bullets, and the supernatural powers of the Great Lama in the background. Whether they had any lurking suspicions that perhaps, after all, these might not be efficacious I know not. But, anyhow, all had to obey the orders from Lhasa. Those orders were not to let us proceed farther, so stop us they must, and that was all they were concerned with. They had formed no plan of what they should do if we did advance contrary to the Great Lama's orders. But for that there was no need; the Lama would provide. Such were their ideas. It was, of course, an impossible situation.

The Generals and their following returned to their camp. The quarter of an hour of grace elapsed. And now the great moment had arrived. But I wished still to give them just one last chance, in the hope that at the eleventh hour, and at the fifty-ninth minute of the eleventh hour, they might change their minds. I therefore asked General Macdonald to order his men not to fire upon the Tibetans until the Tibetans first fired on them. In making this request I well knew the responsibility I was incurring. We were but a handful of men—about 100 Englishmen and 1,200 Indians—in the face of superior numbers of Tibetans, in the heart of their country, 15,000 feet above the sea, and separated from India by two high passes; and the advantage our troops possessed from arms of precision and long-range fire I took from them.

It was the last and final effort to carry out our object without the shedding of blood. The troops responded with admirable discipline to the call. They steadily advanced across the plain and up the hillside to the Tibetan lines, expecting at any moment that from behind the sangars a destructive volley might be opened upon them before they could fire a shot. Some of them afterwards, and very naturally, told me that they hoped they would never again be put in so awkward a position. But I trust their discipline will at any rate show to those in England who so decried this day's action, and spoke about our "massacring unarmed Tibetans"—that men on the remotest confines of the Empire can and do exercise moderation and restraint in the discharge of their duty, and do not always act with that wantonness and reckless cruelty with which they are so often credited at home.

If General Macdonald had had a perfectly free hand, and had been allowed to think only of military considerations, he would have attacked the Tibetans by surprise in their camp, without giving them any warning at all; and even after I had given the Tibetans warning, if he had still been free to act on only military lines, he would have shelled their position with his guns, and with long-range rifle-fire have broken down the defence before advancing to the attack. As it was, in order to give them a chance up to the very last moment, he abdicated both the advantage of surprise and of long-range fire, and his troops advanced up the mountain-side on less than even terms to the fortified position of the Tibetans.

The Tibetans on their side showed great indecision. They also had apparently received orders not to fire first; and the whole affair seemed likely to end in comedy rather than in the tragedy which actually followed. The Tibetans first ran into their sangars and then ran out again. Gradually our troops crept up and round the flanks. They arrived eventually face to face with the Tibetans, as will be seen in the accompanying photograph by Lieutenant Bailey, and things were almost at an impasse till the Tibetans slowly yielded to the admonitions of our troops, and allowed themselves to be shouldered out of their

SEPOYS "SHOULDERING" TIBETANS FROM POSTITION: GURU, MARCH, 1904.

To face page 176.

position and be "moved on," as London policemen would disperse a crowd from Trafalgar Square.

At this point the two Lhasa Majors who had met me previously in the day rode out again, and told me that the Tibetans had been ordered not to fire, and begged me to stop the troops from advancing. I replied that we must continue the advance, and could not allow any troops to remain on the road. There was a post actually on the road, with a wall newly and deliberately built across it, and it was obvious that if we were ever to get to Gyantse the Tibetans behind that wall must be removed. Yet I thought the affair was practically over. The Tibetans were streaming away from their position along the ridge, and had even begun to leave their post on the road.. Then a change came. The Lhasa General, or possibly the monks, recalled the men to their post, and an officer reported to General Macdonald that, though surrounded by our troops, they refused to retreat: they were not fighting, but they would not leave the wall they had built across the road.

General Macdonald and I had a consultation together, and agreed that in these circumstances the only thing to do was to disarm them and let them go. We rode together to the spot, and found the Tibetans huddled together like a flock of sheep behind the wall. Our infantry were in position on the hillside only 20 yards above them on the one side; on the other our Maxims and guns were trained upon them at not 200 yards' distance. Our mounted infantry were in readiness in the plain only a quarter of a mile away. Our sepoys were actually standing up to the wall, with their rifles pointing over at the Tibetans within a few feet of them. And the Lhasa General himself with his staff was on *our* side of the wall, in among our sepoys.

He had, of course, completely lost his head. Though in command of some thousands of armed men, and though I had given him ample warning of our intention to advance, he was totally unprepared for action when our advance was made. He had brought his men *back* into an absurd position; his action when he had got them back was simply childish. I sent Captain O'Connor to announce to him that General Macdonald and I had decided that his men must be disarmed, but he remained sullen and did nothing; and when, after a pause, the disarmament was actually commenced, he threw himself upon a sepoy, drew a revolver, and shot the sepoy in the jaw.

Not, as I think, with any deliberate intention, but from sheer inanity, the signal had now been given. Other Tibetan shots immediately followed. Simultaneously volleys from our own troops rang out; the guns and Maxims commenced to fire. Tibetan swordsmen made a rush upon any within reach, and the plucky and enterprising Edmund Candler, the very able correspondent of the *Daily Mail*, received more than a dozen wounds, while Major Wallace Dunlop, one of the best officers in the force, was severely handled. For just one single instant the Tibetans, by a concerted and concentrated rush, might have broken our thin line, and have carried the Mission and the military staff. But that instant passed in a flash. Before a few seconds were over, rifles and guns were dealing the deadliest destruction on them in their huddled masses. The Lhasa General himself was killed at the start, and in a few minutes the whole affair was over. The plain was strewn with dead Tibetans, and our troops instinctively and without direct orders ceased firing—though, in fact, they had only fired thirteen rounds per man.

It was a terrible and ghastly business; but it was not fair for an English statesman to call it a massacre of "unarmed men," for photographs testify that the Tibetans were all armed; and, looking back now, I do not see how it could possibly have been avoided. The Tibetans afterwards at Lhasa told me in all seriousness that I might have known their General did not mean to fight, for if he did he would not have been in the front as he was. This, no doubt, was true, and, left to himself, he would, we may be sure, have arranged matters with me in a perfectly amicable manner, for at Guru in January, and when he came to see me at Tuna, he had always shown himself courteous and reasonable; and his men had no antipathy towards us. But he had at his side, ruling and overawing him, a fanatical Lama from Lhasa. Ignorant and arrogant, this priest herded the superstitious peasantry to destruction. It is only fair to assume that, somewhere in the depths of his nature, he felt that the people's religion was in danger, and that he was called upon to preserve it. But blind fear of the danger which he believed threatened was so combined with overweening confidence, and there was such a lack of effort to avert the supposed danger by reasonable means, as might so easily have been done, that he simply brought disaster on his country, and, poor man, paid the penalty of his unreasonableness with his life. What to me is so sad is that now, when the Lamas have discovered their errors and are imploring our aid, we can do so little to befriend them.

After the action, General Macdonald ordered the whole of the medical staff to attend the wounded Tibetans. Everything that with our limited means we could do for them was done. Captains Davies, Walton, Baird, Franklin and Kelly, devoted themselves to their care. A rough hospital was made at Tuna. And the Tibetans showed great gratitude for what we did, though they failed to understand why we should try to take their lives one day and try to save them the next. We had been in some anxiety regarding a second body of Tibetans, 2,000 strong, on the opposite side of the lake, but these, on hearing of the disaster near Guru, retreated; and on April 5 we resumed our march in the direction of Gyantse, the thermometer, even thus in April, showing 23 degrees of frost on the morning we started.

I now received a letter, dated March the 27th, from the Resident, who said he was most anxious to hasten to meet me, and had seen the Dalai Lama, but "difficulties arose over transport, which he was unwilling to grant." After considering all this, he had come to the conclusion that Tibetan politics were those of drift; that Chinese officials were too engrossed in self-seeking, and hence the Tibetans shirked action. But a quarrel on his part with the Dalai Lama would only mar matters, so he would "go on" and perform his share of the duties allotted to him, and he had decided to write "a succinct report to

Peking," and then again ask for transport. He hoped I would recognize his perplexities. I had excellent reason for an advance to Gyantse with my escort, he said. But, "notwithstanding the craft and deceit of the Tibetans and their violation of principle," he had compelled them "somewhat to understand the meaning of principle," and if I suddenly penetrated into their country he feared they would lapse into their former temper, and thus imperil the conclusion of trade relations. The Dalai Lama had told him that if I would retire to Yatung he would select Tibetan delegates and request him (the Resident) to proceed there and discuss matters. The Resident added that "this frontier matter had been hanging fire for over ten years because it had been perfunctorily drawn up in the beginning, and because subsequently it was shirked by the different delegates, who did not strive honestly to adjust the difficulties." He was ashamed to mention the question of my retirement to Yatung, but, still, he thought it would be better for me to retire there and "insure the smooth working of a settlement."

This is all we got after waiting for him for fifteen months. I replied, informing him of the circumstances of the Guru fight, and telling him that I was advancing on Gyantse, which I expected to reach in about a week, and I hoped that I should then have the pleasure of meeting him and a high Tibetan official with the power to make a settlement which would prevent any further useless bloodshed.

On the way to Gyantse, at the Tsamdang Gorge, the Tibetans again opposed our progress by building a wall across the narrow passage. But General Macdonald dislodged them and inflicted heavy loss, and on April 11 we arrived at Gyantse.

We found the valley covered with well-built hamlets and numerous trees and plenty of cultivation. Most of the inhabitants had fled, but the jong, or fort, which stands on an eminence in the middle of the valley, was still partially occupied. The Commandant was informed that General Macdonald proposed to occupy the jong on the following morning, and would expect to find it vacated by 9 a.m. On the morning of the 12th we found that the troops had been withdrawn, and the jong was occupied without opposition.

So ended another phase of the enterprise, and on April 14 the Viceroy telegraphed, offering to myself, General Macdonald, and to all the officers and men of the Mission escort, both civil and military, his warmest congratulations upon the success of the first part of our undertaking, and his grateful recognition of the cheerfulness, self-restraint, and endurance exhibited by all ranks in circumstances unexampled in warfare, and calling for no ordinary patience and fortitude.

CHAPTER XIII

GYANTSE

GYANTSE, which had been our goal for so many months, and with which we were to be but too well acquainted before we had finished, has two principal features—the jong and the monastery, called Palkhor Choide. The jong is a really imposing structure built of strong, solid masonry, and rising in tiers of walls up a rocky eminence springing abruptly out of the plain to a height of 400 or 500 feet. It has a most commanding and dominant look. And the monastery immediately adjoining it at a part of the base of the hill is also impressive from the height and solidity of the walls with which it is surrounded, and by the massiveness of the buildings within the walls.*

The town itself was not of much importance, nor so promising as a trading-mart as I had hoped. It lay at the foot of the jong, and the bazaar did not possess shops of any size. The real population, indeed, seemed to be scattered in the numerous hamlets dotted all over the valley, through which ran a considerable river.

The demeanour of the inhabitants was respectful. They brought in supplies for sale, and in a few days a regular bazaar was established by the Tibetans immediately outside our camp, the bartering being carried on, as usual, mostly by women. The people said they had not the slightest wish to fight us, and only desired to escape being commandeered by the Lhasa authorities. The valley proved to be very fertile, with cultivation all down it, and supplies were plentiful.

* An excellent description of the jong and monastery will be found in Chapter VII. of Landon's "Lhasa."

Gyantse was indeed a delightful change from Tuna. It was, in the first place, nearly 2,000 feet lower, so naturally warmer. In addition, spring was coming on. Leaf-buds were beginning to sprout on the willows. The little irises in plenty were appearing. And birds of several rare varieties came to rejoice Captain Walton's heart and fill his collection.

Captain O'Connor, Captain Ryder, and Mr. Hayden rode down the Shigatse road to Dongtse and visited its monastery, besides other houses and estates of note in the valley. They found the people everywhere friendly and very different from what they would have been on the north-west frontier, for instance, under similar circumstances. The peasants were ploughing and sowing their fields, and the whole country appeared perfectly contented and quiet.

From the rear, too, came encouraging tidings. I received a letter from the Dharm Raja, of Bhutan, saying that when he heard that his friends had won a victory he was greatly rejoiced, for nowadays England and Bhutan had established a firm friendship, and he hoped that there would always be firm faith and friendship between the English and Bhutanese.

Yet, with all this ease and quiet, there was not the slightest real sign of the business of negotiation being commenced. I had naturally expected that, when the Resident had been specially deputed by the Chinese Government for these negotiations sixteen months previously, I should have found him at Gyantse, or at any rate on his way there, and that, after the Chinese Government had been urging the Tibetans since the previous summer to send a properly empowered delegate, the Resident would have been accompanied by a Tibetan Commissioner capable of negotiating with me. But on April 22 I received a despatch from the Resident, stating, indeed, his intention of arriving at Gyantse before May 12, but giving no news that a proper Tibetan Commissioner had been appointed. He stated that the Lhasa General had been the aggressor in the fight at Guru, that the fault was on the side of the Tibetans, who had disregarded his advice, and he recognized our compassion in having magnanimously released the foolish and ignorant prisoners, cared for the wounded, and shown humane motives of sternness and mercy. He added that the Dalai Lama was now aroused to a sense of our power. But still there was no mention that the transport which the Resident was "insisting on" had been provided, and the appointment of a proper Tibetan Commissioner was still not made. In fact, the Councillors had all been imprisoned by the Dalai Lama, and there were "but few capable Tibetan officials to settle the frontier and other important questions," which could not, added the Resident, "be disposed of in a peremptory manner." A few days' delay would not, therefore, he considered, be out of place.

Three days later he wrote that in this matter of proceeding to meet me he had exhausted himself in talking with the Tibetans, and trusted I would perceive something of the difficult nature of the circumstances. And on April 29 he wrote that he had received a reply from the Dalai Lama about some representations I had made against monks taking part in the fighting, but in this reply not a word was mentioned about his transport or any other matters.

In these circumstances I telegraphed to Government on April 22 that the best way to meet these dilatory tactics was, at the earliest moment by which military preparations could be completed, to move the Mission straight to Lhasa, and carry on the negotiations at the capital, instead of halfway. This, I said, would be the most effective and only permanent way of clinching matters, besides being the cheapest and quickest. Our prestige, I urged, was then at its height, Nepal and Bhutan were with us, the people were not against us, the Tibetan soldiers did not care to fight, the Lamas were stunned. By a decisive move then a permanent settlement could be procured. I added that, in recommending this proposal at so early a stage for the consideration of Government, my object was that the favourable season might be utilized to the full, and that we might not allow the psychological moment to pass without taking advantage of it. Meanwhile, I said, I would receive the Amban, and would ascertain what power to effect a settlement he and the Tibetan representative really possessed.

In making this recommendation I was counting on a collapse of the Lhasa authorities, which seemed to be indicated by the Resident's statement, by the statement of a Chinese official from Lhasa that Tibetan officers were begging the Resident to intercede, by the fact that the common people even, it was said, at Lhasa did not resent our presence, that there were few troops between Gyantse and Lhasa, and that the Lhasa authorities had been able to produce only 5,000 men to oppose our advance as far as Gyantse.

Whether this collapse would have taken place if we had then set about advancing to Lhasa it is impossible to say. Certainly it did not take place. But this may have been due to the retirement of General Macdonald with the greater part of the force which now took place, in accordance with the plan prearranged between us of leaving the Mission with a good strong escort to conduct negotiations while the bulk of the force remained in support in Chumbi, where supplies were more readily available. This, from a supply point of view, was desirable, and it was in accordance with the policy of Government, but it may have had the effect of re-arousing the Tibetans.

Anyhow, rumours soon began to reach me that Tibetan forces were collecting again. On the 24th came news that they were building walls across the road at the Karo-la (pass) on the way to Lhasa, that camps holding 700 or 800 Tibetans had been established there, that the Dalai Lama was endeavouring to gain time to enlist Tibetans from far and wide to resist a British advance to Lhasa, and that the local soldiers round Gyantse were, under his orders, quietly leaving and proceeding towards Lhasa.

To ascertain the truth of these rumours, Colonel Brander, who was now in command of the Mission escort of 500 men, two guns and two Maxims, and some mounted infantry, on April 28 sent out a reconnaissance party of one company of mounted infantry to the Karo-la; and on

May 1 we received news from Captain Hodgson, commanding the party, that he had advanced with his mounted infantry across the pass, and three miles beyond had found the Tibetans in occupation of a wall, some 600 yards long, built across the valley. The Tibetans, estimated at from 1,000 to 1,500 in number, opened a heavy fire on the mounted infantry at about 300 yards' distance. Our men then retired steadily, firing only a few shots and returned towards Gyantse.

Besides the definite information thus acquired, reports also reached me that other troops were assembling in the Rong Valley, ready to support those on the Lhasa road, and that there was a large gathering, estimated at 4,000, assembled at Shigatse itself, a portion of which was to move up to Dongtse, twelve miles from Gyantse.

Colonel Brander now came to me and asked for leave to go out and attack the Tibetans before these gatherings could come to a head. He had much frontier experience, and I also had some, and we both of us knew that when such gatherings take place it is a pretty sound general principle to take the initiative, and hit hard at them before they have time to accumulate overwhelming strength. It was a bold move, he contemplated, for the Karo-la (pass) was forty-five miles distant, and was over 16,000 feet high; and while he was away with two-thirds of the escort, the Mission, with only one-third of its full escort, might be itself attacked. I said that if he, on his side, did not mind taking this risk, I, on my side, did not mind it, and, as far as my military opinion was worth anything, was quite in favour of the operation.

But it was on political grounds that I had to give the decision, and on those grounds I had no objection. I had come to negotiate, but there was no symptom of negotiators appearing. On the other hand, the Tibetans were still further massing their troops; their position at the Karo-la and between there and Kangma was threatening our line of communication; and they had fired on our reconnoitring party. For these reasons I informed Government by telegram on May 2 that I had raised no objection on political grounds to Colonel Brander's proposal to go out and attack the Tibetans on the pass before they could attack our line of communication. I had stated, verbally and in writing, to the Chinese and to the Tibetans that we came to Gyantse to negotiate. Since our arrival we had evacuated the jong, and General Macdonald, with the greater part of the force, had returned to Chumbi. There could be no question, then, that we meant to negotiate and not to fight. Yet they still neither sent a negotiator, nor said they had any intention to negotiate; instead they massed troops to attack us; and I felt at perfect liberty to let the commander of the Mission escort take whatever means he liked to secure its safety.

On the same day, in view of the rumours of the hostile attitude of the Tibetans towards Shigatse and of their reinforcement by local levies, I placed the Gyantse Jongpen in custody in the British camp.

Colonel Brander set out on May 3, with three companies of the 32nd Pioneers, one company 8th Gurkhas, two 7-pounder guns and two Maxims, accompanied by Mr. Wilton and Captain O'Connor, to assist him in case Chinese or Tibetan officials were met with.

On May 4 Captain Walton's patients warned him that some kind of attack on us at Gyantse was likely, and Major Murray, 8th Gurkhas, who was in command during Colonel Brander's absence, sent out a mounted patrol some miles down the Shigatse road; but they returned, reporting everything quiet.

At dawn the next morning the storm burst. I was suddenly awaked by shots and loud booing close by my tent. I dashed out, and there were Tibetans firing through our own loopholes only a few yards off. From the Shigatse direction a force of 800 men had marched all night, and many, under cover of the darkness, had crept up under the walls of our post. Then at dawn these suddenly jumped up, and, supported by the remainder, made an attempt to rush our post, a substantial house with a garden at one side, the wall of which we had loopholed. In the first critical moment they almost succeeded. They as nearly as possible forced an entrance, but were stoutly held at bay by two gallant little Gurkha sentries till our men turned out. Then, as at Guru, once the single favourable moment had flashed by, nothing but disaster lay before them. The attack began at about 4.30, and did not cease till nearly 6.30, but in that time they had left about 250 dead and wounded round our post.

Personally, I did not deserve to get through the attack unscathed, for directly I was out of my tent I made straight for the Mission rendezvous. I was in my pyjamas, and only half awake, and the first thought that struck me was to go to the rendezvous, agreed upon beforehand, in what we called the citadel. But I ought, as I did on other occasions—and as I think always should be done in cases of any sudden attack—to have made straight for the wall with whatever weapon came to hand, and joined in repelling the attack during the few crucial moments.

Major Murray, as soon as he had repelled the attack, pursued the enemy for about two miles down the Shigatse road. But it now became evident that this attacking party was not the only force of Tibetans in the neighbourhood, and that another of similar strength had occupied the jong, for these latter began firing into our post, and we gradually came to realize that we were now besieged.

It turned out from information received from prisoners that these troops had been collected by a General recently appointed by the Lhasa Government, and that it was accompanied by a representative of the great Gaden monastery at Lhasa, by two clerks of the Dalai Lama, and by other Lhasa officials. It was, therefore, no mere local rising, but an attack deliberately planned by the Central Tibetan Government.

For a few days, till Colonel Brander returned, we were in a critical position, and we were also anxious about Colonel Brander himself. The worst that, in making our calculations at Darjiling in November, we had deemed likely to happen had happened, and we were now at the straining-point. Major Murray, assisted especially by Captain Ryder with his engineering experience, strengthened the post as far as possible during the day, and at night we looked out watchfully for a further attack. For it was at night, when our long-range rifles lost their special advantage, that the Tibetans would have their best chance. We only had 170 men, and the vastly superior numbers which the Tibetans were now collecting ought to have had a fair chance of overwhelming us if they had pressed home a well-planned night attack. They fired a good deal during this and the following nights, but we kept a good watch, and we heard afterwards that the Lamas tried to organize a second attack on us, but the men refused to turn out.

It was an intense relief to me to hear on the 7th that Colonel Brander had been successful in clearing the gathering at the Karo-la, which consisted of 2,500 men, armed with numerous Lhasa-made and foreign rifles, and headed by many influential Lamas and officials from Lhasa. In a short note to me he told me of the anxious moments he had passed when, on the early morning before he made his attack, he received a letter from me saying that the Mission had been attacked at Gyantse. The Tibetans were in a very strong position behind a loopholed wall of great solidity, and 800 yards long, which they had built right across the pass; and to attack such a position at a height of over 16,000 feet above sea-level, surrounded with glaciers, with only a sixth of the numbers opposed to him, and with his communications not over safe behind, Colonel Brander had in truth to set his teeth and steel his nerves. His frontal attack failed. Poor Bethune, a typically steady, reliable and lion-hearted officer was killed. The guns proved absolutely ineffective. Ammunition was none too plentiful. And Colonel Brander said in his letter to me that he was on the point of despairing when, just at the critical moment, the turning movement of the Gurkhas, under Major Row, who had slowly scrambled up to a height of 18,000 feet, proved successful. Panic took the Tibetans. They first began dribbling away from the wall, then poured away in torrents. Colonel Brander hurled his mounted infantry at them, and Captain Ottley pursued them halfway to Lhasa.

It was a plucky and daring little action, and unique of its kind in the annals of any nation; for never before had fighting taken place at altitudes well over the summit of Mont Blanc. I was indeed relieved to hear of its brilliant success, and late at night on the 7th—that is, the very day after the fight—to welcome back Captain O'Connor, Mr. Perceval Landon, and the indefatigable Captain Ottley, with his dashing mounted infantry, already the terror of the Tibetans. They had made a bold dash back ahead of Colonel Brander, and on the very next morning Captain Ottley was to show the Tibetans who were investing us the difference which his presence made.

A party of Tibetan horsemen were seen from our post sauntering unsuspectingly along the valley, out of reach of our rifles, but not out of reach of our mounted infantry, twenty of whom, under Captain Ottley, now dashed out of our post in pursuit. The Tibetans galloped up a side valley; Captain Ottley galloped after them; and now we saw a great body of Tibetan horsemen issue from the jong to cut him off. I held my breath in suspense, fearing he would not see the party behind in his eager pursuit of the party in front. But Captain Ottley was not to be so easily caught. He suddenly wheeled on to some rising ground, dismounted his men as quick as lightning, and was blazing away at *both* parties before they could realize what had happened. In a moment several Tibetans dropped, and the remainder scuttled away as fast as they could.

All this put fresh spirit into our men, for we had had three days and nights of considerable strain; and on the day following Colonel Brander himself with his column returned safely to camp, and arrangements were at once made to harry the garrison of the jong with rifle and Maxim fire.

We now heard full details of the Karo-la fight. It appears that the Tibetans engaged were mostly drawn from the districts of South-Eastern Tibet. They were commanded by a layman and a monk official, and had been organized by a monk State Councillor and another high ecclesiastical official who had been stationed for some time at Nagartse. Representatives of the three great Lhasa monasteries were at the fight, and each monk had been provided by the Lhasa Government with a matchlock and a knife before starting to join the army.

On the morning of the 10th we buried the remains of poor Bethune, and it was my melancholy duty to read the Burial Service over one whom I had known since the Relief of Chitral, whose genial, manly nature attached him to every one of us, and for whose soldierly qualities all had the highest admiration. He was a grand type of British officer, strict and thorough in his duties, yet beloved by his men, and his loss was severely felt in the days that were upon us.

Colonel Brander now reconnoitred the jong to see if it was possible to capture it. He came to the conclusion that an attack was too much to undertake. Our two 7-pounder guns were useless, though they had been brought up specially for this purpose, and our force was too small to carry the place by assault. It will naturally be asked why, when the jong was evacuated on our first arrival, we were not now occupying it instead of a house in the plain. General Macdonald had several excellent reasons for not establishing the Mission with escort in the jong. It was too far from a water-supply; and it was too big to hold. The post he chose was compact and on the river. Here he placed us, with ample supplies to last us till relief could arrive if we were attacked. As I have said, the worst that could happen did happen, and we held out till reinforcements came.

But Colonel Brander, though he could not attack the jong, did not allow himself to be simply invested in his post. He constantly sallied out to clear villages, and demolish any within the vicinity of our post; he maintained a mounted dak service to the rear, and in every way endeavoured to keep as much in the ascendant as was possible in the circumstances.

An important stage had now been reached. The Government of India on May 14 telegraphed to me that His Majesty's Government agreed with them that recent events made it inevitable that the Mission should advance to Lhasa, unless the Tibetans consented to open negotiations at Gyantse. I was, therefore, to give notice to the

Amban that we should insist on negotiating at Lhasa itself if no competent negotiator appeared in conjunction with him at Gyantse within a month.

This was satisfactory to a certain degree, but I was disappointed to have to be still further talking about negotiations when we had been wantonly attacked, when we were now actually invested, and when the Lamas were gathering yet more forces around us. Any mention of negotiating in such circumstances would only lead them to believe we feared them, and it was with much reluctance that I eventually gave this message. But the Government had to contend with many difficulties. They were in the face of a strong opposition in the House of Commons. There was no enthusiasm for the enterprise in the country. We had only recently emerged from the South African War. The Russo-Japanese War was causing anxiety. And we had not yet concluded the agreement and formed the *Entente Cordiale* with France.

General Macdonald was meanwhile making every preparation in Chumbi for supporting the Mission escort and eventually advancing to Lhasa; and he had many difficulties of his own to contend with, through an outbreak of cholera, and through the heavy rains causing many breaches in the road in Sikkim. Supplies, munitions, and transport, had to be laboriously collected, and progress was necessarily slow. But on May 24 strong reinforcements reached Gyantse, and were a most welcome addition to our strength, enabling Colonel Brander to assume a more active attitude. They consisted of two 10-pounder guns of the British mountain battery, under Lieutenant Easton, a company of native sappers and miners, 50 Sikhs, and 20 mounted infantry.

Our little garrison was strengthened, too, by the arrival of Captain Sheppard, Royal Engineers, who, of all the officers I saw during the Mission, struck me as being the most likely to rise to the very highest position in the service. His energy, his never-failing cheerfulness, his daring, and his general ability, were altogether exceptional. He was the champion racquet-player in the army, and he was already known on north-western frontier campaigns for his bravery. Here he added daily to his reputation, and he and Captain Ottley were the two whom I, as an onlooker—seeing a good deal, if not always most, of the game—singled out to myself as having in them the surest signs of military genius. In a military career so much depends on chance that these two may very possibly sink down to the usual humdrum respectable commander or staff officer. But I will stake my reputation as a prophet that, if the chance ever does come to either of them before routine and examinations have quenched their burning vitality, they will make a mark like Lord Roberts or like the daring Hodson of Hodson's Horse.

Here I must in a brief parenthesis criticize some remarks I heard Mr. Roosevelt, for whom otherwise I have the greatest admiration, make to the Cambridge University Union Society. He said that in public life and in the army geniuses were not wanted, but that what was required were average men with the ordinary qualities developed by the men themselves to an extraordinary degree. In this I most profoundly disagree. It is not the ordinary average man, however much he may develop his mediocrity, that is most wanted. It is the exceptional man. It is the man with just that touch which we cannot possibly define, but which we all instinctively recognize as genius. There is a superabundance of ordinary men, and it must be admitted that they do ordinary work very much better than geniuses. But it is the genius alone who, when the occasion arises, will flash a ray through these masses of ordinary men, and make them do what they would never do with any amount of development of their ordinary plodding qualities. And it is of the highest importance to find out these exceptional men. But the way to do this is not by examinations—unless those who are least capable of passing them are chosen. It is by letting the best select the best, by letting the proved best select whom *they* think promise best.

All this, however, is by way of interlude, and is merely one of the many reflections I made while I was myself under enforced inactivity, and had nothing much else to do but watch the action of those others upon whom the responsibility for the time being rested.

With his reinforcements Colonel Brander now took the offensive in earnest, and on May 26 attacked the strongly-built village of Palla, which was only 1,100 yards from our post, and which the Tibetans were holding in strength, and connecting with the jong by a wall. In the dead of night, in utter darkness, the attacking party assembled. All of us who were to remain behind went up to the roof to watch the result. The column moved noiselessly out from our post. A long silence followed. Then a few sharp rifle cracks rang out, and soon from the jong and from the Palla village there was a continuous crackle, with sharp spurts of flame lighting the darkness. Soon after a great explosion was heard, followed by a deadly silence. What had happened we heard afterwards. Captain Sheppard, accompanied by Captain O'Connor, had dashed up to the wall of one of the principal houses in the village, and after shooting two Tibetans with his revolver, placed a charge of gun-cotton, lighted a fuse, and dashed back again to cover. The explosion was the result, and a big breach had been made. Captain O'Connor had then, with his cake of gun-cotton, rushed into another house and successfully fired it. Lieutenant Garstin and Lieutenant Walker in another place tried to make a similar breach, but the fuse did not act, and in making a second attempt the former was killed, while Captain O'Connor also was severely wounded.

This blowing up of houses crammed full of armed men is indeed a desperate undertaking, but except by this method of deliberately rushing up and placing a charge under manned walls, and firing the charge, there was no means of getting in, and Sheppard, Garstin, Walker, and O'Connor deserve all the honour that is due to the bravest of military actions.

Breaches had been made, but the village had yet to be stormed, and Major Peterson, with his Sikh Pioneers, as soon as it was light, gallantly stormed house after house, while Colonel Brander supported him with the guns on the hillside a few hundred yards off. The Tibetans fought stubbornly, as they always did in these villages, but Major Peterson pressed steadily on, and by 1.30 the village was in Colonel Brander's hands.

Our losses were, besides Lieutenant Garstin, Royal Engineers killed, Captain O'Connor, Lieutenant Mitchell, 32nd Pioneers, Lieutenant Walker, Royal Engineers, and nine men wounded. It was a heavy casualty list for our little garrison to sustain, but the capture of the village was a great shock to the Tibetans, who till then, according to a Chinaman whom Mr. Wilton met when accompanying one of our sorties, had become very truculent, and talked of first attacking us and cutting all our throats, and then murdering all Chinese.

The Palla village was occupied by our troops, and at 1.30 on the morning of May 30 the Tibetans, who had for long been trying to screw themselves up for an attack upon us, attacked both this and a Gurkha outpost we had established. It was a beautiful sight to watch, with the jong keeping up a heavy fire on us, and the houses at the foot of the jong firing away hard on the village. But the Tibetans were easily repulsed, for Colonel Brander had been careful to fortify the place well, and the Tibetans after this never ventured to take the offensive against us, and the tide now definitely began to turn.

I therefore now with less reluctance wrote letters to the Resident and Dalai Lama, saying that we were ready to negotiate at Gyantse up to June 25, but that unless by that date the Resident and competent negotiators had arrived, we would insist upon negotiations being carried on at Lhasa. The letters, together with a covering letter to the Tibetan commander in the jong, were sent by the hands of prisoners. Before undertaking their delivery, however, the bearers stipulated that they should be allowed to return to us as prisoners, which was a significant commentary on the method of enlistment of the Tibetan forces opposing us. The next morning the letters were returned by the Tibetan General, who said that it was not their custom to receive communications from the English.

On the afternoon of June 5 I received instructions

from the Government of India to proceed to Chumbi, to confer with General Macdonald as to future plans. We had to a certain degree kept open our communications. Still, there were Tibetans all about, and it was a somewhat unusual, and certainly risky, proceeding for the chief of the Mission to have to ride 150 miles down the lines to consult the military commander. However, I was glad enough of the change from the monotony of our investment at Gyantse, and at four the next morning, while it was still dark, I rode out with an escort of forty mounted infantry, under Major Murray, and accompanied by that gallant doctor of the 8th Gurkhas, Dr. Franklin. We gave a wide berth to the Niani monastery, and arrived safely at Kangma, our first fortified post, forty miles distant, where Captain Pearson, of the 23rd Pioneers, was in command with about 100 men.

All was quiet here, and the post had never so far been attacked, owing probably to the effect of Colonel Brander's action on the Karo-la, from which a route led direct to this place. I had risen at 4.30 the next morning to make an early start, and was just dressed when I heard that peculiar jackal-like yell which the Tibetans had used when they made their attacks at Gyantse. I instantly dashed on to the roof, and there, sure enough, was a mob of about 300 of them weighing down upon the post, and before our men were out they were right up to the walls, hurling stones and firing at me up on the roof, which was flat, and from which I could not for the moment find a way down. We all, dressed or undressed, dashed up to the walls, seizing the first rifles we could find, and firing away as hard as we could. And here again the Tibetans just lost their opportunity. As before, in a moment it was gone, and they suffered terribly for their want of military acumen. Sixty or seventy were killed, and the rest drew off up the mountains.

But this was not the only body of Tibetans about. While these were making the direct attack, two other bodies of 400 men each had appeared, all of them Kham men, the best fighters in Tibet. One party went up the valley and the other down, to cut off our retreat on either hand. This was a great strategical effort on the part of the Tibetan commander, but it failed, because as soon as the attack on our post was repulsed Major Murray sallied forth, and in turn attacked the other Tibetan parties, climbing the hillside and sending them helter-skelter over the mountains.

Then we had some breakfast, and I proceeded on my way to Chumbi. It was twenty-eight miles to the next stage, at Kala Tso, and there was considerable risk of encountering Tibetans on the way; but I argued that there was less risk immediately after a repulse than there might be a day or two later. So I set out with twenty mounted infantry, Major Murray and his men having to return to Gyantse. At Kala Tso I was welcomed by my old friends the 23rd Pioneers, under Colonel Hogge, who had been our escort at Tuna during all that terrible winter.

I now replied to a telegram I had received in the morning from Government, asking me to communicate my views on the general situation by telegram, as they wished to have them as soon as possible. I said, with reference to the contention which had been made by the military authorities that it would be impossible to keep troops at Lhasa after the autumn, that in my opinion "an effort should be made to quarter troops at Lhasa for the winter, for if we retired to Chumbi in November, we risked the loss of all the results of our present efforts, and the Tibetans would be still more obstructive." I computed that the Lhasa and Gyantse valleys would support 1,000 men each. I hoped that while the ample forces now being sent would break down opposition during the summer months, it would be possible to keep in Lhasa a garrison, like that then at Gyantse, capable of holding its own for a whole winter. I added that if it was the case, as the military said, that troops could not be maintained in Lhasa during the winter, I had better not go to Lhasa at all, for there was little use in my commencing negotiations with two such obstructive people as the Tibetans and Chinese in any place where I could not stay a full year, if necessary. I had been eleven months trying even to begin negotiations. I should be quite unable to complete them in two or three months, especially if the Chinese and Tibetans knew we intended to leave before the winter.

The substance of this telegram I still think was perfectly sound, but its tone I do not now in cold blood seek to defend. I must confess that during all this Gyantse period I was not so steady and imperturbable as an agent should be. Perhaps the prolonged stay at very high altitudes was beginning to tell, for even Gyantse was over 13,000 feet. Perhaps it was the greater realization that nothing ever would be effected short of Lhasa, and that this playing about at Khamba Jong, at Tuna, and at Gyantse was merely for the benefit of the distant British elector. Or it may have been the difficulty of reconciling military with political considerations. Or possibly it was reading in the newspapers now arriving from England the accusations of cruelty, injustice, and oppression which were being publicly brought against the Mission, and the prophecies of disaster, such as befell Cavagnari, which were to come on us also. Whatever it was, I certainly became very restive, and now earned a rebuff from the Government of India, which only made me worse, and determined me to give up the whole business. It seemed so easy to carry through if we only went straight at it, so utterly impossible when in England they were only half-hearted. I see now that I ought to have gone stolidly and cheerily on, for Governments, too, have innumerable difficulties of their own. Still, this was not easy at the time.

It was tolerably certain a fortnight after my arrival at Gyantse that the Tibetans did not seriously mean to negotiate, and if we had to go to Lhasa, it was urgently necessary to make early preparations for an advance, so that another whole summer might not pass away without result. Yet I was undoubtedly premature in breathing the word Lhasa so early as the end of April. It was clear to me that if we wished to make a well-thought-out, complete, and lasting settlement with the Tibetans and the Chinese combined, and if we wished—

what I always regarded as much more important than any paper settlement, and as our real object in going to Tibet—the establishment of a good feeling between ourselves and the Tibetans, we must not only go to Lhasa, but be able to stay there for an ample period. Yet when I stated this opinion to Government, I should, I acknowledge, have given it in a less brusque way than I did in the telegram I have quoted.

I had this much in excuse. I had, as I have related, at dawn on the day I sent that telegram, and before having had my breakfast, been attacked by the Tibetans, and had myself to fight with a rifle in my hand. I had had, after breakfast, to ride nearly thirty miles with the constant risk of further attack on the way. I had had to do all this after being cooped up for a month in a house without being able to stir outside it. I had therefore to compose and cipher my telegram when I was physically exhausted and depressed in spirit. I knew that military considerations, and Imperial considerations, and international considerations, and every other consideration which hampers action, were dead against my proposal, and I was not in the mood to be respectful towards them. Still, I was ill-advised to let my telegram have the slightest tinge of brusqueness in it. If I wanted to get the thing done, I should have preserved that marvellous imperturbability and cheery good sense which, from the Strangers' Gallery, I have so frequently admired in British Ministers in the House of Commons. All this I note for the benefit of future leaders of unpopular Missions. For the effect of my telegram was not to further the object I had in view—the making of all preparations for keeping the Mission at Lhasa for the winter, if need be. It merely earned for me a reprimand from Government, who telegraphed back on June 14 that they found it necessary to remind me that any definite proposals I made for their consideration should be, as far as possible, in conformity with the orders and present policy of His Majesty's Government; and I was to remember that the policy of His Majesty's Government was based on considerations of international relations wider than the mere relations between India and Tibet, which were not only beyond my purview, but also beyond the purview of the Government of India. They expected me. therefore, to do my utmost to carry out the present plans until there was unquestionable proof that they were impracticable. It was impossible, I was told, to argue the political necessity for remaining at Lhasa during the winter until I had arrived there and gauged the situation; and the military objections were great and obvious.

My reply to this is not published, so I will not quote it. I will only say that I pretty well despaired of getting this business through. Lord Curzon was away in England, and evidently now military, and not political, considerations were having the upper hand. I knew about the "international relations" and the "wider view," for copies of all the important despatches to our Ambassadors were sent to me. But there were dozens and scores of men to represent those "wider" views, which need not, as is so often imagined, be wiser simply because they are wider, whereas there was only one person, and that was myself, to represent the narrower view, but which, because it was local, need not be inferior or less important.

The narrow local point of view was, then, that for thirty years continuously we in India had been trying to settle a trumpery affair of trade and boundary with a semi-barbarous people on our frontier, and time after time we had been put off by these "considerations of international relations wider than the mere relations between India and Tibet." But now we had the chance of a century of settling this business once and for all. We had, after years of negotiations and correspondence, made our effort. We had taken immense trouble and gone to great expense. And all I wished to do was to represent from my restricted point of view that I ought to have plenty of time to make the most of this opportunity. I should have represented my views in less provocative language, I admit; but the main contention was, I am sure, sound, and it would have been better now if it had been acted on. If I had not been rushed at Lhasa, but had had plenty of time to gauge and report the situation there, and to receive the orders of Government on any modifications which might be suggested by the circumstances, I should have been able to conclude with both the Chinese and Tibetans a treaty which my own Government as well as they would have accepted.

The Russian Government now began again to refer to Tibetan affairs. On April 13 Lord Lansdowne had assured the Russian Ambassador* that "nothing had happened to modify the objects with which we had originally determined to send Colonel Younghusband's Mission into Tibetan territory." And on June 2,† the Ambassador having on several occasions expressed a hope that our policy towards Tibet would not be altered by recent events, Lord Lansdowne informed him in writing that, in sanctioning the advance of the Mission to Gyantse, they announced to the Government of India that "they were clearly of opinion that this step should not be allowed to lead up to the occupation of Tibet, or to permanent intervention in Tibetan affairs. They stated that the advance was to be made for the sole purpose of obtaining satisfaction, and that as soon as reparation had been obtained, withdrawal would be effected. They added that they were not prepared to establish a permanent mission in Tibet, and that the question of enforcing trade facilities in that country was to be considered in the light of this decision." "I am now able to tell you," continued Lord Lansdowne, "that His Majesty's Government still adhere to the policy thus described, though it is obvious that their action must to some extent depend upon the conduct of the Tibetans themselves, and that His Majesty's Government cannot undertake that they will not depart in any eventuality from the policy which now commends itself to them. They desire, however, to state in the most emphatic terms that, so long as no other Power endeavours to intervene in the affairs of Tibet, they would not attempt either to annex it, to establish a protectorate over it, or in any way to control its internal administration."

This, in the sequel, was to be a clinching fetter on the

* Blue-book, III., p. 1.

† *Ibid.*, p. 15.

action of the Indian Government. They still wanted a representative at Lhasa; and in view of the determined hostility of the Tibetans, they wanted discretion to occupy the Chumbi Valley as a guarantee for the fulfilment of the treaty; and when the Russians had permanently stationed thousands of troops in Manchuria, had constructed railways, built forts, and established posts, where seventeen years before I had not seen a single Russian, and when they had Consular representatives all along their border in Chinese Turkestan and Mongolia, it was hard to see on what grounds they could have objected to the very mild measures which the Government of India desired to adopt. In any case, when the Tibetans had shown, not merely passive obstinacy, but downright hostility, and when, even though it might be the case that, in the words of Count Lamsdorff to Sir Charles Hardinge,* "the relations between Russia and Tibet were of a purely religious nature, due solely to the large number of Russian Buriats who regarded the Dalai Lama as their Pope," it was clear that the Tibetans relied on those merely religious relations as a support against us, the Government of India might have hoped that their hands would be freed to enable them to definitely settle up this intrinsically not very important Tibetan affair. But "wider international considerations" were, as so often happens in Indian affairs, to tell hardly against the Government of India. Since the Mission had started into Tibet war between Russia and Japan had broken out. Our relations with Russia were, consequently, at a very delicate stage. War was in the air, and statesmen had to be careful. For the sake of this insignificant business with Tibet, it would be hardly worth while endangering our relations with Russia, especially when her adhesion to our arrangement with France in regard to Egypt was required. Yet when we look at the map at the end of this book, and see how far the Russian frontier is from Tibet and to what a length our own actually touches it, and when we remember, too, that there was actually in Lhasa at this time a Russian subject who had been accustomed to go backwards and

* Blue-book, III., p. 20.

forwards between Lhasa and St. Petersburg, and served therefore all the purposes required of those religious relations which it was very natural should subsist between the Dalai Lama and Russian Buddhists, it does seem hard that the Government of India, now at the climax of all their efforts, should have been tied down through deference to the distant Power.

It is a remarkable coincidence, in this connection, that while the Russians were making protests and representations upon a move of ours which was not within a thousand miles of their frontier, the Chinese Vice-Minister, when Sir Ernest Satow informed him* that we intended to advance to Lhasa, received the news with perfect equanimity, raised no objection, and remarked that the Dalai Lama was ignorant and pigheaded.

I reached Chumbi on June 10, and spent the next few days in discussing details of the advance with General Macdonald. The change from the monotony of the investment at Gyantse and from the barrenness and high altitude of Tibet was refreshing in the extreme. I met old friends again: Colonel J. M. Stewart, who had years before relieved me when I had been arrested by the Russians on the Pamirs; Major Beynon, who had been Colonel Kelly's Staff Officer in the Relief of Chitral; and my brother-in-law, Vernon Magniac, who was to accompany me now as private secretary, and whose companionship was the greatest relief in the midst of a host of the usual official worries. The drop from 13,000 feet at Gyantse to 9,000 feet in Chumbi, and the change from constant risk to absolute security, all eased the tension on me; and the joy of being once more amidst luxuriant vegetation, with gorgeous rhododendrons, dense pine forests, roses, primulas, and all the wealth of Alpine flowery beauty, was a softening and welcome relaxation.

At Phari, on my way to Chumbi, I had met the Tongsa Penlop, now the Maharaja of Bhutan, who had recently come to interview General Macdonald and myself.

* Blue-book, III., p. 19.

Mr. Walsh, who had been in political charge of Chumbi, had interviewed him on June 3, and to him the Tongsa Penlop had admitted the unreasonableness and folly of the Tibetans, but argued that it was due to the bad advice of the Councillors, who had, in consequence, all been put in prison. He said, though, that nothing could be gained by our going to Lhasa, as the Dalai Lama and the Government would all leave before our arrival, and we should find no one there with whom to negotiate. He had written to the Dalai Lama, informing him of what I had told the Trimpuk Jongpen at Tuna we wanted, and the Dalai Lama had replied that the Sikkim boundary must be as it was, that no trade-mart could be established, and that no communication from the Indian Government could be received by the Tibetan Government. The Tongsa Penlop added that the rumour in Bhutan was that Mr. Walsh had been killed at Guru, that I had been killed at Gyantse, and that Russians had landed at Calcutta, defeated the English, and set up five banners.

This was a somewhat gloomy outlook; still, I was a good deal encouraged by my interview with the Tongsa Penlop. Mr. Walsh had been able to dispel many illusions, and at subsequent interviews the Tongsa Penlop had been a good deal impressed by General Macdonald and Mr. White, the latter of whom founded a friendship which has had most beneficial subsequent results.

The Tongsa Penlop I found to be a straight, honest-looking, dignified man of about forty-seven years of age. He bore himself well, dressed well, gave me costly presents, and altogether showed himself a man of importance and authority. He said he was most anxious to effect a settlement between us and the Tibetans. The latter had been very obstinate and wrong-headed, but the Dalai Lama was a young man, who needed good counsellors, and unfortunately there were bad men in Lhasa, who acted in his name to the detriment of the country. General Macdonald had told him that we were prepared to receive negotiators up to June 25, and he (the Tongsa Penlop) had, accordingly, written urgently to the Tibetans to send

THE TONGSA PENLOP (NOW MAHARAJA OF BHUTAN).

To face page 204.

a negotiator before that date. Would not I, therefore, show patience up to then?

I asked him whether he himself would be inclined to be patient if he had been attacked four times at night after waiting eleven months for negotiators to come. He admitted that he would not, and would feel more inclined to go about killing people; but he said I was the representative of a great Government, and ought to be more patient than he would be. I said I had named June 25 as the date up to which I would receive negotiators, but since then I had been again attacked at Kangma, and I could not answer for it that the Viceroy would still allow me to receive negotiators.

I said no Englishman liked killing villagers who were forced from their homes to fight us. We knew they did not want to fight, and we had no quarrel with them. But, unfortunately, it seemed impossible to get at the real instigators of the opposition to us except by fighting, in which the innocent peasant-soldiers, and not the authors of the trouble, suffered most. If these latter would only lead their men I would be better pleased, for then they would appreciate what opposition to the British Government really meant. The Tongsa Penlop was much amused at the suggestion, but said the leaders always remained a march behind when any fighting was likely to take place.

Continuing, I said that, though I had little hope that any settlement would be arrived at without fighting, yet, fighting or no fighting, I had to make a settlement some time, and one that would last another hundred years. If the Tibetans had only been as sensible as the Bhutanese, and come and talked matters over with me, we could easily have arrived at a settlement long ago. All we desired was to be on friendly and neighbourly terms with States like Bhutan and Tibet lying on our frontier. War, though it could have but one result, gave us much trouble, which we had no wish unnecessarily to incur. We, therefore, much preferred peace. I sent my respects to the Dharm Raja, and asked the Tongsa Penlop to write to me often and give me advice regarding the settlement with Tibet, and he fervently assured me of the good-will of the Bhutanese, and said that they would never depart from their friendship with the British Government.

In this interview I purposely appeared indifferent about receiving negotiators, for the less anxious I seemed for them to come the more likely was their arrival. As a fact, when, a fortnight later, there really were signs of their appearance, I asked Government to agree, which they readily did, to grant a few days' grace beyond the 25th to allow them to come in.

Besides this friendly support from Bhutan on our right, we had also further evidence at this time of equally friendly, and much more valuable, support from Nepal on our left. The Nepalese Minister informed Colonel Ravenshaw that he had received a letter and some presents from the Dalai Lama, but that he made no allusion to our Mission, which omission led the Minister to think that the Dalai Lama was kept in ignorance of what was going on. And this surmise was, I think, perfectly correct, and represented one of the great difficulties with which we had to contend. No one dared inform this little god that things were not going as he would like them, and yet they had to get orders from him, for they would do nothing without his orders.

The Nepalese Minister, to remove this difficulty, wrote early in June to the Dalai Lama, expressing his anxiety at "the breach of relations [between India and Tibet] which had been brought about by the failure of the Tibetan Government to have the matters in dispute settled by friendly negotiation." He referred to the letter which he had written to the four Councillors in the previous autumn, and he went on: "Wise and far-seeing as you are, the vast resources of the British Government must be well known to you. To rush to extremes with such a big Power, and wantonly to bring calamities upon your poor subjects without having strong and valid grounds of your own to insist upon, cannot readily be accepted as a virtuous course or wise policy. Hence it may fairly be inferred that the detailed circumstances of the pending questions have not been properly and correctly represented to you." The Minister then urged the Dalai Lama at once to send a duly authorized Councillor to meet the British officers, to desist from fighting with the British Government, and to try his best to bring about a peaceful settlement; otherwise he saw clearly that great calamities were in store for Tibet. He concluded by saying that His Holiness was too sacred to be troubled with mundane affairs, but the present critical condition in Tibet demanded his utmost foresight, and on him depended the salvation of his country.

It is melancholy to think that the Dalai Lama paid no heed to this well-intentioned advice, and then, when calamities had fallen upon his country and we were just outside Lhasa, fled on the pretext of retiring into religious seclusion, and left his country to take care of itself.

CHAPTER XIV

THE STORMING OF GYANTSE JONG

STRONG reinforcements had now come up from India: the remainder of the mountain battery, under Major Fuller, a wing of the Royal Fusiliers, the 40th Pathans, and the 29th Punjabis; and on June 13 I set out to return to Gyantse with General Macdonald to relieve the Mission escort at Gyantse and, if need be, to advance to Lhasa, while Colonel Reid remained in charge of the communications.

At each post we stopped at the officers in charge invariably reported that the people were well content with us on account of our liberal treatment. The villagers themselves were thoroughly friendly. They were making money by selling their produce at rates very favourable to themselves. They were only afraid of the officials and Lamas. Captain Rawling, who had explored in Western Tibet in the previous year, and was well acquainted with the Tibetans, and who was now stationed at Phari in charge of a transport corps, specially remarked this. What the people were now afraid of was not our stopping, but our withdrawing, and leaving them to the vengeance of the Lamas.

This is a dilemma in which we are constantly being placed on the Indian frontier. The people of a country into which we advance are often ready to be friendly with us if they could be certain we would stay and be able to support them afterwards. But if they know we are going to withdraw they naturally fight shy, for those who show us friendship would get into trouble when we left. This is one of the many reasons which make me favour our keeping up a strong continuous influence when once we have been compelled to advance into a semi-civilized or barbarous country. It is often highly inconvenient to have to do this, but it is the most humane course, and I am not sure that it would be so inconvenient if it were followed consistently. It need not mean annexation or petty interference, but it must mean sufficient influence to prevent relapses to barbarism.

We reached Kangma without incident on June 22, and halted a day while Colonel Hogge was sent to disperse a body of 1,000 Tibetans who were holding a sangared position on the road which runs down here from the Karo-la. While halted I received a telegram from the Tongsa Penlop at Phari to say that a big Lama and one of the Councillors were coming to Gyantse, and that a parcel of silk had arrived for me. The Penlop also said he wished to come himself to see me at Gyantse. Thinking this might indicate anxiety of the Tibetans to come to terms at last—at literally the eleventh hour, for there were only two days left up to the expiry of the time beyond which I had signified that I would no longer be able to negotiate at Gyantse—I telegraphed to Government, recommending that a period of five days' grace, up to June 30, should be given to them. Government replied, on June 24, that the advance to Lhasa might certainly be deferred for that purpose, and I so informed the Tongsa Penlop.

On June 26 we reached Gyantse, after encountering considerable opposition at the village and monastery of Niani, which was held by 800 Tibetans. The fight lasted from 10 a.m. till 2 p.m., Colonel Brander from Gyantse assisting by occupying the hills above the village. Major Lye, 23rd Pioneers, was here severely wounded in the hand and slightly in the head. On its arrival our force was ineffectually bombarded from the jong.

General Macdonald had now to break up the Tibetan force investing Gyantse. On the 28th he attacked a strong position on a ridge on which were the Tse-chen monastery and several fortified towers and sangars. The process of clearing the villages in the plain below lasted most of the day. At 5.30 the position itself was stormed by the 8th Gurkhas and the 40th Pathans, supported by the mountain battery. The fight was severe, for the hillside was very steep. Captain Craster, 46th Pathans, was killed whilst gallantly leading his company, and Captains Bliss and Humphreys slightly wounded. The capture of this position much disheartened the Tibetans; communications between Gyantse Jong and Shigatse were cut off, and the jong was now surrounded on three sides.

Hearing that the big Lama from Lhasa, known as the Ta Lama, was at Shigatse, and that the Councillor was at Nagartse, on the road to Lhasa, I made a Lama in our employ write to these two on June 28, saying that the Tongsa Penlop had told me that they wished to come here to settle matters, but were afraid. I promised them, if they had proper credentials to effect a settlement, to guarantee their safety and treat them with respect; but I said they must come at once, for we were about to start for Lhasa. These letters I sent by the hands of prisoners.

One of these messengers was seized by the Tibetans and brought to the jong, where a council was held to consider its contents, as a result of which, on the following morning, a messenger with a flag of truce of enormous dimensions was sent to the Mission post. The whole garrison crowded to the walls to see his arrival, for this was the first indication of peace. He said the Tibetan leaders desired an armistice till the Ta Lama, who was at Penam, halfway to Shigatse, and who could be at Gyantse on the following day, could arrive to negotiate with me. The messenger said that he and the Councillor coming from Nagartse had powers from the Dalai Lama to treat.

After consultation with General Macdonald, I replied to the Tibetans that I would grant the armistice they asked for till sunset of June 30, to enable the Ta Lama to reach Gyantse; but that as I was attacked on May 5 without warning, though I had informed the Tibetan Government that I was ready to negotiate there, and as Tibetan armed forces had occupied the jong and fired into my camp ever since, General Macdonald, who was responsible for the safety of the Mission, demanded that they should evacuate the jong and withdraw all armed force beyond

Karo-la, Yang-la, and Dongtse. A reasonable time for this would be given.

By June 30 neither of the Tibetan delegates had arrived, but both the Tongsa Penlop and the Ta Lama were to arrive the next day, and we allowed the armistice to extend informally till they arrived. The Tongsa Penlop arrived first, though he had had twice the distance to travel, and at once came to see me, and showed me a letter he had received from the Dalai Lama, saying he had heard we had appointed a date up to which we would negotiate, and after which we would fight; but as fighting was bad for men and animals, he asked the Tongsa Penlop to assist in making a peaceful settlement, and he was appointing the Ta Lama, who was a Councillor, the Grand Secretary, and representative of the three great monasteries, to negotiate. The Tongsa Penlop also produced a packet of silks, which he said the Dalai Lama had sent me.

About three in the afternoon the Ta Lama arrived in Gyantse, and as he was already a day later than the date of the armistice, and six days over the date of the original ultimatum, I sent a message to say I should be glad to see him that afternoon. He replied that he proposed to visit the Tongsa Penlop on the following day, and would come and see me some time after that. I returned a message to the effect that unless he visited me by nine on the following morning military operations would be resumed.

Undisturbed by this threat, he shortly after nine on the following morning proceeded to visit the Tongsa Penlop; but as he had to pass my camp, I sent out Captain O'Connor to say that I insisted on his coming to pay his respects to me, unless he wished me to consider he was not anxious to negotiate. He was at perfect liberty to discuss matters with the Tongsa Penlop, but he must no longer delay paying his respects to me, and giving me evidence that the Tibetan Government were sincere in their wish to negotiate.

At eleven I received the Ta Lama and the Tongsa Penlop in Durbar. There were also present the Tung-yig-Chembo (the Grand Secretary, who was one of the delegates at Khamba Jong last year), and six representatives of the three great Lhasa monasteries. As all except the Grand Secretary were men who had not met me before, and were probably ignorant of our view of the situation, I recounted it at length, showing how we had lived on very good terms with Tibet for nearly a century and a half, and it was only after the Tibetans had wantonly invaded Sikkim territory in 1886 that misunderstanding had arisen: that Mr. White had for years tried at Yatung to make them observe the treaty made on their behalf by the Chinese; and that when I came to Khamba Jong, a place of meeting which the Viceroy had been informed was approved of both by the Emperor of China and the Dalai Lama, they still repudiated the old treaty, refused to negotiate a new one, or have any intercourse at all with us; while after my arrival at Gyantse, when I told them I was ready to negotiate, instead of sending me negotiators, they sent soldiers and treacherously attacked me at night. I concluded by saying that the Viceroy, on hearing this, had directed me to write letters to the Dalai Lama and the Amban, announcing that if proper negotiators did not arrive here by June 25 we would advance to Lhasa to compel negotiations there; but these letters had been returned by the commander in the jong, no negotiators had arrived by the 25th, and it was only because on the 24th the Tongsa Penlop had informed me that negotiators really were on the way that the British Government, in their anxiety for a peaceful settlement, had been pleased to grant them a few days' grace. We were ready to go on to Lhasa the next day. If they were really in earnest and had power to make a settlement, I was prepared to negotiate with them. If they were not empowered to make a settlement, we would advance to Lhasa forthwith. Had they proper credentials?

The Grand Secretary replied, on behalf of the Ta Lama, that we had come by force into the country, and occupied Chumbi and Phari, and though the Tibetan soldiers at Guru had strict orders not to fire on us, we had fired on them and had killed all the high officials. He said they did not know I was here when this camp was attacked on May 5; but they now had orders to negotiate with me. They had no special credentials, but the Dalai Lama, in his letter to the Tongsa Penlop, had mentioned that they were coming to negotiate, and the fact of a man in the Ta Lama's high position being here was evidence of their intentions.

I replied that I did not wish to discuss the past except to make clear one point. They were not at the Guru fight, but I was, and I saw the first shot fired by the Tibetans after General Macdonald had purposely restrained his men from firing. But what concerned me was the future. If they made a settlement with me now, would it be observed, or would it be repudiated like the last one? They at first replied that this would depend upon what was in the settlement, but subsequently explained that, though they might have to refer to Lhasa for orders, yet, when once the Dalai Lama had placed his seal on a treaty, it would be scrupulously observed. They said they wished to talk matters over with the Tongsa Penlop, who would act as mediator and arrange matters with me. I informed them that I would be very glad if they could discuss the situation with him, and I was quite willing that he should accompany them when they came to see me, but they themselves must come to me if they desired that negotiations should take place. They said they would have a talk with him the next day, and come and see me the day after. I told them, however, that they must have their talk before noon on the following day, and come and see me again at that hour, as I was not yet satisfied of the earnestness of their intentions.

The same afternoon they had a prolonged interview with the Tongsa Penlop, who asked them what they had gained by their silly attitude of obstruction, and advised them to give up fighting and make terms with us. The Tongsa Penlop informed me he thought the delegates, or certainly the Dalai Lama, were really anxious to make a settlement.

On July 3 the Tongsa Penlop arrived half an hour before the time fixed for the reception of the delegates. At noon I took my seat in the Durbar, which was attended by General Macdonald and many military officers, while a strong guard of honour lined the approach. I waited for half an hour, but as at the end of that time the Tibetan delegates had not arrived, I rose and dismissed the Durbar.

At 1.30 the Tibetans appeared; but as the dilatoriness they had shown in coming to Gyantse and after their arrival in coming to see me was a pretty clear indication that they had not even yet realized how serious the situation was, I saw that I should have to do something yet to impress them with its gravity. The Tongsa Penlop was able to come from much farther and reach Gyantse before them. He had come to see me at once on arrival, while they had delayed till the next day; he had come half an hour before the time fixed for the Durbar, while they had come an hour and a half late. All this indicated that, while they were still so casual and indifferent, no negotiation that I could enter into with them would produce the smallest result. They had yet to be shown that we were not to be trifled with any longer. So on their arrival I had them shown into a spare tent, and informed that I had waited for them in Durbar for half an hour; that as they had not arrived by then, I had dismissed the Durbar, and would not now be at leisure to receive them for another two or three hours.

By four o'clock the Durbar was again assembled, with General Macdonald and his officers, all my staff, and a guard of honour. Captain O'Connor then led in the Tibetan delegates, and showed them to their places on my right; but I made no signs of receiving them, and remained perfectly silent, awaiting an apology. They moved about uncomfortably during this deadening silence, and at last the Ta Lama, who was really a very kindly, though perfectly incapable, old gentleman, and absolutely in the hands of the more capable but evil-minded Chief Secretary, murmured out a full apology. I informed them that the inference I drew from the disrespect they had shown me in arriving an hour and a half late was that they were not in earnest in desiring a settlement. The Ta Lama assured me that they were really in earnest, but that the Grand Secretary was ill. I then informed them that, as I had been attacked at Gyantse without any warning, and after I had written repeatedly to the Amban saying I was waiting there to negotiate, and as I had been fired on from the jong continually for two months since the attack, I must press for its evacuation. General Macdonald was prepared to give them till noon of the 5th—that is, nearly two days—in which to effect the evacuation; but if after that time the jong was occupied, he would commence military operations against it. Irrespective of these operations, I would, however, be ready to receive them if they wished to make a settlement, and prevent the necessity of our proceeding to Lhasa.

The Grand Secretary then said that if the Tibetan troops withdrew from the jong, they would expect that we also would withdraw our troops; otherwise the Tibetans would be suspicious. I replied that the Tibetans did not at all seem to realize that they would have to pay a penalty for the attack they had made on the Mission, and that I could not discuss the matter further. They must either leave the jong peaceably before noon on the 5th, or expect to be then turned out by force. On leaving, the Ta Lama very politely and respectfully expressed his regrets for having kept me waiting, and begged that I would not be angry. But the Grand Secretary went away without a word of apology. He was the evil genius of the Tibetans throughout this affair.

The following morning the delegates had a long interview with the Tongsa Penlop, and asked whether time could not be given them to refer to Lhasa for orders. I sent back a message saying that it was already nearly a week since I had let the Ta Lama know that the evacuation of the jong would be demanded, that they ought to be grateful for the opportunity that had been given them of withdrawing unmolested, and that no further grace could be allowed.

The Tongsa Penlop also informed me that they were very suspicious, and wanted an assurance that we really wished a settlement. I told him he might inform them that the best evidence that we desired a settlement was the fact that the control of affairs was in my hands. If we had intended war the control would have been in the hands of a General.

The delegates and the commanders in the jong were still undecided. No one would take the responsibility of evacuating the jong. On the morning of the 5th the Tongsa Penlop with some Lhasa Lamas came to see me, and I sent one of the latter over to the delegates, saying that at twelve a signal gun would be fired to warn them that half an hour afterwards firing would commence. I told them that if they came over either before or after with a flag of truce they would be given an asylum in the Tongsa Penlop's camp. I begged that the women and children should be taken out of the town; and I sent a special warning to General Ma, the local Chinese official. No notice was taken of any of these warnings. At twelve I had a signal gun fired, and at 12.30 I heliographed to General Macdonald that he was free to commence firing.

The Tongsa Penlop had stayed with me on the ramparts of our post up till noon, and I asked him to remain and see the fight. But he said he would prefer to see it from a little farther off, and I dare say he did not yet feel quite certain that we should win. For it was a tough task that lay before General Macdonald. We were right in the heart of Tibet, with all the strength that the Lamas, with a full year of effort, could put forth. The fortress to be attacked from our little post in the plain looked impregnable. It was built of solid masonry on a precipitous rock rising sheer out of the plain. It was held by at least double, and possibly treble, our own force, and they were armed, many hundreds of them, with Lhasa-made rifles, which carried over a thousand yards. In addition, there were several guns mounted. No wonder the Tongsa Penlop thought it best to be a little distance off, and not too decidedly identified with either side.

General Macdonald probably never would have been able to take the jong if his guns had not just been supplied, on the recommendation of General Parsons, the Inspector-General of Artillery, with "common" shell as well as the shrapnel, which was all that up till now they had carried

GYANTSE JONG.

To face page 216.

with them. Shrapnel is of use only against troops. Common shell is more solid, and can be used against masonry, and against the jong it proved tremendously effective when fired by the accurate and hard-hitting little 10-pounders.

At 1.45 p.m. on July 5 General Macdonald began his operations by renewing the rifle fire on the jong. Then, at 3.30 p.m., two guns, six companies of infantry, and one company of mounted infantry, were sent to make a feint on the monastery side of the jong. This succeeded in inducing the Tibetans to reinforce largely that side of their defences. But after dark this column was withdrawn, and shortly after midnight a force of twelve guns, twelve companies of infantry, one company of mounted infantry, and half a company of sappers moved out in two columns to take up a position south-east of Gyantse.

We in the Mission post naturally spent the night on the ramparts awaiting events. It was 3.30 a.m. by the time the columns had taken up their position. Dawn had not yet appeared. All was still and quiet. The stars shone out in all the brilliance of these high altitudes, and nothing could be more serene and peaceful than this clear summer night. Suddenly a few sharp rifle cracks spat out, telling us that the enemy had seen our assaulting columns. Then the dull, heavy thud of an explosion showed that some doorway had been blown open. And after that came the full blaze of the fight, the whole jong lighting up with the flashes of rifle and jingal fire, and down below our own fire getting hotter and hotter.

As day dawned we could see that we had gained a footing in the town which was the immediate object of General Macdonald's attack previous to the assault on the jong itself. What had happened was this: The Tibetans had opened an unexpectedly heavy fire before the assaulting columns could get close up under the walls of the outlying parts of the town, and our three columns were reorganized into two—that on the right under Colonel Campbell, of the 40th Pathans, a tried and experienced frontier officer, and that on the left under Major Murray, 8th Gurkhas. With Colonel Campbell was Captain

Sheppard, R.E., who, with that dash and effectiveness which always characterized him, succeeded in laying and firing a charge under the walls of the most strongly held house, and blowing in it a breach, which, with the damage done by the fire of the 7-pounder gun, gave an opening for the assaulting column. On the left Lieutenants Gurdon and Burney also succeeded in blowing breaches in the walls of the houses; but, to the grief of all, Gurdon was killed—it is believed by the falling débris of the very wall which he had blown up. He had been with the Mission escort from the very first, and in many of these very dangerous assaults on villages had displayed most daring courage. He was a brother of the Captain (now Lieutenant-Colonel) Gurdon who had so distinguished himself in the Siege of Chitral, and who was one of my closest friends. When the news came in to me from the front, I felt how sad indeed it was that one so young and so full of promise, with a great and useful career most certainly before him, should have been thus in an instant cut off. But he did not fall in vain, for what he had done at the cost of his life enabled the assaulting columns to enter the town, which by 7 a.m. was in our possession.

The troops began to make good their position in the area thus won, but the real business had yet to be accomplished. The jong, with 5,000 or 6,000 Tibetans inside it, still had to be assaulted. During the morning there was a general lull in the proceedings while the troops rested. But about two o'clock Colonel Campbell, who was in command of all the advanced troops in the town, sent back word to General Macdonald, who was in the Palla village, recommending that an assault should be made on the extreme east of the jong. To him in his advanced position, immediately under the walls of the jong, it appeared that if our guns could make a breach in the wall itself an assault could be made, though the storming party would have a stiff, hazardous climb over the steepest part of the rock. General Macdonald adopted the proposal, and as the Tibetans now appeared somewhat exhausted, ordered the assault to be made at once.

At three o'clock General Macdonald ordered forward

four companies of the reserve, and directed the 10-pounder guns to concentrate their fire on the portion of the wall to be breached for the assault. As the reinforcements crossed the open to the town the Tibetans redoubled their fire, but our fire from all parts of the field also increased. The 10-pounder battery under Major Fuller did magnificent work. Stationed only 1,000 yards from the point to be breached, it placed one shell after another in exactly the same spot. Bit by bit the wall came tumbling down. A larger and larger gap appeared, and by four a breach sufficiently large for an assault had been made.

Then the heliograph flashed from post to post that the jong was now to be assaulted. Major Fuller immediately gave the order for "Rapid firing" on the upper buildings. Maxims from three different directions began rattling away with peremptory emphasis. Every man poured in his rifle fire with increasing energy. Then a little cluster of black figures, ever augmenting in numbers, was seen, like a swarm of ants, slowly making its way up the nearly precipitous rock towards the breach. A cheer was raised, which was taken up from post to post all round our encircling force and back to the reserves in the rear. The Tibetans could still be seen firing away in the breach and hurling down stones, but we only redoubled our fire upon them.

Very, very gradually—or so it seemed to us in our suspense below—the Gurkhas, under Lieutenant Grant, made their upward way. First a few arrived just under the breach, then more and more. Then came the crisis, and Grant was seen leading his men straight for the opening. Instantly our bugles all over the field rang out the "Cease fire," so as not to endanger our storming party. The Tibetans, too, now stopped firing; and where a moment before there had been a deafening din there was now an aching silence. We held our breath, and in tense excitement awaited the result of the assault. We saw the little Gurkhas and the Royal Fusiliers, who formed the storming party, stream through the breach. Then we watched them working up from building to building. Tier after tier of the fortifications was crowned, and at last our men were seen placing the Union Jack on the highest pinnacle of the jong. The Tibetans had fled precipitately, and Gyantse was ours.

The Tongsa Penlop next morning came over to congratulate General Macdonald and myself; and we went over the jong together. Till I had got up there and looked down through the Tibetan loopholes on our insignificant Mission post below, I had not realized how certain the Tibetans must have felt that they could overwhelm us, and how impossible it must have seemed that we could ever turn the tables upon them. If one stood in the Round Tower of Windsor Castle and looked down from there upon a house and garden in the fields about Eton, held by some strangers who said they had come to make a treaty, one would get the best idea of what must have been in the Tibetans' minds. They were in a lofty and seemingly impregnable fortress in the heart of their own country. We were a little dot in the plain below. The idea of making a treaty with us, if they did not want to, must have appeared ridiculous. And as I stood there in their position and looked down upon what had till just then been my own, I soon understood how it was that the Ta Lama and other delegates had been so casual in their behaviour.

Yet, in spite of our success, and to a certain extent by reason of it, I was still ready to negotiate with Tibetan delegates. I had disliked, with an intensity which only those can know who have been in a similar position, the idea of making any mention of negotiation during all that critical time in May, while they were firing proudly at us from the jong, and were surrounding me in my little post below. Now that, through General Macdonald's skilful dispositions and the bravery of his troops, I was in the top place, I readily tried to negotiate. And I thought that His Majesty's Government were anxious that further efforts to negotiate here should be made; for on June 25 they had telegraphed that if there was reasonable expectation of the early arrival of the Resident, accompanied by competent Tibetan negotiators, the advance to Lhasa might be postponed. They thought that the advance should not be undertaken unless there was adequate ground for doubting the competency of the Tibetan delegates or the earnestness of the Tibetan Government. Moreover, some few days' delay was necessary for General Macdonald to complete his arrangements for the advance, to collect sufficient supplies, and to establish Gyantse as his secondary base.

I therefore, immediately the jong was captured, asked the Tongsa Penlop to send messengers to tell the Ta Lama and the Councillor at Nagartse that I was still ready to negotiate, as previously announced, but that they must come in at once, as otherwise we would proceed to Lhasa. But the messenger found the monastery in which they had been staying deserted and the delegates fled.

On July 9 the Government of India telegraphed to me that they considered the advance to Lhasa inevitable, but that if the delegates could be induced to come in and negotiate *en route* I might invite them to accompany me, explaining the terms of His Majesty's Government, and warning them that any further resistance would involve a settlement less favourable to Tibet.

By July 13 General Macdonald's preparations were all complete. He had reconnoitred the country both up and down the valley, and found the Tibetans had fled in every direction. He had amassed plentiful supplies. He had set about repairing the jong, in which he was, to my infinite regret, to leave Colonel Hogge, and the 23rd Pioneers, and he was ready to leave for Lhasa the next day. It was sad that the old Pioneers, who had borne the burden and the cold of the day at Tuna all through that dreary and anxious winter should be left behind, while other regiments who had but just arrived from India should have the glory of going to Lhasa, and I would willingly have had it otherwise.

All were now eager and ready for the advance, and I wrote to the Chinese Resident, that as neither he nor any competent Tibetan negotiator had come to Gyantse I was proceeding to Lhasa. I stated that my purpose was still to negotiate, but that I must ask him to prevent the Tibetans from further opposing my Mission, and I intimated that the terms I was demanding would be still more severe if we encountered opposition.

The Tongsa Penlop also, at my request, wrote to the Ta Lama, saying that I was prepared to carry on negotiations *en route*, in order that the settlement might be ready for signature at an early date at Lhasa. And I asked the Tongsa Penlop, further, to write to the Dalai Lama himself, giving an outline of the terms we should demand.

Lastly, I issued a proclamation, drafted by the Government of India, stating that we had no desire to fight with the people of Tibet or to interfere with their liberties or religion, but that it was necessary to impress unmistakably upon the Government of Tibet that they could not with impunity offer insults to the British Government, and that they must realize the obligations they had entered into and act up to them in all respects. The people were warned that any opposition to our advance would only result in making the terms demanded more exacting.

CHAPTER XV

THE ADVANCE TO LHASA

Just a year had now elapsed since we had arrived at Khamba Jong, and now at length all were united in the single purpose of advancing to Lhasa — the Imperial Government, the Indian Government, and the military authorities. A year had been wasted in futile forbearance for the benefit of the British public, but at length what the responsible Government of India had advocated since January of the previous year was to be carried into effect, and on July 14 we left our dreary little post at Gyantse and set out, full of enthusiasm, for Lhasa.

Though we were so high above sea-level, it was quite hot now in the middle of the day, for the sun in these low latitudes and in this clear atmosphere struck down with considerable force. But we also had some very heavy rain in the next few days.

As we approached the Karo-la (pass), the scene of Colonel Brander's gallant little action, I received a letter from the Tongsa Penlop at Gyantse, enclosing a letter he had received from the Dalai Lama. It said:

"We have written to the Yutok Sha-pé, inquiring from him whether it will be easy to effect a settlement or not. Will you also request the English privately not to nibble up our country? Please use your influence well both with the English and the Tibetans. I cannot at present speak with exactness with regard to the frontier, but I have said something on the matter to the Pukong Tulku, so it will be well if the negotiations are begun quickly. Once they have begun, we shall hear gradually who is in the right."

On the next day, July 17, we marched to a camp

immediately below the Karo-la, and there we found the Bhutanese messenger who had carried a letter from the Tongsa Penlop to the Yutok Sha-pé's camp had returned, saying that some Tibetan officials would come over presently to see us. The Tibetans, however, fired at our mounted infantry from the wall on the far side of the pass, and no officials appeared.

This looked as if we were to have another fight. Before we left Gyantse we had heard that the pass was occupied by 2,000 Tibetans, and that there were 2,000 more in support, and the mounted infantry now reported the pass to be strongly held and fresh walls and sangars to have been built. All the villages *en route*, too, had been deserted, so we fully expected a fight.

Our camp under the pass was right in among a lofty knot of mountains, one of which rose to a height of over 24,000 feet above sea-level. A magnificent glacier descended a side valley to within 500 yards of the camp. The whole scene was desolate in the highest degree. And though we were on the highroad to Lhasa, the road was nothing but the roughest little mountain pathway rubbed out by the traffic of mules and men across it.

The afternoon and evening of the 17th were occupied in reconnoitring the position of the Tibetans. They were very strongly posted at a narrow gorge three miles from our camp on the north side of the pass, and their position was flanked by impassable snow mountains. The old wall of Colonel Brander's time had been extended on either hand till it touched precipices immediately under the snow-line. Behind this lay a second barrier of sangars. Like all the walls which the Tibetans so skilfully erected at such places, this was built up of heavy stones. The position was manned, according to our latest information, by about 1,500 Tibetans.

At 7 a.m. on the morning of the 18th, when now, even in the height of summer, there was still a nip of frost in the air, the advance troops marched off. The Royal Fusiliers, under Colonel Cooper, were to attack the centre, and on either side parties of the 8th Gurkhas were to turn the flanks.

CAMP NEAR KARO-LA.

To face page 224.

While the Gurkhas were slowly plodding up the mountain-sides, I seated myself beside Major Fuller's mountain battery, and watched the effects of gun-fire at these altitudes. It was most interesting. The pass itself was 16,600 feet, and the battery was a few hundred feet above it, and was for some time firing at groups 5,000 yards away, and some of them on the glacier at about 18,000 feet above the sea. In such a rare atmosphere ordinary sighting and ordinary fuses were quite useless. The shells would cleave through the thin air at very considerably greater velocity than they would pass through the thicker air at sea-level. All the sighting and the timing of the fuses had, therefore, to be completely readjusted by trial and guesswork. Despite this, however, wonderfully accurate shooting was effected by these splendid little guns, and it would have made all the difference to Colonel Brander if he had had them instead of the useless 7-pounders.

The Gurkhas and Pathans, after a long and difficult climb to 18,000 feet, turned the position, but the Tibetans in the centre had not waited. They knew that the dreaded mounted infantry would be after them, so each determined that he, at any rate, would not be the last to leave the position, and all had cleared off before our troops arrived. Most, indeed, had retreated in the night, and in reality only about 700 Kham men were left to hold the position. Many of these escaped high up over the snows, pursued only by our shrapnel shells. Our mounted infantry reconnoitred up to within two miles of Nagartse Jong, which was found to be occupied, while reports came in that 1,300 more men from Kham were expected.

Nagartse was reached on the 19th, and close to it I was met by a deputation from Lhasa. Here were signs of negotiations at last. I said I would have a full interview at three that afternoon, but must warn them at once that it would be necessary for me to occupy the jong, and to advance to Lhasa, though I was ready to negotiate on the way. The deputation, which consisted of the Yutok Sha-pé, the Ta Lama, the Chief Secretary, and some monks, arrived in my camp shortly before the time appointed.

The Yutok Sha-pé took the chief place. He was a genial, gentlemanly official of good family and pleasant manners. But it soon became apparent that both he and the Ta Lama were in the hands of the Chief Secretary, the monk official who, from our first meeting at Khamba Jong, had ever been an obstacle in our way. This latter official, acting as spokesman, said they had heard from the Tongsa Penlop that we wished to negotiate at Gyantse, and they had set out to meet us when they heard that we were advancing. They were quite willing to negotiate if we returned to Gyantse, and in that case they would accompany us and make a proper settlement with us there.

I repeated for the fiftieth time that I had waited for more than a year to negotiate; that even at Gyantse I had given them many opportunities; that when I had first arrived there I had announced my desire to negotiate; that after the attack upon me I had still declared my willingness to negotiate up to June 25; that on the intercession of the Tongsa Penlop the Viceroy had extended that term for some days; that even after the capture of the jong I had sent messengers over the country to find them, and waited for another week at Gyantse; but that eventually the patience of the Viceroy had become completely exhausted, and His Excellency had ordered me to advance to Lhasa forthwith, as he had reluctantly become convinced that only there could a settlement be made. We were now advancing to Lhasa. I would be quite ready to negotiate with them on the way, and if the Tibetan troops did not oppose us we would not fight against them; but as our troops had on the previous day been fired at from the jong, we must send our troops in to occupy it. We would, however, allow the delegates to remain unmolested, and would see that their property was not disturbed, and that they themselves were accorded proper marks of respect.

The delegates replied that if we went on to Lhasa there was no chance of a settlement being arrived at; that they had come here with the sincere intention of making friendship with us and securing peace, but if we sent troops into the jong they did not see how they could be friends with us; they were the two biggest men in Tibet next to the Dalai Lama, and it was both against their religion and disgusting to them to have soldiers in the same place where they were staying. I said they must, after all, allow that this could not be half so disgusting to them as having their soldiers firing into my camp at Gyantse, while I was asleep, was to me. They continued one after another wrangling and protesting against our occupying the jong. After listening for an hour to their protests, I asked them if they would now care to hear the terms we intended to ask of them. They replied that they could not discuss any terms till we returned to Gyantse. I said I had no wish now to discuss the terms, but merely desired to know if they wanted to be acquainted with them. They continued to protest that they would discuss nothing here, and it was only after considerable fencing that I got them to admit that they had heard the terms from the Tongsa Penlop.

I then said that I wished them to understand that if we were further opposed on the way to Lhasa, or at Lhasa itself, these terms would be made stricter. I said the British Government had no wish to be on any other than friendly terms with Tibet, that we had no intention of remaining in Lhasa any longer than was required to make a settlement, and as soon as a settlement was made we would leave. But I had the Viceroy's orders to go to Lhasa, and go there I must. I desired, however, to give them most earnest advice and warning. They were the leading men of Tibet, and upon them lay a great responsibility. I was quite prepared on arrival at Lhasa to live on as friendly and peaceable terms with the people as I had at Khamba Jong, and as I had when I first arrived at Gyantse; to pay for everything, and to respect their religious buildings. It rested with them now to decide whether our stay at Lhasa should be of this peaceable nature and of short duration, and whether the settlement should be of the mild nature we at present contemplated, or whether we should have to resort to force, as we had been compelled to do at Gyantse, to impose severer terms, and to prolong our stay.

The delegates listened attentively while I made this exhortation to them, but, after consulting together, replied that even if we did make a settlement at Lhasa, it would be of no use, for in Tibet everything depended on religion, and by the mere fact of our going to Lhasa we should spoil their religion, as no men of other religions were allowed in Lhasa. I asked them if there were no Mohammedans living in Lhasa, and they replied that there were a few, but they were not allowed to practise their religious rites—a sad admission in view of the toleration which the Buddhist religion in reality enjoins. I added that we would not have gone to Lhasa unless we had been absolutely compelled to by their incivility in not meeting us elsewhere; that personally I had already suffered great inconvenience, and would much prefer not to have the further inconvenience of going to Lhasa; but no other resource was now left to us, and my orders from the Viceroy were final.

The Yutok Sha-pé throughout was calm and polite, and at his departure was cordial in his manner. The Ta Lama, though more excited, was not ill-mannered. The Chief Secretary was very much excited throughout, and argumentative and querulous. The whole tone of the delegates showed that they—or, at any rate, the Dalai Lama—had not even yet realized the seriousness of the position. The tone they adopted entirely ignored their serious breaches of international courtesy, and was that of people with a grievance against us and quite ignorant of the fact that we had grievances against them; they were, too, excessively unbusinesslike and impracticable, and I anticipated an infinity of trouble in carrying through a settlement with such men. On the other hand, the disposition and manners of the Yutok Sha-pé gave one more confirmation of the impression I had long formed that the laymen of Tibet were by no means inimical, and that but for the opposition of the monks we might be on extremely friendly terms with them.

Under General Macdonald's well-thought-out arrangements the occupation of the jong was effected without any mishap or loss of life. Captain O'Connor accompanied the delegates back towards the jong, which, however, they did not again enter, but took up their quarters in the village, while their followers and baggage were sent down to them there. I expressed my regret to the Yutok Sha-pé that at our first meeting I should have had to put him to such inconvenience. But the occupation of the jong was a military necessity. It was a matter of congratulation that it should have been effected without the loss of life on either side.

The following day the Tibetan delegates held another prolonged interview with me, lasting three and a half hours. They made no further mention of the occupation of the jong, but were very insistent that we should not advance to Lhasa. The Yutok Sha-pé was the chief spokesman at first, but during the course of the interview each one repeated separately much the same arguments. They said that in Lhasa there were a great number of monks and many unruly characters, and disturbances might easily arise; to which I replied that I should much regret any such disturbances, and hoped the delegates would do their best to prevent them, for the result could only be the same as the result of the disturbances at Gyantse.

Another argument the delegates used was that, if we went to Lhasa, we should probably find no one there. To this I replied that this would necessitate our waiting until people returned. I reminded them that they lived apart from the rest of the world, and did not understand the customs of international intercourse. To us the fact of their having kept the representative of a great Power waiting for a year to negotiate was a deep insult, which most Powers would resent by making war without giving any further chance for negotiation. But the British Government disliked making war if they could possibly help it. They had therefore commanded me to give the Tibetans one more chance of negotiating, though that chance could only be given at Lhasa itself. Let them make the most of this opportunity.

The delegates replied that they had intended no insult by keeping me waiting a year; it was merely the custom of their country to keep out strangers. "But, anyhow," they said, "let us forget the past; let us be practical, and look only at the present. Here we are, the leading men in Tibet, ready to negotiate at Gyantse, and make a settlement which will last for a century."

I replied to the Yutok Sha-pé that I had no doubt that if a sensible man like himself had been sent to me sooner, we might have made up a satisfactory settlement long ago, and there would have been no necessity for us to go through all this inconvenience of advancing through an inhospitable country to Lhasa; but after the many chances which had been given them of negotiating at Gyantse, they could hardly consider it reasonable that we should give them any more. Moreover, the Viceroy had formed the opinion, from the fact of the Ta Lama having told me at Gyantse that he had no authority to evacuate the jong without referring to Lhasa, and from the fact of his running away, that he had not sufficient power to make a settlement. For all these reasons we were compelled to go to Lhasa, though I was ready to negotiate on the way, and we would return directly a settlement was made.

They then made further reference to their religion being spoilt if we went to Lhasa, and I asked them to make more clear to me in what way precisely their religion would be spoilt. I said we were not intolerant of other religions, as they themselves were. They had yesterday told me that, though there were some Mohammedans in Lhasa, yet they were not allowed to practise their religious rites. We had no such feelings towards other religions. On the contrary, we allowed the followers of each to practise their religious observances as they liked.

The delegates said that they were not so intolerant to the Mohammedans: they merely forbade building mosques, and prevented any new Mohammedans coming into their country. I said that at any rate some were there, and apparently they had not spoilt the religion of the Tibetans. They replied that the ancestors of these had come many, many years ago, and the Tibetans had become accustomed to them; to which my rejoinder was that if Mohammedans had lived among them practising their religious rites for all these years—apparently for centuries

—without spoiling the religion of Tibet, I could not believe that the fact of our going to Lhasa for a few weeks only could have any permanent ill-effect on the religion of Tibet.

They then remarked that if we now went to Lhasa all the other nations would want to go there, and see the sights, and establish agents there. I told them I had not the smallest wish to see the sights of Lhasa. I had already travelled in many different lands, and seen finer sights than they could show me at Lhasa; and as to stationing an agent there, we had no such intention. Could they tell me if any other nation wished to? They replied that the Russians would be wanting to send an agent to Lhasa. I told them they need not be in any fear on that score, for the Russian Government had assured our Government that they had no intention of sending an agent to Tibet. I added that, though we had no intention of establishing a political agent at Lhasa, we desired to open a trade-mart at Gyantse on the same conditions as the trade-mart at Yatung had been opened—that is, with the right to send a British officer there to superintend the trade.

The delegates would not, however, be led into a discussion of the terms. They said they could only discuss the terms at Gyantse, and the conversation drifted back into the old lines of withdrawing to Gyantse. Each of the four members of the delegation repeated in turn the same arguments for withdrawing to Gyantse, and I gave to each in turn my reasons for advancing to Lhasa. I said I feared they must think me extremely obstinate, and I felt sure that, if they had been deputed by their Government earlier in the day, I should have been able to agree to their wishes, and we could have soon come to an agreement. As matters stood at present, I could do nothing but obey the orders of the Viceroy. They asked if I could not stop here, represent to His Excellency what they had said, and await further instructions. I replied that the Viceroy only issued his orders after very careful deliberation, but once they were issued, he never revoked them.

I endeavoured throughout the interview to avoid being drawn into petty wrangling. Even more important than the securing of a paper convention, which might or might not, be of value, was, I stated to Government at the time, the placing of our personal relations with the officials of Tibet upon a good footing from the start. I had to be severe with them at Gyantse, because they would not pay proper respect to me; but at each interview since they had come well before the appointed time, they were thoroughly respectful throughout, and I was able to treat them with the politeness I preferred to show them when they made this possible. I trusted that, after I had suffered two interviews, one of three and a quarter hours and another of three and a half hours, they would feel that I was at any rate accessible, and that they would have no compunction in coming to see me whenever they felt inclined. Until, however, they received further orders from Lhasa, there was nothing more to be said on either side.

We had halted a day at Nagartse to collect supplies, of which we were short, and some question arose whether, as we had the negotiators here, it would not be better to stop and negotiate. By being too uncompromising we might be simply stiffening them up to renewed fighting, and in the desolate country in which we found ourselves, with practically no supplies and with a lofty pass behind us, we might find ourselves in a very awkward predicament. All this had certainly to be taken into consideration. Still, we should be sure to find supplies in the Lhasa Valley, unless the Tibetans resorted to the extreme course of destroying or carrying off all their foodstuffs; and as the Tibetans were now evidently on the run, I never had any real doubt that we should keep them on the run, and follow them clean through, right up to Lhasa.

On the 21st we found that the delegates had decamped in the night. Perhaps, after all, I had made a mistake, and allowed these very coy birds to escape just as they had come into my hand. On the whole I thought not. I believed others would soon come in. So I marched very contentedly along the shores of one of the most beautiful lakes I have ever seen—the Yamdok Tso. It was 14,350 feet above sea-level. In shape it was like a rough ring, surrounding what is practically an island; and in colour it varied to every shade of violet and turquoise blue and green. At times it would be the blue of heaven, reflecting the intense Tibetan sky. Then, as some cloud passed over it, or as, marching along, we beheld it at some different angle, it would flash back rays of the deep greeny-blue of a turquoise. Anon it would show out in various shades of richest violet. Often, when overhead all was black with heavy rain-clouds, we would see a streak of brilliant light and colour flashing from the far horizon of the lake; while beyond it and beyond the bordering mountains, each receding range of which was of one more beautiful shade of purple than the last, rose once more the mighty axial range of the Himalayas, at that great distance not harsh in their whity coldness, but softly tinted with a delicate blue, and shading away into the exquisite azure of the sky. What caused the marvellous colouring of this lake, which even the Tibetans call the Turquoise Lake, we could none of us say. Perhaps it was its depth, perhaps it was its saline character, or some chemical component of its water. But whatever the main cause, one cause at least must have been the intense blue of the Tibetan sky at these great altitudes, so deep and so translucent that even the sky of Greece and Italy would pale beside it.

This latter theory is what Lord Rayleigh would adopt. In a lecture which he delivered this year at the Royal Institution on the causes of the coloration of water, he gave his conclusion, from careful observations and tests, that the cause of the blueness of, say, the Mediterranean Sea was the Mediterranean sky, which was exactly the theory we had thought must apply to this Tibetan lake.

Marching along by this lake we had much rain, turning into snow at night. Pete Jong, a picturesque little fort close to the shore, was reached on the 22nd, where, as at Nagartse, a company of infantry and a few mounted infantry were left to keep up the line of communications. From here the mounted infantry, reconnoitring ahead, reported the remnants of the Kham force to be retreating in a disorganized condition, and looting the country *en route*.

Another of the Tibetan stone walls, running from the waters of the lake far up the mountain-side, was found deserted on the next day, and that same day we crossed the last pass on the way to Lhasa, the Kamba-la, 15,400 feet. The ascent was steep, but we all eagerly clambered up in the faint hope of getting some distant glimpse of Lhasa, or at any rate of the mighty Brahmaputra River, which still lay in between us and the sacred city. The enthusiastic Perceval Landon was quite certain that through some chink he saw the glitter of a gilded cupola, and refused to be convinced by the prosaic survey officers that whatever it might be it at any rate was not the roof of the Potala.

But if we were not yet to catch a sight of our goal we had many other exciting incidents on that day. We descended rapidly from the pass by a very steep path to a camp on the banks of the great Brahmaputra itself, called here the Sanpo, and presumed to be identical—though this is a great geographical problem yet to be solved—with the Brahmaputra of India. It was here 11,550 above sea-level, and spread out in many channels, but farther down, where it was narrowed into a single channel, it was 140 yards wide and flowing with a strong, swift current. The valley was wide and well cultivated with wheat and barley, and several cultivated valleys ran into it. In these valleys were plenty of trees, poplars and willows, but the hillsides were not wooded, as we had hoped.

General Macdonald sent on his mounted infantry to seize the Chaksam Ferry, and they succeeded in capturing the two large ferry-boats, and occupied Chaksam for the night. This was a great stroke, as if the Tibetans had kept the boats on the other side of the river our difficulties in surmounting this most serious obstacle would have been immensely increased.

Another great event on this day was the receipt of what was, I think, the first written communication which any British official had received from a Tibetan official

BERTHON BOATS ON BRAHMAPUTRA.

To face page 234.

since the time of Warren Hastings. It was addressed to "The all-wise Sahib sent by the English Government to settle affairs, from the Tibetan National Assembly." It ran as follows:

"Recently the Tongsa Penlop sent a letter to the Dalai Lama, and also communicated with the two delegates, but hitherto a treaty has not been effected. The Sahibs say that they intend to come to Lhasa and to see the Dalai Lama and to negotiate there, and that they will there establish friendship. The letter which contains the nine terms of the Convention has arrived here. This is a matter of great importance, and therefore the Chigyab Kenpo (Lord Chamberlain) has been sent to Chisul. Now, our Tibetan religion is very precious, so our Regent, officials, monks, and laymen have consulted together. Formerly we made a National Convention that none was to enter the country. So now, even if the Sahibs should come to Lhasa and meet the Dalai Lama, this will not advantage the cause of friendship. Should a fresh cause of dispute arise, we greatly fear that a disturbance, contrary to the interests of friendship, may follow. So we beg of the Sahibs both now and in the future to give the matter their earnest consideration, and if they will negotiate with the delegates who are now here all will be well. Please consider well all that has been said, and do not press forward hastily to Lhasa.

"Dated the Wood Dragon year."

This letter was brought by a messenger, who said that the new delegates were then at Chisul, on the opposite bank of the river. And now again arose the question whether we should make use of this new chance of negotiating or should still press on to Lhasa. We had in front of us the serious obstacle formed by the Brahmaputra River, which, if we crossed it, would be a nasty impediment to have in our rear. On the other hand, we had negotiators here with more ample credentials than any had had before, and we had the National Assembly itself in communication with us. The fear of our going to Lhasa might have more effect than our actual presence in the place. The mere dread of our advance might make them agree to our terms, while if we actually advanced to their sacred city we might find that the most determined defence had been reserved for the capital; and that we had put our heads into a hornets' nest, and irritated 20,000 monks into buzzing about our ears. This was an eventuality on which I had to count, and of which I had been warned by speeches by responsible men in England which did little to encourage me in my task. An ex-Prime Minister, Lord Rosebery, had said in February in the House of Lords that this Mission bore "in its circumstances so melancholy a resemblance to that first war in Afghanistan, which we conducted under the late Lord Lytton, that it must give all those whose minds and memories recurred to the past serious grounds of misgivings when they saw once more His Majesty's Government proceeding in the same direction to an end which they could not see themselves." A future Prime Minister, Sir Henry Campbell-Bannerman, in pressing for the recall of the Mission, had said in the House of Commons in April that "we had had experience before, and the associations connected with the name of Cavagnari did not seem to invite us to undertake a similar policy again."

If we pressed on to Lhasa, into this swarm of fanatically hostile monks, we might all share the fate of Cavagnari, while if we simply held up the threat of advancing we might get the treaty through. It was an alternative which I had to consider; but I felt fairly sure by now that I had rightly taken the measure of the Tibetans, so I sent a verbal intimation by the messenger that I would be glad to receive the delegates, but that I could not consent to defer my advance to Lhasa. And, in reply to the letter of the National Assembly, I wrote to the Dalai Lama that more than a year ago I had arrived at Khamba Jong, which he had approved as a meeting-place for the negotiations, but that the appointed delegates refused to negotiate. I had advanced to Gyantse, but still no negotiators had arrived, and instead, I was treacherously attacked at night. Now the Viceroy had ordered me to advance to Lhasa to negotiate there. Those orders I had to obey, but I had no desire to create disturbances in Lhasa or interfere with the religion of the country, and as soon as I had obtained his seal to the Convention I had been instructed to negotiate, I would retire from Lhasa. No religious places which were not occupied by Tibetan soldiers would be occupied by British soldiers; our soldiers would not fire if no opposition was offered to them; and all supplies taken from the peasants would be paid for. But if opposition were offered, our troops would be compelled to commence military operations, as they did at Gyantse, and the terms of the settlement would be increased in severity.

This letter I despatched on the 25th, and the same day we marched six miles down the banks of the Brahmaputra River, to Chaksam Ferry. For the purpose of crossing this river we had brought with us from India four collapsible Berthon boats, and with these and the local ferry-boats seven companies of infantry and one company of mounted infantry were crossed over by nightfall.

But a sad accident occurred: one of the boats capsized in the rushing, eddying current, and Major Bretherton, the Chief Supply and Transport Officer, and two Gurkhas were drowned. There was no more capable and energetic officer in the Force. Our success depended much less on fighting than on supply and transport arrangements, and these had been wellnigh perfect. Major Bretherton, in the Kashmir, Gilgit, Chitral, and North-West frontiers, had almost unrivalled experience of rough transport work, and his driving power, his readiness, quickness, far-sightedness, and inexhaustible buoyancy and cheerfulness were of inestimable value in carrying through such an enterprise as that which we had now so nearly completed. It was hard that young Gurdon should lose his life just at the beginning of so promising a career; it seemed almost more cruel that a man who had achieved so much, and who was just within sight of the goal for which he had worked longer and harder than any one of us, should have been swept away in an instant and have never seen his reward. It is in reflecting on cases such as these that one begins to wonder whether our touching trustfulness in the mercy of Providence is altogether justified.

We had to halt some days now, while the troops and baggage were being transported across the river, and on the 27th I had a three hours' interview with this new deputation from Lhasa, which consisted of the Dalai Lama's Chamberlain, a man of some capacity, with an air of great consequence, who was evidently regarded with much respect; the Ta Lama, the somewhat effete, but genial, old gentleman who had met me at Gyantse; and a Secretary of the Council, a brisk, cheery gentleman, with an ever-ready smile, and very different from the other Secretary who had met us at Khamba Jong, Gyantse, and Nagartse.

They brought with them a letter from the Dalai Lama, and repeated the old request that we should not go to Lhasa. The only new argument they used was that our going to Lhasa would so spoil their religion that the Dalai Lama might die. I told them that I should much regret that our arrival in Lhasa should have any such melancholy result, but I had studied their religion, and could hardly believe it was so weak that it would not stand our presence in Lhasa for a few weeks. The delegates repeatedly urged me to realize the personal inconvenience our presence in Lhasa would be to the Dalai Lama. The Ta Lama explained that the Chamberlain was in constant personal attendance on the Dalai Lama, and enjoyed his fullest confidence, and for that reason had been specially deputed by the Dalai Lama. I was given to understand that this was a very unusual favour, and I was earnestly begged to accede to the Dalai Lama's personal wishes; the delegates further told me that if I did not accede to them they would themselves be severely punished by the Dalai Lama.

In reply I expressed my inability to accede to the Dalai Lama's wishes, but trusted they would ask His Holiness to excuse my insistence. They had spoken of the inconvenience our presence in Lhasa would cause the

Dalai Lama, but His Holiness would, I felt sure, realize the inconvenience we had already suffered through the delay in the arrival of negotiators. I could assure them that the Viceroy had every desire to consult the feelings of the Dalai Lama, and it was because we knew that His Holiness was averse to the presence of strangers in Lhasa that His Excellency had not sent me there in the first instance, though the capital of a country was the natural and usual place in which to conduct negotiations. It was only after we had found it impossible to effect a settlement anywhere else that I had been ordered to proceed to Lhasa.

I added that after an Envoy had been kept waiting for a year, and had been attacked and shot at for two months, most rulers would have refused to allow their representative to negotiate till the capital had been captured. We were not, however, advancing with that object. They could see that here we were paying for all supplies we took, and the monastery immediately outside the camp was left unmolested. I was prepared to show like consideration on our arrival at Lhasa if we were unopposed, and I trusted His Holiness would appreciate this concession.

The delegates assured me again that the Dalai Lama was really anxious to make a settlement, that they had come in a peaceful manner, and had let the army they had with them a few days ago disperse to their homes. I had little difficulty in believing these assertions, for we had received accounts that the Tibetan army had scattered in a panic, the Kham levies looting in all directions. A peaceful settlement was undoubtedly, therefore, the sincere desire of the Dalai Lama, though turbulent monks might yet create a disturbance in Lhasa. As to the delegates being punished if we advanced to Lhasa, I said that I myself would be punished if we did not.

A discussion afterwards followed on the question of other foreigners coming to Tibet if we were allowed there. I told them it was the usual custom for neighbouring countries to have representatives at each other's capital, and we would probably have avoided all the misunderstandings which led to the present troubles if we had had a representative at Lhasa and they had had one in Calcutta. We knew, however, their aversion to keeping a British agent at Lhasa; we were not, therefore, pressing the point, and were only insisting upon having trade agents at Gyantse and other marts. There would, however, in any case, have been no reason for other foreigners establishing an agent at Lhasa. Russia had declared that she had no intention of sending an agent to Tibet. The delegates replied that our establishing an agent even at Gyantse would be against their custom, and spoil their religion. I said that I understood, then, that they were not prepared even now to agree to our terms, and they informed me that they were only authorized to discuss them, and they would have to be considered in the National Assembly. "You expect me, then," I said, "to remain out here in a half-desert place discussing terms. I have already remained for months together in desert places in Tibet, and can now negotiate in no other place than Lhasa." I begged the Chamberlain as a practical man to accept this as inevitable, and to turn his mind now to insuring that there should be no more useless bloodshed on the way, and that we should be enabled by the speedy conclusion of the settlement to leave Lhasa at an early date.

Before closing the interview, I had some conversation with the delegates on the general question of intercourse between Tibet and India. I said that we should be very glad if they would more frequently accept the hospitality we were always ready to offer them in India. They would find that in India they could travel wherever they liked, and would everywhere be protected and welcomed. They would see, too, that though we were Christians we not only tolerated but protected Buddhists, Hindus, and Mohammedans. We even spent large sums of money in preserving ancient buildings of other religions. In this camp was an officer, Colonel Waddell, who had spent his life in studying the Buddhist religion, and while reading the ancient books had discovered instructions indicating exactly where the birthplace of Buddha could be found.

The British Government had spent a considerable amount of money in clearing away forests, and the town in which Buddha was born was actually discovered. We did not believe that every religion except our own was wrong. On the contrary, we believed that the same God whom we all worshipped could be approached by many different roads, and we were ready to respect those who were travelling to the same destination, though by a different road to that which we ourselves were following.

The delegates expressed their satisfaction that we should have studied their religion, but the conversation soon returned to the more pressing question of our advance to Lhasa. The Chamberlain was the most sensible, practical man we had so far met, and I was specially polite to him, as in the event of the flight or murder of the Dalai Lama he might be a possible Regent. But even he had evidently very little power, and while he was nervous throughout the interview, was clearly more nervous of his own people than of us.

After the interview had lasted three and a half hours, I asked them to report my words to the Dalai Lama, and I told them that I should be very glad to see them again whenever they liked, either to discuss further official business, or, putting official matters aside, to pay me a friendly private visit. They took one of my Tibetan Munshis with them, and gave him a special present of silk for Captain O'Connor, and also told the Munshi that the man who had brought all this trouble on Tibet was the Tung-yig-Chembo (the Chief Secretary), who was at Khamba Jong, Gyantse, and Nagartse, but who was not present at this interview. It was satisfactory to find that two such influential men as the Chamberlain and the Ta Lama had discovered this, and I thought that if the man was now cast aside, our chance of getting on terms of friendship with high Tibetan officials would be vastly increased.

I now accepted the silk which the Dalai Lama had sent me through the Tongsa Penlop, but which I had at the time refused to accept unless accompanied by a letter or handed to me by one of the Dalai Lama's own officials. The present was mentioned in the Dalai Lama's letter to me, and the Chamberlain also told me the Dalai Lama begged me to accept it. I could therefore accept it without loss of dignity. I sent him in return a large and very handsome silver-gilt bowl.

This letter was certainly the first letter which any Dalai Lama had written to an Englishman, and was addressed "To the Sahib sent by the English Government to settle affairs," and ran as follows:

"In a letter recently received by the Sha-pé from the Tongsa Penlop he says that the establishment of friendship has now become difficult, as the English officers with their escort say that they are about to proceed to Lhasa to make a treaty and to meet the Dalai Lama. With this communication the nine terms of the Convention were also received. The National Assembly has been consulted regarding this matter, and as it has decided for friendship it has sent a separate communication to the British. I too, in accordance with the religious customs of Tibet, am at present in retreat, and it would be a difficult matter for me to meet the Sahibs. I have sent two representatives on ahead to negotiate regarding friendship, and also the Chikyab Kenpo, who lives always near me. It will be well if matters are discussed with my delegates there for the sake of peace. But it is not well for the establishment of an agreement between the two countries if you come to Lhasa contrary to my wishes. Please consider this well. I send a scarf and have already sent some silks separately.

"Dated the 8th day of the 6th month,
"Wood Dragon year."

To this letter I replied that I was sure he would recognize the inconvenience it would be to me now that I had left Gyantse to negotiate at any other place than Lhasa itself, but that I would disturb His Holiness as little as possible in his religious seclusion.

The Dalai Lama's Chamberlain returned to Lhasa immediately, but on the 29th the Ta Lama, accompanied by the same Secretary of Council who was present at the

TA LAMA AND HIS SECRETARY.

To face page 242.

interview of July 27, again came to visit me. He explained that the Chamberlain had returned to Lhasa to report personally to the Dalai Lama the result of his interview with me, and he hoped that I would wait here till the reply of the Dalai Lama should reach me. I informed him that I could not wait here longer than the 31st, that it was not our custom to act in a dilatory manner, and that I was indeed daily expecting a telegram from the Viceroy asking me for an explanation of the delay which had already occurred.

During the interview, which lasted three hours, the conversation was of a discursive nature, as the Ta Lama clearly had no power even to discuss anything else than our advance to Lhasa. I gathered that what he and the other delegates, and probably also the Dalai Lama himself, feared was the turbulence of the war party among the monks of the three great monasteries, leading to some futile collision with our troops which would not have the slightest effect in stopping us, but which would merely irritate us into sacking Lhasa. Probably what the Dalai Lama's party also feared was that these same turbulent monks might turn upon the Dalai Lama himself and make away with him.

I told the Ta Lama that I considered it a great pity that he and the other able councillors who had recently met me had not come to Khamba Jong, for the Secretary of Council who had met Mr. White and me there had not comported himself in at all a conciliatory manner; he had, in fact, irritated us considerably, and made a peaceful settlement impossible. This surprised me the more because the Chinese Government had informed the Viceroy that the Dalai Lama had agreed to Khamba Jong as the meeting-place where negotiations should take place.

The Ta Lama replied that what the Dalai Lama meant was the Khamba *boundary*, not Khamba *Jong*. I told him that this was hardly intelligible, as the Khamba boundary was along the top of mountains. We clearly could not sit on the top of a mountain and negotiate: we had to meet on either the one side or the other, and as the

Amban and Tibetan officials had come to India on the last occasion, it was natural that we should expect to meet in Tibet on this. I added that when the Chinese and Tibetan officials came to India we treated them as our guests, as Mr. White, who was present at Darjiling, could testify; we provided houses, food, and transport for them; allowed them to have their own soldiers as escort; and took them down to Calcutta to visit His Excellency the Viceroy. On the other hand, when Mr. White and I arrived at Khamba Jong last year we were not even allowed to *buy* supplies.

The Ta Lama said that what was meant by the Khamba boundary was not the top of the mountains, but the wall at Giagong. He did not deny that Tibetan officials had been treated as guests at Darjiling, but he said we did not realize the great expense the Tibetan Government had incurred in transporting them to the Indian frontier. I then asked the Ta Lama what reason they had for originally starting this trouble, which after all originated in their invasion of Sikkim in 1886. Why did they send troops into the territory of a British feudatory State? We had lived for so many years without troubling one another: why did they start a trouble which had lasted up to the present time?

He replied that they considered Sikkim to be a feudatory of Tibet, and the Dalai Lama was accustomed at that time to send orders to the Sikkim chief. I said that they must surely have been aware of the treaty which had been concluded more than twenty years previous to the Tibetan invasion of Sikkim, between Sikkim and the British Government, by which the former acknowledged the suzerainty of the latter. If the Tibetans had had any objection, the proper course would have been to make representations at the time, and not twenty years after to send troops into Sikkim.

As regards the treaty we now wished to make with them, how would the negotiations be conducted? I asked, and who had the final authority in the State? The Ta Lama said that Councillors and secretaries and representatives of the National Assembly would meet me and discuss the terms. The final authority was the National Assembly, which was composed of representatives from all over Tibet, but chiefly from the three great monasteries at Lhasa. Both monks and laymen attended as well as many officials, but the Councillors (Sha-pés) were not included in it, and the Dalai Lama had no representative there.

I told the Ta Lama that this seemed rather extraordinary, for the Councillors were presumably the most able men in the State, and yet their counsels were liable to be overridden by the decision of a body of irresponsible and less capable men. "Supposing," I said, "that the Dalai Lama and the Councillors wished to agree to the terms I was asking and the National Assembly declined to agree, whose views would be adopted?" The Ta Lama said that the Dalai Lama and the Councillors never disagreed with the National Assembly, for the decision of the latter was final. I said this made matters very difficult for me; for I negotiated with the Councillors as being the leading men in the State, and yet they could not even enter the National Assembly to report what I had said to them. The Ta Lama said the custom was for the Councillors to send one of the secretaries to present their views to the National Assembly. I asked who presided, what was the number of representatives, and whether the decision was arrived at by votes. He said no one presided, that there were about 500 representatives, and that they arrived at a decision by discussing till they were all of one mind.

I remarked that in these circumstances the negotiations promised to last a considerable time. Did he think they would be concluded in a year? He said a good deal depended upon how we proposed to set about negotiating. If we took each point separately, and had it discussed in the National Assembly till agreed to, the settlement might be made fairly quickly; but if we gave the whole treaty in a lump, and said this and nothing less must be agreed to, he did not think a settlement would ever be made.

I told the Ta Lama that it was a matter of indifference

to the British Government how long the negotiations lasted, for we should expect the Tibetan Government to pay for our expenses from the date of the attack on the Mission at Gyantse till the date of the conclusion of the treaty. The Ta Lama urged that we should not be hard on the Tibetans by demanding an indemnity, for if we did we could never be friends. I answered that we would not have demanded an indemnity if they had been reasonable and had negotiated at Khamba Jong or Gyantse, but as they had chosen to fight, and had been worsted, they must take the consequences of their own actions.

The Ta Lama then dwelt upon the habit of the Tibetans to take plenty of time in making decisions. They liked to think well before taking action, and could not stand being hurried. I informed him that we also tried to think well before taking action, but we thought quickly and acted at once, so as to get on without delay from one thing to another. The lives of men were short, and we wished to get through as much as possible in the little time we were here. The Ta Lama said that their time was taken up with the study of religion, which did not admit of hurry. During this latter part of the discussion the Ta Lama and the Secretary laughed heartily, then the former, after asking leave to depart, repeated, as I was shaking hands with him, another appeal to me not to go to Lhasa.

On the same day as I was having this interview I also received from the Chinese Resident a letter, in which he expressed sympathy with me in the trials of my long journey, and said that the Tibetans were "dull, unlettered men, obstinately averse to receiving advice," and that he was truly ashamed at the state of affairs. He said he was sending me the Chief of the Military Secretariat to acquaint me with the condition of affairs. He had impressed on the Dalai Lama that the Tibetans were on no account to treat me unceremoniously, but he warned me that these Tibetans were "cunning and insincere to a degree, and that it was necessary to obtain guarantees from them before a settlement of anything could be made."

On July 31 all the troops, except a small garrison to guard the ferry, having crossed the river, we set out again towards Lhasa. As I was passing Chisul the Ta Lama asked me to stay for a short time to talk to him. He said he was much surprised at our advancing, as he had understood from me that we wished to make a settlement and be on friendly terms, and, if we advanced, there might be disturbances. I reminded him that I had always said we would advance, and remarked that, if there were disturbances, the responsibility would rest upon the Tibetan Government, for I had informed him many times, and had written to both the Amban and the Dalai Lama to say that we would not commence fighting, and our troops had orders not to fire unless they were fired upon.

The Ta Lama then begged me to stay till the Chamberlain returned with the reply from the Dalai Lama. His Holiness would not at all like our advancing without his permission, but if we waited for his reply, we might find that he was willing for us to advance, and he would give orders to the Tibetan soldiers to allow us to pass. I replied that we had already waited nearly a week at Chaksam Ferry, that there had been plenty of time to issue such orders if there was any intention to issue them, and that, in any case, whatever the Dalai Lama's reply was, I should have to advance to Lhasa.

The Ta Lama then tried to persuade me to advance with only a small following; he said that my entering Lhasa with a large army would alarm the Tibetans, and make the Dalai Lama think that our intentions were not really friendly. I recalled to his remembrance that only a few minutes before he had spoken of the possibility of disturbances. It was to protect ourselves in case of disturbances, and to guard ourselves against such another attack as that which was made upon me at Gyantse in May, that we were taking a sufficient force to Lhasa.

The Ta Lama begged me not to be always harping upon what had occurred at Gyantse. Let all that be forgotten, he said. The Tibetans were now really anxious to make a settlement, and he would give me a promise in writing that no harm would befall us if I went to Lhasa with only a small following. I told him the Tibetans already had a promise in writing from me in my letter to the Dalai Lama that we would not fight unless opposed, and if, with that in their hands, they allowed disturbances to occur, I should presume they were not anxious for a settlement. I required no written promise from them not to harm us, but relied upon their sense of self-interest not to bring on further disturbances.

The Ta Lama, as a final effort, begged me to stay here for a day; and, last of all, as he was shaking hands with me—a ceremony which lasted a quarter of an hour—entreated me not to enter Lhasa city. I told him that I had the highest admiration for his eloquence and power of persuasion, and would have great satisfaction in telling the Dalai Lama that he really had done his utmost to delay us. I, of course, realized the position in which he stood, and that it was his business by every means in his power to prevent us reaching Lhasa. At the same time, I was sure, I said, that a man of his sense knew in the bottom of his heart that the Tibetans were extremely fortunate in having been able to secure our peaceful entry to Lhasa, and prevented the capture of the city by force of arms. We had promised not to occupy Lhasa if we were not further opposed, and with that promise they must be content.

The Ta Lama, though excessively urgent towards the close of the interview, was perfectly polite throughout. But so extraordinarily impracticable are these Tibetans that he evidently thought that, because I had assured him at previous interviews that we wished to make a friendly settlement, we were therefore committing a sort of breach of faith in now advancing to Lhasa. I had never ceased to assure him that we did intend to advance, but now that we actually were advancing he regarded it as a grievance.

For the next two days we marched steadily on towards Lhasa, expecting at each corner we turned to catch sight of the Potala in the distance, or at least to hear from the reconnoitring parties of mounted infantry that they had seen its gilded roofs. On August 2, at our last camp, a dozen miles only from Lhasa, which now really could be seen in the distance, I received the final deputation, which had come to make the last great effort to induce us to stop. It consisted of the old Ta Lama, the General who had met Mr. White and me at Khamba Jong, and had since been promoted to the post of Councillor, and known as the Tsarong Sha-pé, the Chinese official deputed by the Resident, the Abbot in private attendance on the Dalai Lama, a Secretary of Council, and the Abbots of the three great Lhasa monasteries. They repeated the usual requests that we should not go to Lhasa. I reiterated my usual statements that we must go there. They said that if we would remain where we were they would supply us with everything—of course, on payment. The Dalai Lama's private Abbot made a special appeal on behalf of the religion of Tibet. I told him I was particularly interested in hearing his views on religion, but I trusted he would not object to my reminding him that, while he was an eminent authority on religion, he had little experience of politics. In political life, when a country repudiated a treaty, declined to negotiate a new one, and attacked the Envoy who was sent for that purpose, it was considered that that country had committed three very serious offences, any one of which would be justification for the capture of the capital of the offending country. In the present case, out of consideration for the special sanctity of the city, we were prepared, if we encountered no opposition, to abstain from capturing Lhasa, and I trusted the Abbot would appreciate the consideration. Perhaps if he had himself been fired on continually for two months he would not have been equally moderate. The Abbot laughed, but remarked that they also had had to suffer.

I promised the Abbot to respect the monasteries. If they were occupied by soldiers, and we were fired at from them, as we were from the monasteries round Gyantse, we should, of course, have to attack them. But we did not wish to be obliged to resort to force, and as long as we were not attacked we would prevent our soldiers from entering the monasteries. I would also see that soldiers and followers did not enter the city of Lhasa unless in attendance on an officer. The Tsarong Sha-pé asked me to give them a written agreement to this effect. I said I would, provided they would give me a written agreement that traders from the city would not be prevented from coming to sell things to the soldiers in camp, as the Gyantse traders had done. The Tsarong Sha-pé said that this would be impossible without the consent of the National Assembly. I told him that I could not in that case give them the written agreement, and I rose at once and closed the Durbar.

The final effort to stop us had failed, and on August 3 we set out on our last march. The eventful day, to which we had so long looked forward, had at length arrived. We marched up a well-cultivated valley two or three miles broad, bounded by steep snow-capped mountains, and with a rapid river as wide as the Thames at Windsor running through it. We passed numbers of little hamlets and groves of poplars and willows. And then we saw, rising steeply on a rocky prominence in the midst of the valley, a fort-like dominating structure, with gilded roofs, which we knew could be none other than the Potala, the palace of the Dalai Lama of Lhasa.

The goal of so many travellers' ambitions was actually in sight! The goal, to attain which we had endured and risked so much, and for which the best efforts of so many had been concentrated, had now been won. Every obstacle which Nature and man combined could heap in our way had been finally overcome, and the sacred city, hidden so far and deep behind the Himalayan ramparts, and so jealously guarded from strangers, was full before our eyes.

THE GATE OF LHASA.

To face page 250.

CHAPTER XVI

THE TERMS

I HAVE often been asked what were my feelings when I first saw Lhasa—whether I was not filled with a sense of elation. I was filled with nothing of the kind. It was when I left Lhasa that I really had all that feeling of intense relief and satisfaction which everyone experiences when he has set his heart on one great object and attained it. When I left Lhasa I had my treaty, and—what I had always put at more value than the treaty itself—the good-will of the people. When I arrived at Lhasa it was very doubtful if I should be able to get a treaty at all, and still more doubtful if I could get it with the good-will of the people, without which any paper treaty would be useless. To negotiate a treaty with a people acknowledged by those who knew them best—the Chinese, the Nepalese, and the Bhutanese—to be most obstinate and obstructive, time was required. To break through the reserve of so exclusive a people, to make friends of men with whom we had just been fighting, still more time was essential. Yet it was just time that was denied me. I had pressed for it in June, but in too ineffectual a manner, and had been rebuffed. Though this was an avowedly political Mission, military considerations were allowed to preponderate. I could only stay in Lhasa a month and a half or two months. We must be back before the winter. And thus tied, I had to set to work with all speed, but with the outward appearance of having the utmost leisure, to negotiate the treaty. Hurried as I was, I had yet to assume an air of perfect indifference whether the negotiations were concluded this year, next year, or the year after. And irritated though I might be, I had above all to exercise as much control as I could possibly bring to bear to keep down any feelings of hastiness or exasperation, which might ruin our chances of securing the eventual good-will of the people.

I had, then, too much before me and still too much anxiety in regard to the very immediate present, to yet feel much elation on our first arrival at Lhasa, and my chief thought was how to start the negotiations without showing in what a hurry I really was.

Before, however, describing the course of the negotiations which were now to take place, I must give an account of the terms which I had been directed to make with the Tibetans, and the considerations on which those demands were based. Already, before I left Gyantse, I had received from the Government of India a copy of the despatch, dated June 30,* containing their views on the terms which they had sent to the Secretary of State. I was to understand that the proposals contained therein had not yet been approved by His Majesty's Government, but I was, without committing Government, to ascertain how the Tibetan Government would regard them.

It was the terms contained in these proposals—with the exception of asking for the establishment of a Resident at Lhasa—of which I informed the Tongsa Penlop, and asked him, as I have mentioned previously, to communicate to the Dalai Lama.

The first point on which the Government of India laid stress in their communication to the Secretary of State was the acceptance by the Tibetans of an accredited British agent in their country, preferably in Lhasa itself. The arguments against such a measure were largely based on the declarations of His Majesty's Government, and on consideration of international policy. And apart from such considerations, the Government of India declared themselves deeply impressed by the grave responsibilities which they must incur by placing a resident agent at the capital of Tibet. Still, they felt it their duty reluctantly to assume the burden of that measure.

* Blue-book, III., p. 33.

His Majesty's Government had already recognized the necessity of asserting the predominance of British influence in Tibet, and Lord Lansdowne had clearly apprised Count Benckendorff of our attitude in this matter. To establish such an influence it was evident that we must now acquire something more practical than the nominal concessions acquired by the treaty of 1890 as the fruits of our operations in 1888. Our experience then gained showed that we could not trust to our recent military successes leaving any lasting impression. It was difficult to avoid the conclusion that the best guarantee for the due observance of the new Convention, and for the adequate protection of our rights as the only European Power *limitrophe* with Tibet, must be that, in addition to the appointment of officers to watch over our commercial interests at the marts to be established in Tibet, we should demand the acceptance of an accredited British agent in Tibet.

The place at which this agent should reside was a question on which opinions might easily differ, and it might, the Indian Government thought, be left open until they were in possession of the fuller information that would be acquired after the Mission had reached Lhasa. The arguments in favour of placing him at Lhasa were the following: Lhasa was the pivot of the religious and political life of Tibet; it was the seat of the Dalai Lama and his Council, with whom we had to establish official relations; and it was the focus of the priestly influence, which we had to conciliate or overcome. It might be argued that it was undesirable to arouse the resentment of the Tibetans by requiring them to receive a representative of a strange race and a strange religion in the home of their most sacred associations. But after the manner in which for the past fifteen years the Tibetans had repudiated their obligations and had derided the patience with which we had submitted to their insults, Government believed that, even should such a feeling exist, it might be better to face it than to allow of the misconstruction which would be placed upon the location of an agent at any place outside Lhasa.

They saw, however, no reason why the presence of a resident agent in Lhasa should be a lasting source of irritation. For more than eighty years we had now had an agent at Khatmandu, a capital the isolation of which from foreign intrusion had been guarded hardly less jealously than that of Lhasa itself, and that by a people whose prowess had been proved in our own armies. The hostilities which preceded the first appointment of a British Minister at Peking, under the treaty of 1860, were also far more serious than any opposition which had so far been encountered, or was likely to be met with, on the way to Lhasa. The Government of India saw, then, no reason to anticipate greater risk in placing a Resident at Lhasa than was incurred in sending a British representative to Khatmandu or Peking.

Despite the hostility which, under the influence and leadership of the monkish faction, they had displayed against us, the Tibetan people had no dislike for us as a race, and there was nothing in the tolerant Buddhist creed which counselled hostility to strangers of a different faith or encouraged fanaticism. The exclusion of British subjects and Europeans was merely based on a concordat of the present dominant class in Tibet, and was not in any way a religious obligation. The monks were at present opposed to us, fearing the loss of their influence, but their antipathy was based on suspicion and ignorance, and with tact and patience it might be eradicated—a view which was supported by the friendly relations which the Mission was able to establish at Khamba Jong with ecclesiastical Envoys from the Tashi Lama of Shigatse.

It had always to be borne in mind that subjects of all her other neighbours—China, Nepal, and Kashmir—were allowed freely to resort to, and trade in, Tibet, while China and Nepal had official representatives at Lhasa. As at Khatmandu, our agent would, like the Nepal representative at Lhasa, abstain from all interference with the internal administration of the country, and would confine himself to watching over our trade interests and in guarding against the introduction of foreign influences. His presence, therefore, at Lhasa would be in no sense a contravention of the policy declared by His Majesty's Government.

As to the objection which might be raised on the grounds of the difficulty of keeping open communication with the agent at Lhasa, the Government of India contended that such an objection was based upon a misapprehension, and that there was no real difficulty, except on the southern side of the watershed, to such free passage to and from Tibet as might be necessary for the adequate support of a British representative, either at Lhasa or Gyantse; and our recent operations had demonstrated that, however great the physical difficulties of communication might be, they were not insuperable even at the worst time of the year. Moreover, the difficulties on the Indian side of the Himalayas would be obviated by a road through Chumbi, which they were examining, that ran down the Amochu to the plains of Bengal, avoiding the Jelap-la.

The Government of India felt, then, that it was a necessity to have an agent at Lhasa, and they were quite willing to undertake the responsibility. That was the view of the responsible Government on the spot. The Imperial side of the question had still to be weighed, and of that the Imperial Government would be the judge, but in regard to that aspect the Government of India made the following observations:

Lord Lansdowne had given assurances to the Russian Ambassador, but he had expressly added when making them that the policy then announced was not unalterable in any eventuality, and that the action of His Majesty's Government was to some extent dependent on the action of the Tibetans themselves. The Government of India did not desire to depart from the declaration which Lord Lansdowne had made that, so long as no other Power endeavoured to intervene in the affairs of Tibet, no attempt would be made to annex it, to establish a protectorate over it, or in any way to control its internal administration; but they thought that recent developments might make it incumbent upon them to recommend to His Majesty's Government a reconsideration of the opinion they had expressed in their telegram of November 6, 1903, in so far as it concerned the establishment of a permanent Mission in the country.

As to the desire not to accelerate political complications regarding the integrity of China, the Government of India pointed out that no other European Power adjoined Tibet or had any interests there, and that, so far, our arrangements had been made with the cordial co-operation of the Chinese officials deputed to meet the Mission, and it was understood that they met with the sympathy, if not with the avowed approval, of the Chinese Government, as was evidenced by Sir Ernest Satow's telegram of June 15.

So much was urged by the Government in regard to the establishment of an agent at Lhasa. The next cardinal point in the policy which they wished to recommend was the retention of the Chumbi Valley.

They explained that this valley lay to the south of the main watershed, and was Indian rather than Tibetan in character. Our Mission had been well received by the people, and Mr. Walsh, the Political Agent who had been located among them, reported that they regarded our presence with unmixed satisfaction, and that their only fear was lest we might evacuate the valley, and expose them to the vengeance which the Lamas would surely take upon them for having lived on terms of friendliness with us. The occupation of this region was recommended by all the local authorities as far back as 1888, was strongly urged by the Bengal Government in Mr. Cotton's letter, dated July 22, 1895, but was deferred owing to Chinese susceptibilities. The contumacious disregard of the Tibetans for their treaty obligations and for the authority of their Suzerain had culminated in armed resistance to the passage of a friendly Mission despatched by us with the full cognizance of that Suzerain, and accompanied by Chinese representatives throughout. It appeared to Government that recent developments might make it necessary to take material guarantees. They had referred to a road through the Chumbi Valley as desirable in order to secure the position of our representative in Tibet, if such a one should be appointed. The route which was

THE DALAI LAMA.

To face page 256.

projected along the Amo Chu Valley would lead into the foot of the Chumbi Valley, and it was obviously desirable that it should continue under our control up to the point where it debouches on to the open plateau of Tibet beyond the Tang-la. The opening up of such a route into Tibet proper must evidently be the precursor of any real development of trade, and, what was of far greater importance, it would provide one of the surest guarantees for the predominance of our influence and the safety of our Agents in the country.

It had been estimated that, if our forces had all left Tibet by October, the cost of the expedition would not be less than £648,000. The contingency of such an early withdrawal was remote, and it seemed probable that the operations necessary to assert our treaty rights and to exact reparation from the Tibetans would cost us not less than a million sterling.

The Indian Government were, therefore, of opinion that, as a guarantee for the fulfilment of the Convention, and as a security for the payment of the indemnity, that they proposed to require, as well as in the interests of the people of the valley themselves, the occupation of the Chumbi Valley for such period as might be necessary for the due protection of our treaty rights, and international interests would become inevitable.

The next point to be considered was this question of demanding an indemnity.

Now that it had become necessary to send a regular military expedition to Lhasa, Government submitted that they had a good claim to be recouped the expense to which they had been put. It was obvious that the retention of the Chumbi Valley would not, from a monetary point of view, be an adequate return for the outlay in which they had been involved, and Government thought it well to put forward a claim to compensation against the Tibetans. Further, they considered that, having regard to the recent attacks upon their Mission at Gyantse, and as a measure calculated to increase the security of their representative in Tibet, they should follow the precedent of the demands presented by the allied Powers to the Chinese

Government after the events of 1900, and should insist on the razing of all fortified positions which might impede the course of free communication between our frontier and Lhasa, and on the prohibition of the importation of arms into Tibet or their manufacture within the country except with their special permission.

Finally the Government of India discussed what might be done if His Majesty's Government declined to agree to the appointment of a representative at Lhasa. In that case they would urge that a Resident Agent should be posted at Gyantse, whose functions would primarily be to supervise and maintain the trading facilities which we must undoubtedly secure. Although the duties of such an agent would be mainly commercial, they would necessarily comprise that of seeing that the Convention or treaty which we should eventually conclude with the Tibetan Government was observed in all respects. The agent should, therefore, have the right of proceeding to Lhasa, as occasion might require, to discuss matters with the Chinese Amban or with the high officials of the Dalai Lama.

In making the terms of his appointment Government considered that the grounds and conditions of our self-restraint in this matter should be clearly indicated to the Tibetans. It should be explained that His Majesty's Government consented to waive their claim to the appointment of a Resident Agent at Lhasa solely out of regard for the Tibetan desire to maintain their freedom from contact with European influence at the political and religious capital of their country; that they were prepared to forego this demand, so long as the Tibetan Government preserved an attitude of isolation from external affairs, and avoided all intercourse with other European Powers; but that, in the event of any departure by the Tibetans from this policy in the future, the British Government would reserve to themselves the right to require the acceptance of an agent at the capital itself.

Government considered, however, that this alternative, the least which could be contemplated, was not calculated, in the same degree, to afford a guarantee of satisfactory results. An agent at Gyantse, though possibly in greater personal security, would probably not be in so good a position for knowing what transpired in political circles at Lhasa.

But whether or not a British agent was established in Tibet, Government considered that recent events justified their requiring from the Tibetans and from the Chinese Government a formal recognition of our exclusive political influence in Tibet, and an engagement that they would not admit to Tibet the representative of, that they would cede no portion of Tibetan territory to, and that they would enter into no relations regarding Tibet with, any other foreign Power, without the previous consent of the British Government.

Turning to less contentious matter, namely, that of facilities for trade with Tibet, to secure which was the primary object of the Mission when it was originally despatched on an errand, which was then indubitably peaceful in character and intention, Government contended that it was, of course, necessary to insist on access for purposes of trade to convenient centres in Tibet proper in the place of Yatung, which was beyond all question unsuitable for the object for which it was intended. In Central Tibet present information led to the belief that the town of Gyantse provided the site which was best fitted to our requirements. And, in view of recent developments, they thought that it might be advisable to insist on the opening up to trade of the neighbouring town of Shigatse, the seat of the Tashi Lama, and also of Lhasa itself, if a British Resident should be posted to the capital. They considered, too, that the present opportunity should be taken of completing the road to the frontier, and of opening another market at Gartok or some other convenient place in Western Tibet, which, with its vicinity to Chinese Turkestan, might acquire considerable importance in the future.

It would be useless at the present stage, the Government of India thought, to enter into details of the draft Convention, of the trade regulations, of the terms as to

Customs duty, of the arrangements in regard to mining rights and concessions which appeared to be necessary, and of the boundary settlements on the Sikkim and Garhwal Frontiers which stood for decision. These questions must first be discussed by their Commissioner with the representatives of the Tibetan Government.

Summarized, the proposals of the Government of India were: the placing of a Resident at Lhasa, or, failing that, an agent at Gyantse, with the right to proceed to Lhasa; the formal recognition of exclusive political influence; the demand of an indemnity; the occupation of the Chumbi Valley as security; the establishment of trade-marts at Gyantse, Yatung, Shigatse, and Gartok; the settlement of the Sikkim and Garhwal boundaries, Customs duties, and trade regulations. The amount of the indemnity to be demanded was not mentioned in the despatch, but in a telegram to me, giving a summary, and which was also sent to the Secretary of State on June 26, it was suggested that it should be £100,000 for every month from the date of the attack on the Mission at Gyantse until one month after the signature of the Convention.

These proposals appeared to His Majesty's Government to be excessive, and after some telegraphic communication with the Government of India the Secretary of State telegraphed on July 26* the terms which might be named to the Tibetans, and which the Government embodied in a draft Convention which they afterwards sent to me.

Neither at Lhasa nor elsewhere was a Resident to be demanded. Provisions for the maintenance of our exclusive political influence in Tibet were to be made. An indemnity was to be asked, though the sum to be demanded was not to exceed an amount which it was believed would be within the power of the Tibetans to pay, by instalments, if necessary, spread over three years, but I was "to be guided by circumstances in the matter." Trade-marts were to be established at Gyantse and Gartok in addition to Yatung, and a British agent was to have right of access to the Gyantse mart; the Chumbi Valley was to be occupied as security for the indemnity and for the

* Blue-book, III., p. 42.

fulfilment of the conditions regarding the trade-marts; the boundary laid down in the Convention of 1890 was to be recognized; the two Sikkim-British subjects who had been captured in 1903 were to be released; fortifications were to be demolished.

In amplification and explanation of these telegraphic instructions the Secretary of State, on August 5, addressed to the Government of India a despatch,* setting forth the deliberate policy of His Majesty's Government. They had to consider the question, not as a local one concerning India and Tibet alone, but from the wider point of view of the relations of Great Britain to other Powers, both European and Asiatic, and as involving the status of a dependency of the Chinese Empire. Formerly European nations and their interests were, in the main, far removed from the scope of Indian policy, and the relations of India with the States on her borders rarely involved any European complications; but the effect of Indian policy in relation to Afghanistan, Siam, Tibet, or any other dependency of the Chinese Empire was now liable to be felt throughout Europe. This immediate responsibility towards Europe, which Indian policy nowadays imposed on this country, necessarily involved its correlative, and the course of affairs on the Indian frontiers could not be decided without reference to Imperial exigencies elsewhere.

His Majesty's Government had also been consistently averse to any policy in Tibet which would tend to throw on the British Empire an additional burden. The great increase to our responsibilities, however necessary, which recent additions to the Empire had involved, made it obvious that it would be imprudent further to enlarge them except upon the strongest ground. In military and naval matters the resources of Great Britain and India must be considered together. India had from time to time given effective and ready help in the defence of British interests and British Colonies. On the other hand, it had to be remembered that the British army largely existed in order to defend India, and every new obligation undertaken by India was as much a charge upon the

* Blue-book, III., p. 45.

common stock of our heavily burdened resources as if it were placed upon the people of this country.

The satisfactory nature of the assurances given by Russia in regard to Tibet rendered it unnecessary and undesirable that any demand for the recognition of a Political Agent, either at Gyantse or at Lhasa, should be made to the Tibetans. His Majesty's Government held that such a political outpost might entail difficulties and responsibilities incommensurate with any benefits which, in the situation created by the Russian assurances, could be gained by it.

They did not even consider it desirable to claim for the agent, who under the Trade Regulations would have access to Gyantse, the right in certain circumstances to proceed to Lhasa. The effect of this proposal, they considered, would be to alter the character of the duties of the agent, which, it was intended, should be essentially commercial, and to assimilate them to those of a Political Resident.

"As regards the amount of the indemnity," continues the despatch, "our ignorance of the resources of the country makes it impossible to speak with any certainty. The question, in the circumstances, must be left to the discretion of Colonel Younghusband. The condition that the amount should be one which, it is estimated, can be paid in three years, indicates the intention of His Majesty's Government that the sum to be demanded should constitute an adequate pecuniary penalty, but not be such as to be beyond the powers of the Tibetans, by making a sufficient effort, to discharge within the period named."

This despatch did not reach me till after the Treaty was signed.

CHAPTER XVII

THE NEGOTIATIONS

THE very day that we arrived at Lhasa I made a commencement at negotiating a treaty based on the terms set forth in the preceding chapter. I had already, before I left Gyantse and before Government had made up their minds as to the terms which should be asked, told the Tongsa Penlop informally what we were likely to ask, so that the Tibetans might have a rough idea of our demands; and as the Chinese Resident had intimated to me that he would come and visit me on the afternoon of our arrival, I thought it well to make a start with him at once.

The interview was interesting, for I had been waiting a year to see this Amban. I had seen Chinese officials in Peking; I had seen them at the extreme eastern end of the Empire in Manchuria; I had seen them at the extreme western end, in Chinese Turkestan; and I now saw them here at Lhasa. They were always exactly the same; in their official robes, dressed precisely alike, with the same good manners, the same dignity, the same air of something very much akin to superiority, and with the same evidence of solid intellectual capacity and sterling character. The Resident, Yu-tai, was not different from the rest. He was not, indeed, strikingly clever, and I did not see him at his best, for the recalcitrance of the Tibetans had put him in a most humiliating position, which he must have felt or he would not have paid me a visit before I had visited him. But he kept up appearances and made a brave show with all the aplomb of his race, and I had a real feeling of relief in talking to a man of affairs after so many long, dreary and ineffectual interviews with the obtuse and ignorant Tibetans.

I received him, as, indeed, I had received the Tibetans all through, at official interviews, in full dress uniform, with all my Political Staff in similar dress. He made the usual polite inquiries, and then said that he wished to work with me in effecting a speedy settlement with the Tibetans. He had hoped to meet me before, and had hastened to Lhasa at unusual speed, but the Tibetans had refused to furnish him with transport, and he had, therefore, been unable to proceed beyond Lhasa. I said I quite appreciated the difficulties he must have had with the Tibetans, for I had had some experience of them now, and a more obstructive people I had never come across. He agreed that they were an exceedingly obstinate people. He said he feared I must have had a very unpleasant time at Gyantse, and I told him that we had come there to negotiate, and not to fight, and therefore had very few soldiers with us at the time the attack was made. Later on, General Macdonald arrived with reinforcements, and the Tibetans had to suffer heavily for their misconduct. On the present occasion, however, we had come ready either to negotiate or to fight. We were prepared to negotiate; but if the Tibetans were obstinate, we would not hesitate to fight. I should be glad if he would impress upon the Tibetans with all his power that we were no longer to be trifled with.

I added that one of the conditions we intended to impose was an indemnity, to cover part of the cost of military operations, and I should be asking them Rs. 50,000 per diem from the date the Mission was attacked up to a month after the date the Convention was signed. Every day they took in negotiation would cost them Rs. 50,000, so the sooner they concluded an agreement the better. The Amban thought this would be an effective way of dealing with them, and he promised to urge the Tibetans to be reasonable, and make a settlement without further loss of time.

The Resident made a special present of food to the troops, and he had already, at my request, collected two days' supplies.

The next day I had to return his visit, and now arose

THE POTALA, LHASA.

To face page 265.

a problem. His residence was on the far side of the city, and the point was whether we should ride through Lhasa or round it. It was risky to ride through this sacred city, swarming with monks who had organized the opposition against us. We had been so recently fighting against them that we could not be sure of their attitude. Peace was not yet concluded, and they had shown no signs, so far, of really negotiating, but had, on the contrary, been doing their best to stave us off from Lhasa. So our reception was uncertain, and, if anything happened to us, the matter-of-fact, common-sense person at home would, without compunction, have criticized me for running the risk without any necessity. But from my point of view there was a necessity. All this trouble had arisen through the Tibetans being so inaccessible and keeping themselves so much apart; and now I meant to close in with them, to break through their seclusion, to brush aside their exclusiveness, and to let them see us and us see them as the inhabitants of the rest of the world see each other; and I meant to make a beginning at once. So I determined now, on the very first day after our arrival, to ride right through the heart of the city of Lhasa.

The Chinese Resident sent his bodyguard with pikes, and three-pronged spears, and many banners to escort us, and of our own troops I took two companies of the Royal Fusiliers and the 2nd Mounted Infantry. Two guns and four companies of infantry were also kept in readiness in camp to support us at a moment's notice.

Many a traveller had pined to look on Lhasa, but now we were actually in this sacred city, it was, except for the Potala, a sorry affair. The streets were filthily dirty, and the inhabitants hardly more clean than the streets; the houses were built of solid masonry, but as dirty as the streets and inhabitants; and the temples we passed, though massive, were ungainly. Only the Potala was imposing; it rose from the squalid town at its base in tier upon tier of solid, massive masonry, and, without any pretence at architectural beauty or symmetry, was impressive from its sheer size and strength and dominating situation.

We passed numbers of clean-shaven, bare-headed monks from the great monasteries round, one of which alone held 8,000. They were a dirty, degraded lot, and we all of us remarked how distinctly inferior they were to the ordinary peasantry and townsmen we met. The monks, as a rule, looked thoroughly lazy and sensual and effete; the countrymen and the petty traders in the town were hardy, cheery people, and as we rode through the city really paid very little attention to us.

The Resident, with his staff, received me in the usual pagoda-shaped, Chinese official residence. He again referred to the obstinate and insubordinate attitude assumed by the Tibetans, and said that in Eastern Tibet they had given the Chinese a great deal of trouble. I expressed my opinion that the Tibetans were grossly ungrateful, for they owed much to the Chinese, and certainly, after the Sikkim campaign, they would not have come off so easily in the ensuing settlement if the Chinese had not interceded on their behalf. It was merely on account of the friendly feeling we entertained towards the Chinese that the settlement we then made was so light. Now, however, that they had repudiated the settlement which the Amban had made on their behalf, and had otherwise offended us, the new settlement would, of course, be more severe, and I should be greatly obliged if the Amban would make them understand from the start that the terms which I was going to demand from them would have to be accepted.

The Amban asked me if I would give him the terms. I replied that if he would send over one of his Secretaries to Mr. Wilton, he would inform him of them and explain them to him, and the Amban and I could then talk the matter over at an early opportunity.

I then asked the Amban if he would get the Tibetans to depute two or three representatives for the special purpose of negotiating a settlement with me. A variety of delegates had been sent to meet me on the way up, but it was desirable that the same men, without change, should continue to negotiate with me till the settlement was arrived at. The Amban promised to arrange this. After

MISSION QUARTERS, LHASA.

To face page 267.

apologizing for introducing business matters into the conversation during my first visit to him, I took leave of the Amban and returned to camp by a détour through the heart of the city.

Two of the Councillors, with two Secretaries, called upon me on the following day with 280 coolie-loads of tea, sugar, dried fruits, flour, peas, and butter, and bringing also 20 yaks, 50 sheep, and Rs. 1,500 in cash. With the object of getting into the next best house in Lhasa, I made a pretence of wishing to go into the Dalai Lama's Summer Palace, which was in the plain close by, and eventually arranged that the house of the first Duke in Tibet should be at my disposal. This would contain the whole of my staff, as well as an escort of two companies, and was therefore, both for purposes of possible defence and also for receptions, much more suitable than a camp in the open plain.

I had now got into touch with both the Chinese Resident and the highest Tibetan officials, and I was also on the same day—August 5—to see the two men who were eventually to be of the greatest help to me as intermediaries—the Nepal representative who was permanently stationed at Lhasa, and the old Tongsa Penlop of Bhutan, who had just arrived from Gyantse.

Captain Jit Bahadur had been many years in Lhasa, and was much respected. He had very courteous manners, and was much more quick and alert than the Tibetans. He had orders from his Government to give me every assistance, and no one could have been more helpful.

The Tongsa Penlop had neither the local knowledge nor the quickness of Captain Jit Bahadur; but he was a man of more importance—he is indeed now Maharaja of Bhutan—and his representations carried weight. He and Mr. White soon made a firm friendship, and together they did much to bring the negotiations through.

There was still no sign, though, of any definite delegates being appointed to negotiate with me, and on August 8 I had to report to Government that the Tibetan Government was in utter confusion. My old friend the Ta Lama had been disgraced, as, poor man, he always told me he would be if we advanced to Lhasa. My other friend the Yutok Sha-pé, who had met me at Nagartse, had very sensibly, or perhaps naturally, gone sick. Of the two remaining Councillors, one was useless and the other inimical. The National Assembly sat continuously, but only criticized what anyone did, and was afraid to do anything itself without reference to the Dalai Lama. And the Dalai Lama, who had fled on our approach to Lhasa and was three days distant, would not in his turn act without sanction of the Assembly. Everyone was in fear, not now of us, but of his next-door neighbour: and each was working against the other. No attempt at commencing negotiations had been made, though I had given the Resident an outline of our terms. The Tongsa Penlop and the Nepalese representative constantly visited me, but expressed despair at the silliness of the Tibetans, and said their heads ached with arguing with them. The general attitude of the Tibetans, though exasperating, was, I thought, probably more futile and inept than intentionally hostile. But yet it was not easy to see then how in my limited time I was to get a definite treaty signed, sealed, and delivered out of such an intangible, illusive, un-get-at-able set of human beings as I now found in front of me.

The very next day, though, a ray of light appeared which was in the end to show the way to a solution of our difficulties. The Nepalese representative came to inform me that on the previous night he went to see the Ti Rimpoche, the Regent to whom the Dalai Lama had handed over his seal, and had explained to him that matters were getting serious. The Regent replied that he and the Dalai Lama's brother were anxious to make a settlement, and were of opinion that the Government terms might well be accepted with two or three modifications. The Regent thought that the amount of indemnity I had named—Rs. 50,000 a day—was excessive. And he would ask that if they released the two Lachung men we should release the yaks and men whom we had seized last year in retaliation. With those modifications he thought the National Assembly might reasonably accept our terms.

THE COUNCIL.

To face page 268.

The Nepalese representative said the Regent was a moderate man, more inclined to make a peaceful settlement than the generality of the National Assembly. Captain Jit Bahadur having hinted that the Regent and the Dalai Lama's brother were anxious to visit me, I told him to let the Regent know that I would be glad to receive him; and I asked him to tell the Regent from me that we had no wish to be other than on friendly terms with the Tibetans. We had no desire to make war upon them or object to gain by it; we did not wish to annex their country; and the Viceroy had given me the very strictest orders to respect their religion, so that when I heard from him (the Nepalese representative) and the Tongsa Penlop that the Tibetans considered the Summer Palace a sacred building, I had consented to take up my residence elsewhere, even though at inconvenience to myself. But while we had thus no wish to make war, and were prepared to respect their religion, the Tibetans were putting me in a very difficult position. They had asked me to stop hostilities, saying they wished to make a settlement, but although they had been acquainted with the terms for three weeks, and I had already been here a week, yet not one word of negotiation had yet passed between me and them. Nor had they made proper efforts to furnish the troops with supplies. If they failed to negotiate, what could I do? It seemed to me that the Tibetans were like men in a bog. They were sinking deeper and deeper. Last year they were in up to their knees only. A month ago they were up to their waists. Now they were up to their necks. And in a short time, if they would not accept the hand which was stretched out to them by the Regent, they would be in over their heads

I called upon the Chinese Resident on the 10th and impressed upon him the responsibility which lay on the Chinese Government to induce the Tibetans to make a settlement. He said he was most anxious to work with me, and had sent a message to the Dalai Lama to return. But I heard from other sources that the Dalai Lama was now eight marches off, and had with him the Siberian Buriat Dorjieff, to whom the Tibetans attributed all their troubles, but who was reported to have very sagaciously advised the Dalai Lama to retire for a bit, as the English would soon calm down and disappear again like the bubbles in boiling water which subside when the water has cooled.

The Tibetans' so-called reply to our terms was the next day communicated by the Resident's secretary to Mr. Wilton. The Tibetans refused each single point, and said that an indemnity was due from us to them rather than from them to us. The only trade-mart they would concede was Rinchengong, which was scarcely two miles beyond Yatung. I had the document returned to the Resident with a message that I could not officially receive so preposterous a reply.

The Resident called upon me the next day and said he had received a reply to our terms, but it was so impertinent he could not even mention it to me officially. He had sent it back to the Tibetans censuring them for their stupidity, and ordering them to send a more fit reply. He had pointed out to them their folly in not settling with us, and how impossible it was for them to contend against us.

He then made a singularly interesting remark. The ordinary people, he said, were not at all ill-disposed towards us. They liked us, and were anxious to trade with us. Reports of our treatment of the wounded, and of the liberal payment we made for supplies, had spread about the country, and the people in general would be glad enough to make a settlement and be on good terms. Where the opposition came from was from the Lamas, more especially those of the three great monasteries. They and they alone were the obstructionists, and if they were out of the way there would be no more trouble, and the people would speedily be friends with us.

I told the Amban that this was extremely interesting and gratifying to hear, and that what he had said entirely bore out my own conclusions. It made me all the more sorry that so many of these poor peasants with whom we had no quarrel, and who only wished to be friendly with us, should have been killed, and this was one consideration which was restraining us from fighting now. I had on several occasions during the recent fighting gone round the dead Tibetans, and invariably found that they were peasants. A Lama was never seen. If we could be quite sure that the originators of all this fighting would fight themselves, I was not sure that we would have been so ready to suspend hostilities.

Before the close of his visit I asked the Amban if the Nepalese and Kashmiris kept on good terms with the Tibetans here. He replied that they got on well enough with the ordinary people, but avoided the Lamas, as contact with them was liable to lead to trouble. He added that the Nepalese representative had been ordered by the Prime Minister of Nepal to advise the Tibetans to be reasonable and come to a settlement with us, and to tell them that the British respected the religion of others and would not interfere with theirs. I said I had heard of this, and if the Tibetans had only followed this good advice, which was given a year ago, we might have settled up everything at Khamba Jong. What the Prime Minister of Nepal had said about the tolerance of other religions was perfectly true. We had many millions of Buddhists under our rule, about 200,000,000 Hindus, and 70,000,000 Mohammedans. The Tibetan fear that we would interfere with their religion was altogether unfounded. The Amban replied that they were so jealous of their religion that they tried to prevent even Chinese Buddhists of other sects from their own from entering Tibet.

On August 13 two Sha-pés, the Dalai Lama's private Abbot, a Secretary of Council, and the Accountant-General paid me a formal visit. I remarked that the Amban had told me that they had drawn up a document which they had presented to him as a reply to our terms, but which was so impertinent that the Amban had said he could not even mention it to me officially. The deputation replied that they were really anxious to make a settlement, and the document they had presented to the Amban merely represented their views, and was not intended as a reply to me. Their idea was to give the Amban their opinion, and he would give orders upon it.

I asked them whether they were prepared to obey the orders of the Amban. They said that if the Amban gave orders acceptable to both them and him they would obey. I asked them if by that they meant that they would obey his orders if they liked them, but would pay no attention to them if they were not according to their taste. They replied that their idea was that the Amban should act as a sort of mediator. We would both present our views to him, and he would decide between us, and make a settlement satisfactory to both. When they had stated their case to him they had no intention to be impertinent; they were a small people, and ignorant of the ways of great nations; they thought that if they asked much at first, they might not obtain all they asked, but would obtain a part.

I told them I had already warned the Amban that I was not here to act the part of a merchant in the bazaar and haggle over terms. When I arrived at Khamba Jong last year, I had, indeed, then been prepared to discuss the terms of a settlement, and by give and take arrive at a mutually satisfactory agreement. I had, for instance, announced that we were prepared to concede the Giagong lands to them if they showed themselves reasonable in regard to trade concessions elsewhere. But they had declined to negotiate, and had chosen to fight. They had been beaten, and had no further means of continuing the struggle against us. They must, therefore, accept our terms or expect us to take still further action against them. The terms we were now asking were extremely moderate, but if we were compelled to undertake more military operations they would have to be made much more severe.

They begged me to be more reasonable and to discuss things more quietly; they said they were accustomed to talk matters over at great length; they hoped that the Resident would be able to persuade me to be more considerate; and they suggested that I should ask the Viceroy to let me demand easier terms from them. I reminded them that they had been aware of the terms for three weeks now, and I had been ready, on the way up

THE TI-RIMPOCHE.

To face page 273.

here, to explain them to them. I had now been ten days at Lhasa; they had not yet come to talk to me about them; and I had heard from the Resident that, so far from showing any inclination to agree with them, they had written about them in very impertinent terms. They must not be surprised, therefore, that my patience was exhausted. The terms which I had shown them were issued by command of the British Government, and no reference to His Excellency the Viceroy would have the slightest effect in modifying them.

The next day I had a much more interesting interview. The Ti Rimpoche himself came to see me. He was the Chief Doctor of Divinity and Metaphysics of Tibet, and was an old and much respected Lama, to whom the Dalai Lama had left his seals of office and whom he had appointed Regent. He remembered seeing Huc and Gabet as a boy, and he was a cultured, pleasant-mannered, amiable old gentleman, with a kindly, benevolent expression. He was accompanied by the Nepalese representative, and brought with him a present of gold-dust and some silk from the Dalai Lama's brother.

After some polite observations, he asked me whether we English believed in reincarnation. I said we believed that when we died our bodies remained here and our souls went up to heaven. He said that that might happen to the good people, but where did the bad people go to? I replied that we had no bad: we were all good. He laughed, and said that, at any rate, he hoped that both of us would be good during this negotiation. Then we might both go to heaven. I said I had not the smallest doubt that we should.

He then said he would have liked to come and see me before, but was afraid of the Sha-pés. He told me how he had been hastily summoned by the Dalai Lama a few weeks ago, but on his arrival had found the Dalai Lama had fled. He had greatly disliked taking up political business, for he had spent his whole life in religious study, and was altogether ignorant of the methods of public affairs. But the Sha-pés and people in the palace had given him a message from the Dalai Lama, handing over the Dalai

Lama's seal to him, and telling him he was to act as Regent during the Dalai Lama's absence.

The Ti Rimpoche then stated that what he had come to see me about was to ask me to show consideration towards their religion, and not destroy their monasteries. When he had come to look into affairs, he had convinced himself that those responsible for the conduct of them had acted very stupidly, and should have made a settlement with us long ago. Now they were beaten and had to accept our terms, but he hoped we would show them consideration. They were sending to the Dalai Lama to return, and he thought he ought to be here to make a settlement with us.

I told him that I thoroughly sympathized with him in the very unpleasant position in which he was placed. Others had brought trouble upon the country, and he had been called in at the last moment to repair the mischief. But while he was in an awkward position, I hoped he would realize the difficulty in which I also was placed. I had received the orders of the Viceroy to show the utmost consideration to their religion. I had also received orders to make a settlement on the terms which had been determined on by the British Government. But the settlement on these terms had to be made with the National Assembly, which was almost entirely composed of ecclesiastics. The Resident had told me yesterday that the reply which they had made to our terms was so impertinent that he dare not even mention it to me officially. If, then, this assembly of ecclesiastics refused our terms, what was I to do? I had to show consideration to them and their monasteries because of their sacred calling. I had also to get my terms agreed to. Could he suggest any way of doing this except by force?

The Ti Rimpoche said he altogether disagreed with the reply which had been sent to the Amban, but the others were determined to send it; not that they really meant what they said, but they thought that if they put their case strongly at the beginning, they might get easier terms out of me. He again begged me, however, to show consideration.

I said I would be very much obliged to him if he would at the earliest opportunity try to persuade the National Assembly that I was not here to bargain over terms. I was here, by direction of the Viceroy, to carry out the commands of the British Government in making a settlement. The terms of that settlement were drawn up with an especial regard for their religion. We were annexing no part of Tibet; we were not asking for an agent here at Lhasa itself; but we had to ask for an indemnity, because the military operations which had been forced on us in 1888 and in the present year had cost a very great deal of money. The Tibetans had caused the trouble. We had, therefore, to ask them to pay at least a part of the expense. We knew, however, that Tibet was too poor a country to pay the whole. We were, therefore, asking scarcely half of the real cost, and we expected that the Tibetans would give us, who had to suffer by having to pay the remainder of the cost, the advantage of being able to come to Tibet to buy wool and other things which were produced more cheaply here than in India, and of selling to the Tibetans the surplus of articles produced more cheaply in India.

The Regent said he thought this quite reasonable, and he would explain my view to the National Assembly. As to the Dalai Lama, I said I was quite prepared to give him the most positive assurance that he would be safe from us if he returned here. I did not wish to discuss personally with him the details of the settlement, but wished him to affix his seal in my presence; and it would certainly be more convenient if he were nearer Lhasa for reference during the negotiations. The Regent said he would send two messengers to him to-morrow, advising him to return. The trouble was, though, that he had nobody about him to advise him properly. At the close of the interview I told the Ti Rimpoche that I should be glad to see him again. He was an old man, and was, I knew, very busy just now, but whenever he liked to come and talk with me I should be most pleased to receive him.

The first sign of yielding came on August 15, when the Resident intimated to me that he had pressed the

Tibetan Government to make a start towards a settlement by releasing the two Lachung men (British subjects) who had been seized last year beyond Khamba Jong, and that the Tibetan Government had agreed. He wished to know when and in what manner they should be handed over. I informed him that they should be handed over to me the next morning by two members of the Council.

That morning I held a full Durbar, and two members of Council, accompanied by two Lamas, brought the two Lachung men before me. I told the men, who showed the liveliest satisfaction at their impending release, that I had received the commands of the King-Emperor to obtain their release from the Tibetan Government, and they were now free. His Majesty had further commanded that if they had been ill-treated reparation should be demanded from the Tibetan Government. I wished to know, therefore, if they had been ill-treated or not. They said they had been slightly beaten at Shigatse, and their things had been taken from them, but since their arrival in Lhasa they had been well fed and had not been beaten. I told them that they would be examined by a medical officer, to ascertain if their statements were correct.

I then turned to the Tibetan Councillors and said that the King-Emperor considered the seizure, imprisonment, and beating of two of his subjects as an exceedingly serious offence. It formed one of the main reasons why the Mission had moved forward from Khamba Jong to Gyantse, and one of the principal terms of the settlement, which I had been commanded to make at Lhasa itself, was the release of these men. If the Tibetan Government had not cared to have them in Tibet they should have returned them across the frontier, or, in any case, have handed them over to us at Khamba Jong. Their seizure and imprisonment for a year was altogether unpardonable. I trusted they now understood that the subjects of the King-Emperor could not be ill-treated with impunity, and that we would in future, as we did now, hold them strictly responsible for the good treatment of British subjects in Tibet.

The Lachung men were then taken out and examined

by a medical officer, in the presence of Mr. White and two Tibetan officials. The medical officer reported that there were no signs on their bodies of their having been beaten, and that they were in good condition. On receiving this report I expressed my satisfaction that the ill-treatment had not been severe. I would not, therefore, press the matter of reparation; but imprisonment for a year was in itself sufficiently bad treatment to British subjects who had committed no offence, and we expected that no British subjects would ever be so treated again. The Sha-pés promised to respect the subjects of His Majesty in future. They expressed their pleasure that one of the terms of the settlement had been concluded, and hoped, now a start was made, an agreement would quickly be come to. It was, at any rate, their intention to proceed as rapidly as possible in their discussions. It subsequently transpired that the two men had been kept separately in dungeons, twenty-one steps below the surface of the ground, and had not seen daylight for nearly a year. But as they were in excellent health and well fed, and as we had, while at Khamba Jong, seized over 200 yaks in retaliation, I did not pursue the matter farther. The most satisfactory feature in this affair was the fact that the release had taken place entirely on the initiative of the Amban.

I visited the Resident on the following day, and thanked him for procuring the release of the two Sikkim men. He said he would denounce the Dalai Lama to the Emperor if he did not come back, and would summon the Tashi Lama, with a view to making him the head of the whole Buddhist Church in Tibet. He also said that he recognized the Ti Rimpoche, who held the seal left by the Dalai Lama, as the principal in the negotiations. This was a decided advance, though it had taken a fortnight of my precious six weeks to make; and I was also able to report to Government that the general situation was certainly improving; that supplies, which at first we had been only able to secure by the threat of force and by surrounding a monastery, were now coming in steadily; and people were showing growing confidence, while even the National Assembly were slowly giving way, and the party in favour of settlement were increasing in influence.

On August 19 the Resident visited me, and handed to me the second reply of the Tibetan Government to his letter forwarding to them the terms of the settlement we now wished to make with them. The first reply he had been unable to forward, as it was too impudent. This second reply, he said, I would find on perusal was more satisfactory, though it still fell short of what he would expect the Tibetans to agree to.

I told the Resident that I found it difficult to make the Tibetans realize that the main points in the settlement we should expect them to agree to without question. The period in which the indemnity was to be paid might be a matter for discussion, but there was no question as to its having to be paid some time. Similarly, they must agree to having marts at Gyantse and Gartok. I remarked that I had all along been of opinion that nothing could be got out of these Tibetans except by pressure, and I was fully prepared to act. At the same time, it would be much more satisfactory if the needful pressure could be put on by the Resident, as I had no wish to take more action unless absolutely compelled to.

I added that a difficulty I experienced in dealing with the Tibetans was in talking with so many representatives at the same time. Half a dozen delegates would come to me, and each one insist upon having his say, and no responsible head was recognized. The Amban said that he, too, had had this difficulty, but that he had recognized the Regent as the principal in these negotiations, and from now on he intended to negotiate with him alone; he was the best man among the leading Tibetans, and came next after the Dalai Lama in the Lhasa province. I said this seemed to me a wise course, for I had found the Regent a sensible man, and he was much respected by the people.

As regards the Convention itself, the Amban said he would have to discuss the clause regarding trade-marts with me. I said I was prepared to talk the matter over, but we should have to insist upon establishing trade-marts at Gyantse and Gartok, and I did not understand the

Tibetan objections to the establishment of a mart at Gyantse, for we had the right more than a century ago to have one even at Shigatse. This right had not been exercised for a great number of years, but at one time Indian traders visited Shigatse regularly.

We now received certain information that the Dalai Lama had finally fled. He had written to the National Assembly, saying that the English were very crafty people, and warning them to be careful in making an agreement with them, and to bind them tight. He added that he himself would go away and look after the interests of the faith. His departure was not regretted by Tibetans.

The Ti Rimpoche and others came to me on the 21st with silks to the value of Rs. 5,000, which I had imposed as a fine for the assault which a monk with a sword had made just outside our camp on Captains Cooke-Young and Kelly, dealing the former a very severe blow over the head. After this the Ti Rimpoche, the Tongsa Penlop, and the Nepalese representative proceeded to talk over the general situation. The Ti Rimpoche said that he himself had no objection to our terms except in regard to the indemnity, which he thought was too heavy, as Tibet was a poor country. He pointed out the difficulty which the Tibetans had found in paying up the small fine I had imposed on them, and asked how they could be expected to pay the sum of Rs. 50,000 a day which I was demanding. He said, of course, we thought ourselves in the right in this quarrel, but it was difficult for him to make the Assembly acquiesce in this view, and it might be well if I would impress our views upon them.

I said that if only they had behaved more sensibly in the beginning all this trouble would have been saved: there would have been no war, and no indemnity would have been asked. We had not wished for war, and I had gone with Captain O'Connor, without any escort, into their camp at Guru, in January to reason quietly with the leaders there, and ask them to report my views to Lhasa. If we had wanted war I should never have so acted. That I did was proof that we wished for peace. But they refused to report my words to Lhasa, and hence this trouble. The Ti Rimpoche here interpolated that they were afraid to report anything to the Dalai Lama. I went on to say that it was not fair to expect India to pay all the cost of a war brought on by the foolishness of the Tibetan rulers, so we had to ask that the Tibetans should pay part of the sum. Yet even now we were not asking for more than half of the whole cost. I was demanding Rs. 50,000 a day from the date of the attack on the Mission till a month after the date on which the Convention was signed. The Ti Rimpoche would note that I was not asking payment from the date of the Guru fight, because that fight might have been due to mere foolishness on the part of the leaders, but from the date when the Tibetans deliberately attacked the Mission at Gyantse, after I had repeatedly notified that I had come to negotiate. From that date, therefore, we expected them to contribute to the cost of military operations.

The Ti Rimpoche had said that the Tibetans had very little cash. If that was so, I was prepared to consider the question of extending the period in which the payment of the indemnity could be made. I would also consider whether some of it could not be paid in kind to the trade agent in Gyantse and the officer commanding in Chumbi. The Ti Rimpoche said he wished the settlement with us to be fully completed now, so that we could have it over and be friends; but if the Tibetans had to go on paying us an indemnity for some years after, the raw would be kept up, and friendship would be difficult. I replied that if they would now at once pay the indemnity, we should be only too glad. But, in any case, we would not on our side harbour any ill-feelings towards the Tibetans, with whom we had no other desire than to live on terms of friendship.

The Tongsa Penlop then said that Tibet, Nepal, and Bhutan were bound together by the same religion, and all bordered on India. They ought, therefore, to look on England as their friend and leader. The English had no wish to interfere with them, but did not like anyone else interfering. They ought to stand together, therefore, for if one was hurt all were hurt. They could rely, however, on their big neighbour England to help them in time of trouble if they kept on good terms with her. The Nepalese representative agreed with the Tongsa Penlop that all four countries should be on terms of friendship with one another, and that Tibet, Nepal, and Bhutan should always preserve good relations with their neighbour England. The Ti Rimpoche said he trusted that when this settlement was made Tibet and England would always be on terms of friendship. The Tibetans had no wish to have relations with any other Power, and desired now to keep on good terms with England. I replied that we had been on perfectly good terms with Tibet for more than a century up till the time of the Sikkim War, and I hoped that when the present settlement was made we should be friends for ever.

I visited the Resident on August 21, and told him I had perused the Tibetan reply to him which he had handed to me at our last meeting. It was more satisfactory than the first reply, and there were some points which the Tibetans would now evidently agree to. I proposed, then, that we should get these points settled first and out of the way, so as to make a start, and then work on to the more contentious clauses.

I then remarked that I had heard the Dalai Lama had without any doubt whatever fled the country. The Amban said this was true, and he was evidently not flying to China, but to the north—possibly to join the Great Lama at Urga. I said he would hardly be flying to China, for he would surely have obtained the Amban's permission to proceed to Peking, or at least have informed him of his intention. The Amban replied that he had gone off without any warning, and he had now definitely decided to denounce him to the Emperor, and would to-day or to-morrow send me a telegram which he would ask me to have despatched to Peking as quickly as possible. I said I would do this service for him, and I considered he was acting with great wisdom in denouncing the Dalai Lama, for it was he who had brought all this trouble upon his country, and he deserved to suffer for it. I was not surprised, however, at so young a ruler coming to grief, for our experience in India was that a young chief, even when he had only temporal authority in his hands, was very liable to get into the power of unscrupulous and designing men, and rush off in a headstrong way on a foolish course. For a young Dalai Lama, who had not only temporal, but also supreme spiritual power, the tendency to go wrong must have been almost irresistible.

The Amban said this certainly had been the case with the present Dalai Lama, who had always been headstrong and obstinate, and had never followed good advice.

The four hostages which I had demanded, one from the Government and one from each of the great monasteries, for the good behaviour of the monks in future arrived on the 24th. They were in abject terror, and evidently thought they would have their heads cut off before their time was up. On the same day a proclamation was posted up in Lhasa by the Government, forbidding the people to interfere with foreigners in any way. This and the hanging of the monk who had made the murderous assault on the two British officers had the effect of stopping all other fanatical assaults, and after the treaty was signed I returned the fine and let out the hostages, who, much to their surprise, had had a very good time with us and been treated royally.

There was a considerable pause now in the course of the negotiations, though Captain O'Connor the whole time was, day by day and all day long, interviewing innumerable Tibetans of every grade; while Mr. White and I used to see the Tongsa Penlop and the Nepalese representative, and think of any means of getting over the difficulty about the indemnity. On August 28 the Ti Rimpoche, the Yutok Sha-pé, and the Tsarong Sha-pé, accompanied by the Tongsa Penlop, called upon me. They announced that they had been deputed by the National Assembly to discuss the settlement direct with me, as they thought there was delay in dealing through the Resident. I remarked that I understood they were fairly well agreed to accede to all our terms except in regard to the indemnity. They said they had written to the Amban, saying definitely that they would agree to all the terms except that regarding the payment of an indemnity, and except in regard to opening further marts in future. They expressed a wish to make the settlement directly with me, and when we had agreed upon it, then they would communicate the result to the Resident. I said that I should be ready to receive them whenever they wished to discuss matters with me. What I should tell them and what I should tell the Amban would be exactly the same, but if they liked to hear my views from me direct I would gladly receive them.

They then again announced that they were ready to agree to all our terms but one. The indemnity they could not pay. Tibet was a poor country, and the Tibetans had already suffered heavily during the war; many had been killed, their houses had been burnt, jongs and monasteries had been destroyed; and, in addition to all this evil, it was impossible for them to pay an indemnity as well. The little money they had was spent in religious services in support of the monasteries, in buying vessels for the temples and butter to burn before the gods. The peasants had to supply transport for officials, in addition, and there were no means whatever for paying the heavy indemnity we were demanding.

I replied that the war in Sikkim had cost us a million sterling, and the present war would cost another million. After the Sikkim War the Tibetans had repudiated the treaty which the Resident then made, and we might very justifiably now ask for an indemnity for the Sikkim War, as well as for this. We were, however, making no such demand, and we were only asking from Tibet half the cost of the present war. I knew, of course, that Tibet had suffered from the present war, but no such suffering need have occurred if they had negotiated with me at Khamba Jong in the previous year. And, while they had suffered, we also had not escaped without trouble. Captain O'Connor had himself been wounded, and what we looked upon as extremely serious in this matter was that the representative of the British Government should have been attacked. If they attacked the Resident here, they knew well how angry the Emperor of China would be. I quite recognized, however, the difficulty they had in paying the indemnity in cash within three years. I would, therefore, be prepared to receive proposals from them as to modifications in the manner of payment. If, for instance, they thought it impossible to pay the whole indemnity in three years, and would like the term extended to five, I would submit such a proposal for the orders of the Viceroy. Or, again, if they would prefer to pay the indemnity at the rate of a lakh of rupees a year for a long term of years, I would ask Government if the difficulty might be met in that way.

They expressed their disappointment at this answer, as they had hoped that when they had agreed to all our terms except this one I would have given way on it, and excused them paying the indemnity, and they trusted I would not send them back to the National Assembly with so disheartening an answer. In most cases of bargaining, if one party got half the things he had asked he would be satisfied. I had got all the points except one, and still was not satisfied. If I could not agree to that myself, would I not refer it to the Viceroy? If I did this they had great hopes the Viceroy would excuse them the indemnity.

I replied that a reference to the Viceroy would be of no use, for it happened that the terms I was now asking were modifications ordered by the British Government. The Ti Rimpoche said that if the British Government had been lenient once they might be lenient again, and asked me to put their petition before them. I replied that the British Government had considered this matter most carefully before issuing these demands, so if I now dared to suggest that one of them should not be carried out I should be immediately dismissed from my post. I was prepared, as I had said, to submit proposals for alternative methods of payment of the indemnity, and I would be also prepared to submit proposals for privileges of concessions in Tibet which might be taken in lieu of part of the indemnity, but the indemnity, in some manner or other, would have to be paid.

The Tsarong Sha-pé said we were accustomed to fish

in the ocean, and did not understand that there were not so many fish to be got out of a well as could be caught from the sea. A field could only yield according to its size and the amount put into it. A poor peasant got only just enough from his field to support himself and his family, with a very little over for religious offerings. It was hard, therefore, that we should demand so much from Tibet, and the National Assembly would be very much disheartened at the result of this interview.

I replied that what they had agreed to was what cost them nothing, and was, indeed, to their advantage. The opening of trade-marts would in reality prove of much more benefit to them than to us. The only thing that really cost them anything they were consistently refusing. Even on that point I was prepared to make it as easy for them in carrying out as possible, and I could not acknowledge that they had any cause for complaint.

The Tongsa Penlop then said that he hoped I would take into consideration the sufferings the Tibetans had already gone through, and, if I could, lay the matter before the Viceroy. I told the Tongsa Penlop that I was always glad to hear suggestions from one who had proved himself so stanch a friend of the British Government, and if he could think of some way which would save India from being saddled with the cost of this war, and at the same time not weigh too heavily upon the Tibetans, he would be doing a service which would be appreciated by both the Government of India and the Tibetans.

I now came to the conclusion that the Tibetans were trying to make dissension between the Resident and myself, so I asked the Amban when he next came to see me to bring the Tibetan Members of Council with him. He came on the 30th, accompanied by the Acting Regent and three Members of Council. I told him that we had had some misunderstanding with the Tibetans as to what precisely they did and did not agree to. They had informed me on a previous occasion that they had sent him a written agreement to accept all our terms except that regarding the indemnity. I proposed, therefore, on this occasion to ascertain from them precisely what they did agree to point by point. I then addressed the Tibetans in regard to Clause IX., which was the one I understood they had least objection to. I explained to them that by it we had not the least desire to supplant China in the suzerainty of Tibet. The Chinese suzerainty was fully recognized in the Adhesion Agreement, which it was proposed the Resident should sign on behalf of the Chinese Government, and China was not included in the term "foreign Power." We were not placing a British Resident here at Lhasa, and we were not asking for any railway or other concessions. What we asked in this clause was merely what was in accordance with their traditional policy. Did they agree to the clause?

They replied that they did not want to have anything to do with foreign Powers. They would, therefore, be able to agree to it.

The clause regarding the razing of fortifications was then discussed, and they began to raise objections, but I cut them short by observing that all the fortifications named were in our hands, and would be destroyed whether they agreed or not. The clause had been drafted by Government before the fortifications were in our possession. Their agreement was, therefore, merely a formality. They said that in that case they would agree.

We then discussed at length the clauses relating to the opening of new trade-marts. They had an idea we wished them to make a road from Gyantse to Gartok, and to make big roads by blasting. I assured them that all we wanted was that the roads from the frontier to Gyantse, and from the frontier to Gartok, should be kept in repair. We did not expect new roads to be constructed by them, but existing roads kept suitable for trade purposes.

The sentence regarding the opening of more trade-marts in future they very strongly objected to. I pointed out, however, that we were merely asking them to consider this, and not to decide on it now. I said we might reasonably have now demanded a mart here, at Lhasa itself, and in half a dozen other places, and I could not permit them to refuse merely considering the question of future extension. The Resident added that their objections were frivolous, and trade-marts were to their advantage. To the establishment of marts at Gyantse and Gartok they agreed, and the discussion having now lasted two hours, and I having told the Amban that we had done about as much as it was possible to do in one day, he dismissed them.

The next day the Ti Rimpoche, the Tongsa Penlop, and the Nepalese representative came to see me. The Ti Rimpoche said that there was a good deal of opposition to the clause regarding opening other trade-marts in future. The Tibetans did not wish to be bound by anything in regard to the future. I said it was really the least important sentence in the whole Convention. It secured nothing definite for us. It did not say, for instance, that after ten years a third trade-mart should be opened, but merely that the matter should be considered. Now, however, that the matter had, in the last official interview with the Amban, been put forward in official discussion by the Tibetan Council, I was bound to maintain the sentence. While I did not expect that they should now *accede* to the future opening of trade-marts, I could not accept their *refusal* to open them. The matter must remain, as stated in the draft Convention, one for future consideration.

The Ti Rimpoche then again dwelt upon the impossibility of paying what he considered so heavy an indemnity. He said, laughing, that we must remember the losses which not only we, but their own troops, had inflicted on the country. I repeated my old arguments as to the unfairness of saddling India with the whole cost of a war necessitated by the folly and stupidity of Tibetans. It was bad enough to impose on India half the cost, but anything more than that would be a great injustice. The Ti Rimpoche said that we were putting on the donkey a greater load than it could possibly carry. I replied that I was not asking the donkey to carry the whole load in one journey. It could go backwards and forwards many times, carrying a light load each journey. The Ti Rimpoche laughed again, and asked what would happen if the donkey died. I said I should ask the Resident to see that the donkey was properly treated, so that there should be no fear of its dying. Dropping metaphor, I told the acting Regent I was really quite prepared to receive proposals as to easier methods of paying the indemnity. If, for instance, they could not pay the full amount in three years, I would receive and consider proposals as to paying in a larger number of years, or any other reasonable proposal.

The Ti Rimpoche replied that the Tibetans disliked the idea of prolonging the time during which they would be under obligation to us. They wanted to settle the business up at once and have done with it. I asked him if, in that case, he had any other suggestions to make. He made none, but the Tongsa Penlop suggested to him that the Tibetans should let us collect the Customs duties at the new trade-marts, and get the amount of the indemnity from that source. The Ti Rimpoche said that, while he personally saw the wisdom of agreeing to our terms, he could not persuade the National Assembly to be reasonable. I said I quite saw that he was more sensible than the National Assembly, and that he was doing his best to bring them to reason. When, therefore, I used hard words and employed threats, he must consider them as directed at the stupid, obstructive people, and not at himself personally.

CHAPTER XVIII

THE TREATY CONCLUDED

We were now at the end of August; my time was very short, and I was in an awkward predicament. On the 30th I had telegraphed to Government that the Tibetans, in spite of their protests of poverty, could really pay the indemnity, but that I thought trade concessions in lieu of a portion would be preferable. I also asked for liberty to arrange for payment of the indemnity by instalments of one lakh of rupees (£6,666) a year for a long term of years, if that arrangement were preferred by the Tibetans, a proposal which I had also made a month before. On the same day I was told by General Macdonald that September 15 was the latest date to which he could remain at Lhasa. The Secretary of State had telegraphed to the Viceroy* that "the date on which the return of the force from Lhasa is to begin should be fixed by the military authorities in communication with Younghusband." In accordance with these instructions, General Macdonald telegraphed to the Adjutant-General† that he had consulted me with regard to fixing a date for our departure, that I had said I could not fix any date, but thought the beginning of October the earliest, and could not guarantee that. The medical authorities considered September 1 the latest safe date. The officers commanding units thought the 12th might be risked. General Macdonald himself was prepared to stay till September 15, and would delay the departure a few days longer if that would make the difference. There had already been snow on the hills round Lhasa and Nagartse, there was heavy snow on the Karo-la and at Ralung, with severe

* Blue-book, III., p. 51. † *Ibid.*, p. 242.

frost on the Karo-la, and the return march would take nineteen days. General Macdonald concluded that September 13 was the latest safe date for our stay in Lhasa, and would be glad of immediate orders, but, in the absence of orders to the contrary, would fix the 15th for the departure.

From the purely military point of view this was perfectly sound, and latterly the emphasis had been so much laid upon military considerations that I had not much hope of this date being altered. It had, indeed, got into the papers from some military office in Simla, and reached Peking. I was then in a very critical position. The Treaty was almost within my grasp, but I might be pulled back by military considerations before I had time to conclude it.

On the other hand, Mr. White, Captain O'Connor, and I had between us interviewed at length all the principal men in Lhasa, and if we had not fully convinced them, we had, at any rate, broken down most of their opposition. And the Nepalese and Bhutanese, and the Chinese Resident, too, had worked away to bring about the same result. The consequence was that about this time I was pretty well convinced that the bulk of them had at the back of their minds decided to agree to our terms, and put an end to the business. They all realized that the Dalai Lama, or his previous advisers, had blundered into a hopeless position, out of which they had to get as best they might. No one man liked to get up and propose that they should agree to our terms. But if they were put in a position when *all* had to agree, no one would undertake the responsibility of *objecting*. That was how I gauged the situation.

The time to strike had come. If I had moved earlier, before the Tibetans had, each of them, had the opportunity of blowing off steam, I should simply have aroused more armed opposition. If I delayed, I might have to leave Lhasa through military considerations before I ever got the chance. I had asserted fifteen months before, in a letter to my father written when just starting for Tibet, that I would sit tight any length of time, but when my opportunity came, as come it must, I would strike in hard and sharp. The psychological moment had exactly arrived, and I determined to use it. I told the Chinese Resident that I would call on him on September 1 with the full final draft of the Treaty, and that I would like the Tibetan Council and the members of the National Assembly to be present when I met him. In the presence of the Chinese representative, I meant to inform the whole of the leading men of Lhasa, monk, lay, and official, that they must sign the Treaty, or take the consequences of refusal.

On the appointed day, September 1, with my whole staff, all of us in full-dress uniform, I rode through the city of Lhasa to the Chinese Residency. Here the Resident received me with his usual courtesy, and after some general conversation, I intimated to him that I would proceed to business. He thereupon summoned the Sha-pés, who, after salutations, took their seats on stools in the centre of the room. Most of the members of the National Assembly then present in Lhasa also came in, and were huddled into the corners.

I then rose and presented the Resident with the full final draft of the Treaty (precisely as I had received it from Government), in English, Chinese, and Tibetan. The Resident handed the Tibetan copy to the Sha-pés, and when all were seated again, I asked the Resident's permission to address a few words to the Tibetans in regard to the Treaty. The Resident having assented, I said that as this was the first opportunity I had had of addressing members of the National Assembly, I wished to take advantage of it to let them know that if they had negotiated with me at Khamba Jong, or even at Gyantse when I first arrived there, the terms would not have been as severe as these we were now asking. We would merely have arranged trade and boundary questions, and there would have been no demand for an indemnity. By following the advice the Resident had given them, they might have been saved all the trouble in which they found themselves involved. They had chosen to fight, and had been defeated, and had to pay the consequences. Yet even now we were not demanding the whole, but only half, the cost of the military operations. The other half would have to fall upon India. The sum we were now asking would, if the Treaty were signed the next day, be 75 lakhs of rupees, calculated at the rate of Rs. 50,000 a day from the date on which I was attacked at Gyantse till one month after the date of signature of the Treaty. If they signed it on September 3, the amount would be 75½ lakhs. If on September 4, 76 lakhs, and so on. I was prepared to explain any point in the final draft which they did not understand, but I could not further discuss the terms. They had been especially framed with moderation. They embodied the commands of the British Government, and would have to be accepted. I would give them another week within which they might receive explanations and think matters over. But I could not give them any longer time, for while they were punishing themselves by adding day by day to the amount of the indemnity, they were also punishing India, who had to pay the other half of the cost.

They asked to be allowed to take away the final draft and consider it. I said that, as long as they did not mind paying Rs. 50,000 a day, they might consider it, and come to me or my secretary for explanations. They then made an appeal to the Resident to intercede with me on their behalf. The Resident merely acknowledged their request, and then, after asking me if I had anything further to say to them, dismissed them.

When they were gone, I said to the Resident that I was sorry to have to speak to them as I had done, but my experience had been that soft words and reasoning had no effect on their obstinate natures. I then said that the Tibetans were agreeing to all the terms, which did not hurt them in the least, and were, indeed, advantageous, but were refusing the indemnity, the only one of the terms which cost them anything. Excluding foreigners was in accordance with their traditional policy, and was therefore no sacrifice. As to opening trade-marts, that was to their advantage. They were born traders and bargainers, as we were finding to our cost, for they were extorting extravagant prices from us for the articles they brought for sale to our camp.

The Resident and his staff laughed heartily over this, and said that trade-marts were of course to their advantage. As to the indemnity, I said I had had some experience of Native States, and comparing Tibet with them, I should say Tibet was quite able to pay the amount we were asking. If, however, the Tibetans could not pay the whole amount within three years, I was quite prepared, as I had informed them, to receive proposals for the extension of the period of payment. The Resident thought this reasonable, but made no further remark.

I then observed that the draft Convention which I had received from Government was made out between me and the Dalai Lama. Was there any chance of the Dalai Lama returning in time to conclude the Convention with me? The Resident said there was not. I thereupon asked with whom, in that case, I should conclude the Treaty. He said that the Ti Rimpoche would act as Regent, and would use the seal which the Dalai Lama had left with him, and this seal would be supported by the seals of the National Assembly, of the Council, and of the three great monasteries.

My bolt had been shot: what would be the result? This was the thought which I kept asking myself as I rode back through the streets of Lhasa. Would the Tibetans fight? Would they brazen it out, and still remain obstinate? Or would they, perhaps, fly as the Dalai Lama had done? On the whole, I thought they would take none of these courses, or I would not have acted as I had done, for all the way through I had tried to follow the principle of looking before I made a step in advance, so that when my foot was once down, I could keep it down. It was a dull and heavy method of procedure, but was the best way, I thought, of impressing an obstinate people like the Tibetans. I considered, on the whole, that their resistance to our demands would now collapse, though I was naturally anxious as to the result.

On the day following, September 2, one of the Councillors and some other officials visited Captain

O'Connor, and went through the draft Treaty with him word by word. On the same day the Tongsa Penlop suggested, on his own initiative, to the Tibetans that they should let us collect the Customs duty at the marts, and get the amount of the indemnity from that source. I telegraphed to Government that I was making no move in this matter of adjusting the difficulty about the indemnity till the Tibetans made definite proposals, but that I thought it would be advantageous to move, and would like the views of Government.

On September 4 the Ti Rimpoche (the Regent) and a Secretary of Council, accompanied by the Tongsa Penlop and the Nepalese representative, came to me and announced that the Tibetan Government were prepared to conclude the Treaty with me if the term for the payment of the indemnity would be extended, and the payment made in seventy-five annual instalments of one lakh of rupees each.

I kept Captain O'Connor talking with them for a few minutes while I turned the whole question over in my mind once more before I gave a final decision. One very easy course I might have adopted was to say that I must refer the matter to Government and await their orders. But before I could get an answer military considerations might have predominated, and I might find myself forced to leave Lhasa. As the Government of India subsequently said, the language of the communications which they received from the Home Government was such as to impress on them and me alike that they were strongly averse to any prolongation of the stay at Lhasa. I had, therefore, no assurance that I should have time to go on discussing this point with the Tibetans. Then, again, I thought that in the matter of the indemnity a certain amount of latitude had been left me. The Secretary of State's instructions on this point were: "In regard to the question of an indemnity, the sum to be demanded should not exceed an amount which, it is believed, will be within the power of the Tibetans to pay, by instalments, if necessary, spread over three years. Colonel Younghusband will be guided by circumstances in this matter." The full despatch was more definite than this telegram. But the despatch had not yet arrived. Some degree of discretion was left me. Was I justified by the very difficult circumstances in which I found myself in stretching it to seventy-five years? This was the question I had to settle in my mind while the Regent was waiting for my reply.

But this question of the indemnity did not stand alone. It had to be taken in connection with another clause which would give us the right to occupy the Chumbi Valley until the indemnity was paid. I had, then, to ask myself further: Would an occupation of the Chumbi Valley for seventy-five years as a guarantee for the payment of an indemnity run counter to any pledge we had given to Russia? Now, Lord Lansdowne, when he gave his pledge, distinctly said that the action of Government must to some extent depend upon the conduct of the Tibetans themselves, and that His Majesty's Government could not undertake that they would not depart in any eventuality from the policy which then commended itself to them.

This was said to the Russian Ambassador on June 2, before Government had heard the result of our announcement to the Tibetans that we would be prepared to negotiate at Gyantse up to June 25. Since Lord Lansdowne had spoken to the Russian Ambassador, the Tibetans had continued fighting, had attacked me at Kangma, and by June 25 had sent no negotiators. The conduct of the Tibetans had, therefore, been such as might very well cause Government to alter their action.

Further, the Tibetans, during our advance to Lhasa, had opposed us at the Karo-la, and fired on us from Nagartse Jong. This opposition was indeed slight, because we had been obliged, after June 25, to break down at Gyantse the Tibetan forces which intervened between us and our advance to Lhasa. Had General Macdonald not captured the jong and dispersed the Tibetan forces round Gyantse, the opposition to our advance to Lhasa would have been very much greater than it was.

Since Lord Lansdowne had given his pledge to the Russian Ambassador, events had occurred—the failure to send accredited negotiators before June 25 and the continued opposition of the Tibetans—which might, I thought, be considered by His Majesty's Government sufficient justification for departing in some slight degree from the policy which on June 2, before they were completely aware of the nature of the Tibetan position, commended itself to them. Lord Lansdowne had said in April in the House of Lords, referring then to the policy laid down in the telegram of November 6, 1903, that he did not mean to say that, "whatever happened, we were never to move an inch beyond the limits therein laid down." And I thought that the policy settled in London, before Government were aware of the conditions I should find at Lhasa, would admit of some little elasticity.

Then, as regards the nature of the pledges themselves. The pledges given were that, "so long as no other Power endeavours to intervene in the affairs of Tibet, they [His Majesty's Government] will not attempt either to annex it, to establish a protectorate over it, or in any way to control its internal administration."

The question was, "Did the right to occupy the Chumbi Valley for seventy-five years, as security for the payment of an indemnity, involve a breach of this pledge?" Burma, in somewhat similar circumstances, we had annexed, but that meant turning out the native rulers, constituting a Government of our own, and stationing garrisons at the capital and throughout the country. Over Native States in India we established protectorates, but that necessarily involved subordinating their foreign relations to our own. In many of them we controlled the internal administration, but only by agents of Government being deputed especially for that purpose. Would the occupation of Chumbi, a valley lying altogether outside Tibet proper, on the Indian and not on the Tibetan side of the watershed, a valley which had not always belonged to Tibet, mean annexing Tibet, establishing a protectorate over it, or controlling its internal administration? This was the question I asked myself, and I answered it in the negative. I said to myself it involved none of the

THE CHUMBI VALLEY.

To face page 297.

three, and could not, therefore, be taken as breaking our pledges to Russia.

Others might not think likewise. But even if they did not, I could not see that if I agreed to the Tibetan proposals, including, as they would, the right for us to occupy the Chumbi Valley for seventy-five years, I was thereby involving Government in any fresh responsibility. I should not, for instance, be giving to the inhabitants a promise of our protection which it would be impossible for Government to repudiate. I should be simply acquiring for Government the right to occupy the Chumbi Valley for seventy-five years if they wanted to, and if they did not want to, they could go out whenever they liked. I was not "*compelling* the Government to occupy the Chumbi" Valley; I was simply acquiring the right, which they could abrogate if they did not want it.

Arguing thus with myself, I decided finally to seize the golden opportunity. If I let it go I knew not what might happen. The Regent might flee. The National Assembly might sulk. The Chinese might wake up and put in some obstruction. By agreeing I should be doing nothing counter to the wishes of the Government of India, for the amount of the indemnity was what they had themselves suggested, and they had on June 30,* after the pledges to Russia were given, spoken of retaining the Chumbi Valley, the occupation of which had been urged by the Bengal Government as far back as 1888. By agreeing I should also be effecting what my own experience showed me would be by far the most satisfactory permanent solution of the whole question. Chumbi is the key to Tibet. It is also the most difficult part of the road to Lhasa. Situated in the Chumbi Valley, we should have a clear run into Tibet, for the Tang-la (pass) across the watershed is an open plain several miles wide. The Chumbi Valley is the only strategical point of value in the whole north-eastern frontier from Kashmir to Burma. It was the surest guarantee for the fulfilment of the new Treaty which we could possibly get, except the establishment of an agent at Lhasa, and the obtaining of a

* Blue-book, III., p. 36.

guarantee had from the first been placed as one of the chief objects of my Mission.

Our main object was to put our relations with the Tibetans on a permanently satisfactory basis. By saying "yes" to the Regent's proposal I should be concluding a settlement which would admirably meet all our local requirements; which would, as they themselves had made it, best suit the Tibetans; which would not, as far as I could judge, run counter to any international obligations; and which would involve Government in no further responsibility.

I therefore turned to the Tibetans and said that, in view of the representations which had been made to me as to the difficulty of raising the money in cash, I would agree to the payment being distributed over seventy-five years. They must, however, clearly understand that under the terms of the Treaty we should retain the right to continue to occupy the Chumbi Valley till the full amount of the indemnity was paid. They said that they understood this.

I then remarked that the amount due to us was, to-day, 76 lakhs, not 75 lakhs, as two more days had elapsed since I gave them the ultimatum, and for each of those days Rs. 50,000 was chargeable. The Tongsa Penlop, however, asked that this extra lakh might be remitted, and to this I assented. The Tibetans then asked that the amount might be paid in kind—in ponies, for instance. I replied that as the amount was so small it would be better to pay it in cash, for if it were paid in ponies or other articles there would be constant disputes between us as to the value of the articles proffered, and our good relations might be jeopardized. Finally they asked that it might be paid in tangas, the local Tibetan coin. I replied that I had entered rupees in the draft Treaty, and with that they must be content.

The Ti Rimpoche then affixed his private seal to the draft Treaty.

The thing was done, but what I did in saying those half a dozen words agreeing to the Tibetan proposals was considered afterwards to be a grave error of judgment, and was to bring upon me the censure of Government. That, of course, is what I had to risk. I knew that I was not acting within my instructions. I was using my discretion in very difficult circumstances with what the Government of India afterwards described* to the Secretary of State as "a fearlessness of responsibility which it would be a grave mistake to discourage in any of their agents." And if I really was in error, I think that those who tied their agent down for time and bound him within such narrow lines before they were aware in what conditions he would find himself at Lhasa, cannot themselves be considered as altogether faultless.

In another matter also I at this time acted on my own responsibility. In the original proposals of the Government of India regarding the terms about which I was, without committing Government, to ascertain how the Tibetan Government would be likely to regard them,† was one by which the agent at Gyantse was to have the right of proceeding to Lhasa to discuss matters with the Tibetan officials or the Resident. This reached me before I left Gyantse, and when the Tongsa Penlop asked me for our terms to let the Dalai Lama know what we wanted, I gave him this among all the rest. Subsequently, I received instructions not to ask for permission for the Gyantse agent to proceed to Lhasa. I did not, however, at once withdraw the clause from the list of terms, because in the course of negotiations it might prove useful as a point on which I could, if necessary, make concessions to the Tibetans. But when I found the Tibetans raised no special objections to the clause, provided the trade agent went to Lhasa only on commercial, and not political, business, and only after he had found it impossible to get this commercial business disposed of by correspondence or by personal conference with the Tibetan agent at Gyantse, I thought there would be no objection to taking an agreement from the Tibetans to that effect; for, under such limitations and provisions, there could be no grounds for assuming that in going there the trade agent at Gyantse would be taking upon himself any

* Blue-book, III., p. 75. † *Ibid.*, p. 22.

political functions, or adopting the character of a Political Resident.

As this agreement was of a less formal character than the rest of the Convention, I had it drawn up separately. It ran as follows:

"The Government of Tibet agrees to permit the British agent, who will reside at Gyantse, to watch the conditions of the British trade, to visit Lhasa, when it is necessary, to consult with high Chinese and Tibetan officials on such commercial matters of importance as he has found impossible to settle at Gyantse by correspondence or by personal conference with the Tibetan agent."

To this also the Regent gave his consent.

On September 5 the Resident and the principal Tibetan authorities came to arrange final details and formalities regarding the signing of the Treaty. The first point to decide was who should sign it. I asked the Resident whose name should be entered in the place of the Dalai Lama's. He said I might enter the name of the Ti Rimpoche, and he added that representatives of the Council, of the three great monasteries, and of the National Assembly would also affix their seals. To this the Tibetans assented. I then said the next point was to settle the time and place for signature. There could be only one place—namely, the Potala Palace—in which I would sign it, and I was ready to sign as soon as the final copies of the Treaty had been prepared. The Resident said that he had no objection to the Treaty being signed in the Potala. He then informed the Tibetans of our decision. The Tibetans objected strongly, but without advancing any reasons except that they did not wish it. I informed them that they had at Khamba Jong and Gyantse grossly insulted the British representative, and I now insisted that I should be shown the fullest respect. I had been prepared to show, and had shown, the utmost consideration for their religion and sacred buildings, but I expected that they on their part should show the fullest respect to the King-Emperor's representative. They suggested that the Treaty should be signed in the Resident's Yamen, but I said I would be content with no other place than that in which the Dalai Lama would have received me if he had himself been here to sign the Treaty. The utmost respect it was within their capacity to show I expected should on this occasion be accorded. They began murmuring other objections, but the Resident told them the matter was settled, and did not admit of further discussion.

The question of the exact room in the Palace was then discussed, and a certain room was suggested. I told the Resident that I would send officers that afternoon to inspect the Palace, and satisfy themselves that the room suggested was the most appropriate one, and I asked him to have Chinese and Tibetan officials deputed to accompany my officers. To this he agreed. The date for the ceremony of signing was then fixed for the next day. The Resident said he would himself be present, though he would be unable to agree to the Convention till he had heard from Peking.

Messrs. White and Wilton, and Captain O'Connor, with Majors Iggulden and Beynon from General Macdonald's staff, went over the Potala in the afternoon, and reported that the hall suggested by the Tibetans was the most suitable one in the Palace. That, therefore, was the one we fixed on for the ceremony on the following day.

Though it was easy enough to speak decisively like this about signing the Treaty in the Potala, I had many qualms that night as to whether I had not perhaps at the last moment made one false step. Since the days of the eccentric Manning—whose name should never be forgotten when Lhasa is mentioned—no European had been inside this Palace, and these 20,000 turbulent monks in and around Lhasa might flare up at the last moment, or else commit some atrocity when we were once and completely in their power inside the buildings. Such things have happened before now to Political Agents in India. On the other hand, the hall we were to go to was not a temple, and the Dalai Lama himself, though considered a sacred being, was also a political personage. It was not in the temple of a god that I insisted upon signing the Treaty; it was in the audience-chamber of a political chief.

And for the effect upon the Tibetans and upon men in general, upon our own soldiers, British and Indian, and upon the Nepalese, Bhutanese, and Sikkimese, and far away up into Kashmir and Turkestan, it was necessary to do something to strike their imagination, and to give some unmistakable sign that the Tibetans had not been able through all these years to flout us without suffering the penalty.

Here again to the common-sense man it would have seemed ridiculous and foolish to run more additional risk when the Treaty could have been signed comfortably and without any fuss in either my room or the Resident's. But those who have lived among Asiatics know that the fact of signing the Treaty in the Potala was of as much value as the Treaty itself. Few would know what was in the Treaty, but the fact that the British had concluded a Treaty in the Potala would be an unmistakable sign that the Tibetans had been compelled to come to terms. At the commencement of the Mission our prestige all along our frontier with Tibet had been at zero-point. Everywhere it was thought that the Tibetans could defy us with impunity. Our prestige had no value, and prestige in Asiatic countries is a high practical asset. Through prestige a few Englishmen, without a single British soldier, are able to control a district or State in India containing as many inhabitants as Tibet. Because they had allowed their prestige to wane, the Chinese, even with soldiers, were unable to control Tibet. It was to give an unmistakable sign, which all other countries could understand, that our prestige was re-established in Tibet that I insisted on having the Treaty signed in the Potala itself.

To the troops the news that the Treaty was concluded was a completely unexpected announcement. For weeks past they had heard of nothing but Tibetan obstruction. They knew that we should soon be leaving Lhasa, and they had made up their minds that we should have to leave without a Treaty. They were overjoyed, then, when they heard that the Treaty had been concluded and was to be signed next day. On most of the frontier expeditions upon which they had been engaged there was little to show in return for all they went though. Now they had been led to a remote sacred city, and had not only reached their goal, but were also to bring back something with them as the tangible result of their labours. Their satisfaction was therefore great.

All the military arrangements for the ceremonial were in General Macdonald's hands, and no one could have arranged them with greater care and precaution. Every detail both for effect and for defence was regarded. The route to the Palace was lined with troops, equally for show and for use in case of emergency, and a battery to fire a salute or to bombard the Palace, as occasion might require, was stationed in a suitable position.

On the political side we had to arrange the ceremonial in detail, so that there might be no inconvenient hitch at the last moment. The copy of the Treaty which the Tibetans were to keep was written on an immensely long and broad stretch of paper, so that the whole Treaty in all three languages—English, Tibetan, and Chinese—might be on one piece of paper. Four other copies had to be made: one for Calcutta, one for London, one for the Chinese Government, and one for our Minister in Peking. All these were carried on a large silver tray by my Bengali head clerk, Mr. Mitter, who had accompanied me from the Indore Residency Office, and undergone all the hardships and dangers with unfailing cheerfulness. My camp-table was taken in to sign the Treaty on, and on it was laid the flag which had flown over the Mission headquarters throughout.

Half an hour before the time fixed for the ceremony the whole of the route leading up to the Potala, and the inside passages as well, were lined with troops. Soon after 3 p.m. General Macdonald and I, accompanied by the members of the Mission and the military staff, reached the Potala. We were received in the Durbar Hall by the Chinese Resident. The chamber was one in which the Dalai Lama holds Durbars, and was large enough to hold about 200 of our troops (some of whom were formed up as an escort, while others had been allowed to attend as spectators), and also about 100

Chinese, and over 100 Tibetans. The scene as we entered was unique in interest. On the left were all the British and Indian officers and men in their sombre fighting dress. On the right were the mass of Tibetans, the Councillors in yellow silk robes, and many others in brilliant clothing, together with the Bhutanese in bright dresses and quaint headgear. And in front the Resident and all his staff, in their full official dress, advanced to meet me, with the Regent by him, in the severely simple garb of a Lama. The pillars and cross-beams of the roof of the hall were richly painted. An immense silk curtain, gorgeously embroidered, was hung immediately behind the chairs to be occupied by the Resident and myself. And the whole scene was rendered curiously soft and hazy from the light entering, not by windows at the sides, but through the coloured canvas of an immense skylight in the centre.

The Ti Rimpoche (the Regent) sat next to the Resident on his left. I was on his right. As soon as we were seated, Tibetan servants brought in tea, and handed cups to all the British and Chinese officials. Low tables of dried fruits were then set before the two rows of officials. When these were all cleared away, I said to the Resident that, with his permission, I would proceed to business.

I first had the Treaty read in Tibetan, and then asked the Tibetan officials if they were prepared to sign it. They answered in the affirmative, and the immense roll of paper was produced, on which the Treaty was written in three parallel columns in English, Chinese, and Tibetan, according to their custom of having treaties in different languages inscribed on the same sheet of paper. I asked the Tibetans to affix their seals first, and the long process began. When the seals of the Council, the monasteries, and the National Assembly had been affixed I rose, and, with the Ti Rimpoche, advanced to the table, the Resident and the whole Durbar rising at the same time. The Ti Rimpoche then affixed the Dalai Lama's seal, and finally I sealed and signed the Treaty. Having done this, I handed the document to the Ti Rimpoche, and said a peace had now been made which I hoped would never again be broken.

SIGNING THE TREATY.

To face page 304.

The same ceremonial was followed in the case of the copies in the three languages for the Resident, which, having been signed and sealed, I handed to him. The three copies, each in three languages, for the British Government, were then signed and sealed, the whole operation lasting nearly an hour and a half.

When the ceremony was concluded I addressed the Tibetans, saying that the misunderstandings of the past were now over, and a basis had been laid for mutual good relations in future. We were not interfering in the smallest degree with their religion, we were annexing no part of their country, we were not interfering in their internal affairs, and we were fully recognizing the continued suzerainty of the Chinese Government. We merely sought to insure that they should abide by the Treaty made on their behalf by the Amban in 1890; that trade relations, which were no less advantageous to them than to us, should be established with them as they had been with every other country in the world, except Tibet; and that they should not depart from their traditional policy in regard to relations with other countries. They had found us bad enemies when they had not observed Treaty obligations, and shown disrespect to the British representative. They would find us equally good friends if they kept the present Treaty and showed civility. As a first token of peace I would ask General Macdonald to release all prisoners of war, and I should expect that they would set at liberty all those imprisoned on account of dealings with us.

This speech was translated sentence by sentence by Captain O'Connor, and the Resident's interpreter translated it sentence by sentence to the Resident. At its conclusion the members of Council said that the Treaty had been made by the whole people, and would never be broken. We should see in future that they really intended to observe it. I then turned to the Resident and thanked him for the help he had given me in making the Treaty. He said he was glad he and I had been able to work together, and he hoped and thought the Tibetans would keep the Treaty. A copy of the Treaty, as signed, is placed in the Appendix. The three original copies I brought back to India with me.

The Tibetans throughout showed perfect good temper and the fullest respect. They often laughed over the operations of sealing, and when we left they all came crowding up to shake hands with every British officer they could make their way to. The Resident was very courteous, and showed special pleasure when my words regarding the continued suzerainty of China being recognized were translated to him. Altogether the ceremonial very deeply impressed the Tibetans, who, without being humiliated in a way which could cause resentment, had now learnt to accord us the respect which was our due. At the conclusion of the Durbar I had the Lamas of the Potala presented with Rs. 1,000. It was the first present, except to the poor, which I had given since my arrival in Lhasa. My motto had been: The "mailed fist" first and the sugar-plums afterwards. The contrary procedure so often leads to trouble.

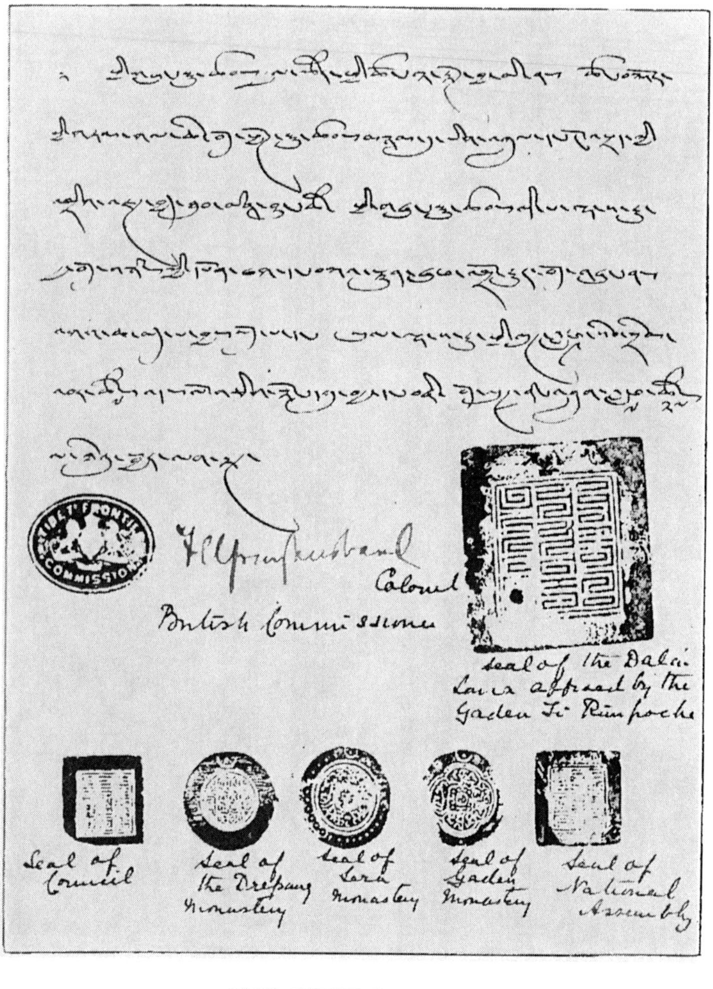

SEALS AFFIXED TO TREATY.

To face page 306.

CHAPTER XIX

IMPRESSIONS AT LHASA

With the signature of the Treaty a tense strain was released, and as I rode down from the Potala I felt at last at ease. That evening General Macdonald, Major Iggulden, his chief staff officer, and the rest of the military staff entertained the Mission at dinner, and among the memories of that eventful day will always be included the recollection of the warmly appreciative speech which General Macdonald made on that occasion.

On the day following two Councillors visited me, and I informed them that General Macdonald had agreed to my request to release all prisoners of war. These were paraded in front of the house, and General Macdonald sent a staff officer to order their release and to give each man Rs. 5 for work he had done.

The Sha-pés then produced two men who had been imprisoned owing to assistance they had given to Sarat Chandra Das, the Bengali traveller, and two men who had been imprisoned for helping the Japanese traveller, Kawaguchi. The two first men had been in chains for nineteen years, and showed signs of terrible suffering. All were in abject fear of the Tibetans, bowing double before them. Their cheeks were sunken, their eyes glazed and staring, their expression unchangeably fixed in horror, and their skin as white and dry as paper. Their release was entirely due to the exertions of Captain O'Connor. I thanked the Sha-pés for their action, which I looked upon as a sign that they really wished to live on friendly terms with us. I trusted that they would never again imprison men whose only offence was friendliness to British subjects.

I returned to the Sha-pés the sum of Rs. 5,000, which I had exacted from them, and released the hostages I had demanded on the occasion of the attack by a fanatical Lama on two British officers. But I demanded back the sum of Rs. 1,000 on account of the murder of one and the brutal torture of another servant of the Mission caught in the town of Gyantse on the night of the attack on the Mission. I said we did not mind fair and square fighting between men whose business it was to fight, but the murder and torture of harmless and defenceless servants was pure barbarity. The Sha-pés acknowledged that what I said was just, but said they were not present, and knew nothing of it. Rs. 1,000 were, therefore, retained to be paid in compensation to the servants' families.

I then remarked that we had now had a general settling up of all accounts between us, and could start fair. The Sha-pés said they hoped now we should always be on friendly terms, and they certainly meant to observe the Treaty.

The Tongsa Penlop paid me a formal visit on the 10th to congratulate me on the successful issue of the negotiations. He said that there was no resentment at the settlement or at the manner in which it had been made, and the Nepalese representative was of the same opinion. The Tibetans were well satisfied with the issue of the negotiations. And I dare say in their heart of hearts, and despite all their protests, they had fully expected us to annex the whole country, as we had annexed Burma, or at any rate to annex up to Gyantse, and were probably quite surprised to have got off so lightly.

Congratulations from India and England soon came pouring in. Only six days after the Treaty was signed came a telegram from the Viceroy conveying the congratulations of the King himself. His Majesty, though away at Marienbad, had immediately telegraphed his congratulations, a particular compliment which is rarely given for work in India. To the troops this was especially gratifying. The telegram was read out to them on a full parade, which General Macdonald ordered for the purpose. The Secretary of State, the acting Viceroy, Lord Ampthill, Lord Curzon, from England, Lord Kitchener, and very many others, also sent their congratulations; and now, while the Chinese Government were making up their minds whether they would allow the Resident to sign his adhesion to the Treaty, I had leisure and inclination to go about Lhasa and see something of the monasteries and temples, and talk with the people in a less forced and formal manner than I had to while the strain of the negotiations was on us.

We had so far seen the Tibetans only on the contentious side. Now that the stress was over I wished to see them as they really were. What especially I wished to see was their monastic life. The priesthood ruled Tibet. Religion was the chief characteristic of the people. Their religion and the character of the Lamas, who both led the religious life of the people and guided their political destinies, were, therefore, the special objects of my interest.

From the first I had insisted that we should not be denied access to the monasteries, for to get rid of misunderstandings it was essential that we should close up with the Lamas and come directly into contact with them. But I had been careful to let only those officers enter the monasteries who could be trusted to comport themselves with propriety, and have all reasonable regard for the feelings and prejudices of the monks.

For this purpose Mr. White, Mr. Walsh, Captain O'Connor, and Colonel Waddell, the well-known writer on Lamaism, who was appointed Chief Medical Officer and Archæologist to the Mission's escort, were invaluable. Each had his special qualification for the work, and each made use of it by "peaceful penetration" to break through the last barrier which separated us from the Tibetans. Mr. White was known in person or by reputation as none of the rest of us were, and had many friends who were also friends of these Lamas. Through them he obtained an invitation to the De-pun Monastery, and from this start made rapid progress. Mr. Walsh, as Deputy Commissioner of Darjiling, and through his long acquaintance with this frontier and intimate knowledge of the language and history of the country, was also able to exert a most useful influence after his arrival from Chumbi, while Colonel Waddell interested himself in the libraries and in historical research. As a consequence, when I visited these monasteries, after the signature of the Treaty, I was received as if the visit from a British official was the same ordinary occurrence as it is in India.

Each monastery is a little town in itself, a compact block of solidly-built masonry—houses, halls, and temples. The streets are narrow and not over-clean, but the halls and temples are spacious. They are mostly of much the same type, with pagoda-shaped roofs, painted wooden pillars, and grotesque demonesque-like figures. In the De-pun Monastery there were from 8,000 to 10,000 monks, divided into, I think, four sections, each with its Abbot and its separate temple hall and institutions.

In outward appearance the monks of some of these Lhasa monasteries are not prepossessing. They look coarse and besotted. Some are bright and cordial, but hardly any look really intellectual or spiritual, and the general impression I took away was one of dirt and degradation. Of the higher Lamas, also, my impression was not favourable as regards their intellectual capacity or spiritual attainments. The Regent (Ti Rimpoche), with whom I carried on the negotiations, had great charm. He was a benevolent, kindly old gentleman, who would not have hurt a fly if he could have avoided it. No one could help liking him, but no one could say that he had the intellectual capacity we would meet with in Brahmins in India, or the character and bearing one would expect in the leading man of a country. And his spiritual attainments, I gathered from a long conversation I had with him after the Treaty was signed, consisted mainly of a knowledge by rote of vast quantities of his holy books. The capacity of these Tibetan monks for learning their sacred books by rote is, indeed, something prodigious; though about the actual meaning they trouble themselves but little.

Some of the Abbots we met were cheery, genial souls, much as we picture to ourselves the jolly friars of olden days in England; but as spiritual leaders of a religious

THE SERA MONASTERY.

To face page 310.

people, I did not find the higher Lamas impressed me any more favourably than the ordinary monks.

These impressions, which in themselves would not have much value, as my period for observation was so very limited, are borne out by the courageous Japanese traveller Kawaguchi, himself a Buddhist, and once Rector of a monastery in Japan, who lived in the Sera Monastery, and in his most valuable work, "Three Years in Tibet," written since we were in Tibet, has given to the English public the results of his study.

For a few Lamas he had a sincere attachment. Like myself, he greatly revered the old Ti Rimpoche, who taught him Buddhism in its correct form, and "truly impressed him as a living Buddha." He struck Kawaguchi as not only having a juster ideal of the real spirit of Buddhism than the other Lamas, but as also having greater ability, which may have been due to what I had not myself known—his father being a Chinaman. For an ex-Minister of Finance, a Lama, Kawaguchi also had great admiration, and certainly from him received unstinted kindness, even when he risked his life in showing Kawaguchi attention. The Head-Priest of Wartang he also thought very clever, and from him he received valuable information on Buddhism.

These, however, were exceptional men, and most of the Lamas were very disappointing to the Japanese. Even the good ex-Financial Minister had the defect of living with a nun. A Lama travelling companion was a "pedantic scholar" who knew nothing of the essential principles of Buddhism, and had only a vague notion of the doctrines. The Abbot of Sakya had a son, though Lamas are not allowed to marry, and Kawaguchi was "loth to remain with so dissipated a priest." The tutor of the Tashi Lama was disappointing in his answers about "grammar."

The doctors of the highest degrees, he said, were unquestionably theologians of great erudition, and at home in the complete cycle of Buddhist works. They had, indeed, he considered, a better knowledge of Buddhist theology than the Japanese divines. But such were few and far between, and he seems to have agreed with the observation of the Ti Rimpoche that it would "be better to have even two or three precious diamonds than a heap of stones." The Tibetan priesthood, he thought, contained plenty of rubbish, with very few diamonds.

To account for this, he says that the main purpose of Tibetans in entering the priesthood is "only to procure the largest amount of fortune, as well as the highest possible fame." To seek religious truth and to work for the deliverance of men was not at all what, according to this Japanese, they wished to do. They simply desired, he says, to escape from the painful struggle of life, and "enjoy lazy and comfortable days on earth as well as in heaven." There is nothing deep that he could see in their religious life and study; service went in their eyes for nothing.

Medicine, logic, engineering, and religious philosophy were introduced into Tibet centuries ago from India; but nowadays, says Kawaguchi, there are almost no Tibetans who are proficient in even one of these subjects.

Of the morality of the Lamas Kawaguchi gives no very pleasant account. Most of these celibate priest-nobles kept women somewhere, and the lower warrior-priests really seem, he says, to be the descendants of Sodom and Gomorrah. Some of the festivals were simply bestial orgies.

These "warrior-priests" of the Sera Monastery, which is one of those I visited, are a peculiar institution. Their daily task is varied. It is to play flutes, lyres, harps, flageolets, and to beat drums; to prepare offerings for the deities; to carry yak-dung for fuel; to practise throwing stones at a target; and to act as a bodyguard. Kawaguchi made friends with them by doctoring, and found them very true to their duties, and though they might look very rough, they were more truthful than the noble and other priests, who, though trustworthy at first sight, were in reality deceitful in seeking their own benefit and happiness, and under their warm woollen garments hid a mean and crafty behaviour.

The ordinary student in these monasteries had certainly to work hard. Kawaguchi worked till he got "a swelling on his shoulder"; and, to get a degree, some work for twenty years, with examinations every year. Besides Tibetans, there were numbers of Mongols, and also some 200 Buriats from Siberia. The Mongols were hard-working and progressive, but "very quick-tempered, proud, and uppish," and every Mongol had it in him to be a great leader, like Jenghiz Khan, whose career was, however, according to Kawaguchi, but a meteoric burst. Compared with these the Tibetan students, though, generally speaking, very quiet, courteous, and intelligent, were lazy and sluggish "beyond the powers of Westerners to imagine," and on account of their laziness very dirty.

Catechism seems to have been their chief study. "The object of the questions and answers is to free the mind from all worldliness, and to get into the very bottom of truth, giving no powers to the devils of hell in the mind." It is by this means, continues Kawaguchi, that the naturally dull and lazy Tibetans are guided to understand Buddhism, and through it they are, for a half-civilized nation, very rich in logical ideas. The catechisms, which I should judge were really more in the nature of philosophical debates which all Orientals love, were carried on in a most excited manner. Many texts and reference books had to be read before anyone could take part in them, and the catechists were always taught that "the foot must come down so strongly that the door of hell may be broken open; and that the hands must make so great a noise that the voice of knowledge may frighten the devils all the world over."

Besides studying and being engaged in ceremonial observances, the monks, however, also carry on business. Most of them are engaged in trade; many are employed in agriculture, others in cattle-breeding, and sheep-rearing; and others, again, in the manufacture of Buddhist articles, the painting of Buddhist pictures; while tailors, carpenters, masons, and shoemakers are also found among the priests. Those of the higher class live very comfortably, building their own villas and temples. Some employ as many as 70 or 80 servants.

The lower-class priests, on the other hand, live in a

pitiful way. No words, says Kawaguchi, can describe their poor condition. The scholar-priests have to earn their living as well as their expenses as students. Yet they are too busy to go out and make money, and what they receive as offerings from believers and as salaries from temples does not amount to enough to support them. They get a drink of tea gratis, but no flour; and such is their pitiable condition that they will often pass a couple of days without eating.

A noteworthy fact is, that though by their religion the Lamas are not supposed to take life, yet they are said not to be able to pass a day without eating meat, and more than 50,000 sheep, goats, and yaks are killed at Lhasa during the last three months of each year. Their punishments, too, are so cruel—gouging out eyes, cutting off hands, beating, etc.—as to excite the Japanese just as much as ourselves.

It is altogether a sorry picture which Kawaguchi draws, but it precisely bears out the casual impressions we got during our limited stay in Lhasa, and from what intercourse we had with the Lamas. Whether Lamaism has on the whole been a success I doubt. It has had a pacifying effect, it is true. If the Tibetans had been Mohammedans, we should not have reached Lhasa as easily as we did. And the Mongols also have lost their old warlike tendencies. The numerous figures of the placid Buddha sitting in calm repose have had their influence. Cut in rocks, erected in imposing statues, or modelled in bronze and brass, and set up in their temples and household altars, they have hypnotized the people to a sense of peace and rest. The Tibetans, who once carried their arms to Peking itself, are now one of the most peaceful of people. And the Mongols, who had set up a dynasty in China, conquered all Central Asia, and laid waste Western Europe, are now an almost negligible quantity in war.

Lamaism has certainly, then, nourished peace in Tibet and Mongolia. But the peace that has been nurtured has been the quiescence of sloth and decadence. The Buddhist idea of repose and kindness all can appreciate.

There are few men who have no kindly feelings, and would not wish, if they could, to be at peace with all the world. Yet the idea may have its danger and be as likely to lead downward as upward. It may lull to rest and render useless passions and energies which ought to be given play to. And the evil of Lamaism is that it has fostered lazy repose and self-suppression at the expense of useful activity and self-realization.

The Mongols in their deserts, the Tibetans in their mountains, have had the amplest opportunity for carrying into effect the Buddhist idea. I have seen the one in the deepest depths of their deserts, and the other in the innermost sanctuary of their mountains, and to me it seems that they have both been pursuing a false ideal. They have sought by withdrawing from the world into the desert and into the mountain to secure present peace for the individual, instead of, by manfully taking their part in the work of the world, aiming at the eventual unison of the whole. Peace, instead of harmony, has been their ideal—peace for the emasculated individual instead of harmony for the united and full-blooded whole.

The Tibetan's main idea, in fact, has been to save his own soul. He does not trouble about others so long as he can save himself. Indeed, he thinks it will require all his energies to do even that much, for at heart he is still full of his original religion of demonology. He looks upon the spiritual world as filled with demons, ready to prey upon him if he makes the slightest slip. Every temple, almost every house, is full of fantastic pictures of the most terrible and blood-curdling devils, with glaring eyes, open fang-studded mouth, extended neck and outstretched arm, ready to pounce upon some miserable victim. The belief in heaven is vague. The belief in hell is the one great fact in their lives, and how real it is may be imagined when we hear of these poor wretches, who, in order to escape its terrors, voluntarily allow themselves to be walled into solitary cells, from which for years they never emerge, but take in their food once a day through a narrow opening. Thus only do those poor deluded creatures think they can escape from demons in the world to come. But that they most sincerely believe in a life hereafter no more positive evidence could be afforded. An interesting detail is that their hell is not hot, but cold. If it were hot, the inhabitants of frozen Tibet would all flock there.

As might be naturally expected, such a people are ready believers in the supposed supernatural powers of certain men. We could hear nothing of the wonderful Mahatmas, and the Ti Rimpoche told Colonel Waddell he was entirely ignorant of their existence. But, according to Kawaguchi, oracles are held in high esteem. The Ngpak-pas, or miracle-workers, the descendants of Lamas who worked miracles, are supposed to possess hereditary secrets, and are held in great awe as being magicians of power. The people showed such practical faith in the efficacy of the charms which the Lamas gave that they rushed right up to our rifles, believing that our bullets could not hit them.

Practically, then, the religion of the Tibetans is but of a degraded form. Yet one does see gleams of real good radiating through. The Tashi Lama whom Bogle met was a man of real worth. His successor of the present day produced a most favourable impression in India, and excited the enthusiasm of Sven Hedin. Deep down under the dirty crust there must be some hidden source of strength in these Lamas, or they would not exert the influence they do. Millions of men over hundreds of years are not influenced entirely by chicanery and fraud. And I think I caught a glimpse of that inner power during a visit I paid to the Jo Khang Temple.

This temple, or cathedral, as it has sometimes been styled, has been fully described by Sarat Chandra Das, Perceval Landon, and others. The latter especially has given a remarkably vivid description of his impression. It is, as Colonel Waddell has aptly styled it, the St. Peter's of Lamadom, and is chiefly noteworthy as containing the image of Buddha, made in India, but brought to Lhasa from China by the Chinese Princess who married a Tibetan King and introduced Buddhism into the country.

I visited this temple with full ceremony after the Treaty was signed, and was received with every mark of cordiality by the Chief Priest. I was even shown round what might be called the high-altar, in spite of my protestations that I might be intruding where I should not go. The actual building is not imposing. The original temple, built about A.D. 650, according to Waddell, has been added to, and the result is a confused pile without symmetry, and devoid of any single complete architectural idea. One sees a forest of wooden pillars grotesquely painted, but no beautiful design or plain simple effect. Moreover, dirt is excessively prevalent, there is an offensive smell of the putrid butter used in the services, and the candlesticks, vases, and ceremonial utensils, some of solid gold and of beautiful design, are not orderly arranged.

Still, this temple, from its antiquity, from its worn pavements marking the passage of innumerable pilgrims, from the thought that for a thousand years those wanderers from distant lands had faced the terrors of the desert and the mountains to prostrate themselves before the benign and peaceful Buddha, possessed a halo and an interest which the beauty of the Taj itself could never give it.

Here it was that I found the true inner spirit of the people. The Mongols from their distant deserts, the Tibetans from their mountain homes, seemed here to draw on some hidden source of power. And when from the far recesses of the temple came the profound booming of great drums, the chanting of monks in deep reverential rhythm, the blare of trumpets, the clash of cymbals, and the long rolling of lighter drums, I seemed to catch a glimpse of the source from which they drew. Music is a proverbially fitter means than speech for expressing the eternal realities; and in the deep rhythmic droning of the chants, the muffled rumbling of the drums, the loud clang and blaring of cymbals and trumpets, I realized this sombre people touching their inherent spirit, and, in the way most fitted to them, giving vent to its mighty surgings panting for expression.

Besides these visits to monasteries and temples, we also saw something of the Tibetans socially during our stay in Lhasa, and Captain Walton, through his skill in medicine, attracted many hundreds to his hospital, and was able to get on terms of intimacy with unofficial Tibetans of the highest position. Many would come and dine with us, for the Tibetans, though they have the ordinary class distinctions which are found in every people, have not those rigid caste barriers which are such a hindrance to social intercourse in India. Even the ladies were very nearly induced by the persuasive Captain O'Connor to come to tea, and the wives of the Councillors had actually accepted an invitation, when at the last moment shyness overtook them. Women are much to the fore in Tibet, and have great influence with their husbands, so we especially regretted not having seen them.

The Tibetans, though they have their reputation for seclusiveness, are not by nature unsociable. We found them quite the reverse, and Kawaguchi says that they were "originally a people highly hospitable to strangers." This more natural sentiment was, he says, superseded by one of fear and even of antipathy, as the result of an insidious piece of advice which, probably prompted by some policy of its own, the Government of China gave to Tibet, and which was to the effect that if the Tibetans allowed the free entrance of foreigners Buddhism would be destroyed and replaced by Christianity. The people had, too, the idea that we sought their gold-mines.

Whatever seclusive feeling they may have had, they abandoned it when the Treaty was concluded. They came to our gymkhanas, and wondered why only the first should be given the prize when all the rest had covered exactly the same distance. They watched with wonder Vernon Magniac and other inveterate sportsmen pulling fish out of the river by pieces of string attached to long sticks. They watched theatrical performances, and marvelled at our display of fireworks; and they did a magnificent business with us in the sale, not only of supplies for the troops, but also of innumerable curios, brass and bronze figures, turquoise ornaments, embroideries, silks, etc.

The Tibetans are, indeed, born traders. Kawaguchi calls them a "nation of shop-keepers." Men and women —and the women more than the men—priests and laity, all trade. And this is another irony of the situation, that a people who are naturally sociable, and who are thus, too, born traders, should have been put for so long in their seclusive position. But of late years the departure of Lhasa merchants to India had been becoming more frequent, and Kawaguchi says that circumstances were impressing the Tibetans with the necessity of extending their sphere of trade, and they realized that if their wool trade was stopped the people would be hard hit, for sheep-rearers constituted the greater part of the whole population.

How it was, from a Tibetan point of view, that of recent years we became estranged is worth hearing. It was, according to Kawaguchi, the explorations of the Bengali gentleman, Sarat Chandra Das, coupled with the frontier troubles which followed, that changed the attitude of the Tibetans towards us. The two events had not the slightest connection with one another, but the Tibetans seemed to have been alarmed that the harmless journeying of Sarat Chandra Das in 1881 was a deliberate design on our part to subvert their religion. As to the frontier troubles—presumably those of 1886—Kawaguchi himself says that it was the Tibetan Government who "most indiscreetly adopted measures at the instance of a fanatic Nechung (oracle), and proceeded to build a fort at a frontier place which strictly belonged to Sikkim."

But the Tibetans were apparently thoroughly nervous about the British, and prejudiced against us on account of our subjugation of India. They were much impressed by the moderation of our rule, by the freedom we gave, and by the hospitals and schools. Tibetans in Darjiling who had these advantages, and who were given small Government posts, were much attached to our rule. And Queen Victoria was believed to be an incarnation of the goddess of the Jo-khang Temple. All this, says Kawaguchi, they quite acknowledged, but when they considered that these same Englishmen annexed other people's lands to their own dominions, their favourable opinion received a shock, and they explained this to themselves by supposing that "there must be two different kinds of Englishmen in India—one benevolent and godly, and the other infernal and quite wicked."

The Dalai Lama, who, though very anxious to clear away all corruption from the Buddhism of Tibet, was "richer in thoughts political than religious," feared the British, and was always thinking how to keep us out of Tibet. The reason why he, "who was at first as timid as a hare towards England, should become suddenly as bold as a lion," was that he had a secret treaty with Russia, which he believed to be the only country in the world strong enough to thwart England. Kawaguchi then proceeds to relate how Dorjieff virtually monopolized the confidence of the young Lama, how he brought gold and curios from Russia and liberal donations to all the monasteries, and even a Bishop's robe from the Czar for the Dalai Lama. He tells how Dorjieff wrote a pamphlet showing that the Czar was an incarnation of one of the founders of Lamaism, and how the Tibetans came to believe that the Czar would sooner or later subdue the whole world and found a gigantic Buddhist Empire. He mentions, too, how one day after Dorjieff's return he saw a caravan of 200 camels, and that he was told they conveyed rifles and bullets, and that 300 camel-loads had already arrived, and the Tibetans were then elated, and said that "now for the first time Tibet was sufficiently armed to resist any attack which England might make, and could defiantly reject any improper request."

These rifles were of American manufacture, and, I believe through neglect, got so completely out of order that the Tibetans were only able to use very few against us. We have the assurance of the Russian Government, too, that no agreement was made with Tibet. But these observations of the Japanese form a remarkable corroboration of the reports we had heard as to the mischief done by Dorjieff's proceedings.

Summarizing the characteristics of the Tibetans, we may say, then, that while they are affable outwardly and crafty within, as most dependent people have to be; while they are dirty and lazy; and while their religion is degraded, and they show no signs of either intellectual or spiritual progress, yet at heart they are not an unkindly or unsociable people, and they have undoubtedly strong religious feelings. Immorality is not entirely unchecked. The Lama who married a nun had his official career blighted. Ministers have been known to refuse their salaries as they had enough to live on without. There is often much affection and staunch friendship among the Tibetans. And there are in them latent potentialities for good, which only await the right touch to bring them into being.

Of the attitude of the Chinese to the Tibetans I took particular note, for I was myself a Resident in an Indian Native State, and I was interested in observing the attitude of a Chinese Resident in a Native State of the Chinese Empire. One point which immediately struck me about it was its tone of high-handedness. A century ago Manning had remarked how "the haughty Mandarins were somewhat deficient in respect," and I noted the same thing. Every British Resident gives a chair to an Indian gentleman who comes to visit him, but I found that the Chinese Resident did not give a chair to even the Regent. He, Councillors, Members of the National Assembly, Abbots of the great monasteries—all had to sit on cushions on the ground, while the Resident and his Chinese staff sat on chairs. In his reception and dismissal of them he preserved an equally high tone of superiority. He did not rise from his chair to receive them, as any British Resident would rise to welcome Indian gentlemen or high officials; he merely acknowledged their salutation on entrance with a barely noticeable inclination of his head. And, in dismissing them, he simply said over his shoulder to his interpreter, "Tell them to go." Our countrymen are often accused, and sometimes with justice, of being too high-handed with Asiatics, but we are not so high-handed with Asiatics as Asiatics are with one another.

In another respect the Chinese are very different from us in their dealings with a feudatory State. Hardly one of the Chinese officials we met in Tibet could speak a word of Tibetan. Except that they married Tibetan wives for the time that they were actually serving in Tibet, they troubled themselves little about the people. They remained quite aloof, took small interest in them, and certainly never worried themselves, as a British Resident would, to improve their lot in some way. The Chinese, both here and in Chinese Turkestan, where I had also observed them, preserved great dignity, were very punctilious in ceremonial, were always, so to speak, in full-dress uniform, and they were ever highly respectful to one another. But the Tibetans were "barbarians" in their eyes, were treated with disdainful contempt, and the Chinese officials thought of little else but how soon they could get back to their own civilized country.

The Tibetans naturally resented this, and hated the Chinese, but they were also greatly awed and brow-beaten by them; and I think, too, that the mere fact of seeing more civilized men than themselves in their midst, and of being attached to a great Empire, with an all-powerful Court in the background, has in itself had much to do with lifting the Tibetans out of barbarism. The aboriginal Tibetans were a savage and warlike race, who constantly invaded China. They have received both their civilization and their religion from China, for Buddhism, as I have said, reached them, not directly from India, but through a Tibetan King's Chinese wife, the daughter of a Chinese Emperor. Books and relics came from India, but it was the personal influence of the Chinese wife which seems to have had the greatest practical effect in establishing Buddhism.

The Chinese have, too, on occasions done great service to the Tibetans in repelling invaders, and the march of the Chinese general, over many lofty passes, to expel the Gurkha invasion in 1792 was a military feat of which any nation in the world might be proud. Chinese prestige in Tibet had, according to Kawaguchi, who lived in Lhasa for three years, dwindled since the Chino-Japanese War; and we had practical proofs even before then that their influence was not as effective as a suzerain's should be. But the memory of the prodigious efforts which China does every now and then make always inspires a certain awe in the Tibetans, and they never feel quite sure when another may not be made.

The Chinese, then, undoubtedly impress the Tibetans, but I am bigoted enough to think that their methods are not practically so successful as our own. Tibet is a protected Chinese State; Kashmir is a protected Indian State. In Tibet the Chinese Resident has, to support him, several hundreds of Chinese soldiers, and in the present year 2,000. In Kashmir the British Resident has not even a personal guard of British soldiers or even of British-Indian soldiers. In Tibet the Chinese are replacing the Tibetan by Chinese police; in Kashmir all the police are of the Kashmir State. Kashmir is 80,500 square miles in extent, and contains nearly as many inhabitants as Tibet, and it borders on Tibet, Turkestan, and through its feudatories on Afghan territory, while Russian territory is only twelve miles distant. But the whole of this is controlled and the bordering tribes are kept in order entirely through Kashmir State troops. British officers are employed, but not a single British or British-Indian soldier or policeman. Yet it is unthinkable that Kashmir troops should, against the wishes and orders of the British Government, invade the territory of a neighbouring State, as Tibetan troops, against the wishes and orders of the Chinese Government, invaded Sikkim in 1886. And it is inconceivable that the Kashmir State should repudiate and refuse to fulfil a Treaty concluded on their behalf by the British Government, as the Tibetans repudiated and refused to fulfil the Treaty made on their behalf by the Chinese in 1890. By all the logic of the case the Chinese, as fellow-Asiatics and as co-religionists of the Tibetans, should have much greater influence in Tibet than we as aliens, with a different religion, have in Kashmir. Yet the contrary is most emphatically the case.

The relations between ourselves and the Chinese at Lhasa I always tried to preserve as cordial as possible. Chinese suzerainty was definitely recognized in the Treaty, and all the way through the negotiations I had tried to carry the Resident with me. It was no part of our policy to supplant the Chinese. We had no idea of annexing Tibet or establishing a protectorate over it. We merely wanted to insure that no one else had a predominant influence in the country, that order was preserved, and that ordinary trade facilities should be accorded us. There was nothing in this to arouse the antagonism or jealousy of the Chinese, and as I always tried to treat the Resident with respect, I expected, and did, in fact, receive, his hearty co-operation. We each of us could and did help the other, to the advantage of both.

CHAPTER XX

THE RETURN

Lord Cromer, when I saw him at Cairo on my way home, made a remark which showed an unusually appreciative insight into situations such as we were in at Lhasa. He said that everyone was praising us for reaching Lhasa, but he thought most Englishman could do that. What he considered really praiseworthy was our getting back again. In such situations ragged ends are often left, resentments incurred, entanglements formed, which make it difficult to retire with grace or even to retire at all. We were happy in this case to be able to return to India on better terms with the Tibetans than we had ever been before.

On September 22 I exchanged farewell visits with the Chinese Resident. In the reserved Chinese way he was cordial enough, and we had always got on well together. But he was in a very nasty position between the Tibetans on the one hand and his own Government on the other, and he was subsequently degraded and put into chains for having, it was locally reported, been too favourable to us.

The Members of the Council also visited me, bringing presents, for the third time, and assuring me of their friendly sentiments. They begged me never again to entertain suspicion regarding them, and to believe that they fully intended to carry out the Treaty.

Before leaving on the following morning, the Ti Rimpoche visited me, and presented each of us with an image of Buddha. He had also visited General Macdonald and given him a similar image. He was full of kindliness, and at that moment more nearly approached Kipling's Lama in "Kim" than any other Tibetan I met. We were given to understand that the presentation by so high a Lama to those who were not Buddhists of an image of Buddha himself was no ordinary compliment. And as the reverend old Regent rose from his seat and put the present into my hand, he said with real impressiveness that he had none of the riches of this world, and could only offer me this simple image. Whenever he looked upon an image of Buddha he thought only of peace, and he hoped that whenever I looked on it I would think kindly of Tibet. I felt like taking a part in a religious ceremony as the kindly old man spoke those words; and I was glad that all political wranglings were over, and that now we could part as friends man with man.

A mile from the town a large tent had been set up by the roadside, and here we found the whole Council, a number of the leading men of Lhasa, and the Chinese Resident's first and second secretaries, all assembled to bid us a final farewell. Tea was served, and then, with many protestations of friendship, we shook hands for the last time, remounted our ponies, and rode away.

When I reached camp, I went off alone to the mountain-side and gave myself up to all the emotions of this eventful time. My task was over and every anxiety was passed. The scenery was in sympathy with my feelings; the unclouded sky a heavenly blue; the mountains softly merging into violet; and, as I now looked towards that mysterious purply haze in which the sacred city was once more wrapped, I no longer had cause to dread the hatred it might hide. From it came only the echo of the Lama's words of peace. And with all the warmth still on me of that impressive farewell message, and bathed in the insinuating influences of the dreamy autumn evening, I was insensibly suffused with an almost intoxicating sense of elation and good-will. This exhilaration of the moment grew and grew till it thrilled through me with overpowering intensity. Never again could I think evil, or ever again be at enmity with any man. All nature and all humanity were bathed in a rosy glowing radiancy; and life for the future seemed nought but buoyancy and light.

Such experiences are only too rare, and they but too soon

become blurred in the actualities of daily intercourse and practical existence. Yet it is these few fleeting moments which are reality. In these only we see real life. The rest is the ephemeral, the unsubstantial. And that single hour on leaving Lhasa was worth all the rest of a lifetime.

We of the actual Mission were now to leave the military escort and ride rapidly back to India to arrange final details with the Government of India. So on the following morning we started early, and as we rode away the whole of the 32nd Pioneers turned out to say good-bye. Some native officers had come to me the previous evening to say the men wanted us to leave camp through their lines. As we rode by, the men all came swarming out of their tents. The native officers clustered round our ponies shaking our hands, and the whole regiment waved and cheered as we passed out of camp. They had been with the Mission from the very start; indeed, they had been working at the road in that steamy Sikkim Valley before the Mission was formed. They had been through all the fighting and through the dreary investment at Gyantse; and it did one good to feel that something substantial had been obtained in return for their labours, and that they would be able to go back to their villages rewarded and happy. Indian troops of the best type have a wonderful capacity for invoking attachment, and for both the 32nd and 23rd Pioneers I shall always have a warm affection.

The behaviour of these Indian troops had also contributed greatly to the change of feeling in the Tibetans. Their discipline was excellent. They had fought hard when fighting was necessary. When the fighting was over they readily made friends with the Tibetans. And the latter more than once told me that the people suffered more from their own troops than they did from ours. This discipline and good behaviour of Indian troops we take for granted. It is none the less very remarkable. We had with us Gurkhas, trans-frontier Pathans, Sikhs, and Punjabi Mohammedans. All of these in their natural state, under their own leaders, and uncontrolled by British officers, would have played havoc in Lhasa. Their good behaviour on the present occasion was one of the main causes of the Tibetans suddenly swinging round as they did in our favour.

With the relays of riding animals and transport which General Macdonald had arranged for us at every stage down the long line of communications we now pressed rapidly on. We did not strive to emulate Mr. Perceval Landon, who had a week or two before made the record ride from Lhasa to India, but we doubled or trebled the ordinary marches, and in a few days reached Gyantse again.

Here a redistribution had to be made. Captain O'Connor, to whom so much of the success of the negotiations was due, was to remain here permanently as Trade Agent under the new Treaty. Also a party had to be sent to Gartok to arrange for the opening of the new trade-mart there. And preparations for some exploration work had to be made.

As soon as the Treaty was signed and I could say for certain that we would be returning to India, I obtained from the Tibetans and Chinese, through Captain O'Connor's and Mr. Wilton's powers of persuasion, leave for three parties to return to India by three different routes besides the one we came up by. One party was to go down the Brahmaputra to Assam; another party was to go up the Brahmaputra to Gartok, and come out by Simla; and Mr. Wilton was to return to China through Eastern Tibet. For all these passports were given, but only the second actually set out.

The journey down the Brahmaputra was the one in which many adventurous officers at Lhasa and Sir Louis Dane, the Foreign Secretary, were keenly interested. No one to this day knows for certain that the San-po of Tibet is the Brahmaputra of Assam. And it was to solve this problem, to discover how and where this mighty river cuts its way clean through the main axis of the Himalayas, and to see the falls and rapids which are involved in a drop from 11,500 to 500 feet, that so many ardent spirits were set. Mr. White was to have had charge of this party, and Captain Ryder was to have accompanied it as Survey Officer. All that was wanting was the sanction of the Government of India, and that, unfortunately, at the last moment was not forthcoming. The party would have had to find a way through some truculent, independent tribes between the border of Tibet and the Assam frontier, and Government were not at that moment prepared to run any further risks. It was a pity, and a sad disappointment to many, for it will be many a year before we again have such an opportunity of solving what is one of the greatest remaining geographical problems.

Mr. Wilton's journey I had myself to stop, though there is nothing I hate more than to block enterprise in travel. The negotiations with the Chinese were not concluded—in fact, had hardly commenced—and I could not afford to part with anyone so valuable to us in India as he had proved himself to be. We Indian officials are like children in dealing with the Chinese, and the help of that special experience with which Mr. Wilton so effectively had aided us was particularly necessary at this time, though it is deplorable to find from the latest Blue-book how little advantage was taken of the advice he gave.

The Gartok party I put in charge of Captain Rawling, as its main purpose was to open the new mart, and he had in the previous year made a remarkable and most useful journey in Western Tibet. Captain Ryder had been detailed for charge of the survey operations of the expedition down the Brahmaputra, and Lieutenant Wood, R.E., who had been engaged for some time in resurveying the peaks round Mount Everest in Nepal, was to have done the survey work with the Gartok party. But now that the project for the former expedition had fallen through, Captain Ryder also accompanied the Gartok party and took charge of the survey. He was an officer of great capacity, and during the Mission had done most valuable work in extending the triangulation of India right up to Lhasa. He had now an even more interesting piece of geographical work before him—the survey of the upper course of the Brahmaputra (San-po) to its source, and the settling definitely of the question whether there was any higher peak than Everest at the back of the Himalayas.

But the party would have to race against time, for they had many hundreds of miles to traverse, and had to cross the Himalayas back to Simla before the winter finally closed the passes. They had also to face the possibility of obstruction in the matter of supplies and transport, and even the possibility of active hostility, for they would be travelling with no other escort than a Gurkha orderly apiece through a country which had only recently been in open arms against us.

Captain O'Connor and Mr. Magniac accompanied them as far as Shigatse, and Lieutenant Bailey, 32nd Pioneers, a keen and adventurous officer, who had distinguished himself with the mounted infantry, and in his leisure moments learnt Tibetan, was also attached to the party to proceed to India.

Captain O'Connor was most warmly received by the Tashi Lama, and laid the foundation of as sincere a friendship as Bogle had with his predecessor. Every arrangement was readily made, and the party was despatched under the best possible auspices. Its result Captain Ryder, who was awarded the gold medal of the Royal Geographical Society, has given in a lecture before that Society.

The survey work had to be conducted under the most trying conditions. Besides the ordinary march, high mountains had to be ascended for purposes of observation, and these observations in winds of hurricane force and in piercing cold were wellnigh impossible to make. From a spot directly opposite Everest the surveyors saw this superb mountain towering up high above the rest of the range with a drop of 8,000 feet on either side, and the point was settled that there was no other peak on the north approaching it in height. They surveyed the Brahmaputra (San-po) to its source, as well as the Gartok branch of the Indus. They established the trade-mart at Gartok, installing a native agent there. They completed the survey of the Sutlej from its source (which they concluded was among the hills on either side of the lake region) to British territory. In all they accurately surveyed 40,000 square miles of territory. And after crossing the Himalayas by the Ayi-la (pass), 18,700 feet, in deep snow and with the thermometer 24° below zero, they reached British territory on Christmas Eve, and Simla on January 11. It was a good piece of work, magnificently executed, for which the greatest credit is due to both Captain Rawling and Captain Ryder, and it was an immense relief to hear of their safe arrival in spite of the risks of hostility and of cold.

In the meanwhile Messrs. White, Walsh, Wilton, and myself had proceeded on to India. It was fairly cold even as we crossed the Tang-la, the thermometer not being much above zero, but we were fortunate to escape the blizzard, the 3 feet of snow, and 27° of frost which General Macdonald and the troops experienced a week or two later, and which caused the death of two men and about 200 cases of snow-blindness.

We had a long, steep, cold ride over our final pass—the Nathu-la—and then we rode down and down through all the glorious Sikkim vegetation into soft and balmy ease. A scientific gentleman once asked what was the chief effect of being a long time at high altitudes, and I told him the principal effect was a desire to get to a lower altitude as soon as possible. Now that we were back at ordinary human altitudes, bathed in delicious air and basking in the glorious sunshine, we realized what the strain of those high levels, combined with the biting cold, had been. Life seemed so easy now. There was no more unconscious effort in breathing; no more conscious fighting against the cold. Existence was once again a pleasure, and in the best season of the year, amid the most splendid scenery in the world, with snowy peaks rising sheer out of tropical forests into a cloudless sky, there was little more a man could wish.

But in the midst of this dream of ease, and just the very day before I reached Darjiling, came the rude shock that the best points I had obtained at Lhasa were to be given up. I will deal with this matter in a subsequent Chapter. It is enough here to state that all the pleasure of my return was dashed from me in a moment, and I bitterly regretted ever having undertaken so delicate a task with my hands so tied.

As we approached Darjiling we passed an enthusiastic tea-planter sitting at his gateway with a gramophone, which, as we neared him, struck up "See the Conquering Hero comes." He said he was by himself, and the gramophone was all the band he had, but he felt he must do something to welcome us; and this, our first greeting in British territory, given with such genuine feeling, went no small way to restoring my spirits.

At the station outside Darjiling I met my wife, and only then realized what the strain and anxiety to her my absence in Tibet must have caused. We went by rail to Darjiling itself, and there I had the unexpected honour of being welcomed on the platform by the kindly Sir Andrew Fraser, Lieutenant-Governor of Bengal, and nearly the whole of the European residents in the place. They had all—and particularly Sir Andrew and Lady Fraser—been so especially kind to my wife I could not thank them enough. Mr. and Mrs. Macpherson, Mrs. Walsh, and many others had never failed in their thoughtfulness, and I hope when they read this they will believe that their kindness will never be forgotten by either of us.

We stopped at Darjiling only a day, which I set apart entirely for our little girl, and then Messrs. White and Wilton, with my wife and myself, set out on our last stage to Simla, where Lord and Lady Ampthill warmly welcomed us to Viceregal Lodge. Lord Kitchener had already asked us by telegram to dine with him our first night at Simla, and from Sir Denzil and Lady Ibbetson, Sir Arundel Arundel, Sir Louis and Lady Dane, and many others we received the greatest kindness.

Nor could anything have been more generous than the support which Lord Ampthill and the whole Government of India gave me in the matter of the disallowed points in the Treaty. But what caused me anxiety was the view which Lord Curzon would take of what I had done. He had recommended me originally on account of my discretion. As long as he was in India he had given me unfailing and ungrudging support, besides the personal encouragement of a real friend; and if he thought that in the end I had failed him I should have been miserable for the rest of my days. I had acted absolutely and entirely on my own responsibility in what, in most difficult circumstances, had seemed to me the best for my country; and I had to take the risk of my action being approved or disapproved. But it would have been indeed a blow if I found Lord Curzon thought I had acted wrongly.

So I hastened home, and at Port Said stopped to meet him on his way out to India again. In one moment he set me right. I dined with him on the P. & O. steamer, and for hours afterwards on deck we talked over all the stirring events which had happened since we had parted in his camp at Patiala. Of all he was warmly appreciative. There is no man more staunch in friendship, and no keener patriot in England, than Lord Curzon; and what he did for the Indian Empire, and still more what he would have done if he had been more amply supported from England, will perhaps some day be more fully recognized than it is at present. If this Mission had been a failure, on him would have fallen the blame. How much its success was due to him no one knew better than I did.

On my arrival in England I had the honour of an audience of His late Majesty, and the reward I most appreciated for my services in Tibet was this opportunity of personally knowing my Sovereign. I saw him quite alone. He placed me in a chair by his desk, and then in some indefinable way made it possible for me to speak to him as I would have to my own father. He was himself most outspoken. He did not merely ask questions in a perfunctory way, but took a genuinely keen interest in our proceedings. He warmly praised the conduct of the troops. He was well aware of the deeds, and even character, of individual officers, and he spoke most feelingly of the loss of Major Bretherton, of whose splendid work he was fully cognizant. It appeared to me that it was men, and not policies, which chiefly interested him: human personalities rather than abstract principles. He was himself, as all the world now knows, a generous personality; and not merely a great Sovereign, but a great man. No one I have ever met has given me such an impression of abounding vitality and warm-blooded humanity, full and overflowing. And I left his august presence not only rewarded, but re-inspired.

Through the kindness of H.R.H. Princess Christian, who informed His Majesty of my wish, the flag* which I had with me throughout the Mission, which was carried before me on every march, which was planted before my tent in camp, which was flown over the Mission quarters at Gyantse, and which was placed on the table on which the Treaty was signed at Lhasa, was deposited in Windsor Castle, and by His Majesty's express commands was hung in the Central Hall over the statue of Queen Victoria.

* The flag known as a "Viceroy's flag"— a Union Jack with a star in the middle and the motto "Heaven's Light our Guide"—flown by political officers in India.

CHAPTER XXI

THE RESULTS OF THE MISSION

Even in the present year I was asked by a Cabinet Minister what good we did in going to Lhasa. Since that question was asked one striking result of our Mission has come to light, in the fact of the Dalai Lama, who before we went to Lhasa would not even receive a communication from the Viceroy, now in person, at Calcutta itself, appealing to the Viceroy to preserve his *right* of direct communication with us. The suspicious and hostile attitude of the Tibetans has so far changed that they have now asked us to form an alliance, and to send a British officer to their sacred city. To attribute this change entirely to the effects of the Mission may not be justifiable. Much is due to the tactlessness of the Chinese treatment of the Tibetans. But the change in direction of Tibetan feeling was visible before we left Lhasa, and there is good cause for assuming that if Lord Curzon had never despatched the Mission to break through the Tibetan reserve, they would have still been as inimical to us and as inclined towards Russia as they were six years ago. The conversion of our north-eastern neighbours from potential enemies into applicant allies may be taken as one result of the Mission.

When the Mission was despatched into Tibet, we had for thirty years been trying to regulate our intercourse with our Tibetan neighbours, but had obtained no success whatever. The Treaty which their suzerain had made with us was repudiated. Boundary pillars were thrown down, trade was boycotted, our communications were returned. And the Dalai Lama showed a decided leaning towards the Russians. As a result of Lord Curzon's policy in sending a Mission to Tibet, there had been signed by the Tibetan Government in the audience-room of the Dalai Lama's palace in Lhasa itself, in the presence of the Chinese Amban and of all the chief men of Tibet, a Treaty which defined our boundaries, placed our trade relations upon a satisfactory footing, and gave us the right to exclude any foreign influence if we should so wish. And in spite of the military operations which we were forced to undertake, and in spite of the Tibetans being compelled to pay an indemnity, the position of the Tibetans towards us was distinctly more favourable when we left Tibet than when we entered it.

In making my final report to Government, I said that I had always regarded the conclusion of a treaty on paper as of minor importance, and the establishment of our relations with the Tibetans on a footing of mutual good-will as of fundamental importance. There was little advantage in bringing back a Treaty which was not framed or negotiated in such a manner as to carry with it a considerable degree of spontaneous assent. And it was especially necessary to secure the good-will of the people in general.

The result of our Mission to Kabul in 1840 was to estrange the Afghans from us from that time to this, and an intense race hatred was engendered. It would be unwise to predict that we shall never have any difficulty in seeing that the present Treaty is properly carried out. But I can safely say that no feeling of race hatred was left behind by the Mission, and that after the Treaty was signed the Tibetans were better disposed towards us than they had ever been before. And this I consider to be incomparably the most important result of the policy which the Government of India had so unswervingly pursued.

A further result was the friendship of Bhutan. When the Mission started, the Bhutanese were practically strangers, and their attitude was uncertain. When the Mission returned they were our firm friends. The chief visited Calcutta. Mr. White has twice been most cordially received in Bhutan. And the former Tongsa Penlop, now the Maharaja of Bhutan, has formally placed himself under our protectorate.

Besides these political results, there were also scientific results of no mean value. Captain Ryder's survey operations have already been referred to. Mr. Hayden made valuable geological collections, which are on view in the Museum at Calcutta, and which are described by him in the Records of the Geological Survey of India. Captain Walton's natural history and botanical collections are placed in the Natural History Museum at South Kensington and in Kew Gardens, and have been described in various scientific works. Colonel Waddell was unable to discover any secrets of the ancient world said to be hidden in Tibet, but he made a collection of Tibetan manuscripts, which are deposited in the British Museum.

If all these political and scientific results may not seem to the ordinary Englishman to amount to much, the most obtuse must at least see one good that came from the Mission—the proving for all time that we can get to Lhasa, and that, even at the cost of crossing the Himalayas in mid-winter, we will see our treaties observed. Anyone practised in affairs knows the advantage of a reputation for enforcing obligations, and this at least accrued to us from the Mission of 1904.

But I have already mentioned that the Secretary of State felt himself unable to approve of the Treaty as signed, and I have now to show how it was that some of the advantages to which the Indian Government attached most importance had to be abandoned.

A week after the signing of the Treaty the Government of India telegraphed to me that the Secretary of State considered that a difficulty was presented by the amount of the indemnity, especially when the provision for its payment was read in conjunction with Clause VII. of the Treaty, the effect being that our occupation of Chumbi might have to continue for seventy-five years. This was, the Secretary of State said, inconsistent with the instructions conveyed in his telegram of July 26, and with the declaration of His Majesty's Government as to withdrawal. The Government of India were, therefore, asked to consider whether, without prejudice to the signed agreement, it would not be possible to intimate to the Tibetans that the amount of the indemnity would be reduced on their duly fulfilling the terms agreed to and granting further facilities for trade.

Some correspondence followed, but, owing to the shortness of my stay at Lhasa and the undesirability of attempting to alter a Treaty directly it had been made, no action was taken, and I returned with the Treaty intact.

The Government of India wrote on October 6 to the Secretary of State* reviewing the conditions under which I had had to make the Treaty, and saying that they considered I was fully justified in using my discretion as I did and in signing the Treaty on September 7 without awaiting approval of the amount of the indemnity and the method of its payment, and pointing out that any alteration in the terms at the critical moment would probably have led to a recommencement of the whole discussion.

They also thought my action in acquiring the right for our Agent at Gyantse to proceed to Lhasa under certain conditions might be approved. They were still of opinion that the right might be of the greatest value hereafter, and, hedged in as it was by the conditions mentioned in it, it could not be held, they thought, to commit us to any political control over Tibet.

At the same time the Government of India expressed their sincere regret that the instructions of His Majesty's Government were not carried out to the letter, as they would have been if communication with their Commissioner had not been a matter of twelve days even by telegraph.

Regarding the amendment of the Treaty to meet the wishes of His Majesty's Government, they proposed by telegram on October 21† that in ratifying it a declaration should be appended by the Viceroy reducing the indemnity from 75 to 25 lakhs, and affirming that after three annual

* Blue-book, III., p. 74. † *Ibid.*, p. 70.

instalments had been paid the British occupation of the Chumbi Valley should terminate, provided the terms of the Treaty should in the meantime have been carried out.

To this proposal the Secretary of State agreed on November 7,* but he added that, as regards the agreement giving the Agent at Gyantse the right of access to Lhasa, His Majesty's Government had decided to disallow it, for they considered it unnecessary, and inconsistent with the principle on which their policy had throughout been based.

Finally, the Secretary of State reviewed the whole affair in a despatch dated December 2. When Lord Curzon, in his despatch of January 8, 1903, made his proposal for a Mission to Lhasa, Tibet, though lying on our borders, was practically an unknown country, the rulers of which persistently refused to hold any communications with the British Government even on necessary matters of business; and if the Tibetan Government had become involved in political relations with other Powers, a situation of danger might have been created on the frontier of the Indian Empire. This risk had now been removed by the conclusion of the Treaty. And it was considered most satisfactory that, having regard to the obstinacy of the Tibetans in the past, I should, besides concluding the Treaty, have good reason to believe that the relations which I had established with them at Lhasa were generally friendly.

In the Treaty I had inserted a stipulation that the indemnity was to be paid in 75 annual instalments, and I had retained without modification the proviso that the Chumbi Valley was to be occupied as security till the full amount had been paid. The effect of this was to make it appear as if it were our intention to occupy for at least seventy-five years the Chumbi Valley, which had been recognized in the Convention of 1890 and the Trade Regulations of 1893 as Tibetan territory. This would have been inconsistent with the repeated declarations of His Majesty's Government that the Mission would not

* Blue-book, III., p. 77.

lead to occupation, and that we would withdraw from Tibetan territory when reparation had been secured.

It had been hoped that it would be possible to alter the Treaty before I left Lhasa, but it was clear in the circumstances that it was not desirable that I should have postponed my departure.

As to the separate agreement, the question of claiming for the trade agents at Gyantse the right of access to Lhasa was carefully considered before His Majesty's Government decided that no such condition was to be included in the terms of the settlement, and a subsequent request made by the Government of India for a modification of this decision was negatived by the telegram of August 3. No subsequent reference was made to the Secretary of State on the subject, and it was not till the receipt of the letter of October 6 from the Government of India that he learned that I had taken on myself the responsibility of concluding an agreement giving the trade agent at Gyantse the right to visit Lhasa to consult with the Chinese and Tibetan officers there on commercial matters, which it had been found impossible to settle at Gyantse. In the circumstances, His Majesty's Government had no alternative but to disallow the agreement as inconsistent with the policy which they had laid down.

Attention had already been drawn to the fact that questions of Indian frontier policy could no longer be regarded from an exclusively Indian point of view, and that the course to be pursued in such cases must be laid down by His Majesty's Government alone. It was essential that this should be borne in mind by those who found themselves entrusted with the conduct of affairs in which the external relations of India were involved, and that they should not allow themselves, under the pressure of the problems which confronted them on the spot, to forget the necessity of conforming to the instructions which they had received from His Majesty's Government, who had more immediately before them the interests of the British Empire as a whole.

Such were the final views and orders of the Secretary of State upon the Mission. The reasons for my action in extending the period of payment, in securing the right to occupy the Chumbi Valley during that extended period, and in obtaining the right for our Agent at Gyantse to proceed to Lhasa, have been already given. I had to act in circumstances that were very exceptional, and I thought I was not taking more latitude than such circumstances naturally confer on an agent. The pledges to Russia were given with a qualification, but the main pledge, that we would not annex Tibet, or establish a protectorate over it, or interfere in its internal administration, had not, in my view, been infringed by the Treaty I signed.

We may assume that Government had some pressing international consideration of the moment which necessitated their taking no account of the qualification to their pledges, but there is some justification for thinking that if the Treaty had not been modified, and the right to occupy the Chumbi Valley and to send the Gyantse Agent to Lhasa had been maintained, we might have prevented the present trouble from ever arising.

CHAPTER XXII

NEGOTIATIONS WITH CHINA

WE had settled with Tibet direct, as was Lord Curzon's chief object, and it had been proposed that China should sign what was styled an Adhesion Agreement, formally acknowledging the Tibetan Treaty. But Yu-tai, the Resident at Lhasa, was instructed not to sign any such agreement, and a Special Envoy was sent by the Chinese Government to Calcutta to treat with the Indian Government in the matter. Yu-tai himself had been specially deputed for these negotiations regarding Tibet, but apparently he was considered too complacent, and first of all, Mr. Tang, and then Mr. Chang, were sent to Calcutta, and from now onwards the Chinese showed first great diplomatic insistence, and then great military activity, in regard to Tibet, till, profiting by the jealousy between us and the Russians, which had prevented our reaping all the fruits of the Mission to Lhasa, they one by one gathered those fruits themselves.

Nothing resulted from Mr. Tang's visit to India, and ill-health caused him to return to China. But on April 27, 1906, in place of an Adhesion Agreement, a Convention was signed at Peking between Great Britain and China which "confirmed" the Lhasa Convention of 1904. In addition, Great Britain engaged "not to annex Tibetan territory, or to interfere in the administration of Tibet"; while the Chinese Government undertook "not to permit any other foreign State to interfere with the territory or internal administration of Tibet." We were entitled to lay down telegraph-lines to connect the trade-marts with India. And it was laid down that the provisions of the old Convention of 1890, and the Trade Regulations of 1893, remained in full force.

The signature of this Convention, far from improving our status in Tibet, or conferring any increased regularity upon our intercourse, seems to have had a precisely opposite effect. The impression was spread abroad in Tibet that this new Convention superseded the Lhasa Convention, and the Chinese assumed that we had virtually recognized their sovereignty in the country. They had obtained from us the engagement not to annex Tibetan territory, and with this and the renewed formal recognition of their rights of suzerainty after they had shown themselves so incapable of carrying out their suzerain duties, we might have expected that they would have shown at least a neighbourly feeling in Tibetan affairs, but we have so far been disappointed in this respect, and the 1906 Convention promises to be as little use to us as the 1890 Convention.

The first indications of the tone which the Chinese were going to adopt in Tibet was furnished by Mr. Chang, who was now appointed a High Commissioner for Tibet. On his arrival in Chumbi there was at once an "incident" with the British officer, Lieutenant Campbell, in political charge there. Lieutenant Campbell had been specially chosen for his knowledge of the Chinese language and customs. He had spent a year in China learning the language, and had carried out a remarkable and interesting journey from Peking to Kashmir by Chinese Turkestan. On Mr. Chang's arrival in Chumbi, Mr. Campbell proceeded in uniform to call on him, but he was first asked to enter by a side door, and afterwards told that Mr. Chang was not very well and was lying down. This may have been the case, but, combined with other acts, it produced the impression that he meant to ignore the British occupation and assert Chinese authority.

Mr. Chang's action at Gyantse gave rise to a similar impression that he was aiming at the belittlement of British influence rather than at cordially co-operating with our officers as Yu-tai had. He posted there a Chinese official named Gow as Sub-Prefect, with the title of

Chinese Commissioner in charge of the Chinese Trade and Diplomatic Agency; and this Mr. Gow proved so contumacious that Sir Edward Grey had eventually to press for his withdrawal. He threatened to stop the supply of provisions by Tibetans to our Trade Agent unless they were paid for at rates to be fixed by himself; and he also, apparently under sanction from Peking, claimed that in all transactions between the Tibetans and British officers *he should act as intermediary*.

This was a clear enough indication of Mr. Chang's line. He meant to get in between us and the Tibetans. And the Tibetans at Gyantse had many rumours just now that he was going to eject the Europeans and the Indian troops from Gyantse; that if the Indian Government did not agree, Chinese troops would be sent to expel us by force from Tibet. It was explained that Chinese troops were not sent to oppose us during the time of the Tibet Mission because there was no time to collect them. It was also reported that Mr. Chang intended to object to British officials and other Europeans travelling in Tibet except between the trade-marts and India. And this is what in fact he did in the case of Sven Hedin. He wrote him a very polite note saying what interest he took in geography and so forth, but adding: "The last treaty between China and Great Britain contains a paragraph declaring that no stranger, whether he be Englishman or Russian, an American or European, has any right to visit Tibet, the three market towns excepted." The Treaty has no such clause. It simply confirmed the Lhasa Treaty, in which was a clause stipulating that the agents or representatives of foreign Powers should not be admitted. As a matter of fact Sven Hedin was not the agent of a foreign Power, but a scientific traveller, and in any case the Lhasa Treaty simply laid down that agents should not be admitted "without the previous consent of the British Government." Sven Hedin was then at Shigatse. He was being most cordially received by the Tashi Lama, who was quite willing to let him travel where he liked. It was merely Mr. Chang who twisted and misquoted the Lhasa Treaty to exclude him.

Later other evidence of Mr. Chang's antipathy came to light. The Tibetan Jongpens at Gyantse informed Captain O'Connor in January, 1907, that since his arrival upon the scene their position had become very difficult, for he had told them that in future the Chinese were to act as intermediaries between the English and Tibetans, and so before complying with any request of his they would be obliged to ask the permission of Mr. Gow. And on March 5 Captain O'Connor telegraphed that he was now completely cut off from personal intercourse with Tibetan officials, as Mr. Gow refused to let the Jongpens see him.

In other directions also the change for the worse since Mr. Chang's arrival was apparent. The Resident Yu-tai, with whom I negotiated in 1904, was reported to have been dismissed from office and imprisoned in fetters in January, 1907. His Secretary was also degraded, and a desire to sweep away all Chinese officials connected with the improvement of our relations with the Tibetans seemed to have inspired Mr. Chang's actions. A similar resentment against Tibetan officials concerned with the recent negotiations was also shown, two Councillors and a General being degraded. These incidents afforded, in the opinion of the Government of India, indubitable proof of Mr. Chang's determination to upset the *status quo* and destroy the position secured to us by the Mission. Mr. Chang's assumption seems to have been that virtual recognition of Chinese sovereignty over Tibet was involved in the signature of the latest Convention with China.

So clear, indeed, had the intention of the Chinese to work against us rather than with us been showing itself that Sir Edward Grey, on February 9, 1907,* telegraphed to Sir John Jordan that, while it was our desire to have matters put right, not by separate action in Tibet, but through the medium of the Chinese Government, he should bring Mr. Chang's action to the attention of the Chinese Government, and point out to them that the recognition by China of the Lhasa Treaty was not con-

* Blue-book, IV., p. 88.

sistent with the punishment of officials for being concerned in its negotiation. Our Minister was further to state that interference by Chinese officers with the freedom of the dealings between the Tibetan Agent and the British Trade Agent at Gyantse could not be permitted by His Majesty's Government.

Again, on March 15,* he telegraphed that "the right of direct communication between the British Agent and local Tibetan authorities must be firmly insisted on," and the Chinese Government must be "urged to send very clear instructions in this sense to Chang."

Later, again, on June 27, Sir Edward Grey had again to telegraph to our Minister to make further very serious representations to the Chinese Government on the subject. He was to draw their attention to the fact that no friction existed between Captain O'Connor and the Tibetans of the locality previous to the intervention of Mr. Chang and Mr. Gow. We wanted nothing more than freedom of trade, for our political interests were safeguarded by clauses in the Treaty, and we had no wish to assert any political influence ourselves. We did not even desire to foster trade. We wished, indeed, to reduce the establishment at the marts, and, if things went on quietly, native instead of British agents might be appointed there. But Sir Edward Grey considered that China was "trifling with her obligations in the matter of Tibet," and he suggested that Mr. Gow should be entirely removed from all employment in that country.

In consequence of these representations Mr. Gow was withdrawn from Tibet, but only to be given a higher appointment in a more popular part of the Chinese Empire—the Directorship of Telegraphs at Mukden in Manchuria—and the attitude of the Chinese in Tibet has not yet really changed. Perhaps the reason may be found in the hint given by Sir John Jordan, who, when the Grand Secretary told him that the Wai-wu-pu had always been puzzled to know the causes of the friction between Mr. Gow and the British Trade Agent, expressed his conviction that they lay in the fact that someone from

* Blue-book, IV., p. 98.

Peking had been inspiring a policy in Tibetan affairs which was hostile to the Treaty and to British interests.

In any case, whether the cause lay in Peking, or with Mr. Chang, or with the Tibetans, the fact was clear that the Treaty had not been carried out; and the Government of India thought it necessary to bring the matter formally to the notice of the Secretary of State in a despatch dated July 18, 1907. Considering what had taken place at Gyantse, it was impossible to admit, they said, that the Gyantse trade-mart had been effectively open during the last few months. Our Agent had been cut off from intercourse with the Tibetan authorities, and no adequate provision had been made for British traders having resort to the mart. The agents whom the Lhasa Government had nominated for the marts had not been allowed freedom of communication with the British Trade Agent. And various minor difficulties had arisen in connection with the opening of the Gartok trade-mart. The Government of India, therefore, suggested that the Chinese and Tibetan Governments should be formally reminded of these various breaches of the Convention which had occurred, and more particularly of the failure to open the marts, which was a matter which struck at the root of the whole Convention.

Mr. Morley thought* the situation at Gyantse constituted undoubtedly a serious cause of complaint, but, in view of the reply of the Chinese Government to the representations recently made to them, he doubted the expediency of making any further reference to the subject at the moment. If, when the negotiations with Mr. Chang regarding the Trade Regulations commenced, the attitude of the Chinese and Tibetan representative should prove obstructive, the question would arise whether the British representative should not be authorized to warn them that our evacuation of the Chumbi Valley depended on a satisfactory settlement of the matters connected with the trade-marts being arrived at, the Chinese and Tibetan Governments being simultaneously warned to the same effect.

* Blue-book, IV., p. 126.

So for the present ended any idea of direct remonstrance regarding breaches of the Treaty. But it was not only locally at the trade-marts that the Chinese were pursuing their policy of separating the Tibetans from us. By an astute move they had already sought to effect the same end through payment of the indemnity. By the terms of the Treaty this was due from the Tibetans. Though we might well have demanded the indemnity from the Chinese, and many think that we should have demanded part, at least, for it was to enforce a Treaty which they had *asked* us to make, which they had assured us they could see observed, but of which, from 1890 to 1904, they were never able to secure fulfilment, that we went to Lhasa, we instead demanded it from the Tibetans, and, on account of their poverty, we reduced the amount payable from 75 to 25 lakhs of rupees—from half a million sterling to £166,666. The Chinese now said that they would pay this reduced indemnity. In an Imperial Decree issued in November, 1905, it was ordered that the indemnity should, in view of the poverty of the people, be paid by the Chinese Government—that is, that the Chinese Government should pay it over to us direct for, and on behalf of, Tibet.

In forwarding this information, Sir Ernest Satow suggested that we should inform the Chinese Government that we could not receive payment from them. He believed that the Chinese Government were trying to make themselves the intermediary of all communications between India and Tibet, and it seemed to him reasonable to conclude that this declaration of their intention to pay the indemnity was intended to force the hand of the Indian Government, and induce them to accept an arrangement which the Chinese Government could afterwards quote as a precedent in other matters.

Lord Lansdowne—these negotiations commenced while the late Government were still in office—felt difficulty in advising the India Office* as to how to deal with the matter. It was on the one hand obvious that the indemnity was required of the Tibetans partly as a punitive measure and

* Blue-book, IV., p. 29.

partly in order that by the annual payment of the necessary instalments they should formally recognize the binding nature of the obligations entered into by them towards the British Government. Should the annual instalments henceforth be paid by the Chinese Government, the punitive effect of the indemnity would disappear, for it did not seem to Lord Lansdowne at all probable that the Chinese Government would be able or willing to recover from the Tibetan Government the sums paid on this account, and past experience had proved that it was not in the power of China to insist effectively on the fulfilment of the other stipulations of the Convention.

Lord Lansdowne felt no doubt that the proposal had been made by the Chinese Government with the object of re-establishing their theoretical rights to supremacy over the Tibetan Government, and probably also with the object of insuring that the non-payment of the instalments at their due date should not stand in the way of the retirement of the British forces. Irrespectively of these considerations, the refusal of the Chinese Government to adhere to the Tibetan Agreement made it doubly difficult for us to entertain the offer, and upon this ground alone Lord Lansdowne considered that it should be rejected. For acceptance would be tantamount to admitting the intervention of China in relieving Tibet from this portion of her obligations while avoiding all responsibility for any other portion of the Convention.

Should the attitude of the Chinese Government undergo a change in consequence of our refusal, and should they intimate that they would adhere to the Agreement, the situation would no doubt be altered, and might be reconsidered by His Majesty's Government. Having regard, however, to the complete inability shown by China in the past to exercise effectual control over the Tibetan authorities, it seemed to Lord Lansdowne that it would be highly inadvisable to agree to any settlement which might be regarded as an admission that responsibility for the behaviour of the Tibetans would for the future rest upon the Chinese Government.

This view of Lord Lansdowne's and Sir Ernest

Satow's, both very able and experienced diplomatists, was justified by the event. It was here that the Chinese began their series of efforts again to thrust themselves in between us and the Tibetans, and prevent that direct relationship between us which, through the futility of the Chinese themselves, we had been compelled at so much cost to establish. If we had stood firm at the start on this point, which was one on which we had a perfect right to stand fast, much future trouble might have been saved.

The Government of India concurred in this view, and thought that the annual payment by Tibetans in Tibet, even though China should provide the money, would be preferable from the point of view of local political effect, to payment of a lump sum by China direct. The course, therefore, which was preferred was, that a notification should first be made by them to the Tibetans under Article VI. of the Convention, to the effect that we desired payment at Gyantse of the first instalment; and that His Majesty's Minister at Peking should then inform the Chinese Government that His Majesty's Government could not recognize the right of intervention on their part, as they had not adhered to the Convention.

A notification was accordingly given to the Tibetan Government that Rs. 100,000, the first instalment of the indemnity, was due on January 1, 1906, and should be paid at Gyantse. They replied in January, 1906, that the revenue of Tibet was not great, and that the Chinese Resident had stated that the payment of the indemnity was to be the subject of discussion with China, in which Tang at Calcutta was to act. Thus, said the Government of India, as a result of the action of the Chinese, the Treaty had been broken by the Tibetans, for no payment of the indemnity had been made on the date fixed. They proposed, therefore, to inform the Tibetan Government that they held them responsible for the payment of the indemnity under the terms of the Treaty.

Mr. Morley, who had succeeded Mr. Brodrick, approved of the proposal, but added that this would not preclude our accepting payment eventually from the Chinese Government if agreement with them as to the

Tibet Convention should be arrived at; and in a later telegram he said that "direct payment by China could not be refused by us after the Adhesion Convention had been concluded."

The principle that the Chinese should pay instead of the Tibetans was therefore practically conceded. But another point arose. The Chinese had said they wished to pay the amount of 25 lakhs of rupees (Rs. 25,00,000) in three annual instalments, but by the Treaty the payment was to be paid in annual instalments of 1 lakh each. The suggestion that the whole indemnity should be paid in three instalments the Government of India thought a Chinese device, having for its object the weakening of our position in Tibet. The Treaty obligation was clear. And the Indian Government preferred, as requested by the Tibetans themselves at the time of signing the Treaty, to receive annual payments of 1 lakh each at Gyantse, both for political effect and because money was required for recurring rent expenditure there.

Mr. Morley felt much hesitation in accepting the views of the Government of India on this point. While recognizing that certain advantages had been supposed by some to arise from the political point of view in maintaining our hold over the Tibetans for the full period of twenty-five years, he was of opinion that such advantages would be altogether outweighed by our relief from the necessity of enforcing a direct annual tribute for so long a period.

Shortly after, on April 27, the Chinese signed the Convention which has been described at the beginning of this Chapter, and the Chinese Government were informed that we agreed to accept the offer to pay the whole of the indemnity in three instalments, and that the first instalment would be accepted from the Sha-pé either by cheque, handed to the British Commercial Agent at Gyantse, or by cheque to the Government of India, drawn on the Hong Kong and Shanghai Bank.

The Chinese had made good their first point, and we had receded from yet another stage which we had reached in 1904. Their next point had now to be made—

to get us to accept payment in India instead of in Tibet. The Tibetan Sha-pé being in Calcutta at the time, we did not raise any difficulty about accepting payment of the first instalment there. But when the question of the payment of the second instalment arose, the Government of India pointed out that under the Treaty it should be paid at such place as the British Government might indicate, whether in Tibet or in the British districts of Darjiling or Jalpaiguri. Permission had been given to pay the first instalment at Calcutta, as the Tibetan Councillor happened to be there at the time, but the Government of India wished that the second instalment should be handed over by a Tibetan official to our Trade Agent at Gyantse. But the Secretary of State telegraphed that it would be in accordance with the present policy of His Majesty's Government to acquiesce in the wish of the Chinese Government, and payment by telegraphic transfer was agreed to. The third instalment was also received in Calcutta. So the Chinese obtained their second point also.

The third point which they tried to make in their policy of excluding the Tibetans, was to get us to receive the indemnity direct from them instead of from the Tibetans. They suggested that they should pay the second instalment "by telegraphic transfer without the intervention of the Tibetans." But the Government of India recommended that deviation from the procedure laid down in the Treaty should not be permitted, as their proposal seemed to them a further indication of the Chinese desire to exclude the Tibetans from relations with us.

His Majesty's Government, however, considered that the formality of payment through a Tibetan representative was "a comparatively immaterial point," and that if China was to make further pretensions we should not be prejudiced by the concession.

Later on, however, as the Chinese had been obstructive in other matters, and the second instalment had not yet been paid, both Mr. Morley and Sir Edward Grey adopted the proposal of the Government of India that payment to the Trade Agent through a Tibetan official at Gyantse should be required, and arrangements recently conceded by His Majesty's Government for payment direct by the Chinese should be cancelled. But this was not eventually insisted on, and payments were received by the Government of India through the Hong Kong and Shanghai Bank.

In regard to the third instalment, Mr. Chang proposed, on December 27, 1907, that he should hand it over in the form of a cheque to the Indian Government. But the latter again stood out for receiving it from a Tibetan. It was due only to a misunderstanding that payment in the previous year had been accepted direct before orders on the subject had arrived. As regards this proposal of the Chinese, Mr. Morley, though he doubted the advantage of raising the point, saw no objection, as the Tsarong Sha-pé was then in Calcutta, to payment being made by the Tibetan Government through him to the Government of India.

But this method of payment Mr. Chang refused, and wrote to Sir Louis Dane: "I regret to say that I am unable to meet your wishes that Tsarong Sha-pé should himself tender payment. I have received very explicit instructions from my Government on this subject, that the third instalment of the indemnity (Rs. 8,33,333 : 5 : 4) is to be handed over in the form of a cheque only by myself." When the matter arose in discussion at a meeting on January 10, Mr. Chang intimated that he based his objection to the proposal on the fact that direct dealings between us and the Tibetan authorities would be involved in it. It was no longer possible, the Government of India thought, to doubt Chang's firm determination that Chinese sovereignty over Tibet, to the exclusion of all local autonomy, should be indicated, and that direct communication of all kinds between our officials and Tibetans should be prevented. It appeared that Mr. Chang was being supported in this attitude by the Chinese Government, and that it was doubtful if we could expect, without further guarantee, loyal fulfilment of the Lhasa Convention as interpreted by His Majesty's Government. Chinese claims might exist which contravened our distinct rights under the Lhasa Convention, as recognized in the Anglo-Russian arrangement regarding Tibet, and confirmed by the Peking Convention. The Indian Government greatly feared the reproduction in an aggravated form of the position of affairs before 1903 if Chinese contentions were admitted.

Mr. Morley proposed to Sir Edward Grey that a representation should be made to the Chinese Government of the serious consequences that would ensue if payment of a third instalment of the indemnity was not made in accordance with the Treaty; and the latter telegraphed to our Minister at Peking to inform the Chinese Government that the transfer of authority in the Chumbi Valley, much as it was desired by His Majesty's Government, would be unavoidably delayed unless payment was made in accordance with the provision of the Lhasa Convention. The result was that within a week a cheque, signed by Mr. Chang, was delivered by the Tsarong Sha-pé, who paid a formal visit to Sir Louis Dane, accompanied by two Tibetan officers.

The Chinese did not altogether gain their third point, but it is to be noted that the cheque was signed by Mr. Chang, and that the Tibetan official was not much more than a messenger carrying it over to the Foreign Office.

All these proceedings have an air of triviality, but that in Asiatic eyes they were of importance we may infer from the insistence of the Chinese. If they really were trivial they might have handed the money to the Tibetans, and saved themselves the worry with us.

Connected with this question of the payment of the indemnity was the question of the evacuation of the Chumbi Valley, to effect which was the most important object of Chinese policy. By the original Treaty we had the right to occupy it till seventy-five annual instalments of the indemnity had been paid, but by the declaration affixed to the ratification of the Treaty we undertook that the British occupation of the Chumbi Valley should cease after due payment of three annual instalments, provided that the trade-marts, as stipulated in Article II., should have been effectively opened for three years, as provided in Article VI.; and that in the meantime the Tibetans should have faithfully complied with the terms of the said Convention in all other respects. On December 23, 1907, the Chinese Government addressed a note to our Minister, stating that as the final instalment was ready for payment on January 1, 1908, we should "withdraw on the above date the British troops in temporary occupation of the Chumbi Valley."

The Indian Government pointed out* that the Chinese ignored the condition that evacuation was contingent on the Tibetans faithfully complying with the Treaty in every respect. Instances tending to show that this condition, and the condition that the trade-marts should be effectively opened had not been fulfilled, had already been reported to the Secretary of State. The fact that the Tibetan authorities had recently failed to provide accommodation, except at extortionate rent, for Indian traders supplied evidence of this. The Tibetans also imposed unauthorized restrictions on trade by accustomed routes across the northern frontier of Sikkim, and on traders going from the United Provinces to marts in Western Tibet. The fact that, in spite of the maintenance of the telegraph service being provided for in Article III. of the Peking Convention, there had been serious recrudescence of interruptions to it since Mr. Chang's visit to Tibet, further illustrated the attitude of the Tibetans. There had also been obstruction to postal communication with Gartok. It could not, then, be said that marts had been effectively opened since Mr. Chang's visit, whatever might have been the case before.

We should presumably have been entitled to claim, under the letter of the Treaty, that, until the trade-marts had been effectively opened for three years, and until the terms of the Convention had in the meantime been complied with in all other respects, the valley should be retained by us. It was not the desire of the Government of India to suggest rigid enforcement of the Convention in this respect. They bore in mind, however, the decision of His Majesty's Government that if, after commencement

* Blue-book, IV., p. 136.

of the negotiations for the Trade Regulations, the attitude of the Chinese and Tibetan representatives proved obstructive, the question of warning the Chinese and Tibetan representatives that our evacuation would depend on matters connected with trade-marts being satisfactorily settled, should be considered.

It was shown by the history of the negotiations that, in regard to important points at issue, the Chinese had been, and still were, most obstructive. Sir John Jordan's requests regarding points which he was pressing had not yet been acceded to by the Wai-wu Pu ; while, in a letter to Sir Louis Dane, which had just been received, Mr. Chang refused to yield other contested points, and forwarded further draft regulations. The transfer of the administration of the valley should, therefore, the Indian Government submitted, be deferred until some guarantee that the marts would be effectively opened, and that they would remain so, was afforded us by the new Trade Regulations. The chief lever which we possessed for securing China's real compliance with the terms of the Lhasa Convention would be lost if the transfer was permitted before the signature of the Regulations. The possibility, in the event of non-fulfilment of conditions, of temporary postponement of evacuation was apparently contemplated by the annexure to the Anglo-Russian arrangement concerning Tibet. And the sincerity of our intention to leave the valley would perhaps be sufficiently guaranteed by the fact that discussion of the Trade Regulations was in progress, and that their settlement was to be followed by evacuation.

Mr. Morley, in reviewing these contentions of the Indian Government, said that it must be remembered that when the Government of India, in July, 1907, raised the question of the failure of the Tibetans to fulfil the conditions on which evacuation was to take place, it was decided by His Majesty's Government that it was "not necessary at present formally to remind the Chinese and Tibetan Governments of such breaches of the Lhasa Convention as have occurred." Nor had the incidents since reported by the Government of India been considered of sufficient importance to justify a warning either to Tibet or China that there had been a failure to comply with the conditions on which our evacuation of Chumbi depended. The fact that we kept silence at the time that these incidents occurred rendered it impossible, in Mr. Morley's opinion, to revive them now without exposing ourselves to a charge of bad faith.

There remained the argument that the evacuation of Chumbi would deprive us of our only practical means of bringing pressure to bear on the Chinese Government to expedite a satisfactory settlement of the negotiations now in progress for the revision of the Tibetan Trade Regulations. But though it might be inconvenient to be deprived of this weapon, it appeared to Mr. Morley that, since by our own action we were precluded, for the reasons stated above, from alleging that there had been breaches of the Lhasa Convention of such a nature as to necessitate our retention of Chumbi, it would be an unjustifiable extension of the interpretation to be placed on the conditions laid down in that Convention to maintain, as we should have in effect to do, that the marts cannot be regarded as effectively open till the revised Trade Regulations have been satisfactorily settled. The Lhasa Convention clearly contemplates the marts being conducted under the old Regulations, which in form were sufficiently comprehensive until the new ones were introduced. It contained no stipulation, as it well might have done, that a revision of the Regulations satisfactory to ourselves was essential before the marts at Gyantse and elsewhere could be held to have been effectively opened.

The possibility had also to be borne in mind, given the peculiarities of Chinese diplomacy, that the continued occupation of Chumbi might have no other effect than to increase the obstinacy of the Chinese Government in the matter of the revision of the Regulations. In that case, as time went on, our position would have become increasingly difficult, and if our occupation was seriously protracted, as might not improbably have been the result of delaying evacuation, the whole policy of His Majesty's Government in Asia would to a certain degree be stultified.

A comparison of the British and Chinese drafts of the proposed Regulations showed that the points at real issue in the Regulations were not only those of political status involved in the wording of the preamble, but practical commercial questions of great complexity and inherent difficulty, such as that, for instance, to which the Government of India drew special attention, of the terms under which Indian tea was to be admitted into Tibet. It could not seriously be contended that our occupation was to continue till terms as to tea, satisfactory to the Indian trade, had been accepted by Tibet and China. On the other hand, no line could be logically and defensibly drawn between those matters in the Trade Regulations which were, and those which were not, essential points in the consideration of the question whether the trade-marts had been effectively opened.

The conclusion at which Mr. Morley had arrived was that, on an impartial interpretation of the Lhasa Convention, by the light of the events of the last three years, there were not sufficient grounds to justify a refusal to withdraw from Chumbi, and that, for reasons of policy and expediency, it was desirable that our occupation should terminate at once. Whatever difficulties might be in store for us from Chinese obstructiveness, Mr. Morley was of opinion that our power of coping with them would be diminished, not increased, if we placed ourselves in what would be an essentially false position by declining to withdraw from the Chumbi Valley, in accordance with our pledges and declared intentions.

Sir Edward Grey concurred in the views expressed by the Secretary of State for India in regard to the evacuation of the Chumbi Valley; but he considered that it would be well to point out to the Chinese Government that His Majesty's Government would expect, in return for evacuation, that their wishes would be met in regard to the Trade Regulations then under discussion at Calcutta, and that conciliatory instructions would be sent to Chang with a view to the speedy conclusion of the negotiations. He had accordingly sent to His Majesty's Minister at Peking a telegram in the above sense.

The final instalment of the indemnity having been paid, orders for the evacuation of the Chumbi Valley were issued on January 27, 1908.

Thus we deliberately abandoned the sole guarantee for the fulfilment of the Treaty. For years prior to the conclusion of the Lhasa Treaty we had had practical experience that Chinese engagements regarding Tibet were useless. Since the signature of the Lhasa Treaty we had three years' evidence that the Chinese were trying to evade its execution. Its provisions had not been fulfilled, and have not yet been carried out, six years after it was signed. Extreme moderation had been shown; concession after concession had been made. With a broad-mindedness in which some might suspect indifference we had given way point after point. In spite of all this, the Chinese were not observing the Treaty. And yet we gave up the one and only material guarantee for its fulfilment.

Now, at least, when we had withdrawn from Chumbi, and when we had been complacent in so many respects, we might fairly have expected that a change of tone would have come over Chinese policy. But, as we have on many other occasions experienced, the Chinese are not always most reasonable when we are most accommodating. And from the time we evacuated the Chumbi Valley they commenced a great forward movement in Tibet, which has resulted in the practical extinction of the Tibetan Government, and necessitated our despatching a much larger number of troops than we had in Chumbi to Gnatong, an inhospitable spot over 12,000 feet above sea-level, where they still have a 15,000-feet pass between them and Chumbi, and can, in consequence, exert only one-quarter of the moral effect they had in Chumbi itself.

But before this movement actually commenced, the Chinese had concluded some Trade Regulations with us; again at the instance of the Chinese Government, who seem to have a shrewd suspicion that these various agreements bind us to a far greater extent than they confer benefit on us.

On April 7, 1907, the Chinese Government had notified our Minister at Peking that if the Government of India would appoint a special representative, Mr. Chang would proceed to Calcutta to negotiate the new Trade Regulations with him. Sir John Jordan, in accordance with instructions he had received, pointed out that under Article III. of the Lhasa Convention it was the Tibetan Government who should appoint a delegate to negotiate a revision of the Trade Regulations. We were, however, willing not to insist on negotiating these Trade Regulations exclusively with delegates of the Tibetan Government. But before the negotiations began a Tibetan delegate should be appointed by the Tibetan Government, with full power to negotiate and sign on behalf of the Tibetan Government in such a manner as to bind that Government to the settlement arrived at. This delegate should then be associated with Mr. Chang and proceed together with him to Simla, to negotiate there with a special representative of the Government of India.

The Chinese Government replied on May 21, suggesting that Tibet should depute a Tibetan and India an Indian Government official to negotiate, and that the actions of the Tibetan representative would be subject to the approval of Mr. Chang, and those of the Indian representative to that of the Viceroy of India. This was a thoroughly Chinese device to put India on a par with Tibet and Mr. Chang on a par with the Viceroy. What reply it met with is not on record, but on July 18 the Secretary of State telegraphed to the Viceroy that he should address to the Tibetan Government a friendly and uncontroversial letter, notifying them of the negotiations to be held at Simla, and requesting that their delegate might be supplied with proper credentials. In carrying out these instructions the Viceroy telegraphed that he had also told the British Trade Agent to give a copy of the communication to Mr. Chang, and that the Foreign Secretary had written a friendly letter to Mr. Chang announcing that he, Sir Louis Dane, had been appointed British delegate.

The Regulations were eventually signed at Calcutta

on April 20, 1908, by Mr. Wilton (who had taken Sir Louis Dane's place), Mr. Chang, and the Tsarong Sha-pé. The questions relating to extradition, the levy of Customs duties, the export of tea from India into Tibet, and the appointment of Chinese Trade Agents, with Consular privileges, were reserved for future consideration.

By these new Regulations it was laid down that the old Regulations of 1893 should remain in force, in so far as they were not inconsistent with the new Regulations. The boundaries of the Gyantse mart were fixed. British subjects were allowed to lease land at the marts for the building of houses and godowns; the administration at the marts was to remain with the Tibetan officers, under the Chinese officers' supervision and directions; the Trade Agents and Frontier Officers were to hold personal intercourse and correspondence one with another, and the Chinese authorities were not to prevent the British Trade Agents holding personal intercourse and correspondence with the Tibetan officers and people; and British subjects were to be at liberty to sell their goods to whomsoever they pleased and to buy goods from whomsoever they pleased. China engaged to afford effective police protection at the marts and along the routes, and on due fulfilment of arrangements for this, Great Britain undertook to withdraw the Trade Agents' guards at the marts and to station no troops in Tibet, so as to remove all cause for suspicion and disturbance among the inhabitants. In a letter accompanying the Regulations Mr. Wilton wrote to the Chinese and Tibetan delegates that the strength of the armed guards at Gyantse and Yatung would not exceed fifty and twenty-five respectively, and the desirability of reducing these numbers even before their actual withdrawal would be carefully considered from time to time, as occasion might offer.

These Regulations would have been of value if they had been observed, but even in 1910 the Indian Government reported that the Chinese did not allow the Tibetans to deal directly with our Agents, and once they were concluded the Chinese seem to have been more engrossed with the great forward movement which, I have stated, they commenced as soon as we had evacuated Chumbi, than in carrying out their part of the agreement.

The first indication of this significant change of Chinese policy was the appointment of Chao Erh-feng, the Acting Viceroy of Szechuan, as Resident in Tibet, in the spring of 1908. It was unusual, said Sir John Jordan in reporting this, to select an official of his standing and record for this position. The appointment was all the more significant because his brother, Chao Erh-hsun, who succeeded Chang Chih-tung as Viceroy at Hankow in the previous September, was suddenly transferred to the less important post of Viceroy of Szechuan at the same time as Chao Erh-feng was sent to Tibet.

A Memorial of the Board of Finance, approved by an Imperial Rescript of March 19, which was published in the Chinese press on March 31, threw some light on these appointments and the intentions of the Chinese Government. Chao Erh-feng was apparently expected to perform in Tibet functions similar to those of the Marquis Ito in Korea, and especially to extend the control of the Chinese Government over the Tibetan Administration. The appointment of Chao Erh-hsun as Viceroy was intended to strengthen his brother's hands and insure harmony of action.

The Memorial of the Board of Finance stated that Tibet acted as a rampart for the province of Szechuan, and, in view of its extent and the backward civilization of the natives, plans for such important measures as the training of troops, the promotion of education, the development of agriculture, mining and industries, the improvement of means of communication, the increase in the number of officials, and the reform of the Government, should be prepared without delay, so that the administration of the country might gradually be put on a better basis. Chao Erh-feng had been appointed to the post of Imperial Resident in Tibet, and, as a mark of the importance of his office, exceptionally high rank had been conferred upon him.

Chao Erh-feng was directed to investigate the local conditions in concert with Lien Yu, to prepare comprehensive schemes for all the measures to be undertaken in Tibet, and to draft Regulations. The officials should receive liberal salaries, and be generously rewarded for meritorious service. They should all be permitted to bring their families with them, and would be required to hold their appointments for long periods. To meet the necessary expenditure, the Board of Finance was to provide a sum of from 400,000 to 500,000 taels every year in order to aid in this important undertaking, and the Viceroy of Szechuan was to give his assistance when required, even beyond the limits of his own jurisdiction.

Sir John Jordan, as events have proved, was amply justified in drawing attention to the significance of this appointment of Chao Erh-feng. He was a man of both ability and energy, but also of severity. His dealings with the semi-independent States of Eastern Tibet will be related in the following Chapter. Here it is important to emphasize the facts that he was turning these States one after another into districts directly administered by Chinese officials, and that he was making a special set against Lamaism*—regulating the numbers who might become priests, curtailing the donations to monasteries, increasing the taxes they had to pay, prohibiting the construction of temples except by Chinese officials, and declaring the inefficacy of the Lama's prayers—excellent reforms in many ways, but when carried out with the severity with which Chao was introducing them in Eastern Tibet, inevitably calculated to arouse anger and suspicion at Lhasa.

Following the appointment of this high-handed Viceroy bearing a special mandate to "reform" the Government of Tibet appeared anti-British articles in a Lhasa newspaper,† published by the Chinese officials and circulated throughout Tibet. The Tibetans were exhorted not to be afraid of Chao and his soldiers; they were not intended to do harm to Tibetans, but "to other people." The Tibetans were to remember how they felt ashamed when the foreign soldiers arrived in Lhasa, and oppressed them with much tyranny. Chinese and Tibetans must all strengthen themselves on this account; otherwise their common religion

* See especially p. 373. † Blue-book, IV., p. 178.

would be destroyed in a hundred, or perhaps a thousand, years. In the west the "foreign frontier" was very close. In that direction, also, was Nepal. The Tibetans were therefore to make friends quickly with the Nepalese, and "become as one to resist the foreigners." In Tibet were "some wicked, aggressive foreigners," with whom intercourse had to be maintained, and for this purpose English schools would be opened. Then, again, in the south was Bhutan, and "Tibet and Bhutan were as inseparable as the cheek from the teeth." It would be even more advantageous to make friends with Bhutan than with Nepal. If at any future time the Bhutanese wanted help, the Chinese Resident would give it. "Bhutan is like a wall of Tibet. The Emperor thinks that the Gurkhas, Bhutanese, and Tibetans should live like three men in one house."

The next Chinese move was the Imperial Decree issued in November, 1908, to which more detailed allusion will be made later,* ostensibly conferring an additional honour on the Dalai Lama, in reality containing, as Sir John Jordan put it, "the first unequivocal declaration on the part of China that she regarded Tibet as within her sovereignty"—sovereignty, be it noted, not suzerainty.

Then, a year later, came the announcement by the Chinese Government to our Minister, that "Chao Erh-feng was faced with a serious state of unrest on the Tibetan marches—so much so that the Chinese Government, having reason to fear complications with Tibet, and desiring to strengthen their influence at Lhasa, were contemplating the despatch of a body of troops to the Tibetan capital."

By a remarkable coincidence, on the very day, November 12, 1909, on which the Chinese Councillor made this announcement to our Minister, the Dalai Lama, from a monastery three marches outside Lhasa, despatched a messenger to him, expressing the Dalai Lama's concern to find, on his return to Tibet, that active measures were being taken in the country by Chinese troops, and adding his hope that the Minister would do what he could in the matter.

* See p. 384.

The events which led up to this will be set forth in detail in the following Chapter. To make the consecutive narrative of Chinese action complete, it will merely be noted here that three months later the Chinese troops arrived in Lhasa; that on the day of their arrival ten soldiers were sent to each of the Tibetan Ministers' houses; that the Dalai Lama thereupon fled to India; that the Chinese sent several hundred soldiers to "attend" and "protect" him, but that he escaped across our frontier; that only a fortnight after he had left Lhasa he was deposed by Imperial decree; that the Chinese then took the Government of Tibet into their hands, preventing the sole remaining Minister from doing anything without the Resident's consent, holding the ferry across the Brahmaputra, and preventing anyone crossing the river without a pass from the Resident, replacing Tibetan by Chinese police, seizing rifles, closing the arsenal and mint; and, what more intimately concerns ourselves, and what was immediately opposed to Treaty obligations, preventing the Tibetans dealing directly with our Trade Agents.

All this was done, moreover, with the object, as our Minister was informed, of "tranquillizing the country," of "protecting the trade-marts," and of "seeing that the Tibetans conform to the Treaties."

Whether the Chinese forward movement extended beyond Tibet to Nepal and Bhutan, there is no official information. But Government evidently expected some such action, for in January, 1910, they concluded a Treaty with Bhutan, increasing the annual allowance from Rs. 50,000 to Rs. 100,000, and securing from the Bhutanese an agreement that they would be guided by the advice of the British Government in regard to their external relations. And on Lord Morley's suggestion, the Chinese Government was informed in February of this year that we could not prevent Nepal from taking such steps to protect her interests as she might think necessary under the circumstances; while in April we went a step farther, and gave a clear intimation to China* that we could not allow administrative changes in Tibet to affect or prejudice

* Blue-book, IV., p. 215.

the integrity either of Nepal or of Sikkim and Bhutan, and that we were prepared, if necessary, to protect the interests and rights of these three States. It was also impressed upon the Chinese Government that it was inadvisable to locate troops upon, or in, the neighbourhood of the frontiers of India and the adjoining States in such numbers as would necessitate corresponding movements on the part of the Government of India and the rulers of the States concerned.

CHAPTER XXIII

THE ATTITUDE OF THE TIBETANS SINCE 1904

IMMEDIATELY following the conclusion of the Treaty at Lhasa, the attitude of the Tibetans was friendly enough. The Ti Rimpoche wrote to the Government of India expressing the gratitude of the Tibetans for the reduction of the indemnity from 75 to 25 lakhs of rupees, and for the promise to restore the Chumbi Valley after three years if the provisions of the Treaty were duly observed. "The two parties have now commenced friendly relations," wrote the Regent, "and we hope that for the future they will be firmly established, and that the Viceroy will vouchsafe his aid in making this friendship last for a very long time to the benefit of the Tibetans."

The Yutok Sha-pé, one of the councillors who had negotiated the Treaty at Lhasa, was appointed a kind of Special Commissioner to Gyantse to arrange about the opening of the trade-mart, and in a speech he made during a visit to Captain O'Connor he said that the Tibetans were quite satisfied with the arrangements regarding the trade-marts, and that they all hoped that the newly cemented friendship would be of long duration, and that a flourishing trade would spring up.

The National Assembly also wrote a letter to Captain O'Connor saying that they were rejoiced in heart, and gave thanks.

Some exception was taken by the Tibetans to our building a house in Chumbi, and to the maintenance of the telegraph-line, both of which had been erected during the course of the Mission. But on the whole the intercourse was friendly, and these written and personal communications showed that the Tibetans had entirely reversed their former attitude of positively refusing all direct intercourse with us.

On the opposite side of Tibet, in that part not directly under the Lhasa Government, but inhabited by people of the Tibetan race and of the Lamaist religion, matters were, however, very different, and in the spring of 1905 serious troubles, including the massacre of both Chinese officials and Europeans, occurred.

Around Batang for years past the Tibetans had been very turbulent. In February, 1905, according to Chinese accounts, a Chinese official was forcibly robbed near Batang, and the Chinese Amban, Feng, sent a hundred Tibetans belonging to a regiment in Chinese employ to arrest the robbers. Thereupon great crowds from the surrounding country assembled in the neighbourhood of Batang, declaring that Feng had no right to establish his permanent residence there. Communication by water was cut off, and on April 2 the people, "in collusion with the Lama brigands of the Ting-lin monasteries, surrounded Batang." The Roman Catholic Mission Chapel was burned, and subsequently Pères Mussot and Soulié were murdered here, and four others at Litang. The Chinese general was shot in the main hall of the Yamen, and Feng only escaped through a back gate. He was, however, followed up and surrounded in a house to which he had fled. He tried to escape from this also with seventy-three men, but of these only three escaped, and all the rest, including the Amban Feng himself, were killed.

A French priest of the Tibetan Mission, when informing Mr. Litton, our Consul at Teng-yueh, that the revolt appeared to be spreading to all the large lamaseries in North-West Yunan, thus analyzed the cause of the disorders.

For some two years past the Szechuan Government had been endeavouring to bring Batang and the adjacent country under the ordinary jurisdiction of the Chinese officials, which was violently resented by the Lamas.

The new Amban, or Assistant Amban, who was murdered, had been delaying his journey at Batang for some months, and his followers had been guilty of pillaging the Tibetans.

The considerable party which was still attached to the deposed Grand Lama had been active in intrigues against the Chinese officials, who, it was argued, had been proved by recent events quite incapable of safeguarding the privileges of the Lamaist body, and incompetent to exercise the rights of suzerain over Tibet—that is to say, the Lamas had realized the utter feebleness of the Chinese Government.

Before the outbreak at Batang the probably false rumour was spread about that the deposed Grand Lama had "descended from Heaven," had arrived in Tachien-lu, and was about to return to Lhasa.

It was said that secret orders had been issued by the great lamaseries at Lhasa to Batang and other places for the murder of all Chinese and Europeans near the Tibetan frontier.

The Lamas about Litang had a further feud with the Chinese officials, who in the previous year seized the kenpu, or chief steward, of their lamasery and chopped off his head.

It may be noted that on March 30—that is, four days before the attack on Feng took place—Consul-General Campbell had written to our Minister saying that Feng was headstrong, and that it was evident that his plans must create serious disturbances unless the Chinese garrisons in East Tibet were strengthened.

Later, on May 12, Consul-General Goffe wrote from Chengtu that a Chinese official at Batang stated that the local tribes had no intention of rebelling against the Chinese Government, and that Feng had brought his death upon himself by his harsh and unpopular measures. The local chiefs also sent a petition to the Chinese Viceroy of Szechuan complaining of the various unpopular changes introduced by Feng, which had incensed the people beyond measure. They repudiated any intention of throwing off their allegiance to China, but they warned the Viceroy that any despatch of troops to Litang and

Batang would exasperate the people and provoke a general rebellion.

The Chinese official view of these transactions is given in a joint memorial from the General and the Viceroy to the Throne. The memorial stated that Feng recognized that unless the power of the Lamas, who had absolute control of the tribesmen, was reduced, there was certain to be serious opposition to the measures of reform he proposed to introduce. He accordingly requested that the old law limiting the number of priests should be put in force, and he further proposed that for a space of twenty years no one should be allowed to enter the priesthood. The Lamas resented this, and spread reports that Feng's troops wore foreign dress and were drilled in the foreign fashion. They also represented that the changes he wished to introduce were solely in the interests of foreigners. His protection of the missionaries was adduced as a further proof of his partiality towards foreigners.

The Tibetan frontier continued in a disturbed condition. The great lamaseries of North-Western Yunan rose against the Chinese, and on August 3 Consul Litton reported from Teng-yueh that the rebellion was the work of the exiled Dalai Lama's partisans. He said it was easy to raise disorders, particularly on account of the ill-judged attempt of the Szechuan authorities to force their jurisdiction on the Batang people. Mr. Forrest, a botanist who was travelling in the district at the time, wrote to Mr. Litton that, so far as the Chinese military were concerned, the whole affair had now become a mere squeezing and looting expedition. The disorderly character of the Chinese troops and the corruption of their officers constituted, he said, a serious danger, because the whole country might be raised thereby.

With more information before him, Mr. Litton wrote, on August 12, that the reason why the great lamaseries which in the previous May, when there were no Chinese troops at Atentse, had refused to join the Batang insurgents had now risen against the Chinese was to be sought in the violence and extortion of the Chinese Prefect. He had been at Atentse since the end of May with some 400 or 500 troops, who had been looting everywhere, which was hardly surprising when, according to a French priest living in the district, he received neither men nor money from his Government in spite of his warnings of the growing seriousness of the situation. Mr. Litton observed, further, that this was the third serious rebellion which had occurred in Yunan during the three years of Viceroy Ting's tenure of office, and that none of these rebellions would have occurred if the most ordinary efficiency and honesty had been exercised. Viceroy Ting's government, he said, was a calamity to his own people and a nuisance to his neighbours.

Only three days after he wrote this he received a report that Mr. Forrest, together with Pères Dubernard and Bourdonné, had been murdered.

The Chinese, in face of these occurrences, now took strong measures to put down the insurrection. Chao Erh-Feng, then Director of the Railway Bureau, and now Resident for Tibet, was ordered in April, 1905, to proceed with 1,000 foreign-drilled troops, and 2,000 more which he could raise on the way, to Tachien-lu. Some difficulty was experienced in collecting together the necessary troops, but in August it was reported that the Tibetans had suffered a reverse near the Batang frontier, and that the Chinese Commander was then at Batang itself. Later information showed that, in consequence of Chao's severity and breach of faith, a serious revolt had again broken out in Batang, that Chao's position was critical, and reinforcements were being hurriedly despatched from Chengtu in response to an urgent demand for them which he had addressed to the Viceroy. But he eventually established his position there, and, as will be related below, converted it from a self-ruling State into a Chinese district.

In January, 1906, Chao set off with some 2,000 foreign-drilled troops, equipped with rifles of German pattern and four field-guns, for Hsiang Cheng, a lamasery at one time the home of over 2,000 Lamas. It is situated about a week's journey south-east of Batang on a high plateau surrounded by mountains, and the territory under its sway had so far been prohibited to Chinese, any who did enter being skinned alive. In the winter of 1905 a small Chinese official with twenty soldiers had come to this stronghold with a summons to the Abbot to swear his allegiance to China, but the Lamas had treated him with contumely.

Chao now bombarded the monastery, but the walls were 20 feet high and 4 feet thick, and at the four corners stood high square towers pierced with loopholes for rifle-fire, and against this the bombardment was ineffective. The country people harassed the besiegers from the surrounding hills, and the Chinese were unable to make an entrance till June 19, and then only by a ruse. The garrison, by deaths, sickness, and desertion, had been reduced to 1,000 men. The Abbot himself had, in despair, committed suicide. But Chao got some friendly Tibetans to say they had come as a relief, and induce the garrison to open the gates. The ruse was successful. The Lamas streamed out of the back gate, but only to find themselves surrounded by Chinese, who slaughtered them almost to a man.

For excessive severity in connection with this siege and in other places, and for extensive looting of the lamasery, Chao was impeached by a censor. He nevertheless succeeded in establishing Chinese authority, and, before the year was closed, in converting Batang into a Chinese province, laying down for its governance regulations* which are particularly worthy of note.

The head T'u Ssu (chief) and the assistant T'u Ssu having been beheaded, the office of T'u Ssu was abolished for ever. Both the Chinese and the tribesmen of Batang were henceforth to be subjects of the Emperor of China, and subject to the jurisdiction of Chinese officials; and the district of Batang, together with the Chinese and tribesmen resident therein, were to be under the administration of Chinese officials. The people were forbidden to style themselves subjects of the Lamas or of the T'u Ssu. And being subjects of the Emperor, every man was to shave his head and wear the queue. Headmen of villages were to be elected for triennial periods by the

* Blue-book, IV., p. 98.

villagers themselves, and were to be removable by the villagers if they acted unjustly. Under each district official (presumably a Chinaman) were to be three Chinese and three Tibetans, to be jointly responsible for the collection of the land tax and the hearing of suits, and all six of them were to know both the Chinese and Tibetan languages. The land tax (payable in cash), according to the fertility of the land, was to be 40, 30, or 20 per cent. of the total yield, which is considerably higher than the land tax in British India. Officials in future were to pay for their transport—a very wise and necessary provision. Highway robbery was to be punishable with death, whether anyone was killed or not. The gross ignorance of the tribesmen having led to the murder of Feng and the French priests, a Government school would be established which all boys from the ages of five or six would have to attend. The barbarous methods of burial practised by the tribesmen were to be abolished. Habits of cleanliness were inculcated. Adult men and women were urged to wear trousers in the interests of morality, and children were to be compelled to wear them. Each family was to take a surname. Slavery was to be abolished. The people were warned against smoking opium. The streets were to be properly scavenged, urinals erected, and cemeteries were to be made in low-lying places, and not on high ground.

Thus in every detail did Chao determine to make Batang a component part of China. But the most significant portion of the regulation is that relating to the Lamas.

The Ting Ling Monastery had been razed to the ground. Orthodox temples would be constructed by officials, but no other places of worship would be allowed, and no Lamas would be permitted to reside even in these. Those Lamas who took no part in the late disturbances might continue to reside in the country villages, and such of them as wished would be permitted to quit their habit. What those Lamas who *did* take part in the disturbances might do is not mentioned. The number of Lamas in each temple was not to exceed 300, and a register was to be kept of the names and ages of the Lamas of each temple.

Temple lands were to pay land taxes like other land,

though previously this had not been done. On the other hand, the custom of making annual donations in kind to the Lamas was to be abolished. So that the Lamas, while they had to pay more, were to receive less. The Lamas were not to interfere in the administration of the districts by the Chinese local authorities. And as a final thrust at the priestly power, it was pointed out to the people of Batang how ineffectual the prayers recited by the Lamas really were, for they had not been able to save the Dalai Lama, himself a living Buddha, from being defeated by foreign troops and forced to fly for his life.

No one, after reading this, will wonder that the Dalai Lama again fled from Lhasa when he heard that this very same Chao, who had since absorbed still other parts of Eastern Tibet, was advancing on Lhasa with a Chinese army.

The introduction of as large a Chinese element as possible into the district was, Chao Erh-Feng informed our Consul-General at Chengtu a year later, what he was anxious to bring about. He desired, by the above outlined means, and by the inviting of Chinamen of the farming class to settle in Batang, to check the Lamas.

Batang being reduced, Chao turned his attention to Derge, the largest State in Eastern Tibet, and also the most favourable to the Chinese. For four years there had been strife, of the type to which we are so accustomed on the Indian frontier, between two brothers. The unsuccessful appealed to Chao. Chao seized the chance; supported him with 500 Chinese and 500 Tibetan soldiers; drove the other brother out; established his protégé on the throne, and constructed a road from Derge to Batang. Eventually he reports to the Emperor that the Chief is a man of no ability, and had made repeated requests to him to be allowed to hand over the whole of his territory to China. He had also handed over his seal of office, saying that the strife between him and his brother had caused indescribable suffering to the people. Chao pointed out to the Emperor that the situation of Derge was important strategically, and that with it under proper control the Chinese would be able to strengthen Central Tibet, and at the same time screen the frontier of Szechuan. If the Chinese Government insisted on the Chief carrying on the succession, there would be no end to the sufferings of the inhabitants, and other States would get drawn into the disturbances. He therefore recommended that China should take measures to guard against such eventualities.

It is not difficult to read between the lines of this report. The Reform Council, in a memorial on this proposal that "the native State of Derge should be allowed to adopt our civilization and come under our direct rule," said that it was laid down in the Imperial institutes that native Chiefs who did not govern properly, must be denounced and punished either by the substitution of other Chiefs or by their territory reverting to China. The present conditions on the frontier were not the same as before, and the Chinese must take proper measures to keep their boundaries secure, and to put an end to tribal feuds. Derge was of great strategical importance to Szechuan and Tibet. The people were extremely anxious to come under Chinese jurisdiction. Chao's proposals should therefore be acceded to, and "the entire State of Derge be brought under Chinese rule." The Chief was to be allowed the hereditary title of captain, and to wear a button of the second class and the peacock feather, and allowed about £500 a year from the revenue of his own State. Whatever he had got out of Chao by his appeal, certainly Chao had taken a good deal out of him.

Chao's next move was to Chiamdo, which, according to a traveller* who was there in 1909, was not a part of Lhasa territory, but had a Government on the Lhasa principle, with an incarnated Lama as ruler and three chief Lamas as his Ministers, all residing within an enormous monastery. The whole population was said to amount to 84,000 families, say about 420,000 people. Chiamdo is the most important place between Ta-chien-lu and Lhasa, and though the State sends tribute every six years to Peking, it only did so because it received much more valuable presents in return, and as a fact, the Chinese

* Blue-book, IV., p. 185. It is not clear whether this was Mr. Toller or someone else.

residents in Chiamdo had to serve the Lamasery. At the end of last year there was a great deal of unrest, this traveller reported, among the Tibetans in this and other parts of Tibet owing to the appointment of Chao, whom they feared and hated, and everywhere they were preparing and drilling soldiers, and in some places had already declared their independence, and refused to give transport to Chinese officials travelling.

Chao, however, early in 1910 was entirely successful in his operations, and occupied Chiamdo, Draya, and Kiangka without suffering any casualties.

Such were the relations between the Chinese and Tibetans in those parts not directly under the Lhasa Government. That they must have profoundly affected the inhabitants of Tibet proper must be very evident, and what the effect was I will relate after I first traced the relations between the Tibetans and ourselves at this time and followed the adventures of the Dalai Lama himself.

Returning, then, to the relations between ourselves and the Tibetans on the other side of Tibet, we find representations being made by both parties as to what each considered breaches of the Treaty by the other. The Tibetans objected to our administering Chumbi during our occupation, and we objected to their reconstruction of the fortifications of Gyantse Jong.

The Government of India replied to the Tibetans that the action taken by us in the Chumbi Valley called for no explanation or defence, as it was in strict accordance with the terms of the Treaty. As we subsequently gave up the Valley, the point is not of any importance.

On the other hand, by levying trade dues at Phari, by the stoppage of free trade *viâ* Khamba Jong, by the stoppage of the letters of the British Trade Agent at Gartok, and by their failure to pull down defence walls on the road between Gyantse and Lhasa, Captain O'Connor considered* that the Tibetans had clearly contravened the provisions of the Treaty.

* Blue-book, IV., p. 41.

This change of attitude the Government of India attributed to fear on the part of the Lhasa authorities lest the Dalai Lama should on his return punish them for complaisance to our demands; and also to expectations that the negotiations which the Chinese Commissioner was at the time conducting in Calcutta might result in a material modification of the Convention in favour of Tibet.

Any real change there might have been at this time was, anyhow, only at Lhasa itself, for the Tashi Lama from Shigatse, spiritually an equal of the Dalai, visited India in the winter of 1905-06, was received by H.R.H. the Prince of Wales and Lord Minto, travelled to all the Buddhist shrines, saw some great manœuvres under Lord Kitchener, and returned to Tibet impressed with the cordiality of his reception.

As to the Dalai Lama himself, after fleeing from Lhasa on our approach in August of 1904, he made his way to Urga, in the North of Mongolia, where there is another incarnate Lama of great spiritual influence. But the two incarnations do not appear to have hit it off very well, and the Dalai Lama's presence is reported to have nearly ruined the other both in revenue and in reputation. They had a disagreement as to the division of fees, and the Dalai Lama accordingly left Urga in September, 1905, for Sining, on the borders of Tibet.

Early in the following year we hear of him sending the indispensable Dorjieff to St. Petersburg with a message and gifts for the Czar. Of this the Russian Director of the Asiatic Department informed our Ambassador, stating that His Majesty had granted Dorjieff an audience, and had accepted the gifts, which consisted of an image of Buddha, a very interesting copy of Buddhistical liturgy, and a piece of stuff. The message was to the effect that the Lama had the utmost respect and devotion for the "Great White Czar," and that he looked to His Majesty for protection from the dangers which threatened his life if he returned to Lhasa, as was his intention and duty. The answer returned to him was of a friendly character, consisting of an expression of His

Majesty's thanks for his message and of his interest in his welfare. The Russian Minister said that he wished the Ambassador should hear exactly what had occurred, as the Press would probably make out that the audience had a political character.

The Czar also sent the Dalai Lama a complimentary telegram, in regard to which our Ambassador spoke to Count Lamsdorff in April, 1906. The Russian Chancellor informed Mr. Spring-Rice that the policy of his Government with regard to Tibet was the same as that of His Majesty's Government—namely, that of non-intervention. They wished the Dalai Lama to return as soon as possible to Lhasa, as they considered his continued presence in Mongolia undesirable, but he had fears for the safety of his person on his return, and had asked for a promise of protection. The telegram had been sent in place of this promise, and was designed to reassure, not only the Dalai Lama himself, but also the Emperor's Buddhist subjects, with regard to whom the Russian Government would find themselves in a very embarrassing position should any mishap befall the Lama. The intention of the Russian Government, Count Lamsdorff informed our Ambassador, was to keep us fully informed in order to avoid all misunderstanding.

Here it may be convenient to interpolate an account of the agreement which was come to in the following year between the Russians and ourselves in regard to Tibet. By the Convention of August 31, 1907, generally known as the Anglo-Russian Agreement, the suzerain right of China in Tibet was recognized, but, "considering the fact that Great Britain, by reason of her geographical position, has a special interest in the maintenance of the *status quo* in the external relations of Tibet," the following arrangement was made. Both parties engaged "to respect the territorial integrity of Tibet, and to abstain from all interference in its internal administration." They, secondly, engaged "not to enter into negotiations with Tibet except through the intermediary of the Chinese

Government." This engagement was not, however, to "exclude the direct relations between British Commercial Agents and the Tibetan authorities provided for in Article V. of the Convention between Great Britain and Tibet of September 7, 1904, and confirmed by the Convention between Great Britain and China of April 27, 1906;" nor was it to "modify the engagements entered into by Great Britain and China in Article I. of the said Convention of 1906." It was to be clearly understood that Buddhists, subjects of Great Britain or of Russia, might enter into direct relations on strictly religious matters with the Dalai Lama, and the other representatives of Buddhism in Tibet; the Governments of Great Britain and Russia engaging as far as they were concerned not to allow those relations to infringe the stipulations of the present arrangement. Thirdly, the two Governments engaged not to send representatives to Lhasa; and they further agreed neither to seek nor to obtain, whether for themselves or their subjects, any concessions for railways, roads, telegraphs, and mines, or other rights in Tibet; and no part of the revenues of Tibet, whether in kind or in cash, were to be pledged or assigned to Great Britain or Russia, or to any of their subjects.

On this agreement I would here make only this remark—that it embodied yet one more concession to Russia of what we had obtained at Lhasa three years before. By the Lhasa Treaty the Tibetans engaged not to cede territory, admit foreign representatives, grant concessions for railways, roads, telegraphs, mining or other rights, "without the previous consent of the British Government"; and in the event of concessions for railways, mines, etc., being granted, "similar or equivalent concessions" were to be granted to the British Government—that is to say, we were not precluded from ourselves acquiring any of these concessions if, at any time, we should want them; but the Russians were precluded from obtaining them until our consent had been given. This was the position under the Lhasa Treaty. Under the Anglo-Russian Agreement we have bound ourselves not to try to get any of these concessions. Out of deference to Russia, we had already given up the right we had acquired to send a British officer to Lhasa, and the right to occupy the Chumbi Valley, and we now gave up the right to exclude Russians from concessions in Tibet if we so desired, and engaged not to obtain any concessions ourselves. I am not here contending that, from grounds of general policy, this deference to Russia may not have had some countervailing advantages. All I am concerned to show is that, in regard to Tibet, we gave up in the Anglo-Russian Agreement yet another of the results we had obtained at Lhasa in 1904.

Annexed to the Agreement was a re-affirmation of the declaration we had made that the occupation of the Chumbi Valley should cease after the payment of three annual instalments of the indemnity, provided that the trade-marts had been effectively opened for three years, and that in the meantime the Tibetans had faithfully complied in all respects with the terms of the Treaty. But to this affirmation was added a most important supplementary statement. "It is clearly understood," it said, "that if the occupation of the Chumbi Valley by the British forces has, for any reason, not been terminated at the time anticipated in the above declaration, the British and Russian Governments will enter upon a friendly exchange of views on this subject."

Before we evacuated the Chumbi Valley the Indian Government represented* that the trade-marts had not been effectively opened since Mr. Chang's appointment to Tibet, whatever might have been the case before, and that in other respects the terms of the Treaty had not been faithfully complied with; and they referred to this annexure to the Anglo-Russian Agreement as contemplating the possibility of a temporary postponement of evacuation. But no advantage was taken of the annexure, and the only material guarantee we had for the observation of the Treaty was given up.

To return to the Dalai Lama. Throughout the year 1906 he seems to have wandered about the borders of

* Blue-book, IV., p. 136.

Tibet in the Kansu Province of China, either in the vicinity of Sining or of Kanchow; but in the spring of 1908 he began making towards Peking. In March he was at Tai-yuan-fu, where he put up in a specially made encampment outside the town; then he marched to Wu-tai-shan, a holy place in North Shansi, the huge following which accompanied him preying upon the country like a swarm of locusts, and tending to create a general feeling of dissatisfaction.

From Wu-tai-shan he sent a messenger and a letter to our Minister at Peking. The letter was merely complimentary, and was similar to what the Dalai Lama had addressed to the other foreign representatives in Peking. The messenger said the intention of the Dalai Lama was to return to Tibet in response to the repeated petitions of the Lama Church. Sir John Jordan told his visitor that he could not say how His Majesty's Government would view his intended return to Lhasa. During his absence relations between India and Tibet had improved, and the rupture of friendly relations in 1904 had been the outcome of misunderstanding, which had arisen under the Dalai Lama's administration. The messenger explained that this had been due to the fact that the Dalai Lama's subordinates had persistently kept him in the dark as to the true circumstances in State affairs; but the Dalai Lama now knew the facts, and was sincerely desirous, on his return, to maintain friendship with the Government of India, whose frontiers were those of Tibet.

Mr. R. F. Johnston, of the Colonial Service, District Officer at Wei-hai-wei, and the author of the most remarkable of recent books of travel, "From Peking to Mandalay," paid the Dalai Lama a private visit in July, and reported that he was treated in a dignified and friendly manner. The Dalai Lama told him that he wished his relations with the British to be friendly, and that "he looked forward to meeting British officials from India when he returned to Tibet." Mr. Johnston said he appeared to treat his Chinese guard with contempt, and that there was bad feeling between the Chinese and

Tibetan soldiers, while the Chinese officials complained that they were ignored by the Lama.

The Dalai Lama informed another visitor that he had received several pressing invitations to go to Peking, and on July 19 an Imperial Decree was issued, summoning him to the capital. He arrived at Peking by rail on September 28, 1908. The reception at the station was not specially remarkable. He was borne in his own chair to an improvised reception-hall, where representatives of the Wai-wu-pu (Board of Dependencies), and the Imperial Household awaited him; he was then escorted to the Huang Ssu (Yellow Temple), outside the north wall of the city. It had been built by the Emperor Shun-chih especially for the reception of the Dalai Lama who came to the Chinese Court in 1653 to pay homage to the new Manchu dynasty. He had been the first Chief Pontiff of Tibet to visit Peking, and the present Dalai Lama was only the second.

An emissary from the Dalai Lama came to Sir John Jordan two days later, with a message of greeting. The Minister acknowledged this, and gathered that the Dalai Lama would be pleased to see him. Sir John Jordan was not, however, prepared to visit the Dalai Lama till he had been received in audience by the Emperor, and about this there was some difficulty. The Chinese Government did not find the Pontiff an altogether tractable personage to manage. In the rules for his reception it had been laid down that "the Dalai Lama would respectfully greet the Emperor, and kotow to thank his Majesty for the Imperial gifts." Kotowing is kneeling and bowing down till the forehead touches the ground. The Dalai Lama was prepared to kneel, but not to touch the ground with his forehead. This might be called "a puerile question of etiquette." But etiquette means a great deal in Asia, and the audience had to be put off eight days, till this point and the question of the interchange of presents had been satisfactorily arranged. The Dalai Lama was to offer forty-seven different kinds of presents, but was to kneel and not kotow; it was likewise laid down that when being entertained at a banquet by the

Emperor, he was to kneel on the Emperor's entrance and departure.

Though the Russian and British Ministers worked in consultation with one another in regard to visits to the Dalai Lama, and agreed to communicate their intentions informally to the Wai-wu-pu, the Chinese evidently did not care to encourage these visits. The foreign Ministers were informed that the Dalai Lama would receive the members of their staffs on any day except Sunday, between the hours of twelve and three, and that the introduction would take place through the two Chinese officials in attendance, one of whom was Chang Yin-t'ang, the negotiator of the recent Anglo-Chinese Convention, and the same official who had done so much in Tibet to stop direct intercourse with us. This was obviously intended to reduce intercourse with the Dalai Lama to the level of commonplace Western functions, and to deprive him of any further opportunity of ventilating his grievances to the representatives of the foreign Powers. That the Chinese should thus assert their claim to control the external relations of Tibet was, perhaps, reasonable enough, but our Minister thought it was open to doubt whether their methods would, in the long-run, further their interests in that dependency. Some Chinese were already beginning to doubt whether the Pontiff's experience at Peking was likely to make him an active partisan of Chinese policy on his return to Tibet.

Sir John Jordan visited the Dalai Lama on October 20, at the Yellow Temple. On arrival he was received by two Chinese officials, one of whom was the afore-mentioned Mr. Chang. After a considerable delay in the waiting-room—whether due to Mr. Chang or to the Dalai Lama is not mentioned—he was conducted to the reception-hall, where he found the Dalai Lama seated cross-legged on a yellow satin cushion, placed on an altar-like table, about 4 feet high, which stood in a recess or alcove draped in yellow satin. The Dalai Lama in appearance was of the normal Tibetan type, thirty-five years old, slightly pock-marked, with swarthy complexion, a small black moustache, prominent and large dark brown eyes, and good white teeth. His hands worked nervously, and his head had not been shaved for ten days.

A few remarks were interchanged regarding the climatic superiority of North China over Tibet, and the Dalai Lama's journey from Wu-tai-shan to Peking, part of which was performed by train, and then the Dalai Lama made reference to the proximity of India to Tibet. Some time ago, he said, events had occurred which were not of his creating; they belonged to the past, and it was his sincere desire that peace and amity should exist between the two neighbouring countries. He desired the Minister to report these words to the King-Emperor. The message was not in the first instance clearly interpreted by the attendant Lama, but that this was the Dalai Lama's meaning appeared from what followed. Sir John said in reply that the desire for peace and amity was fully reciprocated by his country; and, on this being interpreted, the Dalai Lama returned to his point, repeated the language he had previously used, and asked that it should be reported to the King-Emperor. The Minister then added that he would not omit to carry out this request. A pause ensued, and then the Dalai Lama said that if the Minister had nothing further that he wished to discuss, he would bid him God-speed, and, in doing so, presented him with a pound or two of "longevity" jujubes. The reception lasted about eight minutes. The whole proceedings were carried out with perfect dignity.

Under the outward aspect of honouring the Dalai Lama, the Chinese now by Imperial Decree emphatically stated his subordinate position. "The Dalai Lama," said the Decree, "already, by the Imperial commands of former times, bears the title of the Great, Good, Self-existent Buddha of Heaven. We now expressly confer upon him the addition to his title of the Loyally Submissive Vicegerent, the Great, Good, Self-existent Buddha of Heaven." As Sir John Jordan observed, the additional attributes did not leave much doubt as to the rôle which the Pontiff was expected to play in the future. He was, above all else, to be the loyally submissive Vicegerent of the Chinese Emperor, and his dependence on the Imperial favour was to be further accentuated by the grant to him of a small personal allowance, also provided for in the Decree.

The Decree laid down, too, that when he arrived in Tibet, he was "to carefully obey the laws and ordinances of the sovereign State," and in all matters he was to "follow the established law of reporting to the Imperial Resident in Tibet." This, said our Minister, was the first unequivocal declaration on the part of China that she regarded Tibet as within her sovereignty, though in a conversation between Prince Chang and Sir Ernest Satow the former had held that both land and people were subject to China.

In preparing his expression of thanks for the honours conferred upon him, the Dalai Lama sought to improve his position by proposing that he should be able to memorialize the Throne direct, instead of through the Resident, but the Board of Dependencies refused to allow him to do so.

The Dalai Lama left Peking on December 21 to proceed to Lhasa by way of Tung-kuan, Si-ngan, Lanchou, and Kumbun—that is, by the northern route, and not through Szechuan, as the Chinese Residents always travel. The day before his departure he sent two of his Councillors to Sir John Jordan to pay a visit of farewell on his behalf. In addition to some presents of incense and other articles for the Minister, they brought a "hata" (scarf), which they specially begged should be transmitted to His Majesty the King-Emperor, with a message of respectful greetings from His Holiness. The Councillors said that the Dalai Lama's visit to Peking had been a useful educative influence to himself and his advisers, and had resulted, they hoped, in the resumption of the time-honoured relations with China. It had also enabled them to ascertain the views of His Majesty's Government with regard to Tibet, and, after the assurances our Minister had given them, they now went back thoroughly convinced that so long as they faithfully carried out the terms of the recent Convention, they could look forward with confidence to the maintenance of friendly relations with His Majesty's

Indian Government. This they considered one of the most valuable results of their journey. The Dalai Lama had originally intended, they explained, to leave two or three of his Councillors to represent his interests here, but this proposal had for the time being been abandoned in deference to the views of the Chinese Government.

So the Pontiff disappears into space again, and for a year nothing is heard of him till a report comes from our agent in Tibet in October, 1909, that he had arrived at Nagchuka, a fortnight's march from Lhasa. He had by this time evidently heard of the proceedings of Chao (Chao Erh-feng) in suppressing Lamaism and destroying the powers of the Lamas in Eastern Tibet, for he now sends telegrams to the British Agent at Gyantse, to be despatched from there to "Great Britain and all the Ministers of Europe." These reached Gyantse on December 7, 1909. The first of them said that though the Chinese and the Tibetans were the same, yet nowadays the Chinese officer, named Tao (? Chao) and the Amban Len, who resides at Lhasa, were plotting together against the Tibetans, and had not sent true copies of Tibetan protests to the Emperor, but had altered them to suit their own evil purposes. They had brought many troops into Tibet, and wished to abolish the Tibetans' religion; the Dalai Lama asked, therefore, that "all the other countries should intervene and kindly withdraw the Chinese troops." The second telegram, to be sent after some days if no reply were received to the first, said that in Tibet, in the case of several Chinese officers, "big worms were eating and secretly injuring small worms." The third telegram was to the Wai-wu-pu, and contained the same expression, and added: "We have acted frankly, and now they steal our heart."

The Dalai Lama also at this time sent a messenger by Calcutta to Peking with a letter to the British Minister, dated November 7, from the Tacheng Temple, three days' march outside Lhasa. This messenger reached Peking on February 7. The letter gave expression to the Lama's desire that friendly relations with India might be maintained, and begged that the bearer's message might be listened to by the Minister. This message, which was delivered on February 21, was to the effect that, having arrived in Lhasa territory, the Dalai Lama was concerned to find that active measures were being taken in the country by Chinese troops, and hoped that anything our Minister could do would be done. This messenger, though he had denied that he was the bearer of any other letters, as a matter of fact also delivered similar letters to the Japanese, French, and Russian Ministers, and the Russian Minister informed Mr. Max Müller, our Chargé d'Affaires, that the letter to him was couched in more definite terms than that addressed to Sir John Jordan, and asked directly for Russian help against the aggression of the Chinese.

The point to note about these proceedings is that before the Dalai Lama had even reached Lhasa, he was seriously concerned at the anti-Lamaist proceedings of Chao in Eastern Tibet, and very suspicious of Chinese intentions in regard to his own rule in Tibet.

He appears to have actually reached Lhasa on Christmas Day, 1909, and shortly after sent a Lama to the Maharaj Kumar of Sikkim, whom he had met at Peking, with a message to thank the Government of India for the very generous treatment they extended to the Tibetan Government and people during the stay of the British Mission in Lhasa, and for withdrawing from the country after signing the Treaty. The Sikkim Maharaj Kumar understood from this message that the Dalai Lama wished to open friendly relations direct with the Government of India.

The situation in Lhasa on the Lama's arrival was most critical. The Tibetans were alarmed and enraged at the excesses which had been committed by the Chinese troops in Eastern Tibet, especially in the destruction of a large monastery near Li'tang, in retaliation for the murder of a Chinese Amban ; and the Tibetans had a story that when they destroyed the monastery the Chinese soldiers used the sacred Buddhist books for making soles to their boots.

An official was sent by the Dalai Lama and Council to

our Trade Agent to represent the situation to him. He reached Gyantse on January 31 of this year, and said that the Chinese troops were still at Chiamdo, but as Tibetan troops were massed at only half a day's march from that place there was not the least doubt that there would be bloodshed if the Chinese persisted in coming to Lhasa.

At Lhasa itself the Tibetans had continually requested the Chinese Resident to arrange that these Chinese troops should not be brought to Lhasa, but he refused to take any action. After the return of the Dalai Lama to Lhasa, the representatives of Nepal and Bhutan, together with some of the leading merchants and Mohammedan head-men in Lhasa, again approached the Chinese Resident as well as the Dalai Lama, with a request that he should settle the dispute as to whether or not these troops should be allowed in Lhasa. In the meanwhile the Tibetans had sent a considerable force to face the Chinese troops, which, as previously stated, had arrived under Chao-Erh-Feng at Chiamdo, a place tributary to, but not directly ruled by, China. The Tibetan force was meant to intimidate the Chinese, but, like the poor troops at Guru, had orders not to fight.

The account subsequently given by the Tibetan Minister of what next happened was that on February 9 the Assistant Resident, Wen, had an interview with the Dalai Lama in the Potala. The Nepalese representative and Tibetan traders were also present. A promise was then given by Wen not to bring more than 1,000 Chinese troops to be stationed at Gyantse, Phari, Chumbi, and Khamba Jong. Wen further promised that there should be no bringing to Lhasa of fresh troops, by which I suppose he meant that the garrison of Lhasa itself should not be increased. And he undertook to give them a promise to the same effect in writing.

Tibetans are proverbially hazy in their accounts of what was actually said or done on particular occasions, and the Chinese Government afterwards denied that Wen could possibly have given any such promise. But the Ministers did show Mr. Bell, the Political Officer in Sikkim, a letter which they asserted they had received from Wen. Wen wrote:

"I had a personal interview on February 9, 1910, at the Potala, with His Holiness the Dalai Lama, in regard to the orders sent from Szechuan about sending 1,000 Chinese troops to Lhasa. . . ." He then agreed that the distribution of the troops to guard the frontier would be considered on their arrival at Lhasa; the Lamas would not be harmed or their monasteries destroyed, and there would be no diminution in the Dalai Lama's spiritual power. Wen further stated in this letter that the Dalai Lama had agreed that the Chinese troops would have no resistance offered to them; that the Tibetan troops then assembled would be dismissed to their homes; that the Dalai Lama would thank the Emperor, through the Resident, for the great kindness shown him; and that great respect should, as usual, be paid by the Dalai Lama to the Chinese Resident.

This letter was written on February 10, and on the same day the Dalai Lama replied that orders for the withdrawal of the Tibetan troops and for the carriage of the Resident's mails had been issued. The report to the Emperor of his arrival in Lhasa was also forwarded. But the Dalai Lama drew the Resident's attention to the fact that while he had stated that there would be no diminution of his spiritual power, he had made no mention of his temporal power.

From this correspondence, taken with other actions of the Chinese, it was reasonably evident that the Chinese meant to take the temporal power from the Dalai Lama. But the point whether the Resident actually promised that more than 1,000 Chinese troops should not be brought to Lhasa is not clear. Anyhow, there is no mention of any more than 1,000, and no intimation that more than 1,000 were coming, or request that they might be allowed to. In India British troops are not sent into a Native State without at least an intimation, and when the Resident had made no mention of more than 1,000 being sent, the Tibetan Government had some justification for complaining when more than 1,000 arrived.

For this is what now happened. The Chinese, to the number of 2,000, advanced from Chiamdo, where, on

January 20, a small fight took place between the Chinese and Tibetans; eight Chinese and fifteen Tibetans being killed, and eighteen of the latter being captured, all of whom were at once beheaded. The Tibetan troops then withdrew, and on February 12 forty Chinese mounted infantry and 200 infantry arrived suddenly in Lhasa, while 1.000 more were only two marches behind. A crowd of unarmed Tibetans went to look at the new arrivals and the Chinese fired into the midst, killing two Tibetan policemen, and wounding a high Tibetan official and an old woman.

This is the Tibetan version of what happened. The Chinese asserted that, although the Resident had gone to meet the Dalai Lama, yet the latter had refused to see the Resident again to discuss matters amicably; had prevented the Resident and his escort from obtaining the usual supplies, and by refusing transport had endeavoured to cut off communication with China. Bodies of Tibetans had impeded the march of the troops from the first, and finally the supplies collected for the Chinese troops had been burnt, although it had been carefully explained to the Dalai Lama that the troops were coming as police, and to protect trade-marts, and that no alteration whatever in the internal administration or interference with the Church was in contemplation. The right to station troops in Tibet had always rested with China, and the object of sending the recent reinforcements was merely to secure observance of Treaty rights, to protect the trade-routes and to maintain peace and order.

Such was the account given by the President of the Wai-wu-pu to our Minister at Peking. But the Dalai Lama, remembering what had happened just recently in Eastern Tibet under Chao Erh-feng, who was now himself at Chiamdo, was not so confident as to what these additional troops were meant for. When the new arrivals entered Lhasa on February 12, three of his chief Ministers were with him in the Potala, and during the meeting news came that the Chinese had despatched ten soldiers to the house of each Minister to arrest him. Upon hearing this, and that more than the 1,000 Chinese troops had entered Lhasa territory, the Dalai Lama and his Ministers decided to fly, and they left Lhasa that same night.

The Dalai himself gave these to Mr. Bell as his reasons for flying. He said that the promise of the Emperor of China that he would retain his former power and position in Tibet had been broken since his return to Lhasa. The Chinese police already in Lhasa and the forty mounted infantry had fired upon inoffensive Tibetans, and he fled because he feared he would be made a prisoner in the Potala, and that he would be deprived of all temporal power.

He left Lhasa with the Minister and Councillors, who were afraid to return to their houses, at midnight on February 12. Accompanying him were about 200 soldiers and various officials and attendants. The next day they reached the ferry over the Brahmaputra River at Chaksam, where he left the soldiers to check any Chinese who might come in pursuit, while he himself crossed the river and proceeded to Nagartse which he reached on the 15th—very rapid travelling.

The Chinese did pursue him, which is a point to note, as tending to increase the suspicion that they really had meant to make a prisoner of him. A fight took place at Chaksam, in which several Chinese—one report says sixty—were killed, but after which the Tibetans dispersed. And, according to the Dalai Lama, 400 Chinese troops were sent by the direct road from Lhasa to Phari, and another party of 300 along the road to Gyantse, while rewards were promised to anyone who might effect his capture or might capture or kill his Ministers. Some of the Chinese letters offering these rewards fell into his hands.

The Dalai Lama himself had meanwhile pressed rapidly on. On the 16th he crossed the Karo-la, the scene of Colonel Brander's fight, and reached Ralung. Nor was reached on the 17th, Dochen on the 18th, and Phari on the 19th. Here lots were cast as to whether he should proceed *viâ* Bhutan, Khamba Jong, or Gnatong. The lot fell on the last route, and, reinforced by about 100 men of the Chumbi Valley, he was escorted as far as Yatung on the 20th. With still further reinforcements and with fresh supplies he was escorted up to the Sikkim frontier on the 21st, and that same day reached Gnatong, on the British side.

With the British Trade Agent at Yatung he left a message saying that it was his intention to go to India to consult the British Government. He had appointed a Regent and Acting Minister at Lhasa, but he and the Ministers who accompanied him had their seals with them. He looked to the British for protection, and trusted that the relations between the British Government and Tibet would be that of a father to his children.

The Viceroy sent instructions to the authorities at Darjiling to show him every courtesy on his arrival there, about the 27th, but to treat his visit as private. The effect of the flight of the Lama and his Ministers, not only in Nepal, Sikkim, and Bhutan, but also on Indian opinion, would, Lord Minto said, be profound, for in all these countries he was regarded with veneration and awe. He thought it of the first importance, therefore, to treat the Dalai Lama with high consideration.

At Darjiling, on March 3, Mr. Bell, the Political Officer in Sikkim, had an interview with him. The Lama rose from his seat to receive Mr. Bell, and shook hands with him. He asked him to telegraph and thank the Viceroy for the arrangements for the comfort of himself and his party. Then, when he had dismissed his attendants and given an account of his flight and his reasons for leaving Lhasa, he told Mr. Bell that when Ugyen Kazi, the Bhutan agent, had presented him with Lord Curzon's letter, before the time of the Mission, he would not receive it, since he had agreed with the Chinese to conduct his foreign affairs through Chinese intermediaries only. In like manner, when I had written to him in the course of the Tibet Mission, the Chinese refused to let him send a reply. Now the Chinese had broken their promises, as already related, and he had come to India for the purpose of asking the help of the British against the Chinese. He stated that unless the British Government intervened, China would occupy Tibet and oppress it, would destroy the Buddhist religion there and the Tibetan Government, and would govern the country by Chinese officials. Eventually, he added, her power would be extended to India: there were already 2,000 Chinese troops in Lhasa and its neighbourhood, others were following, and it was not for Tibet alone that so large a number of troops were required.

This statement of the Dalai Lama's was borne out by information received from Gyantse, which said that 2,000 Chinese troops from Chiamdo had arrived at Lhasa in February, and that the Tsarong Sha-pé (the General who had met Mr. White and me at Khamba Jong, and who afterwards, raised to the position of Councillor, was one of those who negotiated the Treaty) was the only high Tibetan official left in Lhasa, and had to obtain the Resident's permission for all his acts. The Gyantse report added that the chief opponent of the Tibetans was the Resident Len, who, according to the common talk of Lhasa, desired to take the entire administration into his own hands, and was very suspicious of British influence in Tibet. The Tibetans believed that the first thing he would do if the Ministers returned would be to cut their heads off and force the Dalai Lama to give him the power. Chinese soldiers had been posted on each side of the Brahmaputra at Chaksam to prevent any Tibetan crossing without a pass signed by the Resident.

Later information received from the Ministers showed that whereas the normal Chinese garrison of Lhasa and surrounding country was only 500, there were now altogether 3,400 Chinese soldiers there—viz., 2,400 in Lhasa; 500 at Gyamda, ten days' journey east of Lhasa; and 500 at Lharigo, fourteen days' march north-east of Lhasa. The Ministers also stated that the intention of dismissing the Ministers who accompanied the Dalai Lama to India had been announced by Amban Len. The Dalai Lama's palace near Lhasa, known as Norbaling, was stated to have been taken possession of by Chinese soldiers, who were endeavouring to construct barracks capable of holding 1,000 Chinese troops at Lhasa.

Besides this, the Minister reported that Chinese police were being posted throughout the country by the Amban, and where Tibetan police existed they were being dismissed. The Amban had removed thirty good rifles from the Tibetan armoury, had closed the Tibetan arsenal and Tibetan mint, and proposed the confiscation of all rifles throughout the country in the possession of Tibetans. The Regent had been forbidden by him to perform his religious duties, the Amban saying another Lama would be chosen for this purpose. The Amban had broken open the sealed doors of the Dalai Lama's palace at Norbaling, near Lhasa, was taking steps to deprive the Ministers who accompanied Dalai Lama to Darjiling of their appointments, and had posted soldiers in most of their houses.

From Darjiling the Dalai Lama proceeded to Calcutta, where, on March 14, after an exchange of formal visits, he had a private interview with the Viceroy. He expressed his reliance on the British Government and his gratitude for their hospitality. The difficulties between Tibet and Britain in 1888 and 1903 had been caused by China. The promises of the Emperor and Dowager Empress had been disregarded by the Amban, who had clearly shown that he would leave the Tibetans no power. He appealed to us to secure the observance of the right which the Tibetans had of dealing direct with the British. But he further desired the withdrawal of Chinese influence, so that his position might be that of the fifth Dalai Lama who had conducted negotiations, as the ruler of a friendly State, with the Emperor. There should also be withdrawal of Chinese troops. The Treaties of 1890 and 1906, to which they were not parties, could not be recognized by the Tibetans. He was cut off from communication with the Regent whom he had left at Lhasa, although he and his Ministers were the Government of Tibet, and had the seals of office. All travellers were stopped and searched by the Chinese, and, unless sent secretly, no official letters got through. He had received some private letters. He would not return to Lhasa unless this matter was settled satisfactorily. What his eventual destination would be he could not say; he wished to return to Darjiling for the present. After the violation of the promises which the Dowager Empress gave him, he would not trust the

Peking Government's written assurance. Intrigue on his part against the Chinese he denied. The Amban was altogether hostile, and a hostile policy had been adopted by the Chinese. He repeated his statement that the Chinese had designs on Sikkim, Bhutan, and Nepal. So far as Tibet was concerned, there was no need for the large force of 2,700 troops which, according to his information, the Chinese had in and round Lhasa. The Lama also gave his account of his relations with Dorjieff, who, he said, was a purely spiritual adviser, and of the treatment of the letter from Lord Curzon. He inquired, at the conclusion of the interview, how his appeal was answered. In reply Lord Minto said that at present he could give no reply at all, but that he was very glad to make his acquaintance, to extend hospitality, and to hear his views, which would be placed before His Majesty's Government. The Dalai Lama again thanked Lord Minto warmly for his hospitality and took his leave.

On the return of the Dalai Lama and his Ministers to Darjiling further representations were made by the latter to Mr. Bell. They said that the only offence of themselves and the Tibetan people was the struggle to maintain the freedom of their country, and they asked* that a British officer might be sent to Lhasa or Gyantse to inquire into Chinese conduct, and that "an alliance under which each party should help the other on the same terms as the arrangement which they said exists between the Government of India and Nepal might be concluded by the Government of India with Tibet."

A few days later, on April 18, they requested† that the aggression of the Chinese might be stopped while discussion between the British and Chinese Governments was in progress, and that permission to communicate with their deputies at Lhasa might be given to the Tibetan Government in Darjiling. Failing this, they requested the despatch to Lhasa of British officers with soldiers to inquire into and discuss the present condition of affairs with the Chinese.

* Blue-book, IV., p. 215. † *Ibid.*, p. 217.

Was there ever a more tragic reversal of an old position? Warren Hastings, Bogle, Turner, Lord Curzon, and we in 1904, all trying to induce the Tibetans to be ordinarily civil! And now the Grand Lama and his entire Government come to *us*, come to beg us to uphold their *right* of communicating direct with us, and to send British officers—and not merely officers, but soldiers—to Lhasa, and to form an alliance. In all history there can hardly be a case of a more dramatic turning of the tables. Yet, when all we had been striving after for a century and a half was now being pressed upon us, we informed the Dalai Lama we were precluded from interfering. When the Tibetans did not want us we fought our way to Lhasa to insist upon their having us; when they did want us, and had come all the way from Lhasa to get us, we turned them the most frigid of shoulders.

The reason for this attitude was said to be* that the Anglo-Tibetan and Anglo-Chinese Convention specially precluded us from interfering in the internal administration of the country. But if the Tibetan Government themselves wished a change, there was no reason why the first objection should hold; and if the latter was the obstacle, it is inconceivable why we ourselves should have made it, and thus in yet one other way tied our own hands. It was because the Chinese had so grossly mismanaged Tibetan affairs that the Indian Government had to undertake two expeditions on the Tibetan frontier. And we must have taken some unfortunate step if, when the Chinese were again mismanaging Tibet, we were precluded by an engagement with them from taking what action we liked to keep this frontier quiet.

We were, however, not altogether inactive. On January 31, 1910, the Government of India, when they had first heard through the official sent by the Dalai Lama to our agent at Gyantse that the Chinese were advancing into Tibet, had suggested† that a representation should be made at Peking pointing out that disorder on our frontier could not be viewed by us with indifference,

* Blue-book, IV., p. 218. † *Ibid.*, p. 188.

resulting as it possibly might in the *status quo* being entirely changed, and in conditions being set up wholly inconsistent with the spirit of our agreements with Tibet and China, agreements by which the continuance of a Tibetan Government was recognized. The Chinese Government might also be told, they considered, that we should be compelled in self-defence to strengthen our escorts at Yatung and Gyantse if unsettlement of the country continued, though assurance might at the same time be given to both China and Russia that the maintenance of the *status quo* under the Treaties and Trade Regulations was all that we desired.

There was nine days' delay—perhaps due to the General Election—in considering this telegram in the India Office, and during those fateful days events were advancing apace at Lhasa. But on February 9, the day when the Dalai Lama and the Chinese Associate Resident were consulting together in the Potala, Lord Morley informed* Sir Edward Grey that he would be glad if he would see fit to address the Chinese Government in the sense suggested by the Indian Government.

Sir Edward Grey fully appreciated† the serious complications which might arise upon the Indian frontier as the result of an attempt on the part of the Chinese to deprive the Tibetans of their local autonomy, but before deciding on the course to be adopted he thought it desirable to ascertain the views of Sir John Jordan, who was accordingly telegraphed to in this sense on February 11, the day before the Dalai Lama fled from Lhasa.

Sir John Jordan, one of the best Ministers we have had in Peking, had unfortunately to leave Peking at this time, and since the reply of the Chargé d'Affaires, Mr. Max Müller, was received the situation had so altered that the terms in which the Chinese were to be addressed had to be reconsidered. It was true, said Lord Morley, in addressing the Foreign Office, that, in view both of our Treaty relations with China and Russia and of the history of our past policy in regard to Tibet, the position of Great Britain is somewhat delicate, and that it is

* Blue-book, IV., p. 189. † *Ibid.*

difficult for us to make an effective protest. But he was strongly of opinion that it should be pointed out emphatically to the Chinese Government (1) that Great Britain, while disclaiming any desire to interfere in the internal administration of Tibet, cannot be indifferent to disturbances of the peace in a country which is both our neighbour and is on intimate terms with other neighbouring States upon our frontier, and especially with Nepal, whom we could not prevent from taking such steps to protect her interests as she might think necessary in the circumstances; (2) that, in view of our Treaty relations with both Tibet and China, His Majesty's Government had the right to expect that the Chinese Government would at least have tendered friendly explanations before embarking on a policy which, in the absence of such explanations, could not but appear intended to subvert the political conditions set up by the Anglo-Tibetan Convention and confirmed by the Anglo-Chinese Convention; and (3) that His Majesty's Government must claim that, whatever the intentions of the Chinese Government might be as regards the future of Tibet, an effective Tibetan Government should be maintained, with whom we could, when necessary, treat in the manner provided by those two Conventions.

Sir Edward Grey concurred in Lord Morley's views, and directed Mr. Max Müller on February 23 to make a representation to the Chinese Government in the above sense. In reply to this, Liang-tun-yen, the President of the Wai-wu-pu, informed Mr. Max Müller on February 25 that the force despatched to Lhasa consisted of not more than 2,000 men, under a Brigadier, but not under Chao Erh Feng, who was apparently still at Chiamdo. He wished to assure the British Government that the Chinese intentions were merely to enable the country to be policed and more effective control than formerly to be exercised, particularly in regard to Tibet's obligations to neighbouring States. The Chinese desired no modification of the *status quo*, and no alteration in any way of internal administration. It had not been their intention that the Dalai Lama should be deprived of his power, and repeated messages to that effect had been sent him. His title had already been taken from him in 1904, and subsequently restored to him. He would now be punished personally by deposition and by a new Dalai Lama being appointed; but unless unforeseen circumstances rendered such a course necessary, no further aggressive action in Tibet was contemplated.

On returning home from his interview Mr. Max Müller found a note from the Chinese Government communicating the terms of an Imperial Edict issued that morning deposing the Dalai Lama and giving instructions for the election of a successor. This note said that "the Dalai Lama had flown from Tibetan territory in the night of February 12; he [the Resident at Lhasa] knew not whither, but that officers had been sent in all directions to follow him up, attend upon him, and protect him."

The Imperial Decree said that the Dalai Lama had been the recipient of Imperial favour and abounding kindness, but that since he assumed control of the administration he had been proud, extravagant, lewd, and slothful beyond parallel, and vice and perversity such as his had never before been witnessed. Moreover, he had been violent and disorderly, had dared to disobey the Imperial commands, had oppressed the Tibetans, and precipitated hostilities. In July, 1904, he had fled during the disorders, and was denounced by the Imperial Resident in Tibet as of uncertain reputation, and a Decree was issued depriving him temporarily of his title. When he came to Peking he was received in audience, given an addition to his title, and presented with numerous gifts. Every indulgence was shown to him in order to manifest the Emperor's compassion. The past was forgiven in the hope of a better future, and the Emperor's intention was generous in the extreme. The present entry of Szechuan troops into Tibet was specially for the preservation of order and the protection of the trade-marts, and the Tibetans should not have been suspicious because of it; but the aforesaid Dalai, after his return to Tibet, spread reports and became rebellious, defamed the Resident, and stopped supplies to Chinese officers. Numerous efforts were made to bring him to reason, but he would not listen; and when Lien-yü telegraphed that, on the arrival of the Szechuan troops in Lhasa, the Dalai Lama, without reporting his intention, had fled during the night of February 12, and that his whereabouts were unknown, the Emperor commanded the Resident to take steps to bring him back and make satisfactory arrangements for him. The aforesaid Dalai Lama had been guilty of treachery over and over again, and had placed himself outside the pale of the Imperial bounty. To his superiors he had shown ingratitude, and he had failed to respond to the expectations of the people below him. He was not a fit head of the saints.

He was, therefore, to be deprived of the title of Dalai Lama as a punishment, and to be treated as an ordinary person, and the Resident in Tibet was to at once institute a search for a number of male children bearing miraculous signs, to inscribe their names on tablets, and, according to precedent, place them in the golden urn, from which one should be drawn as the true re-embodiment of the previous generations of Dalai Lamas.

In a written communication to the British Minister, dated February 27, the Chinese confirmed their verbal reply. They were sending troops "to tranquillize the country and protect the trade-marts." The troops which were entering Tibet were "in no way different from a police force," and were to protect the trade-marts and "see that the Tibetans conformed to the treaties." "But the Dalai Lama does nothing but run away on one pretext or another," continued the note "and must really be considered to have renounced his position voluntarily." But "under no circumstances would the dismissal or retention of a Dalai Lama be used to alter the political situation in any way."

In a further interview which Mr. Max Müller had with the Chinese Grand Councillor, Natung, on March 5, the Chinese position was again stated. He showed, by sketching his career, how impossible it was to place any confidence in the Dalai Lama. Ever since the Lama assumed direction of affairs in 1895 he had been a constant source of trouble to China, and our expedition in 1904 was the result of his intrigues and wild disregard of Treaty obligations. On that occasion he had fled from Tibet without permission, but all along he had been treated with consideration, and his insubordination borne with, by the Chinese Government; the latter had, however, been compelled to depose him and appoint another, owing to his proceedings since his return to Lhasa territory and his flight from Lhasa without just cause. On Mr. Max Müller asking for definite instances of insubordinate conduct, Natung said that although, on the Lama's arrival, the Amban had gone to meet him, yet the former, during the fifty days he was in Lhasa, had refused to see the Amban again to discuss matters amicably; had prevented the Amban and his escort from obtaining the usual supplies, and by refusing transport according to regulations had endeavoured to cut communications with China. Bodies of Tibetans had impeded the march of the troops from the first, and finally the supplies collected for the Chinese troops were burnt, although it had been carefully explained to the Dalai Lama that the troops were coming as police and to protect trade-marts, and that no alteration whatever in the internal administration or interference with the Church was in contemplation. On Mr. Max Müller telling Natung of the incidents reported to have occurred in Lhasa at the time of the flight of the Dalai Lama, he said that no such information had reached the Chinese Government; he would not assert that no incidents had accompanied the entry of the Chinese troops, but, seeing that the strictest orders to the contrary had been given to the troops, he could not credit statements as to the unprovoked attacks on Tibetans. It was not true, moreover, that there had been any diminution of position or power of the Dalai Lama, and he could not believe that a promise that only 1,000 troops would come to Lhasa had been made by the Amban; without the Chinese Government's authorization, which had not been given, such a promise could not be made.

Natung emphatically stated that newspaper reports as to the proposal by the Viceroy and Chao Erh-feng for conversion of Tibet into a province of China were without a shadow of foundation. His Excellency said that the

Chinese Government entertained no thoughts of such a course, which would be a contravention of the treaty stipulations between England and China. Mr. Max Müller was reminded by Natung that blame was formerly imputed to the Chinese Government because they did not enforce observation of Treaty engagements on the part of the Tibetans, and that the signature of the Trade Regulations of 1908 by a Tibetan delegate had been insisted on by His Majesty's Government, because they thought that Regulations would otherwise not be conformed to by Tibetans. He stated, as regards troops in Tibet, that none of Chao Erh-feng's force had entered Lhasa territory, that force being still in Derge and Chiamdo. The 2,000 men sent to Lhasa were a separate body of troops from Szechuan, and, beyond the Amban's normal escort and the guard at the post-stations, these were the only additional troops in the country. The right to station troops in Tibet had always rested with China, and the object of sending the recent reinforcements was merely to secure observance of Treaty obligations, to protect the trade-marts, and to maintain peace and order. The person of the Dalai Lama himself, he assured the Minister repeatedly, was alone affected by the steps which the Chinese Government had taken. Precedents for removing Lamas were numerous; in 1710, owing to misconduct, the sixth Dalai Lama had been removed. No action would be taken which would disturb the Lama Church or the existing administrative system in Tibet. It was absurd to suppose that the Chinese Government would interfere with Lamaism, as there were Lamaist functionaries at the Peking Court, and millions of Lamaists among the Mongol subjects of China. With regard to the charges that monasteries had been burnt, one only had been destroyed by Chao Erh-feng, more than a year previously, because a Chinese Amban had been ambushed and killed, together with thirty of his escort, by the Lamas.

On the receipt of the Chinese reply, Lord Morley telegraphed to the Viceroy for the views of the Government of India; but at the same time he impressed on them that they should bear in mind that it was essential that a strictly non-committal attitude on all points at issue between China and Tibet should be observed.

The Viceroy replied on March 12* that it appeared that all power at Lhasa had been taken by the Chinese into their own hands. The only high official left could not act without consulting the Chinese Resident. Reports from Trade Agents stated that the Chinese did not allow the Tibetans to deal with them direct. Various reports as to Chinese aggressive and oppressive action were in the possession of Government, but their authentication was difficult. It appeared to be the case, however, that there was no longer any Tibetan authority in existence, and it was impossible to reconcile with established facts the statements of the Chinese that the power and position of the Dalai Lama had not diminished, and that no alterations in internal administration were contemplated. Copies of the correspondence that had passed between the Dalai Lama and the Assistant Minister at Lhasa had been given to Mr. Bell. This correspondence, in the genuineness of which there was every reason to believe, showed (1) that the intention was that the Dalai Lama's temporal power should be taken from him; and (2) that the despatch of only 1,000 troops was contemplated. Lama Buddhists and Tibetans would not recognize that the Dalai Lama had been deposed spiritually, and the latter would, therefore, be a source of trouble to the Chinese. There was no reason why the Dalai Lama should have our support, but confidence would be restored on the frontier by his restoration, and it would be proof of a desire to maintain the *status quo*. The Suzerainty of China was denied by Tibetan Ministers in conversation with Mr. Bell, but if China wished to be friendly it might still be possible to bring about a *modus vivendi*.

The Viceroy suggested that in any case our own interests must be protected. There was unsettlement in our frontier States. Rumours of location of a garrison at Yatung and the number of troops in Tibet constituted, in the opinion of the military authorities, a menace to the peace of our border. The reform, not the abolition,

* Blue-book, IV., p. 205.

of the Tibetan Government was contemplated in the edict of March 9, 1908. The Trade Regulations of 1908 had been violated in the following respects: Administration and policing of trade-marts had, inconsistently with Article III., been taken over by Chinese, and direct dealings between our Agents and Tibetans had been prevented. The Tibetan Government was recognized by the Convention of 1904, which was recognized by Article I. of the Convention of 1906. A large slice of Tibetan territory had been lopped off by the Chinese, who had forcibly occupied and dispossessed the Tibetans of Chiamdo, of Troya, and of Tsa Kalhö—provinces of Eastern Tibet. It seemed necessary in any case, therefore, that the Chinese Government should be required to give definite assurances on the following points : (1) The limitation of the Chinese garrison in Tibet to a number adequate for maintenance of order internally. (2) The maintenance of a real Tibetan Government. (3) The policing of the trade-marts by Tibetans under Chinese officers, if necessary. (4) The appointment at Lhasa of an Amban less hostile to British interests. (5) The issue of instructions to Chinese local officers to co-operate with British Trade Agents and not to hinder our officers and the Tibetans from dealing direct with one another. It might be advisable that at this stage the Chinese Government should be informed that the British Government must reserve the right to retain and increase the escorts at Yatung and Gyantse, if necessary, in view of the change in the *status quo*, unfriendliness of local Chinese officers, and disturbed state of Tibet. Individual Chinese might get out of hand, though it was improbable that our agencies would be attacked by the Chinese.

Lord Morley, in forwarding these views of the Indian Government to the Foreign Office, observed that it appeared that the Chinese Government was deliberately making its suzerainty over Tibet effective, and that the result of its proceedings would be the substitution of a strong internal administration for the feeble rule of the Dalai Lama. It was necessary, therefore, to consider how this change would affect, in the first place, British-Indian relations, commercial and political, with Tibet;

and, secondly, the relations of the three States of Nepal, Sikkim, and Bhutan, lying outside the administrative border of British India, but under British control or protection, with the Government of India and with their neighbour in Tibet. As to the first of these questions, it seemed to be sufficient at this stage to take note of the assurance of the Chinese Government that it would fulfil all treaty obligations affecting Tibet, and to inform it that His Majesty's Government would expect that pending negotiations and representations on the subjects of tariff, Trade Agents, monopolies, tea trade, and so forth, would not be prejudiced by delay or by any change of administration. The second question was, however, one of greater urgency and importance, because delay might create mistrust in the States concerned, and even encourage China to raise claims which would hereafter lead to trouble. It seemed to be advisable that a clear intimation should at once be made to China that the British Government could not allow any administrative changes in Tibet to affect or prejudice the integrity of Nepal or the rights of a State so closely allied to the Government of India. Sikkim had long been under British protection. By a recent Treaty the foreign affairs of Bhutan were under the control of the British Government. The communication, therefore, which it was proposed to make to the Chinese Government relative to Nepal might well cover the other two States on the borders of British India. While, then, it was suggested that the Chinese Government should be informed that the British Government expected the Treaty obligations of Tibet and China in respect to Tibet to be scrupulously maintained, and, moreover, were prepared to protect the integrity and rights of their allies, the States of Nepal, Sikkim, and Bhutan, the Secretary of State for India proposed to instruct the Viceroy to check any action on their part which was not authorized by the Government of India.

Should China fail in performing her Treaty obligations in Tibet after the receipt of the intimation, the breach of agreement could form the subject of precise protest and negotiation. But in the meantime it was undoubtedly desirable to press the Chinese Government to send strict orders to their local officials to co-operate with our own officers in a friendly manner, since without such friendly relations (of which there had recently been a marked absence), friction between the two Governments was certain to arise. It might also be well, thought Lord Morley, to impress upon the Chinese the inadvisability of locating troops upon or in the neighbourhood of the frontiers of India and the adjoining States in such numbers as would necessitate corresponding movements on the part of the Government of India and the rulers of the States concerned. The Tibetans, though ignorant, were peaceable people, and it was unlikely that a very large Chinese force would be necessary for such simple police arrangements as were contemplated by Article 12 of the Trade Regulations.

Adopting these proposals, Sir Edward Grey telegraphed to Mr. Max Müller on April 8, to make a representation to the Chinese Government in their sense.

All we know further than this is that two battalions of infantry, four guns, and some sappers have been sent by us to the Sikkim frontier, to be ready, if necessary, to proceed into Tibet to protect the Trade Agents. And so the story ends much as when it began, except that while formerly it was the Tibetans who were supposed to be the most impenetrable and unsociable, it is now the Chinese who are presenting the real obstacles to any reasonable intercourse between India and Tibet.

CHAPTER XXIV

SOME CONCLUSIONS

THE close of the long narrative of our efforts since 1773 to effect the single object of harmonizing our relations with Tibet having now been reached, it may be useful to draw here some practical conclusions from our past experience which may be a help for future action. And first I would make some observations on the agency through which our intentions have been carried into effect.

On several occasions in the course of this narrative I have referred to the relations of local officers with their Provincial Governments, of these Local Governments with the Supreme Government in India, and of the Indian Government with the Imperial Government in England. Since the days of Warren Hastings there has been a marked tendency towards centralization. More and more control has been exercised by London over Simla, by Simla over the Provincial Governments, by them, again, over their local officials. This tendency has been accentuated in the last few years. It has never been more pronounced than at the present time. And if the conduct of Tibetan affairs since 1873 may be taken as an example—as I think it may—there is not much evidence that it is producing satisfactory results.

It has been said, indeed, that if ever we lose India it will be in London. I am not of those who think we ever shall lose India, for I have much too great a faith in the common sense and spirit of my countrymen. Nor do I say that we are worse than other peoples in "trusting the man on the spot." I think we are very much better. It requires a really big people to give their representatives rope; and a big people we are, and in the main the

British nation has supported its Viceroys, Governors and their Agents better than any other nation have supported theirs, or we should not be in India now.

But of late the discretion and responsibility of the Government of India have been most seriously diminished. Secretaries of State, partly of their own initiative, and partly because active bands of faddists exert a disproportionately great influence upon them, while the more sensible members of the House of Commons, on account of their silence, exercise a disproportionately small influence, have interfered more and more in even the details of Indian administration. The system is no longer one of selecting the best available men, and then supporting them, on the assumption that in the unusual conditions under which we govern India, they will rule it better than anyone can from England. The system is now becoming one of directing the Government from England on lines which an ignorant British electorate is most likely to approve. The result is a general weakening all down the line. No one feels responsibility. And the British elector, who has been held up to the Englishman in India as the man who ultimately controls his actions, and who should, therefore, have the responsibility, simply shrugs his shoulders and asks what India has to do with him.

And while British administrators in India thus have less and less confidence placed in them, they on their part have little cause to be placing increasing confidence in their controllers and rulers. Those who control Indian affairs from London have, in ninety-nine cases out of a hundred, never been in India. They are as a rule personally unacquainted with Indian conditions. And the Cabinet is not composed of men with a wide and long experience of Imperial affairs; of Indian and Colonial, as well as English, questions; and of European and Asiatic diplomacy. It may occasionally include an ex-Viceroy of India, but it never includes a Colonial statesman, or an ex-Colonial Governor, or an ex-Ambassador, much less an Anglo-Indian administrator. It is almost exclusively composed of men with purely English Parliamentary experience, and a Minister is put in control of India who has not even seen it from the window of a railway-carriage, or probably spoken to a single Indian or Anglo-Indian in his life. Even when there does happen to be available a politician who has visited India and specially studied it, who, being a peer, has naturally some sympathy with the aristocratic inclination of Indian methods of rule, and who, being a Liberal, might be expected to infuse into any too aristocratic methods a sufficiency of the English democratic spirit, he is put (like Lord Crewe) to control Colonial affairs, while another politician who is noted for his specially democratic inclinations, and whose knowledge of India is purely literary, is put to control India. Such methods may in practice produce very fair results, just as the House of Lords does, on the whole, work remarkably well. But better methods would produce better results. By the present system the confidence of administrators can never be secured, and for that reason alone it stands in need of revision. The composition and action of the House of Lords are now subject to criticism, because peers, not being elected, are supposed to be out of touch with the feeling of the people. But, after all, the peers do live in Great Britain, they do know the country and the people and the conditions to a very great extent; and if, knowing all this, they do not yet possess the confidence of the people, how much less can it be expected that Englishmen in India could have any real confidence in the present method of governing India from England? If the composition and methods of the House of Lords need revision, how much more do the composition and methods of the Imperial Cabinet need reform?

Again, agents in India can hardly help feeling that under the existing system less attention is paid to their matured views than to the opinions of inexperienced British electors. Not only is it that the latter are near, while the former are distant, but also that the latter can turn the London controllers of Indian affairs out of office, while the former have to run the risk of being turned out themselves. It stands to reason that the Indian Secretary must be looking more to the will and wishes of the electors who put him where he is, and who may remove him, than to the advice of the agents in India whom he controls, and that he will be more influenced by the English agitator than by the Anglo-Indian subordinate. Indian administrators may say that a particular course is necessitated by local conditions. The Secretary of State will say that the man in the street in England will not understand or give his approval, and the Indian administrator will go by the board without appeal. An English Member of Parliament, holding strong views on an Indian question contrary to those held by the Secretary of State, may, by expressing them with sufficient force, help to remove a Secretary of State for India from office, or at least make him abandon or modify his policy. An Anglo-Indian administrator, if he holds views in opposition to those of the Secretary of State, will not damage the latter, but he may ruin his own career, as Sir Bampfylde Fuller ruined his, though events have shown his views to have been right. Under such conditions, Englishmen in India cannot be expected to have confidence in the present plan of ruling India directly from England.

One very natural result of this system is a resort to half-measures—deporting seditious agitators, and letting them out again a few months afterwards; allowing an agent in Tibet, but not at the capital, only halfway to it, where he runs every bit as much risk and has one-tenth part of the practical effect.

Secretaries of State lecture the Indian Government about the "wider view," the "larger Imperial interests," and so on; but administrators in India have a suspicion that, however broad the views of a Secretary of State may be, they are probably not much longer than the distance which separates him from the next General Election. In any case, whether or no he is looking—as indeed he ought, under the theory of our Constitution, to be looking—to the next General Election, he cannot be expected to have the same *length* of view as the Indian Government; for he is, after all, a bird of passage, in the India Office for a few years and then not heard of there again. And as to the larger Imperial interests, most British administrators are aware of them, for they have been about the world more than British politicians. They are well enough aware that Indian considerations must be weighed in the balance with other Imperial considerations, and that in the last resort it is the British statesman who must decide. But what they doubt is whether the full weight of the Indian considerations is ever put into the Imperial scale. Since 1873 every sort of consideration has been given more weight than the Indian in these Tibetan affairs, and the consequence is that they still drag on in as unsatisfactory a state now as they were thirty-seven years ago.

These are some defects of the present system, but there is little use in criticizing if no remedy is suggested for the supposed evil. The main remedy I would, with all deference, suggest is that the Parliamentary control, which must always exist, should be exercised, less by means of meddlesome and mischievous questions, and more by means of full debates, in which, on Indian affairs, both Houses always show great sense and dignity and restraint. Such debates, critical though they may be of the work of British administrators, assist, encourage, and educate rather than hamper them, and do not tend to impair that responsibility which should be theirs if India is to be well governed. They put faddists in their proper place, and let rounded common sense and wide experience in large affairs have their due influence. The British public probably do not expect any more than this of their Parliamentary representatives. In all likelihood they would be quite willing to allow a greater freedom to their representatives in India, and have no desire for their Parliamentary representatives, by incessant bombardment on trifling points, to be putting such pressure on the Secretary of State as to encourage any natural inclination he may already have to increased interference in the details of Indian administration.

If this be really the wish of the British people, then a much ampler latitude might be allowed to the Viceroy, Lieutenant-Governors, and high Frontier Officers, and a greater deference be shown to their views. If agents abuse this latitude, then they can be censured, as I was censured, or punished in any way that is necessary. And if the present men are not good enough to be entrusted with responsibility, then means might be taken for sending out better. Competitive examinations are not the only or the best means of obtaining rulers for India. And there is no reason why India should not be provided with just as good men as go to Whitehall or Westminster. But never can it be seriously believed that it is the wish of the British people that the principle of trusting the man on the spot be abandoned, or the sense of responsibility in their agents damped down.

For the good working of this principle, which I would here again remark is much more fully carried out by the British Government, with all its imperfection of constitution, than by any other Government in the world, there must, however, be much more intimate relationship than there is at present between these men and their principals in England. The men in India and the politicians in England must be better known to each other, and have more confidence in one another. And it is upon this point that I would make a few suggestions of a practical nature.

Politicians who aspire to control the affairs of our most complex Empire might, like our Royal Family, make an effort at some periods of their lives to become personally acquainted with the local conditions of the more important parts of the Empire. Communication is rapid and easy nowadays, and a week in a railway-train through India would be better than not seeing India at all. If you have seen a man for a couple of minutes you understand him, and, above all, take an interest in his actions, more than if you had never even seen him. And if it is impossible for all Secretaries of State to have visited India before they come to the India Office, there does not seem any inseparable impediment to a Secretary of State visiting India during his term of office. There are many and great objections, I know, but these surely cannot be more numerous or more serious than are the objections to the present system. Mr. Chamberlain's visit to South Africa benefited him and the Dominion, and the precedent would be well worth consideration.

But if this is quite out of the question, the corresponding idea of the Viceroy visiting England at least once in his five years' term of service should not be so utterly impracticable. A swift cruiser would take him home or out again in twelve days very easily, and the rest and the advantages of personal conference would be of inestimable value. The Agent-General in Cairo comes home every year.

More practicable and feasible, and probably more useful, than either of these suggestions is that the India Office, instead of being manned half by officials who have never been to India and half by officials who will never go there again, might be completely manned by officials who have both been to India and who will return there—men of the Indian Service in active employ. At present it consists of officials of the Home Civil Service and of retired Indian officials. What is wanted is an ebb and flow—a strong, fresh current running to and fro from England to India. It is bad to keep men out in India too long at a time, and it is bad to have a Secretary of State who knows nothing about India surrounded by men who have either never seen it or who have left it for good. A Secretary of State would, moreover, if the India Office were filled with men of the active Indian Service, have a better acquaintance than he now has with the personnel of the Indian Services; while, on their side, the latter would experience an infiltration of men who were acquainted with English conditions, and of the especial difficulties and influences which beset Secretaries of State in London.

Another direction in which improvement is possible is in politicians in England making more effort to see men serving in India who are home on leave. Lord Morley has done far more in this direction than any other Secretary of State, and his courtesy in this respect has been much appreciated. His is a good precedent for other Secretaries of State to follow and develop; and if English politicians could regard men of the Civil Service in India as something more than clerks it would be well. A Lieutenant-Governor who had successfully ruled a great province in India told me he was convinced they looked upon him as a clerk, because they were always so "damned polite" to him.

Especially at the present time, too, men who are actually holding high positions in India should be taken notice of and brought forward when they come to England. The old East India Company used to take great pains in this respect, realizing the importance of their agents being known among the best men in England, and having the opportunity of gaining their confidence, and realizing, too, that for the efficient discharge of their duties in India they should be armed with the prestige which high public recognition in England gives. This will be a specially important point in the time to come. From one cause and another, the Service in India has been losing its prestige, and this when, as at no previous time, it requires all the prestige that is its rightful due. The abandonment of Lord Curzon in his controversy with Lord Kitchener, and of Sir Bampfylde Fuller in his efforts to suppress sedition in Eastern Bengal at its rise, have been severe blows to the Viceroyalty and Lieutenant-Governorships, which have to be amended.

Lastly, there is scope for much fuller personal intercourse between local officers and superiors in India itself and between India and England. Facility of communication is not taken sufficient advantage of in this way. To refer again to this case of Tibet. During all that time occupied in the correspondence leading up to the Mission an Indian official, thoroughly well posted in the local conditions and with the views of the Government of India upon them, might have been sent to Peking, St. Petersburg, and London, to put the Indian and local view before our Ambassadors and the Home Government, to be informed in return of the Chinese and Russian and Imperial views, and to be the bearer of the final decision thereon of the Imperial Government, which he could explain with much greater effectiveness than is achieved by letters and telegrams. An advantage, additional to the better settlement of the actual question in hand, would be that the Indian official so employed would be gaining some all-round experience, which would be of value on future occasions.

By all these means that personal, intimate contact will be increased which alone can beget mutual confidence. At present men in India feel that they are regarded with suspicion by English politicians, as if they were guilty till they could prove themselves innocent. No strong inspiration comes from England to them. They have to carry on the greatest Imperial work that any country has ever undertaken, chilled by distant critics who know them not. These are conditions which obviously call for improvement, and perhaps these suggestions would go some way to this end, and render it more possible for English politicians to place that trust in the men on the spot, which is the bed-rock principle on which England should carry on the government of her great Dependency.

All this, however, is a matter of machinery. I have touched on it first because it is, in my opinion, through the machinery being of a defective type that the object of our policy in Tibet has not been attained. It is now time to examine the results of our efforts there since 1773.

The net result is that at last we find the Tibetans anxious to be on neighbourly terms, and, indeed, to form an alliance with us, but that the action of the Russians on the one hand and of the Chinese on the other, together with lukewarmness in England, stands in the way of our being as intimate with the Tibetans as they now wish us to be. It has proved in the result that the Tibetans are not really the seclusive people we had believed. By nature they are sociable and hospitable and given to trade. They are jealous about their religion, but as long as that is not touched they are ready enough for political relationship, for social intercourse, and for commercial transactions. The present obstacle to neighbourly intercourse is the suspicion of the Chinese. There is some reason to think that from the first they have instilled into the Tibetans the idea of keeping themselves secluded. Anyhow, now they are quite evidently keeping us apart. And any means we had of preventing the Chinese insinuating themselves between us and the Tibetans have been taken from us through the jealousy of the Russians. Owing to this, we are not now in Chumbi and we have not an agent at Lhasa. The Chinese fear we may absorb Tibet and press them in Szechuan, and the Russians fear a predominant influence with the Dalai Lama might be used by us detrimentally to their Buddhist subjects present and to be. Both, therefore, stand in the way of that close relationship with the Tibetans which is now desired even more by them than by us.

This in brief is the situation at which we have arrived, and in drawing conclusions as to any future action we must first make our minds clear as to what we want in Tibet.

Many say that we do not want anything at all. They argue that the Tibetans live at the back of a stupendous range of snowy mountains, and we had much better leave them alone. Some go so far as to say that it was actually wicked of us forcibly to enter Tibet in 1904. The Mission was styled in the House of Commons "an ignoble little raid," and even the then leader of the Opposition, after its successful conclusion, said that it had "lowered our prestige." Before, then, I proceed to examine what we actually do want I will deal with this question as to whether we really want anything at all, and whether there was anything inherently wicked in the Lhasa Mission of 1904.

This idea of the immorality of in any way coercing a people like the Tibetans is, I believe, largely based on the assumption lying unconsciously at the back of people's minds that Tibet is as distant and as much separated from India as it is from England, that it is some remote and inaccessible country into which no one but meddlesome adventurers should want to enter. And they think that for us to go out of our way deliberately to interfere with a people who only wanted to be left alone was sheer wanton wickedness, and nothing else—except, perhaps, inane folly and wastefulness of human life and good money. This view proceeds, I am convinced, from the quite intelligible lack of appreciation by those in England of the actual conditions prevailing on the spot. For the men who act on the confines of the Empire in this supposedly evil way are, after all, kith and kin with themselves. They were born and bred in England, and are probably not more naturally wicked than an ordinary Member of Parliament.

Now, I have shown that, however remote Tibet is from England, it is not remote from India, but, on the contrary, adjoins and marches with India for 1,000 miles. And if Russia, whose border nowhere comes within hundreds of miles, can yet take such a practical interest in the country as to protest time after time at each little move we make in relation to the Tibetans, surely there is some probability that we also have a necessity for interesting ourselves in it? If the Russians as well as ourselves take practical interest in Tibet, and feel it necessary to have some fairly sharp diplomatic correspondence about it, the probability is that any action we take is not merely inspired by inquisitiveness, idle curiosity, or love of adventure, but that animating this interest must be some real practical necessity.

What that necessity is must, I think, be evident to those who have read the previous pages. Though it is the fact that Tibet is divided from India by the lofty Himalayas, it is also the fact that there is connection and intercourse between the inhabitants of the two countries. Tibet is not isolated like an oceanic island. The inhabitants of India and the inhabitants of Tibet have always had relation and intercourse with one another. And it is the necessity for regularizing and harmonizing the intercourse, and for putting it on a business-like footing, that has been the cause of our interest in the country.

Let me bring the point a little nearer home. Supposing there were in the far Highlands of Scotland a people who had drawn their religion from England, who always looked with veneration upon and made pilgrimages to the sacred cities of Canterbury and York; who were accustomed to come and trade in Perthshire, and occasionally in Glasgow and Dundee; who pastured their flocks and herds along the Grampians; and who intermarried with the people in the Lowlands; and, supposing that this people said they wanted to keep to themselves in their own country in the far Highlands, and not admit anyone from outside, we would say that we could sympathize and understand such a wish, though it certainly seemed somewhat one-sided, considering they had all the advantage of coming into the Lowlands of Scotland and into England whenever they liked. For the benefit of these Lowlanders and Englishmen we might send some emissaries to the Highlanders, as Hastings sent Bogle and Turner to the Tibetans to try by amicable methods to get them to admit our traders, to the reciprocal advantage of both. But if they resented them strongly, we should probably say to ourselves that as long as they did not worry us we would not worry them, and would leave them in their isolation in the Highlands.

But if they *did* worry us, would not the whole situation be changed? If 10,000 of them came down one day and built a fort in the Perth Hills and refused to move, would not that change our ideas as to leaving them alone? And if, in addition, after they had refused to receive a letter from us, they sent an emissary with letters to the German Emperor and his Chancellor, would not that yet further change our ideas as to respecting their seclusion? The Chancellor might explain that the letter to him was merely to inquire after his health, and that the business with the German Emperor was of a "purely religious nature"; but we should, all the same, think it was about time to be bestirring ourselves to come to some practical understanding with these inhabitants of the Highlands. We should say to them: "We do not in the least mind your keeping yourselves absolutely to yourselves, though we think it inhospitable and unneighbourly; but now you have begun to worry us and to have communications with our rivals, we must come to a clear understanding with you."

But supposing we found it impossible to discover anyone to make an understanding with, and that the emissary we had sent to them, at the first place inside their border, accompanied with a just sufficiently large escort to protect him in venturing into these wild regions, could find no one to communicate with, and had his letters returned, would the proper thing then have been to bring him back home, and say that as we could do nothing further except by using force—and the use of force was wicked—we must give up the whole business, not mind how many letters were written to the German Emperor, and whether the Highlanders did exclude our traders, and occupy our pasture-lands, and throw down our boundary pillars? We might say that the game was not worth the candle, that the coming to an understanding was not worth all the expense and trouble of sending our emissary by force into the very heart of the Highlands. But can it really be contended that there would be anything unjustifiable, wicked, or immoral in increasing our emissary's escort and sending him still farther into the Highlands, with orders that, by the use of force, if necessary, he must proceed till he could find someone of authority sufficient for us to make a lasting understanding with him, so that this intercourse with our neighbours might for the future be properly regulated, and any risk of their entering into undesirable connection with possible rivals be removed?

There surely would be nothing *wicked* in that. Yet that is precisely similar to what we in India did in Tibet, and for which we were accused of lowering British prestige.

Allowing, however, that the proceedings were strictly in order as far as their morality went, it might still be contended that by using force we should defeat our ends —we should make enemies when we wanted to make friends. This argument was, indeed, used in Parliament. "You cannot make friends by force," it was said. And nothing would seem more obvious to the ordinary Briton, who had never left his island. But, contrary to expectations, we not only can make friends by force, but we actually did. The Tibetans were more friendly with us after we had fought our way to Lhasa than they were before, and, still more extraordinary, while they invaded our territory when we countermanded the Macaulay Mission, they came and sought our alliance after we had sent a Mission to Lhasa by force. When we had really got to close quarters with the Tibetans at Lhasa itself, when they had seen that their preconceived ideas about us were false; that, with all our power, we had moderation; that, fighters though we were, we yet treated their leading men with politeness and respect—with far greater respect, indeed, than they received from their fellow-Asiatic suzerain; that we interfered in no way with their religion; that their traders could do an excellent business with us, and their peasantry got fine prices for their produce and plenty of employment as well, they entirely reversed their attitude towards us, and, if I had held up my little finger, would have gladly come under our protection.

This being the case, I hope the idea that it was either wicked or needless to send a Mission to Lhasa will be no longer entertained, and that it will be recognized that in practice it is impossible to leave the Tibetans alone, however much we might like to. If, then, relationship of some kind has to subsist between India and Tibet, what we clearly want is that that relationship should be as harmonious as possible. We want to buy the Tibetans' wool, and to sell them our tea and cotton goods. And, apart from questions of trade, we want to feel sure that there is no inimical influence growing up in Tibet which might cause disturbance on our frontier. That is the sum total of our wants. The trade is not of much value in itself, but, such as it is, is worth having. We have no interest in annexing Tibet, and we have definitely declared against either annexation or protectorate; but we most certainly do want quiet there and the removal of any influence which would cause disquiet. Disorder begets disorder. When Lhasa is unsteady Nepal and Bhutan are restless. What we want, then, is orderliness in Tibet and some means of preventing disorder from ever arising.

Before the Lhasa Mission, Russian influence—not necessarily exerted with deliberate intention by the Russian

Government, but existent nevertheless—was the disturbing factor; now it is Chinese influence, exerted beyond its legitimate limits and with imprudent harshness. Either of these causes results in a feeling of uneasiness, restlessness, and nervousness along our north-eastern frontier, and necessitates our assembling troops and making diplomatic protests, and might require us to permanently increase our garrison on this frontier. That is the practical point we have to meet.

Inimical Russian influence we have no longer any cause to fear. Not only has Russia assured us that she has no intention or desire to interfere politically in Tibet, but the whole set of her policy is now towards Eastern Europe rather than towards India. So altered, indeed, is the situation that in future years I should say that there would be an increasing likelihood of her acting with us rather than thwarting us in Tibet, and I believe the day will come when British and Russian Consuls will be sitting together in Lhasa, as in Kashgar, Mukden, and dozens of other places in the Chinese Empire.

There remains the need of preventing Chinese influence being exercised in such a fashion as to cause disorder. Chinese influence in Tibet, as long as it is neighbourly to us and not irritating to the Tibetans, we have no cause to mind; it is, indeed, what for years we tried to believe existed. So we never questioned China's suzerainty over Tibet, and in any dealings with the Tibetans their suzerainty always has been and would be recognized. It is of many hundred years' standing, and as long as it is not used inimically to us, or in such a tactless way as to cause disorder on our frontiers, we may be very well satisfied that it exists. The Chinese are good neighbours, and in the sense of any invasion of India by way of Tibet, we have no need to fear a Yellow Peril. We have nothing to complain of, therefore, if the Chinese were established as effective suzerains in Tibet, able to preserve order there, and co-operating with us in a friendly manner. A reference to the account of our negotiations at Lhasa will show that throughout I worked with the Chinese Resident, and never directly with the Tibetans, to the exclusion of the Chinese, and when I suspected an inclination of the Tibetans thus to exclude them, I addressed both Chinese and Tibetans together. Further, on leaving Lhasa I presented the Resident with the eight or ten repeating-rifles I had among my articles for presentation, and I gave no rifles to the Tibetans. My estimate of the situation was that any influence we had should be exerted to sustain the authority and position of the Resident. Our presence in Chumbi would give us the means of exercising physical pressure more readily than the Chinese ever could ; the presence of the Chinese at Lhasa itself would enable them to exert personal and moral pressure more readily than we could. By working together we could keep the Tibetans in order. They are exceedingly childish and foolish, besides being excessively obstinate in practical affairs. And if we and the Chinese worked together, as the Amban and I had done at Lhasa in 1904, we should, I thought, be able to preserve harmonious relations between all three of us—Tibetans, Chinese, and British alike.

But when Chinese action is such as to create unrest instead of preserving order, when it upsets all the border people and necessitates our assembling troops to keep the frontier steady, then we have a need to intervene. And this has been the nature of Chinese action lately. Except the Afghans, I have not known any people quite so tactless and provocative as the Chinese in dealing with a subject race. Their haughtiness and the hatred they inspired were remarked on a century ago by Manning. Long years of slackness, indifference, and supercilious disdain of the people, for whom no attempt is made to do anything, are every now and then broken by some sudden and violent effort. Chao Erh-feng's methods have formed the subject of an impeachment by his own countrymen, and apart from the question whether he used treachery or beheaded prisoners, his regulations to the Tibetans of Batang to adopt the queue and to wear trousers, the measures he ordered for the breaking down of Lamaism, and his annexation of Derge, were all calculated to rouse the whole Lamaist world. No one is more fully aware than myself that the priestly power required to be broken, for it had become a curse and drag to the people. What I doubt is whether the Chinese have gone the right way about it. To me it seems they are more likely to have roused rumblings among the Tibetans and Mongolians for many years to come rather than have secured peace. Our own victories had reduced the Tibetans of Tibet proper to order. The recalcitrant Dalai Lama had been obliged to fly, and the Chinese were masters of the situation; and, especially after we had withdrawn from Chumbi, they had nothing to fear from us. That, even with these advantages, they should have pursued this active policy in Tibet, driven the Dalai Lama from Lhasa, turned the suzerainty into sovereignty, and practically transformed Tibet from a native State into a Chinese province, indicates to me that they are wanting in political sagacity, however much diplomatic acumen they may possess, and that their action is much more likely to cause disorder than order on our frontier.

The problem reduces itself to this, then—that we have to find some means of preventing Chinese action causing disorder. Now, though I disagree with our policy of the last few years, I recognize that it does now give us a strong position. We have been most accommodating to the Chinese, and especially in regard to the evacuation of the Chumbi Valley, when the conditions under which they might claim evacuation had not been fulfilled. If we erred, it was in the direction in which we always should err—in the direction of conciliation and broad reasonableness. We have, therefore, some ground to stand on. So standing, we have to work back to the situation there was at Lhasa in 1904, when Yutai was Resident, and before Tang and Chang and Chao ever appeared upon the scene.

It is conceivable that this present burst of the Chinese will not last long. It is expensive, and the Chinese cannot afford unnecessary expenditure. What they want, we may conjecture, is, above everything, to "save their face." The Tibetans had been flouting them for years, and the Chinese wanted to kick them. They now have kicked them, and their faces are saved. What we have to do is to make them realize that to proceed any farther will obviously bring them to unpleasant contact with us. It might conceivably drive us into going to Lhasa again. We have been there once, and could go there again. We ought, therefore, to be able to make the Central Government see that their best chance of quiet on their frontier—which is, after all, even more essential to them than to us—is to send to Lhasa a Resident of the Yutai type rather than of the Chang and Chao description. As long as the Chinese showed themselves willing to co-operate with us, we have for a long series of years shown ourselves ready to co-operate with them, and we are just as interested in their faces being properly saved as they are. And if they would send a Resident with the general hint to "get on" with us, there would be quiet in Tibet without their dignity being interfered with. On our side, to insure smooth working, we might send one or other of the officers on the frontier to Peking or to Chengtu to talk matters over with our representatives in China, find out where the shoe is pinching, and acquire hints as to the methods of dealing with the Chinese to avoid friction. Or a Consular officer from China might visit our trade-marts and give the Indian Government suggestions. Anyhow, in these or similar ways we might do what we can to remove any unnecessary local causes of friction while we are pressing the Central Government for a more conciliatory manner to be observed in the Chinese officials sent to Tibet.

As regards the Tibetans, our difficulty will always be to keep up direct relations with them without interfering with the legitimate and desirable authority which the Chinese should always possess. The Chinese forfeited their right to be the *sole* medium of communication with the Tibetans by their total inability to get them to withdraw from Sikkim in 1886, and to induce them to observe the Treaty which they asked us to make with them on behalf of the Tibetans in 1890; and we acquired the right to deal directly with the Tibetans by the expenditure we were put to in 1888 and in 1904.

These direct relations, within the assigned limits, we should studiously maintain. The touch and contact may be light, but it should never be allowed to drop, for we have many instances of bad blood and estrangement arising through dropping a people and letting them lapse back into isolation once we have been forced into relationship with them. The Tibetans want to preserve what they themselves call the right of direct relations with us, and it is to our interest to preserve it.

How far the Tibetans are entitled to our support is a more delicate question. We who fought against them would probably like to go farther in this direction than those who have had no personal contact with them. We had a square stand-up fight, and we made friends afterwards. We should always, therefore, like to see a guiding and protecting hand extended to them. And what especially rankles with us is that, when *we* had knocked them over, and while they were still down, the Chinese should have proceeded to kick them. While the Tibetans were strong the Chinese did nothing. Even after they were down the Chinese did not touch them while we were about; only after we had left Chumbi did the kicking commence. And I do not myself see why we should have regarded the process so placidly.

One thing, however, we can stand up for is that an effective Tibetan Government should still be maintained—a Government with whom we could, when necessary, treat in the manner provided for in the Treaties with the Tibetans and Chinese. This, on Lord Morley's suggestion, was what Sir Edward Grey pressed on the Chinese Government in February, 1910, reminding them, at the same time, that the Lhasa Treaty made with the Tibetans was confirmed by them, and that, in consequence, we had a right to expect that the Tibetan Government should be maintained. The Chinese Central Government have themselves assured us that they have no desire to interfere with local autonomy in Tibet, and for the preservation of order upon our frontier it is highly desirable that we should see that these intentions are carried out. As I have admitted, the Tibetans do require being kept in control up to a certain limit. They have been very recalcitrant, and must expect to be brought to book. But when the Chinese go beyond merely keeping order, when they drive the Dalai Lama from his capital, depose him, seize his Government, garrison the whole country, and direct the administration themselves, then they simply cause a general discontent and uneasiness upon our frontier, and, from the point of view of expediency alone, we are then justified in intervening, as we intervened in Egypt when the Turks tried to increase their degree of suzerainty beyond its normal limits.

As to the method of intervention, my own view is decidedly in favour of sending a British officer to Lhasa itself. The Tibetans have actually asked for this to be done, so there is no difficulty on that score, and it is within the Chinese Empire, so the Chinese, if they wish to be considered in any way a civilized Power, should have no objection on their side. It is at Lhasa that a British officer could most effectively explain to the Chinese the limits beyond which it is impossible for us to countenance their proceeding, and it is there also that he could best impress the Tibetans of the bounds within which alone we can have relationship with them, or render them support. If such an officer could find it feasible to visit Peking and London before proceeding to Lhasa, he ought to be able to put Tibetan affairs upon a footing adapted to all the interests concerned. And as to risk, if we keep an officer at Gyantse we might as well send one to Lhasa.

Whether this is done or no we ought, in my view, to alter our whole attitude to the Tibetan question. Instead of expecting to secure peace by shrinking from having anything to do with the people, we should rather put ourselves forward to acquire increased intimacy. We should seek to secure quiet by the more effective and certain method of deliberately making use of every means we have of keeping up and increasing contact with the Tibetans. We have given the one line three great trials, and it has failed. We have given the other line three trials, and on each occasion it has succeeded. All the forbearance and patience which we showed in countermanding the despatch of Macaulay's Mission, and in trusting to the consideration of the Chinese and Tibetans, only led to the Sikkim campaign. Similar forbearance after 1888 merely led to the armed Mission of 1904. And the desire to have as little as possible to do with Tibet since 1904 has, after all, resulted in the reassembling of troops upon our frontier and protests to Peking. I am not contending that no forbearance, moderation, and patience should be shown. My own proceedings are good enough testimony of my belief in the efficacy of these qualities. My contention is that there must be moderation even in moderation, and forbearance even in forbearing, and that the obstinate determination to have nothing, or as little as possible, to do with Tibet has brought on exactly what we wanted to avoid. On the other hand, when we have gone forward and made efforts to get in touch with the Tibetans, to understand them and explain ourselves to them, a more settled state has always resulted. After Bogle's and Turner's Missions in the eighteenth century, and after the Mission of 1904, there was a perceptibly better feeling between us and the Tibetans, all tending to that orderliness on our frontier which is what we most desire. The closer contact and more intimate touch, besides being the more humane method, diminishes rather than increases the risk of trouble. As a case in point, I consider that if we had had a representative at Lhasa this year, or even if our agent at Gyantse had been able to proceed to Lhasa, the present trouble need not have arisen. Knowing what British officers are by their personal influence able to accomplish, I believe that if Major O'Connor, or Major Gurdon, or Major Dew, or one or other of a dozen similar officers who are to be found in India, had been at Lhasa last winter, he would have been able to nip this trouble in the bud. And this not by giving the Tibetans out-and-out support against their legitimate suzerain, but by telling them frankly what the limits were beyond which it was quite impossible for them to expect support from us, the Russians, or anyone else; and by similarly impressing upon the Chinese that there is a point at which we should be bound to protest if they attempted to go beyond it. He would have been the friend of the Tibetans, and he would have been the friend of the Chinese; and as friends of both he would have made them friends with one another.

I am, then, for a forward policy in Tibet as elsewhere, though by forward I do not mean an aggressive and meddlesome policy. I mean rather one which looks forward into the future, and shows both foresight and forethought—a policy which is active, mobile, adaptive, and initiative. I imply a policy which recognizes that great civilized Powers cannot by any possibility permanently ignore and disregard semi-civilized peoples on their borders, but must inevitably establish, and in time regularize, intercourse with them, and should therefore seize opportunities of humanizing that intercourse, and, by promoting neighbourly association, minimize that risk of war which isolation, aloofness, and estrangement, invariably bring about. It is because we are islanders that we are such inveterate upholders of isolation. But by so doing we are working against the grain of the world, and must indubitably suffer in the long-run.

If I might personify the spirit of such a forward policy, I would choose the personality of the late King Edward. As he drew England out of her "splendid isolation," so, would I urge, should we be brought out of our Indian isolation. And the means he employed in Europe are equally applicable to Asia. At the bottom of all would be the same broad, generous humanity, great-heartedness, and wealth of sympathy; there would be the same tactful vigilance and the unceasing efforts to know our neighbours and to give them opportunities of knowing us. There would be the same staunch loyalty to friends, and, above all, there would be that same courage and initiative which prompted King Edward, in his first State visit to Paris, to go in among the French people, to dispel the hostility which existed, and to win his way to their hearts by the sheer grace of his personality.

This is the forward policy I would urge for Tibet, as for the frontier generally—far-seeing initiative to control events, instead of the passivity which lets events control us; the use of personality in place of pen and paper; and the substitution of intimacy for isolation.

CHAPTER XXV

A FINAL REFLECTION

"THAT strange force which has so often driven the English forward against their will appears to be in operation once more," wrote the *Spectator* in May, 1904; "it is certain that neither the British Government nor the British people wished to go to Lhasa."

This reflection was criticized by other journals at the time as savouring of hypocrisy. One paper said that no mention was made of the Viceroy, and that it was obvious that "the advance was a perfectly gratuitous move on the part of Lord Curzon." Another leading London paper attributed the whole movement to "the designs of the little group of intriguing officials"; it said that "the raid was conceived and engineered as a part of the forward policy which has always been the peril of India and of the Empire," and added that it had been "based upon the most trivial and factitious excuses ever invented by designing bureaucrats."

This matter is worth going into. Bureaucrats, of whom presumably I was one, are only too painfully aware that they have not a tithe of the power which is attributed to them. They certainly have not the means of making the whole British Government and British people act against their will. I sometimes wish they had. To attribute to them such miraculous power is as shallow as to believe that the Lamas exercise their hold over Tibetans and Mongols only by trickery and chicanery. Bureaucrats and priests must have something far more powerful behind them than intrigues and trickery. The question is, What is it? What does impel us? Is there really, as the *Spectator* suggested, some strange force driving us forward? and if so, whither is it driving us?

These questions are not applicable to the Tibetan affair alone, but to the British Empire generally; and not only to the British Empire, but to the Russian Empire, the Chinese Empire, the Japanese Empire; to the French in Tongking and Annam, Algeria and Tunis; to the Americans in the Philippines, the Germans in Asia Minor, the Austrians in Bosnia and Herzegovina. They are of fundamental importance, and go to the very root of things. They are therefore worth examination by so practical a people as ourselves.

In all these cases where one country advanced into the territory of another the forward movement has been attributed to the intrigues of bureaucrats or the crafty designs of scheming politicians. If the Germans advance to Paris, the action is attributed to the Machiavellian designs of Bismarck; if the Austrians openly declare what is already the accomplished fact of their sovereignty over Bosnia, Baron von Ahrenthal is believed to have deliberately schemed some devilment; if the French attempt to assert a predominance in Morocco, Delcassé is accused of plotting against Germany; if the British laboriously straighten out the affairs of Egypt, Lord Cromer is said to be designing to establish a permanent occupation of the country; and if we advance to Lhasa, Lord Curzon is accused of bureaucratic designs upon Tibet.

To take one very noteworthy case, the German invasion of France in 1870. To this day the action is ascribed to the deliberate designs of Prince Bismarck, and the story of his alteration of the Ems telegram is regarded as a proof positive of his set design heartlessly to make war on France. Yet quite recently there has appeared in the "Reminiscences of Carl Schurz," the American statesman, who was originally a German subject and revolutionist of 1848, the account of a very remarkable interview* he had with Bismarck *before* the Franco German War. In a tone quite serious, grave, and almos solemn, Bismarck said to Schurz: "Do not believe that I

* "Reminiscences of Carl Schurz," vol. iii., p. 272.

love war. I have seen enough of war to abhor it. The terrible scenes I have witnessed harass my mind. I shall never consent to a war which is avoidable, much less seek it. But this war with France will surely come. It will be forced upon us by the French Emperor." The Ems telegram was "edited," but no mere editing of a telegram by a bureaucrat could by itself have produced a war, much less a victorious war. We read that when King William returned from Ems to Berlin, he was quite stupefied by the outburst of popular enthusiasm which greeted him from every side, and gradually came to see that it was in truth a national war which the people needed and craved for. What Bismarck did was simply to express and personify the feelings of the people. And in a recent work by a French writer a letter by Napoleon III. is mentioned, in which he admitted that the French Government had been the aggressor in 1870.

So far as the British are concerned, it is an undeniable fact that we have over and over again been forced forward against our deliberate wish and intention. Our presence in India is the best possible example. There could not by any means have been a deliberate intention on the part of the inhabitants of an island in the North Sea to establish an Empire over 200,000,000 people at the other end of the world, at a time when they could only be reached by a six months' voyage round the Cape, and when the islanders were engaged in a life-and-death struggle with their powerful neighbours across the Channel. "International considerations," the "wider purview," the "interests of the Empire as a whole," should in all conscience have prevented the English from establishing their rule in India. And yet, in spite of all these considerations, in spite of peremptory orders from England, in spite of Governor after Governor being sent out to stop any further aggressions, English rule did extend over India. The British Government and the British people never intended, never even wanted, to supplant the Moghul Emperors. They tried their very best, from motives of clean, sheer self-interest, to leave the Sikhs in the Punjab alone, just as they are now trying desperately to leave the Afghans and frontier tribes alone. But yet they supplanted the Moghuls at Delhi and annexed the Punjab.

It is absurd to put all this down to scheming bureaucrats. There must have been something bigger than bureaucrats behind it all. And in the case of Tibet, though the advance to Lhasa was undoubtedly due to a very large extent to Lord Curzon's strenuous advocacy, and without that would not have taken place for some years later, yet it is a clear absurdity to suppose that his words alone, or his words, supported only by the opinion of Mr. White, myself, and a few other bureaucrats, would have been able to prevail against the deliberate wish and intention of the Cabinet in England, then faced by an opposition which the subsequent General Election showed had the great bulk of public opinion behind it. Lord Curzon is a man of great force and ability, and a most strenuous advocate of any cause he takes up, but even he could not make a British Cabinet reverse their opinion unless he had some strong compelling force behind him.

Or, again, take the case of Lord Morley and Sir Edward Grey in this matter of Tibet. No one could have desired less than they did to intervene in Tibet. They had come into office supported by an enormous majority in the country—a majority which had had the very question of Tibet before them.. They had to fear nothing from opposition in Parliament or in the country. They had shown themselves most amenable and compliant to Chinese wishes and Chinese methods. We had a right to say that the Tibetans should pay the indemnity, but we forebore to press this point, as the Chinese undertook to pay it on their behalf. We had a right to occupy the Chumbi Valley till the trade-marts had been effectively opened for three years. The trade-marts were not effectively opened—our Agent reported, indeed, that they were effectively closed—but again we did not want to press the point, and the Chumbi Valley, our sole material guarantee for the observance of the Treaty, was evacuated. We also engaged in a definite Treaty "not to annex Tibetan territory or to interfere in the administration of Tibet." Even travellers such as Sven Hedin we refused to allow across our border into Tibet. Everything we could do to avoid interference and irritation we did. And every sign of intriguing official had disappeared from India. Lord Curzon had left, Mr. White and I had retired, Captain O'Connor was in Persia, and there was a new Foreign Secretary. Yet just as many troops as accompanied the Mission at the start were moved to the frontier ready to advance into Tibet at any time. If men like Lord Morley and Sir Edward Grey so act, may it not be inferred that bureaucrats also are carried along against their will by some strange force?

To attribute these forward movements merely to the designs of bureaucrats is, then, to take but a shallow view. Single men of great force and ability and little knots of men can do a great deal, but to accomplish anything big they must have a solid backing of some kind behind them. They may, as it were, accentuate an impulse and carry it forward a stage or two farther than without them it would have gone. But unless they have this propulsion from behind they can accomplish nothing. That great men are not only the creators, but the creatures, of their time is now a truism. Born at any other period than the French Revolution, Napoleon might have been no greater than Lord Roberts or Lord Kitchener. Born in the Revolution, Cecil Rhodes might have been a Napoleon.

The overwhelming probability is that there *is* some strange force working in the affairs of men, and when British Governments and the British people are driven along against their will it is more reasonable to attribute this phenomenon, not to the designs and intrigues of a few officials, but to some inward compulsion from the very core of things. The paragraph in the *Spectator* must have been either written or inspired by Mr. Meredith Townsend, then its co-editor and author of "Asia and Europe," a man who had lived in India, who had made a life-long study of Asiatic politics, and who honestly did not like the idea of advancing to Lhasa.

When such a man wrote of the action of a strange force the matter is worth close examination.

Intrinsically, there is nothing improbable or unnatural in the idea. Individually, we all feel ourselves at times in the possession of some unknown power. We are often carried along by an irresistible impulse in spite of ourselves. Each of us must at some time or other in his life have felt that within him which will not let him rest, but impels to expression. Everyone must have experienced deep within him a great source of power which ever and anon comes welling up in forceful spiritual fountains. Some inner necessity compels us onward—longings, dreams, aspirations, greater than can ever be satisfied coming surging up from the inmost depths of our beings.

This internal force which probably most of us individually feel to be within ourselves we also feel must be working in others around us. And we have the further feeling that we are not each of us separate and isolated geysers, but are connected together and impelled by some common interior, hidden, urge and impulse. Each of us is a living centre of action, but we all draw from some one original source and spring of being. Deep in the heart of things, inherent in the very life itself, we feel there is an indwelling eternal energy or vital impulse —the "life-force" of Bernard Shaw; the "potent, felt, interior command" of Whitman; the "élan vital" of Bergson; the "impulse from the distance of our deepest, best existence" of Matthew Arnold; surging ever upward and outward, and straining to express itself through our personalities.

To many of the deepest thinkers this is of all things the most real—to some it is the only thing that is real. The solid mountains may be merely an aspect or appearance of the true reality behind. But to many this "great world-force, energizing through Nature"; this "creative and urging principle of the world"; this unseen cosmic impulse; this indwelling spirit pervading every human being, and ever striving to unfold itself; this pulse and motive, "the fibre and the breath," is the one certainty, the one genuine reality.

We may, then, very safely assume that there actually is a strange force driving us on. The highest intelligence affirms that it is so, and intuition, a still higher guide, confirms the view. The practical question is: What is the direction in which it is driving us?

It has been expressed in various ways—as harmony, as freedom, as the union of all with all, as unity in multiplicity and multiplicity in unity. The direction in which this impulse is believed to press is towards fuller individualization and completer association. Each is driven to express his own individuality more completely, but he equally feels impelled to associate others more closely with him. There is a tendency towards the balancing between individualization and association, till the individuals become more and more free and perfect individuals, but only as they become more and more closely united in harmonious association. And, according to McTaggart, the closer the unity of the whole, the greater will be the individuality of the parts, and at the same time the more developed the individuality the closer the unity; the impulse may be towards greater differentiation, but it is not to separation or opposition, and our harmony with our fellow-beings will always be more fundamentally real than our opposition to them. Towards isolation, unsociability, or dissociation, there are no signs of the impulse tending. It seems to be all in the opposite direction.

And perhaps it is here that we may find the true reason why, as the *Spectator* observed, we English have so often been driven forward against our own will. It is when we have found ourselves in contact with disorder or repugnance to association that we have been so often compelled to intervene. We find by practical experience that the affairs of the world will not work while there is disorder about. We find that except on ocean islands there can in practice be no such thing as real isolation. And experience proves to us in the everyday working of human affairs that in one way or another order has to be preserved. It was the existence of disorder that drew us into both India and Egypt, and it is fear of disorder recurring if we leave that keeps us there. It was the anticipation of disorder which Russian influence might cause which drew us into Tibet in 1904. It is a similar anticipation of the disorder which Chinese action may bring about that is causing even the pacific Lord Morley to sanction the assembly of troops on the Tibet frontier in 1910. In none of these cases have we ever really *wanted* to intervene. We have intended, and we have publicly and solemnly declared our intention, not to intervene, or, if we have to intervene, to withdraw immediately. But yet the impulse comes. Somehow we have to intervene; somehow we have to stay. And not only we find this, but other great nations find the same. Practical statesmen find nothing so disturbing to their wishes and intentions as contact with a weak, unorderly people. They try for years to disregard their existence, but in the end, from one cause or another, they find they have to intervene to establish order and set up regular relations—they are, in fact, driven to establish eventual harmony, even if it may be by the use of force at the moment.

Yet all the time they feel that there is a delicate mean to be observed in these matters. If they think only of order and nothing of individualization they will find those among whom they are preserving order impelled against them. This balancing of order and freedom, of association and individualization, is always the difficult task. It is our trouble now in India, though it may be parenthetically noted that in isolated and secluded Tibet there is far less freedom for the individual than in Bengal under our alien rule, and that there is less freedom in a native State than in a British province in India, for we try in India as in Egypt to give the individual all the play we can within the limits of order.

That there is a strange force driving us on, and that it is impelling us in the direction of freedom with union, or of the one through the other, is, then, a reasonable assumption to make. And if this is so, we are not merely drifting along on a mere tendency—we are being driven onward by a forceful impulse. If, then, we find that the direction in which we are thus being impelled is towards what is, in itself, obviously good and desirable, should we not be wiser, instead of standing stubbornly athwart the impulse, to throw our whole selves in with it, to immerse ourselves in it, to let it permeate us through and through, and to utilize our intellects to give this general impetus practical, definite effect?

Instead of fostering isolation, acquiescing in seclusion, and encouraging unneighbourliness in Tibet, in Afghanistan, and all along our frontier, would it not be better to work whole-heartedly with the great World-Impulse towards more and more intimate union combined with ever-increasing freedom? Independence, indeed, we may respect, but surely not isolation. To individuality we may allow the fullest play, but hardly to unsociality.

Further, recognizing that forceful impulses mean flux and movement, and that therefore we can never expect finality, should we not place less and less faith in settlements and treaties, and repose increasing trust in personal contact, flexible and adaptable, ever ready for change in details, but ever deepening and tightening the essential attachment of man for man? It is through personalities that individuality is brought out, association fostered, and harmony attained. It is through living human beings that suspicions are dispelled, jealousies melted, prejudices dissolved, and peoples united. The Tibet Treaty was good; would not an agent at Lhasa have been better?

APPENDIX

CONVENTION BETWEEN GREAT BRITAIN AND CHINA RELATING TO SIKKIM AND TIBET.

WHEREAS Her Majesty the Queen of the United Kingdom of Great Britain and Ireland, Empress of India, and His Majesty the Emperor of China, are sincerely desirous to maintain and perpetuate the relations of friendship and good understanding which now exist between their respective Empires; and whereas recent occurrences have tended towards a disturbance of the said relations, and it is desirable to clearly define and permanently settle certain matters connected with the boundary between Sikkim and Tibet, Her Britannic Majesty and His Majesty the Emperor of China have resolved to conclude a Convention on this subject and have, for this purpose, named Plenipotentiaries, that is to say:

Her Majesty the Queen of Great Britain and Ireland, His Excellency the Most Honourable Henry Charles Keith Petty Fitzmaurice, G.M.S.I., G.C.M.G., G.M.I.E., Marquess of Lansdowne, Viceroy and Governor-General of India,

And His Majesty the Emperor of China, His Excellency Shêng Tai, Imperial Associate Resident in Tibet, Military Deputy Lieutenant-Governor.

Who having met and communicated to each other their full powers, and finding these to be in proper form, have agreed upon the following Convention in eight Articles:

ARTICLE I.—The boundary of Sikkim and Tibet shall be the crest of the mountain range separating the waters flowing into the Sikkim Teesta and its affluents from the waters flowing into the Tibetan Mochu and northwards into other rivers of Tibet. The line commences at Mount Gipmochi on the Bhutan frontier and follows the above-mentioned waterparting to the point where it meets Nepal territory.

II.—It is admitted that the British Government, whose protectorate over the Sikkim State is hereby recognized, has direct and exclusive control over the internal administration and foreign relations of that State, and except through and with the permission of the British Government, neither the Ruler of the State nor any of its officers shall have official relations of any kind, formal or informal, with any other country.

III.—The Government of Great Britain and Ireland and the Government of China engage reciprocally to respect the boundary as defined in Article I., and to prevent acts of aggression from their respective sides of the frontier.

IV.—The question of providing increased facilities for trade across the Sikkim-Tibet frontier will hereafter be discussed with a view to a mutually satisfactory arrangement by the High Contracting Powers.

V.—The question of pasturage on the Sikkim side of the frontier is reserved for further examination and future adjustment.

VI.—The High Contracting Powers reserve for discussion and arrangement the method in which official communications between the British authorities in India and the authorities in Tibet shall be conducted.

VII.—Two Joint-Commissioners shall, within six months from the ratification of this Convention, be appointed, one by the British Government in India, the other by the Chinese Resident in Tibet. The said Commissioners shall meet and discuss the questions which by the last three preceding Articles have been reserved.

VIII.—The present Convention shall be ratified, and the ratification shall be exchanged in London as soon as possible after the date of the signature thereof.

REGULATIONS REGARDING TRADE, COMMUNICATION, AND PASTURAGE TO BE APPENDED TO THE SIKKIM-TIBET CONVENTION OF 1890.

I.—A trade-mart shall be established at Yatung, on the Tibetan side of the frontier, and shall be open to all British subjects for purposes of trade from the first day of May, 1894. The Government of India shall be free to send officers to reside at Yatung to watch the conditions of British trade at that mart.

II.—British subjects trading at Yatung shall be at liberty to travel freely to and fro between the frontier and Yatung, to reside at Yatung, and to rent houses and godowns for their own accommodation, and the storage of their goods. The Chinese Government undertake that suitable buildings for the above purposes shall be provided for British subjects, and also that a special and fitting residence shall be provided for the officer or officers appointed by the Government of India under Regulation I. to reside at Yatung. British subjects shall be at liberty to sell their goods to whomsoever they please, to purchase native commodities in kind or in money, to hire transport of any kind, and in general to conduct their business transactions in conformity with local usage, and without any vexatious restrictions. Such British subjects shall receive efficient protection for their persons and property. At Lang-jo and Ta-chun, between the frontier and Yatung, where rest-houses have been built by the Tibetan authorities, British subjects can break their journey in consideration of a daily rent.

III.—Import and export trade in the following Articles—

arms, ammunition, military stores, salt, liquors, and intoxicating or narcotic drugs,

may at the option of either Government be entirely prohibited, or permitted only on such conditions as either Government on their own side may think fit to impose.

IV.—Goods, other than goods of the descriptions enumerated in Regulation III., entering Tibet from British India, across the Sikkim-Tibet frontier, or *vice versâ*, whatever their origin, shall be exempt from duty for a period of five years commencing from the date of the opening of Yatung to trade, but after the expiration of this term, if found desirable, a tariff may be mutually agreed upon and enforced.

Indian tea may be imported into Tibet at a rate of duty not exceeding that at which Chinese tea is imported into England, but trade in Indian tea shall not be engaged in during the five years for which other commodities are exempt.

V.—All goods on arrival at Yatung, whether from British India or from Tibet, must be reported at the Customs Station there for examination, and the report must give full particulars of the description, quantity, and value of the goods.

VI.—In the event of trade disputes arising between British and Chinese or Tibetan subjects in Tibet, they shall be enquired into and settled in personal conference by the Political Officer for Sikkim and the Chinese frontier officer. The object of personal conference being to ascertain facts and do justice, where there is a divergence of views the law of the country to which the defendant belongs shall guide.

VII.—Despatches from the Government of India to the Chinese Imperial Resident in Tibet shall be handed over by the Political Officer for Sikkim to the Chinese frontier officer, who will forward them by special courier.

Despatches from the Chinese Imperial Resident in Tibet to the Government of India will be handed over by the Chinese frontier officer to the Political Officer for Sikkim, who will forward them as quickly as possible.

VIII.—Despatches between the Chinese and Indian officials must be treated with due respect, and couriers will be assisted in passing to and fro by the officers of each Government.

IX.—After the expiration of one year from the date of the opening of Yatung, such Tibetans as continue to graze their cattle in Sikkim will be subject to such Regulations as the British Government may from time to time enact for the general conduct of grazing in Sikkim. Due notice will be given of such Regulations.

General Articles.

I.—In the event of disagreement between the Political Officer for Sikkim and the Chinese frontier officer, each official shall report the matter to his immediate superior, who in turn, if a settlement is not arrived at between them, shall refer such matter to their respective Governments for disposal.

II.—After the lapse of five years from the date on which these Regulations shall come into force, and on six months' notice given by either party, these Regulations shall be subject to revision by Commissioners appointed on both sides for this purpose, who shall be empowered to decide on and adopt such amendments and extensions as experience shall prove to be desirable.

III.—It having been stipulated that Joint Commissioners should be appointed by the British and Chinese Governments under the 7th Article of the Sikkim-Tibet Convention to meet and discuss, with a view to the final settlement of the questions reserved under Articles 4, 5, and 6 of the said Convention; and the Commissioners thus appointed having met and discussed the questions referred to, namely: Trade, Communication and Pasturage, have been further appointed to sign the agreement in nine Regulations and three General Articles now arrived at, and to declare that the said nine Regulations and the three General Articles form part of the Convention itself.

CONVENTION BETWEEN GREAT BRITAIN AND TIBET, SIGNED AT LHASA ON THE 7TH SEPTEMBER, 1904.

Whereas doubts and difficulties have arisen as to the meaning and validity of the Anglo-Chinese Convention of 1890, and the Trade Regulations of 1893, and as to the liabilities of the Tibetan Government under these agreements; and whereas recent occurrences have tended towards a disturbance of the relations of friendship and good understanding which have existed between the British Government and the Government of Tibet; and whereas it is desirable to restore peace and amicable relations, and to resolve and determine the doubts and difficulties as aforesaid, the said Governments have resolved to conclude a Convention with these objects, and the following articles have been agreed upon by Colonel F. E. Younghusband, C.I.E., in virtue of full powers vested in him by His Britannic Majesty's Government and on behalf of that said Government, and Lo-Sang Gyal-Tsen, the Ga-den Ti-Rimpoche, and the representatives of the Council, of the three monasteries Se-ra, Dre-pung, and Ga-den, and of the ecclesiastical and lay officials of the National Assembly on behalf of the Government of Tibet.

I.—The Government of Tibet engages to respect the Anglo-Chinese Convention of 1890, and to recognize the frontier between Sikkim and Tibet, as defined in Article I. of the said Convention, and to erect boundary pillars accordingly.

II.—The Tibetan Government undertakes to open forthwith trade-marts, to which all British and Tibetan subjects shall have free right of access at Gyantse and Gartok, as well as at Yatung.

The Regulations applicable to the trade-mart at Yatung, under the Anglo-Chinese Agreement of 1893, shall, subject to such amendments as may hereafter be agreed upon by common consent between the British and Tibetan Governments, apply to the marts above mentioned.

In addition to establishing trade-marts at the places mentioned, the Tibetan Government undertakes to place no restrictions on the trade by existing routes, and to consider the question of establishing fresh trade-marts under similar conditions if development of trade requires it.

III.—The question of the amendment of the Regulations of 1893 is reserved for separate consideration, and the Tibetan Government undertakes to appoint fully authorized delegates to negotiate with representatives of the British Government as to the details of the amendments required.

IV.—The Tibetan Government undertakes to levy no dues of any kind other than those provided for in the tariff to be mutually agreed upon.

V.—The Tibetan Government undertakes to keep the roads to Gyantse and Gartok from the frontier clear of all obstruction and in a state of repair suited to the needs of the trade, and to establish at Yatung, Gyantse, and Gartok, and at each of the other trade-marts that may hereafter be established, a Tibetan Agent, who shall receive from the British Agent appointed to watch over British trade at the marts in question any letter which the latter may desire to send to the Tibetan or to the Chinese authorities. The Tibetan Agent shall also be responsible for the due delivery of such communications, and for the transmission of replies.

VI.—As an indemnity to the British Government for the expense incurred in the despatch of armed troops to Lhasa, to exact reparation for breaches of treaty obligations, and for the insults offered to and attacks upon the British Commissioner and his following and escort, the Tibetan Government engages to pay a sum of pounds five hundred thousand—equivalent to rupees seventy-five lakhs—to the British Government.

The indemnity shall be payable at such place as the British Government may from time to time, after due notice, indicate, whether in Tibet or in the British districts of Darjeeling or Jalpaiguri, in seventy-five annual instalments of rupees one lakh each on the 1st January in each year, beginning from the 1st January, 1906.

VII.—As security for the payment of the above-mentioned indemnity, and for the fulfilment of the provisions relative to trade-marts specified in Articles II., III., IV., and V., the British Government shall continue to occupy the Chumbi Valley until the indemnity has been paid, and until the trade-marts have been effectively opened for three years, whichever date may be the later.

VIII.—The Tibetan Government agrees to raze all forts and fortifications and remove all armaments which might impede the course of free communication between the British frontier and the towns of Gyantse and Lhasa.

IX.—The Government of Tibet engages that, without the previous consent of the British Government,—

(*a*) No portion of Tibetan territory shall be ceded, sold, leased, mortgaged or otherwise given for occupation, to any Foreign Power;

(*b*) No such Power shall be permitted to intervene in Tibetan affairs;

(*c*) No Representatives or Agents of any Foreign Power shall be admitted to Tibet;

(*d*) No concessions for railways, roads, telegraphs, mining or other rights, shall be granted to any Foreign Power, or to the subject of any Foreign Power. In the event of consent to such concessions being granted, similar or equivalent concessions shall be granted to the British Government;

(*e*) No Tibetan revenues, whether in kind or in cash, shall be pledged or assigned to any Foreign Power, or to the subject of any Foreign Power.

X.—In witness whereof the negotiators have signed the same, and affixed thereunto the seals of their arms.

Done in quintuplicate at Lhasa this 7th day of September in the year of our Lord one thousand nine hundred and four, corresponding with the Tibetan date, the 27th day of the seventh month of the Wood Dragon year.

DECLARATION SIGNED BY HIS EXCELLENCY THE VICEROY AND GOVERNOR-GENERAL OF INDIA, AND APPENDED TO THE RATIFIED CONVENTION OF 7TH SEPTEMBER, 1904.

His Excellency the Viceroy and Governor-General of India, having ratified the Convention which was concluded at Lhasa on 7th September, 1904, by Colonel Younghusband, C.I.E., British Commissioner for Tibet Frontier Matters, on behalf of His Britannic Majesty's Government; and by Lo-Sang Gyal-Tsen, the Ga-den Ti-Rimpoche, and the representatives of the Council, of the three monasteries Sera, Dre-pung and Ga-den, and of the ecclesiastical and lay officials of the National Assembly, on behalf of the Government of Tibet, is pleased to direct as an act of grace that the sum of money which the Tibetan Government have bound themselves under the terms of Article VI. of the said Convention to pay to His Majesty's Government as an indemnity for the expenses incurred by the latter in connection with the despatch of armed forces to Lhasa, be reduced from Rs. 75,00,000 to Rs. 25,00,000; and to declare that the British occupation of the Chumbi Valley shall cease after the due payment of three annual instalments of the said indemnity as fixed by the said Article, provided, however, that the trade-marts as stipulated in Article II. of the Convention shall have been effectively opened for three years as provided in Article VI. of the Convention; and that, in the meantime, the Tibetans shall have faithfully complied with the terms of the said Convention in all other respects.

CONVENTION BETWEEN GREAT BRITAIN AND CHINA, DATED 27TH APRIL, 1906. (RECEIVED IN LONDON, 18TH JUNE, 1906.)

(*Ratifications exchanged at London, July* 23, 1906.)

Whereas His Majesty the King of Great Britain and Ireland and of the British Dominions beyond the Seas, Emperor of India, and His Majesty the Emperor of China are sincerely desirous to maintain and perpetuate the relations of friendship and good understanding which now exist between their respective Empires;

And whereas the refusal of Tibet to recognize the validity of or to carry into full effect the provisions of the Anglo-Chinese Convention of the 17th March, 1890, and Regulations of the 5th December, 1893, place the British Government under the necessity of taking steps to secure their rights and interests under the said Convention and Regulations;

And whereas a Convention of ten Articles was signed at Lhasa on the 7th September, 1904, on behalf of Great Britain and Tibet, and was ratified by the Viceroy and Governor-General of India on behalf of Great Britain on the 11th November, 1904, a Declaration on behalf of Great Britain modifying its terms under certain conditions being appended thereto;

His Britannic Majesty and His Majesty the Emperor of China have resolved to conclude a Convention on this subject, and have for this purpose named Plenipotentiaries, that is to say:

His Majesty the King of Great Britain and Ireland, Sir Ernest Mason Satow, Knight Grand Cross of the Most Distinguished Order, St. Michael and St. George, His said Majesty's Envoy Extraordinary and Minister Plenipotentiary to His Majesty the Emperor of China; and His Majesty the Emperor of China; His

Excellency Tong Shao-yi, His said Majesty's High Commissioner and Plenipotentiary, and a Vice-President of the Board of Foreign Affairs;

Who, having communicated to each other their respective full powers, and finding them to be in good and due form, have agreed upon and concluded the following Convention in six Articles:

ARTICLE I.—The Convention concluded on the 7th September, 1904, by Great Britain and Tibet, the texts of which in English and Chinese are attached to the present Convention as an annex, is hereby confirmed, subject to the modification stated in the Declaration appended thereto, and both of the High Contracting Parties engage to take at all times such steps as may be necessary to secure the due fulfilment of the terms specified therein.

ARTICLE II.—The Government of Great Britain engages not to annex Tibetan territory or to interfere in the administration of Tibet. The Government of China also undertakes not to permit any other foreign State to interfere with the territory or internal administration of Tibet.

ARTICLE III.—The concessions which are mentioned in Article IX. (*d*) of the Convention concluded on the 7th September, 1904, by Great Britain and Tibet are denied to any State or to the subject of any State other than China, but it has been arranged with China that at the trade-marts specified in Article II. of the aforesaid Convention Great Britain shall be entitled to lay down telegraph lines connecting with India.

ARTICLE IV.—The provisions of the Anglo-Chinese Convention of 1890 and Regulations of 1893 shall, subject to the terms of this present Convention and annex thereto, remain in full force.

ARTICLE V.—The English and Chinese texts of the present Convention have been carefully compared and found to correspond, but in the event of there being any difference of meaning between them the English text shall be authoritative.

ARTICLE VI.—This Convention shall be ratified by the Sovereigns of both countries, and ratifications shall be exchanged at London within three months after the date of signature by the Plenipotentiaries of both Powers.

CONVENTION BETWEEN GREAT BRITAIN AND RUSSIA, 1907.

His Majesty the King of the United Kingdom of Great Britain and Ireland and of the British Dominions beyond the Seas, Emperor of India, and His Majesty the Emperor of All the Russias, animated by the sincere desire to settle by mutual agreement different questions concerning the interests of their States on the Continent of Asia, have determined to conclude Agreements destined to prevent all cause of misunderstanding between Great Britain and Russia in regard to the questions referred to, and have nominated for this purpose their respective Plenipotentiaries, to wit:

His Majesty the King of the United Kingdom of Great Britain and Ireland and of the British Dominions beyond the Seas, Emperor of India, the Right Honourable Sir Arthur Nicolson, His Majesty's Ambassador Extraordinary and Plenipotentiary to His Majesty the Emperor of All the Russias;

His Majesty the Emperor of All the Russias, the Master of his Court Alexander Iswolsky, Minister for Foreign Affairs;

Who, having communicated to each other their full powers, found in good and due form, have agreed on the following:

ARRANGEMENT CONCERNING TIBET.

The Governments of Great Britain and Russia recognizing the suzerain rights of China in Tibet, and considering the fact that Great Britain, by reason of her geographical position, has a special interest in the maintenance of the *status quo* in the external relations of Tibet, have made the following Arrangement:

ARTICLE I.—The two High Contracting Parties engage to respect the territorial integrity of Tibet and to abstain from all interference in its internal administration.

ARTICLE II.—In conformity with the admitted principle of the suzerainty of China over Tibet, Great Britain and Russia engage not to enter into negotiations with Tibet except through the intermediary of the Chinese Government. This engagement does not exclude the direct relations between British Commercial Agents and the Tibetan authorities provided for in Article V. of the Convention between Great Britain and Tibet of the 7th September, 1904, and confirmed by the Convention between Great Britain and China of the 27th April, 1906; nor does it modify the engagements entered into by Great Britain and China in Article I. of the said Convention of 1906.

It is clearly understood that Buddhists, subjects of Great Britain or of Russia, may enter into direct relations on strictly religious matters with the Dalai Lama, and the other representatives of Buddhism in Tibet; the Governments of Great Britain and Russia engage as far as they are concerned, not to allow those relations to infringe the stipulations of the present Arrangement.

ARTICLE III.—The British and Russian Governments respectively engage not to send Representatives to Lhasa.

ARTICLE IV.—The two High Contracting Parties engage neither to seek nor to obtain, whether for themselves or their subjects, any Concessions for railways, roads, telegraphs, and mines, or other rights in Tibet.

ARTICLE V.—The two Governments agree that no part of the revenues of Tibet, whether in kind or in cash, shall be pledged or assigned to Great Britain or Russia or to any of their subjects.

ANNEX TO THE ARRANGEMENT BETWEEN GREAT BRITAIN AND RUSSIA CONCERNING TIBET.

Great Britain reaffirms the Declaration, signed by His Excellency the Viceroy and Governor-General of India and appended to the ratification of the Convention of the 7th September, 1904, to the effect that the occupation of the Chumbi Valley by British forces shall cease after the payment of three annual instalments of the indemnity of 2,500,000 rupees, provided that the trade-marts mentioned in Article II. of that Convention have been effectively opened for three years, and that in the meantime the Tibetan authorities have faithfully complied in all respects with the terms of the said Convention of 1904. It is clearly understood that if the occupation of the Chumbi Valley by the British forces has, for any reason, not been terminated at the time anticipated in the above Declaration, the British and Russian Governments will enter upon a friendly exchange of views on this subject.

INDEX

THE END